Thomas A. Lewis

THE GUNS OF CEDAR CREEK

"ALL OF THE ELEMENTS OF EXCITING FICTION . . . Lewis paints the battle in the hues of colorful personalities, detailing these long-dead heroes in a way that the reader comes to know them well. His narrative brings the battlefield to thunderous life, and places the reader shivering before dawn beside a little creek in the Shenandoah Valley, watching through the morning mists for the sun, which was to rise that morning on a Confederate victory and set that night on a Union triumph."

—*Tulsa Tribune*

"SHOULD BE ON YOUR MUST-READ LIST . . . exquisitely detailed . . . it's as good as you'll get anywhere."

—*Santa Maria Times*

"THOROUGHLY RESEARCHED . . . a style combining the formality of those times with a more contemporary lightness that makes for interesting reading throughout. The reader becomes so involved with the individuals on whom Lewis concentrates . . . these are no cardboard cutouts to be shuffled about on toy battlefields; Lewis brings them alive again."

—*Roanoke Times*

"THE GUNS OF CEDAR CREEK, whose key figures are presented in exceptional depth and are brought sharply to life, is a riveting combination of factual scholarship and human drama."

—Richard Wheeler, author of *Witness to Gettysburg*

Also by Thomas A. Lewis

THE SHENANDOAH IN FLAMES:
THE VALLEY CAMPAIGN OF 1864

THE GUNS OF CEDAR CREEK

Thomas A. Lewis

FOR MARGARET FEARER,
formerly of Gough School,
who asked to see more stories

A LAUREL BOOK
Published by
Dell Publishing
a division of
Bantam Doubleday Dell Publishing Group, Inc.
666 Fifth Avenue
New York, New York 10103

ISBN: 0-440-20514-X

Reprinted by arrangement with Harper & Row,
Publishers, Inc.
Printed in the United States of America
Published simultaneously in Canada

March 1990
10 9 8 7 6 5 4 3 2 1
OPM

Contents

CONTENTS

PART II: THE GUNS • 197

Preface

James Kidd, a colonel of cavalry in the Shenandoah Valley Campaign of 1864, was sure we would never forget its final battle, fought at Cedar Creek. We would write about its drama and glory, he thought, "as long as literature lasts," and thought it appropriate we do so: "Thus doth poesy erect monuments, more enduring than bronze or marble, to the memory of the brave."

He had many reasons to presume that Cedar Creek would be immortal. The events of that October day wrote themselves large, sounding mystic themes and immediately taking on the hues of legend. There was the brilliant, flawed Jubal Early with his ragged band of Confederate heroes attacking a sleek, well-fed, superbly equipped army twice its size—and winning. But there, too, was Phil Sheridan, a misshapen little terror of a man with an unholy aptitude for the arts of war, galloping a dozen miles to save his routed Union army, single-handedly turning defeat into triumph.

The battle assured the re-election of Abraham Lincoln as president of the Union, something that had not seemed possible a few months earlier. The story of that remarkable day was told and retold in the North as if it were a morality play, confirming the virtues and high destiny of the Union cause, standing in stark contrast to the endless, grinding slaughter going on in the trenches around Petersburg and Richmond. The refreshing effect was amplified in verse by an underinformed and overwrought poet named Thomas Buchanan Read, whose version of events—"Sheridan's Ride" (see page 350)—was read to every possible gathering of voters before the war-weary north went to the polls. It was, on the other hand, the battle that consigned Robert E. Lee and his Army of Northern Virginia to an even harder famine in the winter of 1864 than they had known the year before—a famine that had been almost unbearable.

It was the battle that removed most of the official reservations and all of the public doubts about Phil Sheridan's brilliance, paving the way not only to his pivotal role in the final engagements of the War—at places such as Five Forks and Appomattox—but to eventual supreme command of the United States Army. It was, contrarily, the battle that ended the career of Jubal Early, that rasp-tongued, large-hearted sourpuss who had turned himself from a devoted supporter of the Union into one of its most fervent foes, from an ardent suitor into a woman-hater, and from a mediocre country lawyer into one of the Confederacy's highest-ranking and most valued generals—only to lose it all just before the Cause was lost.

It was the battle that boosted John Gordon, that sleek, bantam-rooster of a general, toward the command of Early's corps in the final days of the War; the battle that helped turn the taciturn George Crook from Phil Sheridan's lifelong friend—they had been Ohio playmates and West Point comrades—into his bitterest enemy; the battle that provided joyful confirmation of the stardom of that dashing young cavalry general, George Armstrong Custer, and stained the career of one of the army's finest commanders, Horatio Wright—and neither outcome was deserved. It was the battle that contributed to the future election of two participants as presidents of the United States—Rutherford B. Hayes and William McKinley—and that took the lives of two young officers, Stephen Dodson Ramseur and Charles Russell Lowell, who, had they lived, would undoubtedly have taken their places in the highest ranks of their country's leaders.

With so many consequences flowing from this day of high drama, it is small wonder that there was, from the moment the firing stopped, a great clamor of voices raised to assign and avoid blame, to give and claim credit, for what happened. Few battles of the Civil War stimulated such long-lived, heated debate among the survivors, with the most acrimonious exchanges taking place between men who had fought on the same side: Early versus Gordon on why the attack halted at noon, and how many of their men actually broke ranks to loot the Federal camps; Crook versus Sheridan on whether Sheridan deserved all the credit for saving the day; George Custer versus Wesley Merritt on which Federal cavalry division captured more guns in the battle's final moments; and so on.

Yet Colonel Kidd was wrong. The debate flickered out with the lives of the last survivors, and what had been one of the Civil War's most noted battles became one of its most obscure.

Perhaps it is time to take another look. This is one of those rare stories that resonates on several levels, and rewards each effort of investigation with fresh insights. Especially, it gives us the chance to see, clearly outlined against the fiery backdrop of this most bitter war, several remarkable men whose backgrounds and characters shaped the war's final outcome, and it is indeed character that is the real subject here. It is no longer enough simply to identify winners and losers, heroes and villains; we have come to understand that heroes are not always brave and true, that villains *can* often be heroic. We have come to appreciate the knots and whorls of true character, the contradictions that coexist in the lives of real people. We want a great deal more information than our ancestors did before we are willing to give, or withhold, our admiration.

We are still trying, moreover, to comprehend what it was that drove people much like ourselves—Americans who had lived under the same flag, benefited from the same bright experiment in freedom and opportunity—to slaughter one another with such ferocity for four years. None of the simple, abstract explanations suffices when we ask ourselves whether we, barefoot and hungry and dejected, would have followed Jubal Early on that cold October morning; or whether we, after years of bloodshed and struggle, having been chased for miles by a howling enemy lunging out of the fog and dark, would have followed Phil Sheridan back to the line to face the guns again.

Nor was it only the combatants whose mettle was on display at Cedar Creek. Jubal Early and Phil Sheridan were in the

Valley that autumn because they were selected by their commanding generals to accomplish missions of the highest strategic import. Thus, their characters and their performances reflect directly on that of their mentors—Robert E. Lee and Ulysses S. Grant—and throw a different quality of light on those much-studied men.

It is fortunate that a great many of those who fought at Cedar Creek were moved by their own meditations on the event, by the many controversies surrounding it, or by other motives, to leave a record of what they saw and felt and heard and thought. From the graceful prose of the novelist John De-Forest to the curmudgeonly, artless harpings of the wardog George Crook; from the studied, self-conscious gracefulness of the aging Senator John Gordon to the florid self-promotion of the incorrigible George Custer (both of whom were less concerned with the facts than with how they appeared, after the fact); from the impassioned defensiveness of Jubal Early to the crisp arrogance of Phil Sheridan; the versions of events are plentiful and, when superimposed, reveal fascinating inferences the writers did not intend to state.

For present purposes it is especially fortunate that among those who witnessed the battle—or at least important parts of its afternoon phase, from the Union side of the lines—was a young artist from *Leslie's Illustrated Newspaper,* James E. Taylor. Some years after the war, Taylor put together his sketches made at the scene, the stories he heard from soldiers immediately after the battle, and some of the written material published later in an illustrated account titled "With Sheridan up the Shenandoah Valley in 1864: Leaves from a Special Artists Sketchbook and Diary," which he never published. If he got some things wrong and drew a few things that never happened, his drawings nevertheless convey to us not only the look and feel or the fighting, but something of the nature of the men whose faces he captured in near-photographic detail. I am grateful to the Western Reserve Historical Society in Cleveland, Ohio, and especially to Ann Sindelar of the Society's museum, for making possible the illustration of this book entirely with Taylor's sketches.

The work of many other people has made this a far better

book than it would have been without their help. Foremost among these individuals is Brian Pohanka, who provided much-needed research assistance. Brian's expert knowledge of the war, combined with an artist's eye for telling detail and a musician's ear for the memorable phrase, has provided constant inspiration and education. If I have managed, despite his efforts, to inject errors of fact or of interpretation into this book, he cannot be blamed. Ben Ritter, of the Handley Memorial Library in Winchester, Virginia, has the tenacity of a terrier when given the scent of a fact or a book, and his gifts to this effort are considerable. I owe another special debt to Lieutenant Colonel Joseph W. A. Whitehorne, historian of the U.S. Army Inspector-General's office in Washington, D.C., for sharing with me his detailed knowledge of the battlefield. Many others, at the Library of Congress, the National Archives, the Lloyd House annex of the Alexandria, Virginia, library, the Valentine Museum in Richmond, and the U.S. Army Military History Institute at Carlisle, Pennsylvania, have contributed vital pieces.

I am grateful to Russ Adams for running his feral editor's eye over the manuscript and catching some of the infelicities, and to the other members of the venerable Martini Mafia whose regular deliberations at Ted's place have been invaluable, not especially to the book, but to the mental health of the author, which, in this and all other enterprises, continues to depend utterly on the love and support of Patricia, Jason, Kimberly and Andrew Lewis.

Thomas A. Lewis
Berryville, Virginia
March 1988

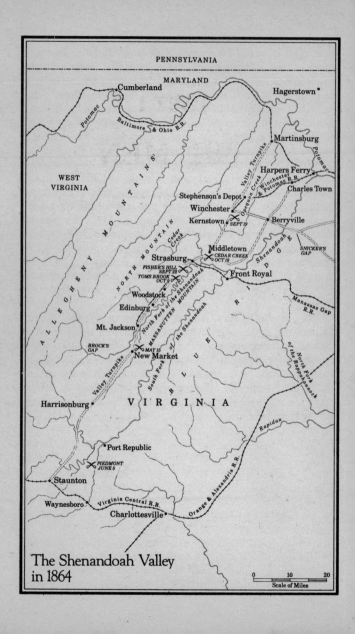

The Shenandoah Valley
in 1864

PART I

THE MEN

Chapter 1

Old Jube:
October 1, 1864

In a cold October rain the rider came, ambling his horse back down into the Valley of Humiliation. He was riding alone into enemy country—hard to believe, but the Yankees had held the Shenandoah for a week now—along the road that eased off the Blue Ridge from Waynesboro and wound eastward toward Staunton. He rode alertly, but without the careful wariness of a man alone; seeing him, one who had lived through three hard years of war would have sensed that something was coming.

And soon there were more horsemen, in a loose line, picking their way across the fields and through the woods on either side of the road. They hunched cold and dripping under the relentless rain that announced the approach of the winter of 1864. Then, behind their arrowhead advance, a denser body of cavalry, column of fours at the walk, a hundred hooves spattering the rainwater, horses nodding and snorting in protest, riders grumbling. Behind the cavalry, marching men; the whole Confederate Army of the Valley was on the move again.

The trickle of incidental noises swelled slowly to a broad and shallow river of sound as the infantry came into view. There were clinks and creaks and mumbles and steps, here a sudden oath, there a snapped order, as they loped along four abreast in the formless but ground-eating route step of the veteran foot soldier, rifles pointing at all quarters of the sky from the slovenly but comfortable right-shoulder shift. In the center of the desperately small regiments the cased colors jutted up like

stripped trees in winter, while to one side the glum officers rode
their gaunt mounts.

Armies have moods, and this one's was sour. It had little to
do with the fact that the men were ill fed and ill equipped,
although how they marched despite these privations is hard to
imagine. One of their number was examined closely that fall by
one of the Federals who had killed him, who in a kind of tribute
recorded exactly how he had been equipped for his last fight:
"His feet, wrapped in rags, had coarse shoes upon them, so
worn and full of holes that they were only held together by
many pieces of thick twine. Ragged trousers, a jacket, and a
shirt of what used to be called 'tow cloth,' a straw hat, which
had lost a large portion of both crown and rim, completed his
attire. A haversack hung from his shoulder. Its contents were a
jack-knife, a plug of twisted tobacco, a tin cup, and about two
quarts of coarsely cracked corn, with perhaps an ounce of salt
tied in a rag."[1]

But this had been the lot of the Confederate soldier for most
of the time he had been fighting his second war for independence, and he had for some time now taken pride in his pov-
erty. He had fewer bullets than the Yankees, so he made them
count for more; fewer men, so they had to be smarter and faster
to attack; less to eat, so they would be tougher. All of this was
especially true in the Shenandoah Valley, home to many of the
men in this army, a hallowed place to every Virginian for its
beauty and productivity, and special even to those who came
from far away.

Most people in America, and many in foreign lands, knew
something about the Shenandoah. Schoolboys learned that a
young George Washington had landed his first surveying job
there, had held his first military command there, had learned
how to fight a war without food or ammunition there. Most
people knew where it was, angled to the northeast from Lexington to Harpers Ferry where the Shenandoah joined the Potomac. Others, who had no idea what or where the Shenandoah
was, had heard of it: for a century or so, riverboat men on the
Mississippi and blue-water sailors all over the world had been
singing out the haunting plaint: "Oh Shenandoah, I long to
hear you."

Since the fearsome decade of outrage and death known as the French and Indian War, the history of the Valley had been a quiet one, always off to one side of the main hard thrust of revolution and war and consolidation that made a country. Yet its presence was always felt, its special character always shone a muted light into the grand events. In each hour of necessity the Shenandoah sent out politicians and generals and heroes equal to the task; otherwise the Valley kept its own countenance, husbanded its surpassing peace.

Then the War Between the States began, and for the first time since the Indian outrages, the Shenandoah shuddered to the sound of guns. As a sheltered highway leading to the rear of the Federal defenses of Washington; as an avenue southward toward the railroads knitting together eastern and western states of the Secession; and most importantly—when embargo, devastation, and depopulation began to claim their terrible tolls—as the granary for Robert E. Lee's Army of Northern Virginia, the Valley was a linchpin of the Southern Cause and a primary target of the Northern war machine.

These considerations, along with the Valley's special hold on all Virginians, invested every conflict in its confines with a special zeal and imbued every campaign with a mythic quality. This had been especially true in 1862. The Confederates had been outnumbered and outgunned and short of supplies already, but that did not matter when they had on their side the quirky brilliance of a Thomas Jonathan Jackson, the Presbyterian deacon who could cripple a Federal army's advance on Richmond by bewildering three Federal armies in the Valley a hundred miles away. Surely, it had seemed then, the Federals would soon tire of being whipped, would see the inevitable as they and the rest of the world began to hunger for King Cotton, and would recognize the Confederacy, make a place for it on the continent, and stop the fighting.

Two years later, as predicted, the Union was tired—bone tired. Weary of war, racked by dissension, weakened by voices shouting for peace on any terms. Lee was still punishing each and every mistake the Federal generals made, still making up for his deficiencies of men and material with the power of his will and the force of his mind. But the world had somehow learned to do without cotton, and somehow the Federals kept coming back. Now, under the sandy gaze of their new general in chief, Ulysses S. Grant, they were coming faster and harder than ever, and were driving on Richmond more powerfully by far than they had in 1862. Once again it was necessary to draw off the Federal strength and deflect disaster. But this was 1864, and things were different. Hope was almost gone.

"It was not disaffection or disloyalty for the cause for which they had so long fought," a Georgia veteran mused later about the thinking of his comrades in the Valley that October, "but they reasoned this way: 'We are confronted with an army four times that of our own; Lee is besieged at Richmond and Petersburg; Sherman is marching through Georgia; we are cut off from the Trans-Mississippi Department; our ports are blockaded; our army is daily diminishing, with no material for recruiting; our families are in want and destitution at home, while the Federal government has abundant resources at home and all Europe from which to recruit their armies.' With these conditions, they felt and maintained that there was no hope for our success."[2]

Yet they advanced, under the lowering clouds, with the mist streaked in tattered wisps like gunsmoke along the flanks of the mountain palisades behind. They balanced their rain-slicked rifles (most of them Federal makes, snatched up from some battlefield) with hands that had been numbed and stiffened by the cold. It had been a long time since there had been the time or the opportunity for a bath, and in warmer weather, it was said, this army could be smelled long before it could be seen.

At its side, trailed by a knot of staff officers, rode Lieutenant General Jubal Anderson Early, commanding the Army of the Valley. They had called him "Old Jubilee" back when he had turned the Federal right at First Manassas in 1861, had held his ground at Antietam in 1862 and had healed a broken line at Fredericksburg a few months later. But at Gettysburg, and since, things had not been quite right with him. Maybe it was bad luck, maybe bad orders, but the men were not disposed to be understanding; whenever a battle had gone awry, General Early had found a reason, and the reason was always that his men had let him down. Now they called him "Old Jube."

He rode along, hunched and brooding, rain dripping from the broad-brimmed white hat that was turned sharply up along the right side and bedecked with a single, rather sorry-looking ostrich feather. As the black eyes darted here and there, taking in the smoking desolation that had been brought to this hallowed Valley by the Federals, tobacco juice and profanity squirted incessantly from behind the gray-brown beard.

"I never saw a man who looked less like a soldier," John S. Wise wrote of Early. Wise, whose father had been governor of Virginia, was a young infantry officer who never served with Early but saw him often, and thanks to a political upbringing saw people clearly. "His eyes were very small, dark, deep-set and glittering, and his nose aquiline," Wise wrote. "His step was slow, shuffling, and almost irresolute." A booming voice of command might have helped, but Early's was "a piping treble, and he talked with a long-drawn whine or drawl."[3]

The first thing one noticed, however—before one thought of an Old Testament prophet calling down damnation, or pictured some spread-winged raptor eyeing a meadowful of mice—was the severely stooped and rounded shoulders. While in Mexico during the war of 1847, Early had been stricken with something he called rheumatism—it was probably spondylitis, a painful affliction of the spinal muscles—that had bent him until he had difficulty holding his head upright, and looked both older than his forty-seven years and shorter than his six feet.

Some came up with an easier explanation for his infirmity; there were persistent rumors of drunkenness. But a courier, Joseph D. Shewalter of Missouri, who was close to Early for fully half of the war, testified that "I never saw him in my life under the influence of liquor." Instead, wrote Shewalter, because of the effects of the "rheumatism" and a wound Early suffered at Williamsburg in 1862, the general "was unable to get on his horse without assistance. I assisted him repeatedly in mounting. It is owing to this fact, and perhaps malice, that it is believed he was constantly drunk."[4]

It was hard to figure the balance sheet on Old Jube, but there was no doubt that, look like it or not, he was a soldier. Only three living generals—the wounded and convalescing James Longstreet, the interim First Corps commander Richard Anderson and Ambrose Powell Hill of the Third Corps—stood as high in the estimation of Bobby Lee. (Since his canonization it is breathtaking to see him referred to as anything other than General Robert E. Lee; but the fact is that the Valley boys expressed their affection and respect by calling him Bobby Lee, just as the men from plantation country called him Marse Robert.) Lee's trust conferred upon Early a large measure of respect; the reverence in which the men held Lee was boundless, and he could spend it in any way he chose.

Standing second to Lee in the pantheon of Confederate sainthood was Stonewall Jackson—in the Shenandoah Valley it was a close second—and Early had met with his approval as well. Jackson had said after Antietam that Early had "attacked with great vigor and gallantry," and from the flinty Stonewall that was exuberant, almost hysterical, praise.[5]

Old Jube's military reputation had not been handed down from above; he had been a hard charger from the first, and had moved steadily toward high command through the fires of every major campaign in the eastern theater of the war. Major Henry Kyd Douglas, who was Early's adjutant general in the fall of 1864 and had served Jackson in the 1862 Valley campaign, wrote that "there were none of General Lee's subordinates, after the death of General Jackson, who possessed the essential qualities of a military commander to a greater extent than Early." No one doubted his courage, his coolness under fire, his aggressiveness, his tenacity; and almost no one liked him.[6]

"Arbitrary, cynical, with strong prejudices, he was personally disagreeable," said Douglas; "he made few admirers or friends either by his manners or his habits." John Wise, who saw Early in a different time and setting, caught the same whiff of bitterness, and suspected a perverse stagecraft: "His likes and dislikes he announced without hesitation, and, as he was filled with strong and bitter opinions, his conversation was always racy and pungent. His views were not always correct, or just, or broad; but his wit was quick, his satire biting, his expressions were vigorous, and he was interestingly lurid and picturesque." Not to mention "startlingly profane."[7]

Both young men glimpsed fissures and whorls in the man's

many-layered character. Douglas saw behind the loud and studied cynicism a startling gentleness. "If he had a tender feeling, he endeavored to conceal it and acted as though he would be ashamed to be detected in doing a kindness; yet many will recall little acts of General Early which prove that his heart was naturally full of loyalty and tenderness." The thoughtful young major also judged the impressive military record to be equivocal: "Quick to decide and almost inflexible in decision, with a boldness to attack that approached rashness and a tenacity in resisting that resembled desperation, he was yet on the field of battle not equal to his own intellect or decision." There is a strange and terrible indictment: to be unequal to one's own intellect.[8]

Such were the glimmerings, in 1864, of the savage conflicts that had soured Jubal Early's soul. He seems to have been born knowing, deep in his bones, that nothing was ever going to turn out right for him. It was his special curse also to nurture, in his innermost soul, a bright, hard flame of ambition, a lust for public acclaim. He was from time to time a military man who detested uniformity and rejected discipline; an elected official who loathed politicians; a fervent Union man until April 15, 1861, from which date until the end of his life he reviled the Union and everything it did; and the heroic protagonist of a youthful, Byronic romance who became a renowned woman-hater, yet remained capable of disarming charm. His was a life that had begun with great gifts and high promise, but that had always somehow retreated from achievement, slowly but implacably, toward star-crossed disappointment and rage.

He never seemed to get what he wanted, or to want what he got. He did not want a military career, but as one of ten children of a prosperous Franklin County farmer (in far southwest Virginia), he wanted a first-class education, and for that he looked to the United States Military Academy. The local congressman was a neighbor and family friend—Jubal's father, Joab, had served his county as sheriff, colonel of militia and state legislator—and the appointment was easily arranged. In June of 1833 the sixteen-year-old rustic became a plebe.

The "clear, direct and comprehensive" mind that Kyd

Douglas would admire thirty years later was already in evidence. Jubal consistently ranked near the top of his class in academics, but he stayed near the bottom of the entire corps of cadets when ranked for behavior. The final year was typical; at graduation he ranked 18th in a class of 50, based on general merit, but for conduct he was judged to be 195th in a corps of 211 cadets. The accumulation of 200 demerits in any class year meant automatic dismissal from the Academy; in his third year Jubal had 196 demerits, and in his best year, the first, he had 142. As he explained it, years later, "I had very little taste for scrubbing brass."[9]

Although he intended to resign from the army and study law, he became infected with thoughts of war and glory. In 1835 he was smitten by the cause of Sam Houston and the Texicans, and pleaded with his father for permission—and the means—to leave West Point and go fight Santa Anna for the independence of Texas. Joab denied both permission and money, and the Alamo was denied another martyr. As it turned out, the army was to be denied another glory-hound. When he graduated in 1837 he was sent to dreary duty in Florida chasing Seminoles, then in Tennessee policing Cherokees. This was not what he wanted, and Early resigned.

Meanwhile he found that Romance, like War, did not measure up to its reputation. It happened when the handsome young six-footer, mounted on a splendid black stallion, took a brief vacation from his academy studies with a trip to White Sulphur Springs in Greenbrier County. And there he met his one true love.

She was a comely Quaker debutante from Philadelphia, also staying at White Sulphur Springs, and their meeting was the stuff of a young man's heated daydreams. She was touring the countryside in a rented carriage when the driver attempted to cross a storm-swollen stream. The horses were knocked off their feet by the torrent, the carriage was being swept away and was threatening to overturn when, with timing that defies belief, young Lochinvar galloped up on his black charger, swept the screaming damsel from the jaws of death and bore her away to safety. (No one seems to have bothered to record the fate of the driver.) With the lady prettily recovered, the heroic rescuer and demure rescuee danced and walked and chatted the days away until harsh duty called him hence. But first, an exchange of fervent promises to meet again, next summer, at the scene of their enchantment.

By that time he had quit the army, but since his resignation would not be processed in time for the rendezvous, he applied for leave. Approval was soon forthcoming, but in the same mail came an envelope addressed to him in a familiar, feminine hand. There was no letter, just a Philadelphia newspaper containing a description of his true love's long-planned wedding. Jubal Early never allowed himself to like, let alone love, another woman.[10]

There were other things to want. He took up law and politics in 1840, applied himself for five years, and made a good start. By the time war with Mexico threatened in 1846, Early had built up a decent practice and had been elected twice to the Virginia General Assembly. Governor William Smith, whom Early would meet again, appointed him a major of volunteers for the war. But where other officers in that conflict got brevet promotions, honorable wounds and decided boosts to their careers, Early got garrison duty, boredom, and the "rheumatism" that bent his back and prematurely aged him.

More disappointments. After the war he lost his seat in the general assembly. He managed to hold on to a lesser position—county commonwealth's attorney, or prosecutor—and he made a living practicing law, but just a living. Thus a decade passed, and Jubal Early passed from his thirties into his forties, the time of life when a man confronts his limitations and realizes how many things he will not achieve. He had a small reputation as an honest and capable country lawyer, but substantial wealth and a glittering career were clearly beyond his reach; he had firm hold on a minor political office, but he would never be a Stephen Douglas or a Henry Clay, shaping a growing nation or guiding a powerful state with his words; he enjoyed a modicum of esteem among his friends, clients and neighbors, but by his own choice he would never know the warmer comforts and the gentling influence of a loving wife and children.

The record seems straightforward and innocuous, yet something lurks here. Young John Wise, seeing Old Jube in Rocky

Mount int he summer of 1862, sensed shadows reaching back before the war. By then Early had been wounded in the Peninsular Campaign, and while convalescing was holding court on a tavern porch overlooking Rocky Mount's steeply inclined main street. "He was the hero of Franklin County," Wise remembered, "and although he professed to despise popularity and to be defiant of public opinion, it was plain that he enjoyed his military distinction. It had done much to soften old-time asperities, and blot out from the memory of his neighbors certain facts in his private life which had, prior to the war, alienated him from many of his own class."[11]

Whatever those facts were, they did not deter the people of Franklin County from turning to Jubal Early for representation in the ultimate crisis of their time. When the Virginia General Assembly called for a convention to be held in the spring of 1861 to decide the question of secession, Franklin County sent Jubal Early and another delegate to vote against secession and for the Union. Their attitude was shared by a large majority of the convention delegates and by virtually every one of the delegates from the western part of the state, between the Blue Ridge Mountains and the Ohio River.

The westerners had little in common with the delegates from the other side of the Blue Ridge, where lay plantations, aristocracy, high society, old money and slavery. Slavery was never successfully transplanted across the Blue Ridge, not from any moral superiority or tenderness of feeling, but for the most implacable of reasons: it simply did not work. Cotton and tobacco did not do well west of the mountains, while other, less labor-intensive crops did. The farms that evolved were small in scale, the people who prospered were tough-minded, unpretentious, self-reliant folk who might never have amounted to anything had it not been for the freedoms offered by the Union. Thus the threat of losing the right to take slavery into the territories—the most powerful impetus to civil war in 1861— did not strike the westerners with anything like the power it held for the planters.

But one thing shared by all the delegates to the 1861 convention in Richmond was a powerful sense of being Virginians. Whether a baronial planter from the Tidewater or a hardscrabble farmer from some narrow, penurious valley in the Alleghenies, the delegates and the people they represented had powerful and emotional bonds to their state, the Mother of States and Presidents, the largest state save only Texas, the richest state, whose capital was claimed to be the center of the most glittering intellectual, artistic and political society to be found on the continent.

Jubal Early was extraordinary in this gathering not for what he believed—that Virginia should remain in the Union—but for the asperity with which he argued his beliefs. One Virginian remembered him as "the most extreme anti-secessionist and anti-war man in the Virginia Convention." He defended President Lincoln even after the creation of the Confederate States of America and the beginning of the siege of Fort Sumter. He told the delegates on February 20 they need not worry about the armaments being rushed to Federal military installations in Virginia. The president was doing his job in protecting public property, Early said, and Virginians would not be in danger from these guns "unless they may foolishly run their heads into the mouth of one of them." Jubal's colleagues called him the "Terrapin from Franklin," undoubtedly having in mind the snapping turtle.[12]

On April 4 the convention recorded a vote of 88–45 against a proposed ordinance of secession, but remained in session out of fear of the General Assembly. That group was radically pro-secession, and had the power to summon another convention if it did not like the work of the first one. On April 12 Fort Sumter was fired on. On April 15 President Lincoln issued a call for 75,000 volunteers to join the army and suppress the rebellion. Thus required by the Union president to take up arms against their fellow Southerners, most Virginians instantly became secessionists. On April 17 the Virginia convention adopted an ordinance of secession by a vote of 88–55. (It took Early a little longer; confused and disbelieving on the day of the stunning proclamation, he continued to vote against secession, but endorsed it immediately after the ordinance was passed.)[13]

The conversion of the Old Dominion was swift, total and accompanied by unrestrained emotion; they were embarking on the second American Revolution, they were defending their state, their homes, their families, and, yes, their sacred honor. The issue was not slavery but coercion; the desire was not to sunder the Union but to protect the United States from a tyranny being attempted by a national government that existed only to serve the states. They had not chosen war until they were forced to choose between war on the one hand and on the other submission, cowardice and disloyalty to kindred states. Then they did not merely choose war, they embraced it with consuming ardor. The same man who had noted Early's extremism in opposing secession and war now found him to be "the most enthusiastic man in the Commonwealth in advocacy of the war and personal service in it."[14]

Jubal went home briefly to put his personal affairs in order before going off to defend Virginia. It must have been an exhilarating time, a chance to shuck off all at once the encrusted strictures of a mundane life and ride toward the sound of guns, where glory was. A man seldom gets a chance to reorder his life completely, to come suddenly within reach of the dreams of power and renown that nurtured his youth but have been almost forgotten. Such is the hidden and terrible appeal of war.

The great gifts and high promise that Jubal Early brought to this new arena were immediately apparent. A colonel at the first battle of Manassas, Early brought his brigade swinging around to the Confederate left at the crisis of the day. "He reached the position intended just when the Federal army was about to assume the offensive, and assailed its exposed front," recalled the Confederate commander, General Joseph E. Johnston. "The attack was conducted with too much skill and courage to be for a moment doubtful. The Federal right was at once thrown into confusion. A general advance of the Confederate line, directed by General Beauregard, completed our success, and won the battle."[15]

(Beauregard had seen Early's brigade approach, but could not tell if it was friend or foe because the colors were hanging limply in the still air. He watched tensely, knowing he would have to retreat if the men were Federals, until a breeze revealed the Confederate flag. Afterward, Beauregard agitated for a new flag, easier to identify on the battlefield; the Stars and Bars, with its three horizontal red and white stripes and its white-starred blue field in the top left quarter, too closely resembled the U.S. flag. A few months later the Confederate Battle Flag—a blue St. Andrew's cross bedecked with seven white stars, on a red field—was adopted.)

In the long, shocked pause that followed that unexpectedly harsh initial taste of civil war, Jubal was promoted to brigadier general for his achievement; but, prophetically, another officer garnered the lion's share of the public acclaim for the victory. Just before Early's counterattack, a brigade of Virginians under Brigadier General Tom Jackson, just rushed in from the Shenandoah, held against a Federal turning movement and got their commander compared to a stone wall, the very antithesis of his approach to warfare.

Jubal achieved some notoriety the next year, however, when in the first battle of the Peninsular Campaign, near Williamsburg, he led his Virginians in a race with D. Harvey Hill's North Carolinians for the privilege of taking some Federal guns. The guns were not taken, his brigade suffered heavy casualties, and Early, shot twice, was out of the war for two months. Instead of fame, he got a reputation for being a bit of a hothead.

When he returned to the army at the end of June, he was assigned to a brigade in the Army of the Valley, and began an apprenticeship for high command under two of the best there were: Richard Ewell, whose division Early joined, and Stonewall Jackson, who had just completed his brilliant Valley Campaign and had now come east of the Blue Ridge to maneuver toward Second Manassas.

Both sides in the war were doing a great deal of reorganizing. Early's old brigade no longer existed, and he was given temporary command of another brigade, in place of a wounded general. It was not an unusual or demeaning arrangement, but for some reason Early was offended. Perhaps he was galled by the fame and rank achieved by Jackson and Ewell, who had been fellow brigade commanders at First Manassas; perhaps his sense of being underappreciated was heightened by the after-effects of his wounds; whatever the reason, he wrote a petulant complaint that came to the attention of Lee himself. In the soothing tones of a father dealing with a very young son, Lee assured Early that "confidence in your zeal and ability has been increased instead of diminished by your service," and that Early's wounds were seen as "a badge of distinction and a claim for high consideration instead of a crime, as you suppose."[16]

During the engagement at Cedar Mountain that began the campaign of Second Manassas, Early was in the thick of the fighting and distinguished himself by his intelligent handling of his men, his prompt and cool response to emergency and his personal courage. Jackson noted crisply that Early had held his position with "great firmness," and Ewell strongly recommended a promotion to major general. If Early began to think that with Ewell's patronage he was finally beginning to get somewhere, the feeling lasted less than three weeks; on August 28 at Groveton, during the opening engagement of Second Manassas, a rifle ball shattered Dick Ewell's knee and took him out of the war for eight months.

In the battle of Second Manassas that began the next day, Jubal Early's part was active but not particularly distinguished. With his newfound mentor wounded, Early apparently felt the need to blow his own horn afterward, and to his official report he appended a remarkable, self-congratulatory sentence: "I hope I may be excused for referring to the record shown by my own brigade, which has never been broken or compelled to fall back or left one of its men to be buried by the enemy, but has invariably driven the enemy when opposed by him and slept upon the ground on which it has fought in every action, with the solitary exception of the affair at Bristow Station, when it retired under orders covering the withdrawal of the other troops."

Two and a half weeks later, Lee's first invasion of the North took the opposing armies to the bloody crucible of Antietam. No soldier of dubious mettle could escape the harsh, clear light thrown by this most awesome of battles, and Jubal Early stood up to the worst it had to offer, which was the worst there ever was.

It had hardly begun when Ewell's replacement went down wounded and the command of the division devolved on Early. In fact, however, only his own brigade remained intact on the field, and it was that force he maneuvered, with characteristic nerve and effectiveness, throughout the fighting on the Confederate left. By his prompt movement he stopped a division-sized Federal breakthrough, then joined in the repulse of a Federal corps. The splendid cavalier Jeb Stuart was impressed enough to mention in his official report that Early had attacked with "great coolness and good judgment." Jackson was impressed enough to leave Early in command of the division, but not enough to recommend a promotion. Most important for Early, however, was the fact that Lee had noticed, praised Early's "great resolution" and recommended him for promotion to major general. The promotion was not forthcoming; Jackson, on the other hand, was made a lieutenant general and was given command of the newly organized Second Corps.[17]

Instead of going into winter quarters that year, the Federals decided to make another push toward Richmond, by way of Fredericksburg. The Army of the Valley was called to help, and on the way east there occurred an exchange between the testy Jackson and the irascible Early that was recounted over campfires for years to come. After a hard day's march during which Jubal's division had been in the lead, he received a note from Jackson's headquarters: "General Jackson's compliments to General Early, and he would like to know why he saw so many stragglers in rear of your division today." The response was immediate: "General Early's compliments to General Jackson, and he takes pleasure in informing him that he saw so many stragglers in rear of my division today, probably because he rode in rear of my division." One veteran who recorded the story marveled that "not another officer in the Army of Northern Virginia would have dared send such an impertinent note to Jackson."[18]

Although not nearly fast enough to satisfy him, Early's stock was rising, both with Lee, whose eye was on the new division commander now, and with the men. They were telling each other stories about Old Jubilee, and they were liking the way the stories told. During the battle of Fredericksburg in December, they loped confidently forward, under fire, to stop a potentially disastrous Federal breakthrough of A. P. Hill's line on the Confederate right. They had saved some of Hill's guns at

Cedar Mountain, and they had saved his flank at Second Bull Run, and now as they charged they yelled, "Here comes Old *Jubal*! Let Old Jubal straighten that fence! Jubal's boys are always getting Hill out of trouble!" Early may have been gratified to hear that evidence of respect, or he may immediately have reflected that Hill had made major general six months earlier.[19]

On the way into combat, as the first casualties fell to the preliminary shocks of stray shells, Jubal saw a chaplain streaking for the rear. At once, the general's oddly tilted humor whined its way to the mark: "Chaplain, I have known you for the past 30 years, and all that time you have been trying to get to heaven, and now that the opportunity is offered you are fleeing from it. Sir, I am surprised!" Then Early's division swung into the breach in the Confederate line, slammed it shut and drove the Federals back into the bottomlands along the Rappahannock River. One of his brigades threatened for a time to drive right through the Federal army, but for lack of ammunition and support had to fall back.

That was the first starving winter for the Army of Northern Virginia. It was an unusually harsh one, made worse for the men by shortages of shoes, overcoats, blankets and food. They endured with remarkable cheerfulness, not imagining how many more such winters were in store for those who lived. For Jubal Early, huddled in his winter quarters south of Fredericksburg near the Rappahannock, spring came early that year; January brought him the long-awaited promotion to major general and assignment to permanent command of Ewell's division, which now became Early's division.[20]

When campaigning resumed in May, Early and his division were denied a major role in the intense drama of Chancellorsville. It was Jackson, again, who took the glory with his stunning flanking maneuver and rout of the Federal right—the right of an army that was itself attempting a flanking maneuver against Lee's smaller force. This, however, was Jackson's final glory, won at the expense of a mortal wound inflicted by his own men.

While all of this was happening ten miles west of Fredericksburg, Early had been left behind to hold the city. Although he faced overwhelming odds, and at a critical juncture received mistaken orders to withdraw, he held for as long as anyone could have expected. Then he rushed west in time to help drive the rest of the Federal forces back across the Rappahannock again. Jubal was performing competent service, he was doing precisely what Lee asked, but he was hardly becoming a legend in his own time. And that, unquestionably, is what he wished to become.[21]

After Chancellorsville, Lee reorganized his army for his second invasion of the North—his ultimate gamble that he could rise above his shortages of men and material and so stagger the Union that it would negotiate a peace. Now that Jackson was gone, Lee believed his two corps to be too large and unwieldy for effective control, and he put his 60,000 men into three corps. Old Pete Longstreet continued in command of the First Corps, of course, and Jackson was succeeded at the helm of the Second by an obvious choice—Dick Ewell. (Old Bald Head had returned to the army in May of '63, without his leg and with a wife. This formidable widow lady, whom the old bachelor persisted in introducing as "Mrs. Brown," firmly deprived him of chewing tobacco and cuss words, introduced him to home life and religion and, in the opinion of the army, ruined him.) The new Third Corps was the plum requiring that someone be promoted, and Lee's selection must have aggravated Jubal Early's biliousness: the anointed officer was the very one Jubal's men had so often bailed out—Ambrose Powell Hill.[22]

On the march toward Maryland and Pennsylvania, the Second Corps had the responsibility of clearing the lower Shenandoah Valley of Federals. Under Ewell's close supervision, Early's division won a fine victory at Winchester, after which Lee's invasion route was clear. Dick Ewell, a year younger than Early, had been greatly aged by his grievous wound and by his infirmity. But he still felt younger than Jubal, apparently, for when the attack on Winchester began, Old Bald Head, watching excitedly, yelled, "There's Early! I hope the old fellow won't be hurt!"[23]

They marched north then, to the ragged, unplanned, uncontrolled meeting engagement at Gettysburg. Once again Jubal Early's thirst for unequivocal glory was to go unslaked. He was caught in a web of failure. His corps commander's nerve failed, inexplicably, and despite repeated urgings by Lee, Ewell for some reason could not bring himself to attack the Federal right on Cemetery Hill until it was too late. Truth to tell, the army commander's generalship failed that day, and Lee displayed none of the vigor and aggressiveness that always before had taken him to the heart of the enemy's weaknesses; on these three fateful days he battered away at strong points. Jeb Stuart, the legendary cavalier, failed to show up in time to do what cavalry was supposed to do, and Old Pete Longstreet, in a monumental snit because his advice on strategy was being ignored, failed to prosecute his orders.

Old Jube came on the field like a thunderclap during the first day of battle, with a charge that broke the Federal left and won possession of Gettysburg itself. Thereafter, however, he was held on a short leash by the unnerved Ewell, and did his duty. When finally unleashed, near dark on the second day of the three-day battle, Early's men clawed their way to the very top of Cemetery Hill and for a time threatened the Federal army headquarters. But they were unsupported, the Federals soon threw in reinforcements, and the Confederate lodgement on Cemetery Hill was short-lived.[24]

The wounded Army of Northern Virginia, blessed again by a slow and unenthusiastic Federal pursuit, made its way back through the Valley and took position along the south side of the Rappahannock River. It was a perilous position, depending for its safety on a bridgehead at the north end of the ruined Rappahannock Bridge of the Orange and Alexandria Railroad. On November 7, 1863, the vital sector was the responsibility of Jubal Early, and here he confronted what he had so long avoided—unmitigated military disaster.[25]

During the afternoon the Federals appeared in front of the bridgehead, which was held by one of Early's brigades, and pushed across the river at another ford four miles downstream. For several hours they made no further progress. A howling wind and approaching darkness made it difficult for Early to assess the danger to his brigade across the river, but the Federals were not known for night attacks, and Lee, who was anxiously watching over the situation, agreed that the dispatch of one more brigade should be a sufficient response.

But the Federals attacked in force at dusk, and for once moved smartly, in an exquisitely planned and executed attack that overwhelmed the bridgehead before the Confederates realized what was happening. Early had roughly 2,000 men on the north side of the river; of these almost 1,700 were lost, most of them taken prisoner, along with four guns and eight regimental flags. The Army of Northern Virginia was forced to fall back nearly ten miles and take up a new line along the Rapidan River.[26]

"This was the first serious disaster that had befallen any of my commands," Early wrote in his memoirs, adding a qualification that was to become familiar: "I felt I was not responsible for it." His official report, written at the time, strained mightily to confer upon himself absolution. Or at least, to preempt severe criticism by admitting to a lesser crime: "I must candidly confess," he wrote fatuously, "that I did concur in the opinion of the commanding General that the enemy did not have enterprise enough to attempt any serious attack after dark." With the blame for any error of judgment thus shifted to Lee's capacious shoulders, Early went on to add that he had "felt there would be very great danger in a night attack if vigorously made," but that he "had no discretion about withdrawing the troops." Then he pointed out that he had previously done well, and that on the whole he had captured more guns and prisoners, thus far in the war, than he lost at Rappahannock Bridge.[27]

That Jubal was stridently explaining things that Lee did not need explained, and thrusting forward a record that Lee knew intimately, was demonstrated a little more than two weeks later when Dick Ewell became so ill he had to leave his command. His temporary replacement as commanding general of the Second Corps was Jubal Early. But the fires of ambition soon had to be banked again, when Ewell recovered.

Now began the second starving winter for the Army of Northern Virginia, and Lee became ever more engrossed with the problem of finding food for his men. Thus when a Federal raid threatened the Shenandoah Valley, his army's one unfailing source of flour, cornmeal, beef, pork, fruit and forage, Lee was determined to hold it. Jubal Early was the man to do it for him.

Flattering as it might have been to be relied upon by the great chieftain, it was perhaps the worst assignment of Jubal's life. He who had recently commanded the Second Corps found himself conducting a months-long, comic-opera chase up and down the Valley, in and out of the Alleghenies, all to no effect. Time and again a brigade of Federal cavalry, led by Brigadier General William W. Averell, slipped away, threading the myriad little valleys and hollows of the western mountains, feinting and dodging. It drove Jubal Early to distraction, and as was becoming usual, he found someone to blame.

The local commander, John Imboden, led a collection of cavalry units that more closely resembled Mosby's Rangers than any Army of Northern Virginia regiment in spirit, conduct, discipline—and achievement. Imboden and his fellow partisans, of whom the best known were John "Hanse" McNeil of West Virginia and Harry Gilmor of Maryland, shared Jubal Early's dislike for scrubbing brass, fought with unbridled ferocity and effectiveness when protecting their homes but became listless and indifferent when the assignment was too far afield. They were used to darting about in the enormous folded wilderness of the Alleghenies, raiding and skirmishing and maneuvering in a way that a sea captain would understand more easily than an infantry officer.

Jubal Early found all this insubstantial, unsatisfactory and irritating. To hear him tell it he was surrounded by incompetents, and to be sure there were foul-ups aplenty. The Federal raiders escaped northward, as did a regiment of infantry—the 34th Massachusetts under Colonel George D. Wells—that pushed into the Valley as a diversion. Early chased the infantrymen for a while but had no cavalry with which to run them to ground; all his horsemen were off on wild-goose chases in the mountains.

All this set Early to smoldering and carping, to shifting his plug of tobacco and spitting with rage. It could not have helped his mood, after the escape of Averell, to be told that since all was quiet along the Rapidan he should stay with his ragtag Valley command and go foraging in the West Virginia valleys.

He was to scour enemy territory for livestock, cloth and shoe leather, Lee said, buying what he could and requisitioning the rest. (He was to pay for what he took, Lee stressed, and leave enough behind for the subsistence of the local people.)

Even years later, when he wrote his memoirs, Early remained reverent in all his references to Lee, and gave no hint that he found his duty unpleasant. Nor did he have anything unkind to say about the commanding general's nephew, Fitzhugh Lee, who with his cavalry brigade assisted for a time in the chase of Averell. The only clue that Early might not have been entirely sanguine about acting as a commissary agent and forager exists in his savage treatment of John Imboden, who had no friends in Richmond. The partisan's brigade was "wholly inefficient, disorganized, undisciplined and unreliable," Jubal was quoted as saying; it was made up of deserters and shirkers. These comments and doubtless other, more profane observations were repeated so often, over so long a period of time, that Imboden, who shunned official proceedings, was goaded into demanding a court of inquiry. Lee responded, a deep sigh almost audible between the lines of his carefully phrased response, that such a proceeding, at such a time, would not be "advantageous."[28]

When Fitz Lee went back to the Rapidan and another cavalry brigade under Brigadier General Thomas L. Rosser joined Early, Old Jube promptly mixed it up with Rosser, too. In one report Early disparaged Rosser's brigade, much as he had Imboden's, but in a later communication he praised the unit and recommended the young man's promotion. Rosser was one of those people who liked to have his wife nearby, a practice that Jubal found insufferable, and Mrs. Rosser took up residence in Staunton that winter. At least once, Rosser visited her when Early thought he should have been on duty elsewhere, and Early complained about it to the long-suffering Lee.[29]

As Early's disappointment with one woman had soured him on all women, so his difficulties with cavalry that winter apparently prejudiced him against the entire mounted arm of the service. Henceforward, his attitude was unmistakably that all cavalry units were "disorganized, undisciplined and unreliable." Cavalrymen did not appreciate such generic contempt

any more than women do, and Jubal Early's military career
was diminished by the one harsh judgment just as his personal
life was impoverished by the other.

Having rounded up and sent to Richmond 1,700 cattle and
sheep, Early took a two-week leave and went home to Franklin
County. The respite did nothing to mellow him. His craving for
the recognition he pretended to spurn was taking on a shrill,
desperate, reckless edge. He had not been back with the army a
month when something happened between him and Dick
Ewell. Nothing is known about the specifics except that Ewell,
who had been Old Jube's constant friend and mentor, actually
placed the Second Corps' senior major general under arrest.
The charge was conduct "subversive of good order and military
discipline." Whatever Old Jube had done, Lee pronounced it
inexcusable, but restored him to command nevertheless. Lee
needed his officers working together. Grant was coming.[30]

In the dreadful spring of 1864 he came from every direction,
with everything. The Federal Army of the Tennessee punched
into Georgia, driving for Atlanta, Savannah and the Carolinas;
the Army of the James came up the Peninsula again, toward
Richmond; the Army of the Shenandoah moved up the Valley
from Harpers Ferry; and George Meade, with Grant smoking a
cigar and peering over his shoulder, began to hook around and
slam into Lee's right flank with a fired-up Army of the Potomac.

If ever there was a time for a man to keep his date with
destiny, this savage campaign should have been it. The Federals
maneuvered; were outmaneuvered; attacked; were beaten off;
then with stunning tenacity maneuvered and attacked again.
They shrugged off appalling losses—50,000 casualties in a single month—and kept coming, through the Wilderness, past
Spotsylvania Court House, to the banks of the North Anna and
the stunning slaughter at Cold Harbor. Through it all Lee reacted brilliantly, anticipating and outfighting his enemy, yet
being borne steadily back by the awesome weight of Federal
numbers. In these desperate battles Jubal Early took full part,
and achieved much, and won advancement. Yet nothing came
to him untainted, and that special state of grace he sought
eluded him.

Ewell's corps was the first to be attacked in the Wilderness—a nasty, trackless area of scrub oak, jack pine and thick underbrush—and the two leading divisions had been roughly handled by the time Early brought his three brigades up. He quickly stabilized the line and oversaw a counterattack that sent the Federals reeling. But much of the credit went not to Early but to one of his brigade commanders, Brigadier General John Gordon, a young Georgia lawyer whose remarkable, unschooled aptitude for battle had caused Lee to mark him as a rising star. It had been bad enough for Old Jube to see his contemporaries raised up ahead of him; now his juniors were coming up from behind and calling for the right-of-way.

Lee lost two of his three corps commanders in the Wilderness. Longstreet went down with a bad wound, shot by his own men just as Jackson had been at nearby Chancellorsville the year before. At the same time A. P. Hill, suffering from the effects of a wound received at Chancellorsville, became so ill that he could no longer command. This meant opportunity for Early, of course, who once again was given temporary command of a corps—this time Hill's Third Corps. But it was hardly a triumphal promotion, and it could not have delighted Old Jube to turn over command of his division to John Gordon; or to see Richard H. Anderson, a man five years his junior who had made major general almost a year ahead of him, now given command of Longstreet's First Corps; or to see Anderson, in his first battle, turn up at the right place and the right time to do the heaviest fighting and achieve the best results at Spotsylvania Court House.

Two weeks later, on May 22, A. P. Hill resumed command of the Second Corps and Early returned to his division. John Gordon was promoted to major general and was given command of another division in Ewell's corps. This galling situation of equality lasted only a week, however, whereupon the ailing Dick Ewell once again had to ask Early to take temporary command of the corps. Stubbornly refusing to give in to his infirmities, Ewell was struggling to return to duty when Lee gently relieved him from the command that was killing him, and sent him to take charge of the defenses of Richmond. Jubal

Early had command of the Second Corps in his own right at last.

The first thing he did was to bungle a battle. Sent out by Lee to sting the Federals badly enough to stop their constant reaching to the southeast, Early attacked at Bethesda Church without coordinating his move with Anderson's adjacent First Corps, and without determining that the Federal line was entrenched. The result was a costly repulse.

This was an odd failure, because Early had been known for his careful reconnaissances before engaging, and had reaped the rewards of preparation on such fields as Cedar Mountain, Fredericksburg and Second Winchester. He had proved brilliant at surveying and comprehending the ground over which a brigade of under 2,000 men would move; skillful, under the close direction of Ewell, at controlling the operations of a division of perhaps 10,000; but seemed frequently nonplussed by the awesome scale of movement of a 20,000-man, 12-brigade, 13-gun corps. Thus at Mine Run the previous November, while handling the Second Corps for the first time, Early had lost track of a division.[31]

However forceful, decisive and courageous an officer might be at handling smaller units, he could not succeed in corps or army command without a mystical ability to envision what he could not see, to comprehend chaos, to wrest from smoke and noise and confusion the essential trends of battle. Old Jube had proved himself at one level, but whether he could make the quantum leap to the next was still in question.

The question was not resolved by the fateful battle of Cold Harbor, which followed on June 3. While the Federals smashed into the Confederate right and center, Early held the left, merely skirmishing, while one of the bloodiest battles of the war raged a short distance away. He held his lines firmly, he counterattacked with telling effect, he remained alert and steady. But History did not visit him there.

Then, at last, with breathtaking suddenness and from an unexpected direction, Jubal Early's time arrived. On June 12 came a summons from Lee, a long discussion of strategy and prospects, and finally orders, heavy with responsibility, tingling with possibility. Save the Shenandoah. Invade the North.

Wreck the Federal railroads, raid the Yankee farms, threaten Washington, free the Confederate prisoners at Point Lookout, Maryland, but above all: save the Shenandoah. Surely Old Jube's glory days, so long awaited, had arrived at last.

He would take with him nearly one-third of the Army of Northern Virginia, despite the grave danger posed by Grant's incessant pounding at the gates of Richmond. Without those men, Lee had to abandon his plans to attack the Federal army, which had lain unmoving for days as if stunned by the slaughter at Cold Harbor. Such was the importance Lee attached to the disaster that had just occurred in the Shenandoah Valley.

John Breckinridge had broken Franz Sigel's Federal army at New Market in May, and had cleared the invaders from the Confederate granary. Such a defeat had always immobilized the Federals for months, and Lee had brought Breckinridge east to help at Cold Harbor. Grant, meanwhile, had put Black Dave Hunter in command of the Army of the Shenandoah and immediately sent it back up the Valley, where it wiped out the small Confederate garrison force left behind, cut the Virginia Central Railroad, sacked Staunton and advanced on Lynchburg. By thus cutting off the Valley's irreplaceable food supplies, Hunter had within his grasp, in the words of his chief of staff, "the vitals of the Confederate."

Early's mission was twofold: retake the Valley, because without its ripening wheat, tasseling corn and fattening cattle the Army of Northern Virginia would starve; and threaten the North, as Lee had done in 1862 and 1863, so that the politicians in Washington City would demand protection and weaken Grant's tightening stranglehold on Richmond.

The glory days had come indeed. The Second Corps went swinging into Lynchburg, confronted Hunter's advancing army, snapped his nerve like a cheap sword and chased him back into the Valley he had conquered, across it, and then out of it again into the fastnesses of the West Virginia mountains. Then, reorganized as the Army of the Valley, Early's men punched into the soft underbelly of the North, smashed another Federal army on the banks of Maryland's Monocacy River, and staggered through the searing July heat to the very gates of Washington. They formed up in Silver Spring, Maryland, in sight of the United States Capitol, and opened fire. They nearly changed history when they shot down a man standing next to the Federal president, watching the affair from the ramparts of an earthen fort. But at the very least, as Early put it, they "scared Abe Lincoln like hell."

They had had to fall back, through Leesburg into the Shenandoah again, but that was all right, no one had really expected that they could capture Washington or stay for long in the North. The important thing was that they had drawn off nearly two full corps from Grant's Army of the Potomac, had taken that much pressure off Lee. They lashed and stung the invaders over and over again, surprising them at Snicker's Ferry, routing them at Kernstown, confusing them at Berryville. Every so often they dashed north and tore up the Baltimore and Ohio Railroad, and the cavalry went back into Pennsylvania and burned Chambersburg, until the Federals from Abe Lincoln on down were beside themselves with helpless fury. It was like the old days under Stonewall, when another Federal drive on Richmond had been sapped of its strength by the need to swat flies in the Valley.

A terrible weariness afflicted the North. Newspapers and politicians decried the lack of victories, the terrible cost of the war, the incompetence of Lincoln. The president privately despaired of his chances for reelection, and began laying plans for turning over to his successor a fatally diminished office—President of the Divided States. His opposition nominated as his opponent George McClellan, who once boasted he would win the war but now simply said he would declare it over.

Yet somehow, for a third time the Federal army came rolling south in the Valley, now reinforced and led by Grant's vigorous young protégé, Major General Philip H. Sheridan. On the morning of September 19, the Federals came boiling west out of Berryville Canyon, up from Opequon Creek to smash into the young Major General Dodson Ramseur's division west of Winchester, with the rest of the Army of the Valley strung out for miles along the Pike. Ramseur's men fought ferociously, the rest of the army struggled to their support and at midday were still holding off the massive Federal assault. Then the Federal cavalry and George Crook's Army of West Virginia crashed in on their left, they couldn't stand it any more, and they ran.

Only as far as Fisher's Hill. That was their Gibraltar, a sharp hill across the throat of the main valley south of Strasburg. Early had almost enough men left to cover the four miles from the snout of Massanutten Mountain, looming over Strasburg, to North Mountain, the first range of the Alleghenies to the west. But not quite, and on the morning of September 22 there came Crook again, he had got up in the woods to the west and flanked them completely, and the army ran again, then skulked around in the Blue Ridge watching the bastards burn the Valley.

Early would not admit defeat. Even years later he continued to take an odd, inverse pride in having avoided "utter annihilation" at Winchester. He claimed that his escape demonstrated the "incapacity of my opponent," who, Early thought, "ought to have been cashiered." Nor did he feel responsible for the debacle at Fisher's Hill. "The enemy's immense superiority in cavalry and the inefficiency of the greater part of mine," he told Lee, "has been the cause of all my disasters."[32]

Thus the sullen look as the sodden men filed back out into the Valley on October 1; thus when their commanding general rode along their column they did not raise a cheer as they used to do for Stonewall, they did not even acknowledge him. No one saluted. The men did not look at him, and he did not look at them. He rode and they walked, for the moment in the same direction, out into the Valley after an army that had whipped them twice, and outnumbered them two to one. They were going, but they were not sure that they were going to follow Old Jube into another battle. The soldier who had written pessimistically about the cause of the Confederacy was similarly somber about the state of the Army of the Valley. "Many of the rank and file expressed the belief," he wrote, "that our army would not repel an attack with the same courage and composure as formerly.[33]

The strands that bound each individual soldier to his duty— concern for his comrades, pride in his unit, confidence in his commanders, belief in his cause, and of course courage—when unbroken formed a web strong enough to propel men unflinchingly toward chaos and death. But the individual threads were fragile, especially vulnerable to incompetence and pointless sacrifice, and in Jubal Early's army they were fraying badly.

This frailty was spotted from above as well as below. Lee, for all his ruthlessness in battle, was the gentlest of commanders when it came to his subordinates; he made suggestions rather than gave orders, and sketched objectives in the broadest possible outline, trusting his commanders to achieve them in their own way. He was exceedingly slow to criticize, and in this light the gentle admonition sent to Early after Fisher's Hill takes on a sharper edge than is immediately apparent: "As far as I can judge, at this distance, you have operated more with divisions than with your concentrated strength." There was truth in this, but even though Lee consistently underestimated the number of Federal troops opposing Early in the Valley, he had not lost confidence in Old Jube. "One victory," he added, "will put all things right."[34]

What Lee did not say was that the victory had better come soon, for powerful forces were gathering to bring Early down. They were being led by none other than the governor of Virginia—William ("Extra Billy") Smith. (The nickname derived from his extraordinary ability to think up additional charges to sweeten a Federal mail-carrying contract he once had.)

Old Jube and Extra Billy had had a long acquaintanceship. Smith had been governor of Virginia before—it was he who commissioned Early a major of volunteers for the Mexican war. He had been elected to the Confederate Congress and commissioned a colonel of volunteers at the outset of the War Between the States, and had divided his time since between fighting and debating. His regiment had been in Early's brigade at Antietam, where Smith had been wounded; and when the following year the former governor was promoted to brigadier general and given command of a brigade, it was in Early's division. In May of 1863 Smith had been elected to a second term as governor, but since he did not take office until January he first went along on the Gettysburg campaign. During the maneuvering that preceded that fateful battle, there occurred an incident that may have contributed to Smith's interest in procuring Early's scalp.

On the evening of June 27, Extra Billy had been leading his brigade through York, Pennsylvania, thirty miles from Gettysburg, watched by a fearful assembly of the town's citizens. It was just not in Smith's makeup to resist a situation like this; he drew up his horse, halted his men and commenced making a speech. It was, as he recalled it, a "rattling, humorous speech" designed to reassure the locals that the Confederates, as he put it, "are not burning your houses or butchering your children. On the contrary, we are behaving ourselves like Christian gentlemen, which we are." The problem was that Smith's brigade was in the van of the division, and just as he was getting warmed up and comfortable with his captive audience, an enraged Jubal Early came clawing his way through the jammed street to grab the orator by the shirt-front and roar, "General Smith! What in the devil are you about, stopping the head of this column in this accursed town?" The governor-elect resumed the march, but perhaps he did not forget the humiliation.[35]

At any rate, during the last week of September he began an exchange with General Lee on the subject of relieving Jubal Early from command. A long Sunday conversation on the subject on September 25 had apparently encouraged Smith to follow up. So when he received a letter from one of Early's officers complaining about the march of October 1, and whining about things in general, Smith gleefully forwarded it to Lee. The men had marched, the unnamed officer wrote, "in the hardest, coldest and bleakest storm of the season." They had left Waynesboro just when a shipment of shoes was expected, only to march twenty-five miles to Mount Crawford, on the Valley Pike south of Harrisonburg, to camp for several days. And that was not all. The disjointed litany of complaints condemned Early for being "surprised at Winchester," for not putting his whole army into his battles at once, for losing 25 cannon to the enemy, and for his character. "I believe the good of the country requires that General Early should not be kept in command of this army," Governor Smith's informant wrote, "and I believe it is the sentiment of the army."[36]

He had other such reports "from high sources," Extra Billy told Lee, but saw no need for further evidence. The case was clear, and the helpful governor had even worked out a whole series of changes and transfers that would accomplish the object of removing Early: "I implore prompt and immediate action."

General Lee's response was uncharacteristically brusque. "I regret to see such grave charges made against General Early," he said. "As far as I have been able to judge at this distance, he has conducted the military affairs in the Valley well." Nothing more could or would be done, Lee said, unless he was given the name of the officer who had written the letter: "Justice to General Early requires that I should inform him of the accusations made against him and of the name of his accuser."

This was not at all what Extra Billy had in mind. In a huffy response that repeatedly emphasized his exalted station, Extra Billy quoted Lee as having said that if public opinion turned against Early, he should be removed: "I respectfully ask how you were to learn that sentiment? Certainly by communications from some quarter, and what quarter more entitled to respect and appreciation than the Governor of Virginia?"

Lee then terminated the exchange with a letter whose tone managed to be at the same time correct and scornful, respectful and unyielding. He had never intended to be guided by "public opinion," Lee said, but by the opinion of the army—which was to say, by people who knew what they were talking about. "You necessarily know only what others tell you, and, like myself, are dependent for the accuracy of your information upon the character of your informant. The reports that have reached me as to several of the subjects of complaint against General Early differ from those you have received." And there was no doubt in Lee's mind about whose informant had more character.

"You will readily perceive," wrote Lee, flirting with sarcasm, "the little importance to be attached to the statement of a subordinate officer as to the propriety of any movement when he does not profess to know the reasons which induced his superior to order it." Lee professed not to know himself why Early had advanced again, and then explained exactly why: Lee had directed that Early advance as soon as the enemy force showed signs of retreating, in order to inflict "such injury as he could," to force the Federals to concentrate instead of spreading out "to devastate and plunder," and to "restore confidence and heart to his own command." In any case, said Lee in tones as curt as he ever used, "I do not propose to enter into any argument on these points." Extra Billy was for the moment rebuffed, but he and others like him were wheeling over Old Jube's reputation like the turkey buzzards that blackened the Valley's sky after a battle.

Thus under attack from superiors and subordinates, plagued by unfulfilled ambitions, strange failings and secret doubts, Jubal Early put his discouraged army into camp on the Valley Pike in that cold October rain, ready to do what the beloved Lee had asked of him. Tom Rosser was on the way from Richmond with a brigade of cavalry, and as soon as he arrived Early was going to attack, outnumbered or not.

Repeatedly, Lee urged him on, almost begging him to be equal to his own intellect: "I have weakened myself very much to strengthen you. It was done with the expectation of enabling you to gain such success that you could return the troops if not rejoin me yourself. I know you have endeavored to gain that success, and believe you have done all in your power to insure it. You must not be discouraged, but continue to try. I rely upon your judgement and ability."[37]

If Old Jube's persistence seemed to some more demented than courageous, that was because they did not know what was being required of him—and because they did not yet know the end of the story. As it stood on October 1, it had all the ingredients of a triumphant epic—or an inevitable tragedy. The final chapter would cast its shadow backwards over all that had gone before, and the final chapter would be written on the banks of Cedar Creek.

Chapter 2

Little Phil:
October 1, 1864

Ten miles north of the Confederates' chilly bivouac, in the pleasant mid-Valley town of Harrisonburg, the commanding general of the Federal Army of the Shenandoah was having his own struggle with higher authority. While Early was under fire for advancing his poverty-stricken army, General Sheridan, with all his superiority of numbers, arms, supplies and equipment, was trying to get permission to retreat. Sheridan had no idea that Early was within striking distance; "The rebels have given up the Valley," he said flatly in a telegram to Washington. "Early is, without doubt, fortifying at Charlottesville," across the Blue Ridge, eastward.[1]

Sheridan knew what he should do next; withdraw to Harper's Ferry, leave a few men to guard the railroad there and take the rest back to Richmond, where the serious fighting was. One reason he got along so well with Grant was that neither man believed in defending real estate; instead of guarding their territory, they preferred to go out and destroy the force that threatened it. Sheridan believed he had done this. It was time to move on.

The secretary of war, Edwin Stanton, disagreed. The chief of staff of the Federal armies, Henry Halleck, also thought otherwise. This was as usual; both men were excessively defensive in their military thinking—protect Washington, defend the railroads, guard this and guard that—and it was thanks in part to their influence that Robert E. Lee had retained the initiative through most of the war. They had been at cross purposes with

General Grant ever since the scruffy little westerner had been promoted to supreme command. They had been opposed to Sheridan's appointment as chief of the cavalry corps of the Army of the Potomac, and they had resisted his elevation to command of the enormous Middle Military Division and its Army of the Shenandoah. Now they opposed Sheridan's plan to leave the Valley, and this time Grant was on their side.

Taking on the entire Federal high command, including the formidable Grant, bothered Phil Sheridan not one whit. He was in no way restrained by the fact that at the age of thirty-three he was one of the younger major generals in the Federal service, or that two generals more senior than he had wrecked their careers in the Valley within the past few months, or that Grant had found it necessary to come to the Valley in person to settle their previous misunderstanding. Nor was Sheridan indulging in an exercise in arrogance fueled by the acclaim for his recent victories. It was simply that he had learned his trade in a very hard school, he knew what he knew, and that was that.

Phil Sheridan and Jubal Early had a great deal in common. Each was one of the very few commanders who enjoyed the complete confidence (although not the personal affection) of his commanding general; each had demonstrated beyond doubt his steadiness, aggressiveness and personal courage in combat; neither man had married, or felt comfortable in the company of women; and neither man looked the part he had been given to play.

They never met except across a battlefield, but had they been seen together the effect would have been incongruous to the point of comedy. The sight of Early—the lanky, stooped, six-foot-tall, bushy-headed Virginian—next to the wiry, almost petite, five-foot-five, 115-pound Ohio Irishman with the bullet head and the close-cropped hair would have suggested anything but a portrait of two of the preeminent generals of the age. But a careful and sensitive observer, such as Captain Wise or Major Douglas, would have noted in the two pairs of midnight eyes the identical glitter of untrammeled ambition.

Jubal Early had become physically misshapen in adulthood, but Sheridan had been an ugly duckling since birth. The newspaper illustrator James Taylor sketched the general shortly after Sheridan took command in the Valley, and was struck by the lack of symmetry: "His head was abnormally large with projecting bumps which from a phrenologist's point of view denoted combativeness. His body and arms were long while his pedals were disproportionately short—'duck legs,' in fact." Abraham Lincoln, who felt free to remark on odd physical specimens since he was one, wisecracked that if Sheridan's ankles itched he could "scratch them without stooping."[2]

When not mounted, and not in combat, Sheridan's martial qualities were invisible. His face was perpetually red—some thought from drinking, others explained that he was made florid by an abnormally fast heartbeat. His gestures were quick and jerky, suggesting nervousness. Taylor was not impressed by Sheridan's voice, either. It was, he said, "anything but musical and when exercised under excitement had a rasping sound." In normal conversation, Taylor added, Sheridan croaked.

The bumps on his head—at the hatline in back, invisible in his portraits—had a curious effect on his image. Artists who saw him in action usually depicted him waving his hat; as Lieutenant Colonel Frederic C. Newhall of his staff observed, "that action probably suggests cheering something on." The more prosaic fact, as Newhall explained, was that "there being no general demand for hats that would fit him, the general never has one that will stay on his head." This probably accounts as well for Sheridan's frequent use of an odd, porkpie slouch hat instead of a forage cap. Otherwise, according to Colonel Newhall, even in the hottest of weather Sheridan was always neatly and properly uniformed: "a double-breasted frock coat; pantaloons outside his boots, strapped down, and chafing against small brass spurs," one of them broken off. Shortly before coming to the Valley, Sheridan tried out a full beard, as he had briefly in 1862, but within a few months would resume shaving everything but his habitual, clipped mustache.[3]

Taylor, like others who tried to comprehend Sheridan at the time, did not feel himself to be in the presence of a profound intellect— "Sheridan possessed great common sense," he said. But he felt something extraordinary. After only a few minutes with the odd little general, Taylor mused that he had been in the presence of a "little mountain of combative force."

No one who saw Sheridan transformed by the sound of guns doubted his inner power. His stumpiness disappeared when he mounted, and the suddenly graceful form was suffused with a fiery, blissful energy. Had it not been controlled, this demonic ardor could have become hysteria, but Colonel Newhall of his staff recalled that in the heat of combat, "the general leans forward on his horse's neck, and hunching his shoulders up to his ears, gives most softly spoken orders in a slow, deliberate way, as if there were niches for all the words in his hearer's memory, and they must be measured very carefully to fit exactly, that none of them be lost in the carrying." All this went on within a cloud of pungent smoke, for Sheridan was as enthusiastic a consumer of cigars, especially when under fire, as General Grant was. It made Colonel Newhall suggest that cigar smoke was an "ally of military genius."[4]

Like Grant, Sheridan seemed impervious to apparent defeat. "A serious check or reverse affects him peculiarly," Colonel Newhall wrote. "To most temperaments disaster is disheartening, but it passes by General Sheridan as an eddy glides around a pier. Show him an opening promising success, and he will go in and widen it while an impressive man would be thinking about it. But he is slow to confess defeat.[5]

Sheridan's manner and successes in combat contributed to, but did not explain, the extraordinary hold he had on the affections of the men under his command. As General Grant would say of him later with undisguised envy, "He had that magnetic quality of swaying men which I wish I had—a rare quality in a general."[6]

A cavalry surgeon, Captain Henry A. DuBois, marveled at this emotional bond. The men regarded Sheridan, DuBois wrote, as they would "a brother in whom they had unlimited confidence and whose interests were also theirs. His appearance in front of the line of battle, without his saying a word, changed the character of every man in a moment." DuBois was mystified; it seemed to him that Sheridan did little to cultivate his troopers. "His ideas of duty are peculiar," Colonel Newhall wrote in support of this view, "he has never issued orders of encouragement or congratulation to his troops before or after campaigns or battles. He has apparently taken it for granted that all under his command would do as well as they could, and that they did so quite as a matter of course."[7]

Even Sheridan professed to be amazed sometimes by the depth of feeling he evoked from the troops. He remarked on it once to his brother and aide-de-camp, Captain Michael Sheridan, and asked if he ever affected Michael the same way. "No," came the brotherly response, "I know you too well."[8]

Colonel James H. Kidd of the 6th Michigan Cavalry thought perhaps the secret was in Sheridan's eyes: "In his manner there was an alertness, evinced rather in look than in movement. Nothing escaped his eye, which was brilliant and searching and at the same time emitted flashes of kindly good nature." (In one or two of Sheridan's photographs, most of which depict a man in an agony of self-consciousness, this glimmer of kindliness can be detected.) "One had a feeling that he was under close and critical observation, that Sheridan had his eye on him, was mentally taking his measure and would remember and recognize him the next time. No introduction was needed." Colonel Kidd went on in this vein at length, struggling to describe Sheridan's impact, then gave up. "There were perhaps no special, single, salient points," he concluded. "He had to be taken 'all in all.' So taken, he was Sheridan."[9]

Thus mystified by Sheridan's appeal, observers looked in vain for the overbearing military presence, the ostrich plumes, the trumpeting speeches or the vainglorious proclamations that might have explained it to them. Meanwhile they missed the prosaic, utterly ordinary foundation of the bond between him and his men. The cornerstone had been set in 1856, during his first combat command, in one of the frequent Indian wars of the far Northwest.

Then a twenty-five-year-old lieutenant, he had taken over a detachment of 40 dragoons, a "medley of recalcitrants," he called them, from a popular officer. The pint-sized shavetail had "some difficulty" controlling this band of brigands, but he chose not to fall back on rank or military regulations to save himself. Instead, he wrote later, "by forethought for them and their wants, and a strict watchfulness for their rights and comfort, I was able in a short time to make them obedient and the detachment cohesive." These were peculiar ideas of duty, indeed, but they worked, and Sheridan never forgot their effect on the men: "The disaffected feeling they entertained when I first assumed command soon wore away, and in its place came a confidence and respect which it gives me the greatest pleasure to remember."[10]

To begin to appreciate what balm such effusions of respect and love must have been to Phil Sheridan's soul, one would have to have grown up in the 1830s on the western frontier, an undersized, black-Irish, immigrant schoolkid beset by larger classmates and violent teachers, with a father who was always away and no one to rely on but a God-fearing mother.

The exact location of Phil Sheridan's birth, on March 6, 1831, remains a minor mystery. The previous year his parents, John and Mary Sheridan, had been living on a small tenancy on an estate in County Cavan, in north-central Ireland. It was a time of relative peace and prosperity in that long-troubled country, but centuries of oppression had left Irish Catholics perpetually fearful, and especially susceptible to the dreams of religious freedom and economic opportunity being realized in the New World. In 1830 John Sheridan sold his leasehold and bought passage to America.[11]

Phil Sheridan recorded in his memoirs that he was born the following year in Albany, New York, a place that later erected a statue of him in honor of the blessed event, but never produced an official record of it. During his life Sheridan also claimed, on various official forms, both Boston and Somerset, Ohio, as his birthplace. Some researchers later deduced, without conclusive evidence, that he was born in Ireland, or in mid-Atlantic during the crossing. The confusion mattered only once, when certain people were thinking of running him for president.

Whatever dreams John Sheridan had nurtured about his new life, he soon saw that they were not to be realized in Albany. He moved west to Ohio, where a frenzy of development was knitting the productive young state into the iron fabric of the industrial North. John Sheridan found work on the National

Road, then being extended from Wheeling, in western Virginia, through Ohio to St. Louis, Missouri. The family settled in the village of Somerset, Ohio, thirty miles southeast of Columbus and ten miles south of the National Road (later U.S. 40).

In later years, Phil Sheridan had little to say about family life in Somerset except that he was raised mostly by his mother, to whom he paid a brief, obligatory tribute in his memoirs. Others remembered that she was quiet, devout and patriotic, and that John Sheridan was always off somewhere working on various road, canal and railroad projects. He wanted to be more than a laborer, and began operating as an independent contractor, but despite the boom his profits were modest.[12]

In 1841, a year after Jubal Early hung out his lawyer's shingle in Rocky Mount, Phil Sheridan began attending the one-room school in Somerset. His was a typical nineteenth-century frontier education; brief (four years in duration), rudimentary and punctuated by frequent whippings (one teacher, when unable to identify a transgressor, simply switched the entire student body). Such treatment did nothing to blunt the natural savagery of schoolchildren, who when running in packs can shred the self-confidence of anyone displaying the slightest degree of difference. Phil Sheridan's small stature and unconventional appearance drew their attention as blood draws sharks. Some children respond to such torture with clowning, or servility, but little Phil fought back. He learned that a quick, brutal assault usually overcame even heavy odds, and before long only newcomers risked igniting his gunpowder temper.

It must have been a relief for everyone when, at the age of fourteen, he went to work in a grocery store in town. Conscientious and bright, he was soon promoted to bookkeeper for Fink and Dittoe's dry goods store. And despite his scanty education, he became, he says, "quite a local authority in history, being frequently chosen as arbiter in discussions and disputes that arose in the store." It was no small thing for one so young to have standing in one of the major social, political and communications centers of the community.

After 1846, discussions in the store centered on the war with Mexico. The stories filtering back to the quiet Ohio main street from places such as Matamoros, Palo Alto, Santa Fe and Buena

Vista, telling of the triumphs of American heroes over the demoniacal legions of Santa Anna, butcher of the Alamo, were more than enough to inflame a young store clerk's heart with dreams of martial glory. He had always been susceptible; a childhood friend wrote that he never saw "Phil's brown eyes open so wide or gaze with such interest" as they did one Fourth of July, when an aged veteran of the Revolutionary War was carried out in public to be acknowledged.[13]

Another occasional visitor to Somerset must have intrigued young Phil. A West Point graduate from nearby Lancaster, he had known the Sheridans and had courted his wife in Somerset, where she went to school, before leaving for the Mexican War (which, in the event, he sat out in California). His name was William Tecumseh Sherman.[14]

Little Phil was too young to fight in Mexico, but his resolve to become a soldier was firmly set by the time that war was over in 1847. The way to a military career as an officer in the shrinking U.S. Army (which within ten years would number a mere 16,000 soldiers) was through West Point. To be considered for that invaluable four free years of schooling, he would have to be nominated by a member of Congress, and neither he nor his family was in a position to exert much political influence. But he waited and watched for a chance, and when it came in 1848—a young man who had been nominated to the academy failed the entrance examination—he immediately wrote to his congressman asking for the appointment, "reminding him that we had often met in Fink and Dittoe's store, and that therefore he must know something of my qualifications. He responded promptly by enclosing my warrant for the class of 1848." Phil Sheridan had won his first battle.[15]

Despite his indifferent education, Sheridan was confident he could pass the oral entrance examinations given in June, and did. This won him admittance to the class that formed in July, but he and his classmates were on probation until they passed the first academy examinations of the following January, and these he feared, for they held the terrors of algebra. Little Phil slugged it out with his intractable enemy, huddling long after taps with his helpful roommate Henry W. Slocum, pounding into his reluctant mind the mysteries of Higher Mathematics.

He did not distinguish himself in the January examinations, or in subsequent academic tests, but he held on, and doggedly carved out for himself a niche in the middle of his class rankings.[16]

Whereas Jubal Early had come to the academy fifteen years before to obtain an education for his own purposes, Phil Sheridan was there to become a soldier. Yet the prospective general was no better than the would-be lawyer had been at polishing brass and observing the school's myriad regulations. Sheridan thought his official initiation into the academy "pompous," and the unofficial hazing that followed "senseless." He and his rustic Western friends (prominent among them two fellow Ohioans, George Crook and John Nugen) were forever excluded from, and put down by, the school's dominant clique of refined, aristocratic Southerners. Through all this Sheridan tried to keep reined in the hot temper of a pint-sized Irishman who had learned to fight slights with fire. He almost made it.

In September of 1851, the beginning of what should have been Sheridan's last year at West Point, he suffered a spectacular loss of control. During a parade, cadet sergeant William R. Terrill of Virginia gave him an order in what Sheridan considered to be an "improper tone." Sheridan lowered his bayonet and charged. "My better judgement recalled me before actual contact could be made," he said, but Terrill of course reported the infraction. Learning of this later, Sheridan went after Terrill and tore into him, this time using his fists. A nearby officer saved Sheridan from a thrashing at the hands of the larger Virginian, but nothing could save him from suspension from West Point for a year.

It was bitter medicine; eleven months of clerking back at Fink and Dittoe's store, followed by a return to West Point at the foot of a strange class—under a new commandant of the academy, one Robert E. Lee—while his friends had received their commissions and their first assignments. The three Ohio buddies, Crook, Sheridan and Nugen, got together that fall for a photograph that Sheridan probably never displayed; in it Crook and Nugen are wearing the uniforms of second lieutenants, while Sheridan is still decked out in the gray academy jacket. The diminutive, wavy-haired cadet is gripping his friends by the shoulders and glaring at the camera.[17]

By the time his final year was over he was a mere 11 demerits short of expulsion (which, oddly enough, was Jubal Early's demerit standing in his final year). But he hung on, and in June of 1853 graduated 34th in a class of 52 (Early had been 18th among 50). His standing was not high enough to give him any choice of arm or assignment. He was made a brevet second lieutenant in the First U.S. Infantry.

Sheridan never referred to it, but he must have felt a sting of shame when he learned that year that his father had been caught in the bankruptcy of a construction company and had lost everything except the little house in Somerset, where John Sheridan went to live out his days a ruined man. It was a house Sheridan would seldom enter again. In March of 1854 he headed west to fight Indians.

There was an interlude at Fort Duncan, Texas, with little to do but run patrols, during which the young shavetail developed two habits that were to stay with him; he studied the local ground, making maps where none were available, and he learned the local language, which was of course Spanish. He retained the habit, although in the first instance it did him little good; he was soon transferred, to Fort Reading, California, at the northern end of the Sacramento Valley.

The frenzy of the gold rush of 1849 was about played out by then; the romantic '49ers had been replaced by the pragmatic mining corporations, and the far West was becoming civilized. A major barrier to that process was the continuing misbehavior of the various Indian tribes, whom the crazed fortune-seekers of the gold rush had cheated, uprooted, humiliated, intoxicated, raped and killed. With the prospectors being replaced by equally rapacious and even more numerous settlers, railroad men and developers, the Indians continued to disrupt progress by clinging stubbornly to their ancestral ways and lands. Correcting their attitude and protecting the vanguard of civilization was the army's job.

It was a job the young Sheridan pitched into with uncritical enthusiasm. His view of the task was uncomplicated by any musings about justice or feelings of sympathy. "They were a pitiable lot," he said of one group, "almost naked, hungry and cadaverous. Indians are always hungry, but these poor creatures were particularly so, as their usual source of food had grown very scarce from one cause and another." He knew the cause. Their "usual source of food" was salmon, and these fish, as Sheridan later explained dismissively, had been obliterated from the streams of California by alluvial mining. The Indians' attempts to sustain life by eating grasshoppers, handouts, and the leavings found in abandoned camps amused Sheridan, and confirmed him in his low opinion of the "miserable wretches."[18]

The wretches gave Sheridan little chance to test his military prowess. Their transgressions usually were minor, and the army's various expeditions often turned out to be pointless rambles led by incompetents and drunks. A highlight was a skirmish in March of 1856, at the Cascades of the Columbia River—a series of rapids about fifty miles east of Fort Vancouver. Sheridan, with 40 dragoons (the command whose gentling had proved so instructive to him), faced a few dozen Indians. After some demonstrating and skirmishing, during which history was nearly changed by a bullet that grazed Sheridan's nose and killed the man next to him, most of the hostile Indians ran away. Sheridan gathered up some misfortunates from another, nearby tribe who had somehow been drawn into the shooting. A civilian posse wanted to shoot the dozen or so prisoners, but Sheridan would not hear of it. Instead, he turned them over to a superior officer, who hanged them. Civilization had come to the Cascades.

It was not much of a battle, but it was experience under fire. There were a few more such confrontations, but for the next five years Sheridan's job was to police an Indian reservation in western Oregon. It was the kind of thankless, promotionless, mind-numbing duty that drove scores of West Pointers to drink or resignation during the years after the Mexican War. Jubal Early had been able to take it for only a few months. Another officer who had resigned in disgust and had gone back east the year Sheridan had come west was Captain Ulysses S. Grant (whose departure was clouded by a dispute with a commanding officer who accused him of drinking on duty).

But Sheridan soldiered on with no visible signs of discontent, learning to speak Chinook (the *lingua franca* of the Northwestern tribes), making his maps and staying ready for whatever his government might ask. He remained contemptuous of the Indians and their "absurdly superstitious practices," and developed a simplistic formula for their management: "a practical supervision at the outset, coupled with a firm control and mild discipline." Presumably he applied the formula to Frances, the Rogue River Indian woman who shared his hut during these years.[19]

Sheridan suffered no anguish over the conflict of principles that was carrying the country toward war in 1861. Being from Ohio, he was of course spared the problem of deciding whether his loyalty belonged to his state or his country. But above everything else, Sheridan was Regular Army, and felt no need to puzzle out his loyalties or his duty. "My patriotism was untainted by politics," he wrote smugly of this time, "nor had it been disturbed by any discussion of the questions out of which the war grew, and I hoped for the success of the Government above all other considerations." He always spelled government with a capital *G*.[20]

Fort Sumter fell, and Bull Run was lost, and still Sheridan was stuck in his remote western fort. "I earnestly wished to be at the seat of war," said Sheridan, "and feared it might end before I could get East." Finally, on September 1, 1861, the thirty-year-old captain headed for Missouri to join a new regiment, the 13th United States Infantry, lately commanded by Colonel William Tecumseh Sherman. Sheridan, well used to the glacial pace of promotions in the peacetime army, expressed the hope that if the war lasted long enough he might win promotion to major.[21]

Neither Sheridan nor anyone else in the country was prepared for the awesome scope of the war to come. Herds of boisterous volunteers in thousand-man regiments, their colonels elected by the men or appointed by political figures, more than quadrupled the armed strength of the Union. The military bureaucracy, consisting largely of aged time-servers enjoying the rewards of the seniority system, was swamped.

At first the regular army tried to keep its distance from the untrained volunteers, decreeing that regular officers could not command volunteer units. This was folly, and soon changed, but in the meanwhile it had the effect of denying rank to the officers who had remained faithful through the army's fallow years. Meanwhile those who had quit and gone home were sought out by civilians and made field-grade officers of volunteers.

Phil Sheridan had remained loyal, dedicated and obedient—in a word, regular army to the core—and for his reward was made a bookkeeper again. The inept Major General John Fremont had made a hash of the financial affairs of the Western Department; Fremont's successor, Major General Henry W. Halleck, selected Sheridan to head a board of auditors to clean up the mess. He spent several months as a military accountant —"the duty was not distasteful," he said stoutly—then became chief commissary and quartermaster for the little Army of the Southwest Missouri District.[22]

As always, Sheridan did his best, first straightening out the enormous muddle left behind by Fremont, then untangling the snarled supply and transportation systems of Brigadier General Samuel R. Curtis. The year 1862 found Sheridan counting hardtack and horses in Missouri while two hundred miles to the east, Union forces under a little-known general named Grant were driving along the Mississippi River into Tennessee. Once again there were predictions that it would be a short war.

In March Sam Curtis's little army ran into and defeated a slightly larger Confederate force at Pea Ridge, Arkansas, but the diligent Captain Sheridan was off scrounging grain and repairing flour mills, and missed the action. Worse, he got into a dispute with his commanding officer that made the possibility of command even more remote.

Sheridan found himself buying for the army horses that had been stolen from Missouri farmers; he confiscated the horses and refused to pay the thieves. General Curtis, apparently seeing no reason to protect the interests of farmers who were Southern sympathizers, ordered the payments made. Sheridan refused. Facing a court-martial, he appealed to General Halleck, who obliged by transferring him out of Curtis's command.[23]

Thus on April 6, 1862, the "forlorn and disheartened" Captain Sheridan was in Chicago buying horses when Grant's forces were attacked by a Confederate army not far from the Mississippi border, near a Methodist meetinghouse called Shiloh Church. Grant won a victory that was tainted by the unprecedented cost in casualties and by allegations that he had been taken by surprise. Sheridan was beside himself with frustration. He hitched a ride on a hospital ship and went to Shiloh to see Halleck again.[24]

Old Brains was a formidable man with an enormous temper, and it is strange that he tolerated all this botheration from a mere captain. But for some reason he did, and gave Sheridan some work to do around camp, but no command. Sheridan's chance finally came on May 27, when the governor of Michigan offered him the colonelcy of the volunteer 2nd Michigan Cavalry. The regiment was riddled by dissension and needed a commander with regular-army training and no knowledge of Michigan politics. It was a volunteer regiment, technically off limits to Sheridan, but he was inspired to such levels of oratory in his pleadings with Halleck that Old Brains approved the arrangement without even getting dispensation from Washington. At eight o'clock that night Captain Sheridan pinned on some borrowed eagles and took command of the 2nd Michigan. At midnight he led them south on a four-day, 180-mile raid into Mississippi.[25]

A few days later, on June 11, Sheridan's brigade commander was promoted, and Sheridan took over the brigade. By this time he had already gentled his fractious regiment by applying the lessons of the frontier: "I had striven unceasingly to have them well fed and well clothed, had personally looked after the selection of their camps, and had maintained such a discipline as to allay former irritation." His care extended beyond physical well-being, too: "Whenever my authority would permit I saved my command from needless sacrifices and unnecessary toil; therefore, when hard or daring work was to be done I expected the heartiest response, and always got it." As before, his approach worked. Within a few weeks, "I had gained not only their confidence as soldiers, but their esteem and love as men."[26]

Sheridan took the brigade to Booneville, Mississippi, to set up camp and guard the front of the Federal army, which was bivouacked twenty miles to the north at Corinth. There he immediately cultivated his old habit of making maps of his surroundings. A few weeks later his leadership and his maps were put to their first supreme test. On the morning of July 1, with virtually no warning, he found himself under attack by a force of Confederate cavalry that outnumbered his 800 troopers by six to one.

Sheridan could easily have withdrawn. In fact, given his situation and the relatively minor importance of his position, he probably should have withdrawn. Instead, while the enemy force advanced with its lines extended far beyond his left and right flanks, Sheridan prepared to attack. He had recorded on his maps a trail that led through a wood, around the Confederate left, to the road on which they had advanced. He sent four companies of troopers out on this road to get behind the enemy and attack from the rear while Sheridan led a frontal attack. It was essential that they attack at the same time, but all Sheridan could think of by way of coordination was to recommend loud yelling.

Fortune often seems to smile on such lunatic undertakings, and it did in this case; just as things were getting under way, a locomotive pulled into Booneville, its whistle convincing both sides that the Federals were being reinforced (in fact, the train carried grain for the horses). Implausibly, the two Federal attacks came off simultaneously, and the Confederate force broke and ran.

It was not a large or an important engagement, but it revealed that Sheridan was made of rare stuff. The case was put succinctly in a telegram sent shortly afterward to General Halleck, signed by no fewer than five brigadier generals. "Brigadiers scarce; good ones scarcer," it read. "The undersigned respectfully beg that you will obtain the promotion of Sheridan. He is worth his weight in gold."[27]

For the moment, however, the only change made was to give Sheridan another regiment and pull him in to Rienzi, a post less removed from the main army. There, on August 27, while half his men were away scouting and the other half were lounging around camp in the blast-furnace heat of the Mississippi summer, there was a sudden burst of firing. Sheridan and his men emerged from their tents to see enemy riders among their tents; the Federal pickets had been so unnerved by the sudden charge that they had simply fled into camp with the Confederates close behind. "We were literally caught napping," Sheridan recalled, and his men were in various states of undress, but they grabbed their rifles and cartridge boxes and promptly drove the enemy off. Not long afterward one of Sheridan's officers presented him with an exceptionally strong Morgan gelding, a jet-black, white-stockinged three-year-old that Sheridan named Rienzi.[28]

Sheridan's scouts discovered that the Confederate army, now commanded by General Braxton Bragg, was headed eastward. Halleck, moving with his usual lethargy, sent an army under Major General Don Carlos Buell lumbering over to try to hold Chattanooga, but Bragg got past the Federals and lunged northward into east Tennessee toward Kentucky. (Meanwhile the dilatory Halleck plodded off to Washington to take over as general in chief of the Union armies.) Suddenly the midwestern heartland of the Union, including the major cities of Cincinnati and Louisville, was in jeopardy. Among the forces hastily pulled from southern Tennessee to meet the threat was Sheridan's brigade.

In Corinth he came face to face for the first time with Ulysses Grant, who had succeeded Halleck as department commander. Their first conversation quickly became an argument. Grant had heard of Sheridan's exploits, but not of his transfer to Louisville, and Grant was upset at the thought of losing a fighter. He intended to countermand Sheridan's orders, but Sheridan wanted to go where the action was, and told Grant so, "somewhat emphatically, I fear. Our conversation ended with my wish gratified." It also left Grant nursing a decided dislike for the pushy little cavalryman.[29]

On reporting to the commanding general at Louisville, General William Nelson, Sheridan was asked curtly why he was not wearing the proper insignia of his rank. Nonplussed, Sheridan defended himself. There was nothing wrong with his uniform, as it turned out, it was simply Nelson's way of announcing a promotion. (Such heavy-handedness had earned Nelson the nickname "Bull," and would contribute to his untimely end; in a pointless argument a few days later, Nelson would be shot by a fellow officer.) Sheridan, who had hoped the war would last long enough for him to become a major, was a brigadier general and a division commander in the Army of the Ohio.

Generals Buell and Bragg marched their armies around each other like wary boxers looking for an opening, and by the end of September the audience was restive; Lincoln complained, and Halleck nearly removed Buell from command. Thus energized, Buell on October 1, 1862, marched his army of 60,000 men southeast from Louisville, boring in on Bragg's divided force of little more than two-thirds that size.[30]

It took Buell a week to find and close with the enemy, but when he did—at Perryville, Kentucky, on October 8—the division commander whose three brigades led the army into contact, and who seized and held the vital high ground as a prelude to battle, was Phil Sheridan. His corps commander, worried that Sheridan was getting too far ahead of the army, repeatedly enjoined him not to bring on a general engagement yet. Sheridan had never seen a battle of this size, let alone commanding an infantry division in one, but his arrogant reply, as he recalled it, was "that I was not bringing on an engagement, but that the enemy evidently intended to do so."[31]

Sheridan held the center, but it was the left that became engaged first. Shortly after midday the Confederates delivered a crushing blow against a brigade commanded by another newly minted brigadier general—William Terrill, the Virginian whom Sheridan had used for bayonet practice on the parade ground at West Point. Terrill's decision to remain in the Federal service had caused him and his family a great deal of pain; "Your name shall be stricken from the family records," his outraged father had written him. Terrill had nevertheless distinguished himself as an artillerist, especially at Shiloh, and had been given command of an infantry brigade. Meanwhile his brother James was making an equally brilliant career as colonel of a Confederate regiment fighting in Virginia under Jubal Early.

Sheridan had rather shamefacedly resumed his acquaintance with William Terrill in St. Louis, and on this day tried to warn the column on his left of the blow about to fall on it. But the brigade was routed, and Terrill was killed. Two years later, his Confederate brother James would die in combat near Cold Harbor, and after the war the family would erect in remembrance of the fallen brothers a memorial bearing an anguished inscription: "God Alone Knows Which Was Right."[32]

Buell, from his position two miles in the rear of his lines, badly mismanaged the battle of Perryville. While his left was being driven in, one of his three corps was unengaged, off to the right awaiting orders. Sheridan's division, meanwhile, fended off several attacks and then counterattacked, driving into the town itself. His advance was neither supported nor followed up, and the battle ended a draw, although Bragg relinquished the field the next day. Disgusted, Sheridan called the battle "an example of lost opportunities."[33]

Buell was sent home to await orders, as the euphemism went, and Sheridan enjoyed his first taste of military glory—some newspaper, in gushing over his achievements, dubbed him "The Paladin of Perryville." Major General William S. Rosecrans, a big, bluff man who took his liquor and his religion to excess and had an eerie ability to go without sleep, replaced Buell, reorganized things and soon got the army feeling better. On Christmas Day Rosecrans advanced the army, now numbering 65,000, to confront Bragg along Stones River, southeast of Nashville near the town of Murfreesboro.[34]

Rosecrans intended to attack the Confederate right on the morning of December 31, but before he could begin, the enemy attacked his right. The assault crushed and routed two Federal divisions, whereupon it came up against Sheridan, who counterattacked. Outgunned and outnumbered, he was stopped and forced back to a second position. He fought there until his division ran out of ammunition, then fell back stubbornly, keeping his men well in hand, to a third. General Rosecrans rode by just as Sheridan, enraged by the failure of supply that had forced this second retreat, was leading his men to the rear, swearing fervently. Even in the midst of disaster, Old Rosy could not resist a pious admonition: "Watch your language. Remember, the first bullet may send you to eternity."[35]

The entire Federal line had been swung back like an enormous gate until it was perpendicular to its original position.

Bragg shifted the weight of his onslaught to the center, but the center held. When nightfall ended the firing, Rosecrans decided to withdraw his battered army as soon as Bragg attacked again. But the next day Bragg did nothing, and after a single, ill-conceived stab on the following day it was Bragg who retreated, thus snatching defeat from the jaws of victory.

Sheridan had done well before, but this was the first time he had had to endure savage, day-long fighting. Much as Jubal Early had done three months earlier at Antietam, Sheridan had weathered his introduction to division command with flying colors. It had not been an easy test; total casualties at Stones River exceeded those of Bloody Shiloh, and Sheridan had been in one of the hardest-fought positions.[36]

Sheridan was justifiably proud of himself and of his 4,000 men. "It was plain to see that they felt a self-confidence inspired by the part they had already played." Here was a unit that had been driven from two lines, whose army was apparently falling apart, which had lost all its brigade commanders, many of its regimental officers and more than enough of its men —40 percent—to justify a complete loss of organization, and it was feeling self-confident. Sheridan had confirmed another central truth about combat leadership, which he expressed most succinctly in the negative: "Soldiers are averse to seeing their comrades killed without compensating results, and none realize more quickly than they the blundering that often takes place on the field of battle." In other words it is not death that disheartens surviving soldiers, but pointless death.[37]

Sheridan would not do quite so well in the next test of his hard-earned lessons, but it did not happen for eight long months. It came on the banks of the Chickamauga River in Georgia, after Rosecrans had maneuvered Bragg's army out of Tennessee and in a burst of confidence had chased the enemy south from Chattanooga into the rugged mountains of northwest Georgia. For days the two armies groped for each other through the tortuous hollows, until after a day of confused skirmishing on September 18 they were facing each other— although the forest was so dense and the country so rough that neither commander knew what he was facing—along the Chickamauga.

The next day they stumbled into a full-scale battle. It started by accident and developed by happenstance, neither side knowing where the other was deployed, Bragg grimly committing division after division in piecemeal attacks ("the sparring of an amateur boxer," one of his own generals scoffed later) and Rosecrans feeding reinforcements to the hot spots. Sheridan's division was not engaged until mid-afternoon. When he was finally ordered in to bolster the wavering Federal right, some of his staff officers galloped in his path shouting to the embattled men they were passing, "Make way for Sheridan! Make way for Sheridan!" Attacking immediately, Sheridan's division ran into a firestorm that had them stumbling back in confusion minutes later. As they did so the troops they had passed called out, "Make way for Sheridan! Make way for Sheridan!"[38]

By the end of the first day of the battle the Federal army was badly battered, and in real trouble. Bragg had been reinforced —most ominously, by two divisions from Lee's Army of Northern Virginia, under the formidable James Longstreet— and outnumbered the Federals by about 8,000. Bragg was applying his heaviest pressure to the north, trying to turn that flank and cut the Federals off from Chattanooga, and Rosecrans was responding by continually edging his units to the left —an extremely tricky thing to do while engaged.

Early on January 20 a mistake in that lateral movement opened a hole in the Federal line between Sheridan's division and the next one to his south; and into that hole poured the divisions of James Longstreet. Sheridan was overwhelmed and driven from the field. He made a commendable effort to re-form his men and return to the fight, but he was able to do nothing of significance. He was, after all, neither infallible nor invincible.

On that day it was Major General George Thomas who, as Sheridan had done at Stones River, held on against impossible odds and saved the army. Thomas's XIV Corps endured a brutal pounding that doubled both its flanks in until the men were fighting back to back, yet held on until dark, then withdrew in good order. For the achievement Thomas was dubbed the Rock of Chickamauga, but the Paladin of Perryville was mildly disdainful and thought Thomas's demeanor on the field much too gloomy. Sheridan's reaction may have had something to do with the fact that George Thomas was a Virginian.[39]

The Army of the Cumberland had been whipped in the bloodiest battle of the war in the western theater (34,624 casualties), and had all it could do to drag itself back to Chattanooga, where it was immediately bottled up by Bragg. The Confederates, whose lines along Missionary Ridge and Lookout Mountain enclosed Chattanooga against the Tennessee River, were not able to surround the city, but did so restrict its supply routes that the Federals were soon on the verge of starvation. The alarmed authorities in Washington sent out from the Army of the Potomac three divisions of reinforcements under Major General Joseph Hooker. And in mid-October they named a new department commander—Ulysses S. Grant.

Grant joined the besieged army, replaced Rosecrans with General Thomas, summoned Sherman's reinforcements and his own Army of the Tennessee, punched open a supply line and on November 23 attacked Bragg's lines. The main assault—Sherman's, on the northern extremity of the enemy line—stalled, while a diversionary probe of the opposite flank by Hooker succeeded; Lookout Mountain fell after a battle above the clouds that instantly became a legend and greatly improved the morale of the Federals watching from below. But the Confederate center was still firmly in place on Cemetery Ridge when Grant and Thomas sent in the Army of the Cumberland.

Sheridan's division, now 25 regiments strong, advanced in the center. Unleashed in a charge after frustrating months under siege, the men took their objective—a line of enemy entrenchments at the bottom of Missionary Ridge—and would not stop. They began to scramble up the steep, four-hundred-foot face of the ridge toward Bragg's main line. It was against orders, but it was fine with Sheridan. With a borrowed hip flask he drank a mock toast to an enemy battery firing from atop the ridge, and followed his men to glory. While Grant watched in admiring disbelief, Sheridan and his division clambered up the slope, cracked the Confederate center, took 1,762 prisoners, captured 17 guns—Sheridan straddling one of them and howling in triumph—then chased the retreating army off into the twilight.[40]

The Federal victory at Chattanooga confirmed, in the mind
of Abraham Lincoln and in the opinion of the northern public,
that Grant was a winning general, destined for higher command. And wherever Grant went, he would remember the
spectacular charge up Missionary Ridge. Sheridan's immediate
reward was to be sent into East Tennessee to spend a miserable
winter defending Knoxville. But on March 12, 1864, Grant was
named general-in-chief of the Union armies, and on March 23,
Sheridan received a summons to Washington.

Sheridan arranged to leave the next day without making the
usual formal farewell to his troops. "I could not do it," he
wrote; "the bond existing between them and me had grown to
such depth of attachment that I feared to trust my emotions."
They found out he was going, however, and when he boarded
the train for Chattanooga the hillsides around the station were
dark with the assembled 25 regiments of his command, come to
say farewell in their own way.[41]

In Chattanooga Sheridan found out he was to be named chief
of cavalry for the Army of the Potomac. He was "staggered,"
he wrote, by the thought of the "great responsibilities," but it is
clear that is not what bothered him most. The Army of the
Potomac was infamous as a snake pit of political infighting.
Closely watched by all factions in Washington, many officers
were playing to a political gallery instead of taking care of
military business; those who were trying to do their duty were
ensnared in power plays and personality cults.[42]

With good reason, Sheridan was uneasy when he reached
Washington on April 4, and his experiences there were hardly
reassuring. After a perfunctory meeting with Halleck, he was
taken into the presence of the formidable secretary of war, Edwin Stanton. Sheridan was keenly aware that his own appearance had not been enhanced by the hard winter he had just
endured. As Lieutenant Colonel Horace Porter of Grant's staff
described him later, Sheridan "had been worn down almost to a
shadow by hard work and exposure in the field; he weighed
only 115 pounds, and as his height was but five feet six [actu-
ally four] inches, he looked anything but formidable as a candidate for cavalry leader." Sheridan suffered: "If I had ever possessed any self-assertion in manner of speech, it certainly

vanished in the presence of the imperious Secretary, whose name at the time was the synonym of all that was cold and formal."[43]

Sheridan had still more sweating to do, for Halleck now hustled him out of the war department and across the White House lawn to see the president. Lincoln sized up the bantam officer with crinkly-eyed amusement, grasping both his hands in a warm greeting and expressing generalized good wishes. "A brown, chunky little chap," Lincoln noted later, with "not enough neck to hang him." To Grant, Lincoln opined that Sheridan was "rather a little fellow to handle your cavalry." Grant's reply was serene: "You will find him big enough."[44]

It was undoubtedly a relief for Sheridan to get away from this skeptical scrutiny and to his new headquarters at Culpeper, Virginia, where he arrived the next day. The problems he confronted there were daunting, but preferable to the stresses of Washington.

With Grant about to launch a massive spring campaign in which every Federal army was to exert maximum pressure on the Confederacy, Sheridan found the cavalry corps in ruins. Federal troopers had fought Jeb Stuart's vaunted horsemen to a draw at Brandy Station the previous June, in the first big cavalry battle of the war, and had done effective service in the Gettysburg campaign. But now the units were widely scattered, their camps filthy, the horses broken down and the men poorly armed.

Then, too, they resented being put under the command of an infantry officer of whom they had heard little, and a Westerner at that. Brigadier General Henry Davies, a New York lawyer, stated the case with typical sarcasm: "Some experiences from which the Army of the Potomac had previously suffered had not induced the belief that the West was the point of the compass from which the advent of wise men bringing rich gifts of victory and success was to be confidently expected."[45]

The troopers soon changed their minds about Sheridan. He straightened out the routines, reestablished discipline and cleaned up the camps. Quietly and without pomp he assembled his men, looked them over and saw to their needs. He would not be deflected; when an officer questioned the recall of a regiment that had been detailed to act as bodyguard to a prominent infantry general, Sheridan snarled, "I have been placed in command of the cavalry of this army, and by God I want it *all.*" Nor did he hesitate to take on the nasty-tempered army commander, Major General George Meade, with all the headlong dash of the assault on Missionary Ridge.[46]

Sheridan was no theorist, then or later. His previous cavalry command had been a two-regiment brigade, hardly a preparation for his enormous new command. But he knew what he knew: that Meade, along with all the army commanders before him, was wrong to use cavalry as a mere servant of the infantry. The cavalry corps was broken down because it was constantly at work carrying messages, escorting infantry officers, patrolling enemy territory and guarding a perimeter sixty miles in circumference so the infantry would not be disturbed while it rested in winter quarters.[47]

It was all part of the defensive mind-set of the political army; protect the capital, protect the wagons, protect the line of retreat, provide for anything the enemy might do. There was seldom enough time or energy left over to think of attacking, which was all Sheridan ever thought about. Instead of hovering on all sides of the infantry waiting for the enemy to attack, Sheridan shouted at Meade, the cavalry should concentrate, ride out and destroy the enemy cavalry. Then the infantry could stop worrying about where the enemy horsemen would attack, and Sheridan could take his riders anywhere in the Confederacy, to break up Lee's communications and help end the war.

"My proposition," wrote Sheridan, "seemed to stagger General Meade not a little." The army commander "deemed the cavalry fit for little more than guard or picket duty," and his only concession was to ease its duties for two weeks before the beginning of the campaign so the horses could be nursed back to health. Sheridan prepared his 10,000 troopers for action (meanwhile, of course, making an intensive study of the topography of Virginia), but his fundamental disagreement with Meade remained unresolved.[48]

When the Army of the Potomac headed into the Wilderness on May 4, 1864, to engage Lee's army in the first of the many heavyweight slugging matches to come, the cavalry was ordered to guard the wagon trains and screen the advance. This passive duty was anathema to Sheridan, and he did not perform it to Meade's satisfaction. Two tempers, one famous at West Point and in Somerset, Ohio, the other legendary throughout the Army of the Potomac, were on the rise.

When the savage infantry fighting in the Wilderness ended inconclusively, and Grant surprised both armies by ordering an advance around the Confederate right, Sheridan was determined to do more than provide a screen. The next objective was Spotsylvania Court House, and Sheridan ordered one of his divisions to take the town on the morning of May 8 and hold it until the infantry arrived, while his other two divisions seized the bridges over the Po River to forestall any advance by the Confederate infantry.

His men took Spotsylvania as ordered, but before the other divisions broke camp Meade found them and changed their orders, assigning one of them to screen the infantry. The subsequent advance was so slow, and Lee's response to the threat was so quick, that the Confederates got between the main Federal force and Spotsylvania. Meanwhile Stuart's cavalry made a thrust around the Federal left and rear, toward its 4,000 wagons. Sheridan had to round up all available troopers to fend Stuart off in heavy fighting at Todd's Tavern, and had to pull his men out of Spotsylvania—which had to be attacked again the next day.[49]

But for this Meade used the infantry, pulling in the cavalry and letting its 10,000 men sit their horses while the serious fighting was done by others. Before long, Meade had another battle on his hands—in his headquarters tent. By mid-morning on May 8, according to Colonel Porter of Grant's staff, Meade "had worked himself into a towering passion" over the events of the previous day. The army commander summoned Sheridan and "went at him hammer and tongs, accusing him of blunders," mainly of getting in the way of the infantry. "Sheridan was equally fiery," Porter recalled, "all the hotspur in his nature was aroused." It was Meade who had blundered, the junior officer yelled, by countermanding Sheridan's orders, and tying the horsemen to the infantry. Sheridan's language, reported the tender-eared Porter, "was highly spiced and continuously italicized with expletives."[50]

Eventually, Sheridan brought his tantrum to a close by saying that Meade could just go ahead and run the cavalry; that he (Sheridan) would not give them another order, so there; and that if he could do what he wanted, he would mass the cavalry, go out and whip Jeb Stuart. Then Sheridan stamped away to sulk while Meade ran off to tell Grant.

The general in chief listened quietly to the purple-faced Meade's account of the remarkable exchange of views. Meade probably did not expect Grant to have Sheridan shot, although he might have been forgiven for asking—however inappropriate Meade's temper had been, he was after all the commanding general of the Army of the Potomac, and Sheridan's words had been seditious. But Meade surely expected more comfort than he got; when he concluded the saga with Sheridan's quote about whipping Jeb Stuart, Grant responded mildly, "Did he say that? Well, he generally knows what he is talking about. Let him start right out and do it."[51]

Somehow, Sheridan had won the argument, and the next morning he led the entire cavalry corps away from picket duty and toward Jeb Stuart. Such raids had been done before, of course, but never on such a scale—the 10,000 men and 32 guns formed a column thirteen miles long, which took at least four hours to pass a given point on its route—or with such deliberation. On previous raids, Colonel Kidd explained, the idea had been "to ride rapidly through the country and avoid the enemy as much as possible, never fighting unless forced into it unwillingly." Sheridan, on the other hand, went out "looking for trouble—seeking it—and desiring before every other thing to find Stuart and fight him." To be precise, Sheridan knew he did not have to look for Stuart; he had merely to set a course for Richmond, and Stuart would be forced to find him.[52]

The riders first headed east toward Fredericksburg, then south toward Richmond, well behind the Confederate army. To the surprise of his men, Sheridan walked his horses, conserving their strength while holding his command ready for battle at any moment. The steadiness of the pace, wrote Kidd, "calmed the nerves, strengthened self-reliance, and inspired confidence."

When at night Sheridan coolly ordered his men to unsaddle their horses as if in the safety of a bivouac far behind their own lines, recalled another trooper, "the boys began to get acquainted with Sheridan."[53]

As Sheridan had foreseen, the moment he was on the move with such a force, the Army of the Potomac was in no further danger from enemy cavalry—Stuart had to chase Sheridan, while leaving nearly half his cavalry behind to guard the army. By pushing his men and horses ferociously, Stuart on May 11 managed to get in front of Sheridan with 4,500 troopers a mere six miles from Richmond, near a dilapidated old crossroads inn called Yellow Tavern.

The Confederates were exhausted and hopelessly outnumbered, but Stuart had to keep Sheridan away from Richmond until the city's garrison could get in place. The Southerners dismounted and, electrified as usual by their magnificent chief, withstood attack after attack until a Federal private got off a chance shot and brought Stuart down with a mortal wound. Sheridan's men bulled their way to the first line of Richmond defenses, and could have gone ahead into the city, but Sheridan was too disciplined to indulge in a pointless escapade for the sake of glory alone. Men would die in the course of such a caper, and since they would not be able to hold Richmond, and would gain "no permanent advantage," Sheridan declined the temptation.[54]

Within two months, for much the same reasons, Jubal Early would decline to enter Washington City, and would be roundly berated for it.

Chased by every man and rider Lee could spare, Sheridan continued eastward, above Richmond, into a narrowing wedge formed by the flooded Chickahominy River to his left and the fortifications of Richmond to his right. The Confederates thought they had Sheridan trapped, and most of his men had the same opinion. But Sheridan was serene—at least he remembered it that way, thirty years later—and "wished to demonstrate to the Cavalry Corps the impossibility of the enemy's destroying or capturing so large a body of mounted troops." Accordingly, he accepted battle, trounced the forces arrayed against him, and at his leisure made his way back to the Army of the Potomac.[55]

With his victory over Meade and Jeb Stuart, Phil Sheridan had made a dramatic point about the proper use of the mounted arm; had shattered the myth of the innate superiority of Southern horsemen; and had confirmed General Grant's high opinion of Little Phil's ability. After the awful slaughter at Cold Harbor in June, when Grant decided to shift the entire Federal army to the south of the James River, he needed protection from Lee's cavalry during the dangerous maneuver. Sheridan had demonstrated how this was done, and Grant asked him to do it again, this time raiding westward to threaten Lee's railroad communications. Wade Hampton led the Southern cavalry in a mad race to get in front of Sheridan, and this time the fight—at Trevilian Station on June 11 and 12—was a draw, and Sheridan had to break off and head home ahead of schedule. But by the time he got there, the army was safely across the James.

Thus in July, when Jubal Early rattled the gates of Washington, scared the politicians and the bureaucrats to within an inch of their pensions, and danced away unharmed from a fumbling pursuit, a deeply embarrassed Grant turned to Sheridan for a remedy. Grant hammered the encrusted machinery of four military departments into one big new one called the Middle Military Division, gave Sheridan the command despite the objections of Halleck and Stanton, and sent to the Shenandoah five divisions of infantry and two of cavalry from the Army of the Potomac.

Sheridan had everything he needed to do the job. Or to put it another way, he had enough rope to hang himself. Of all assignments available to a civil war general, independent army command was the most dangerous. No prior test could determine whether a man was tough-minded enough to face crises, take risks and clean up his own mistakes when far from help and supervision. Usually, an officer was judged ready for promotion if enough time had passed without a foulup, but Phil Sheridan's record was too short to give much assurance.

And his successes were not well known enough to comfort

the men of his new command, who reacted in much the same
way as had his first group of 40 dragoons. "Many were the
expressions of surprise," recalled a member of a veteran New
York outfit serving in the Valley, "that an officer of so little
distinction should be placed in charge of such an immense command." Nor were they assured, said the New Yorker, by the
sight of "the nervous little man with smiling face and black,
glistening eyes." But the moment Sheridan arrived, the men
began to notice little things going right. Mealtimes became
more regular, supplies started showing up when they were expected, and marches were more carefully managed, with proper
rest intervals and much less tangling of traffic. "His influence
was instantly felt," wrote the New Yorker. "It became a common remark among the troops: 'We can see now that somebody
had got hold of this machine who knows how to run it.'" They
began to call him "Little Phil."[56]

Having taken David Hunter's footsore, beaten and confused
army firmly by the scruff of the neck on August 7, Sheridan
shook it, reorganized it, reinforced it and marched it south
from Harpers Ferry on August 10. It seemed that Jubal Early's
days were numbered. But three days later, without making contact with the enemy, Sheridan retreated to the Harpers Ferry
area. What followed, instead of a vigorous advance and a decisive battle, was five weeks of marching, countermarching, maneuvering and skirmishing. The North erupted with denuncia-
tions of yet another hesitant general courting failure in the
Shenandoah. Jubal Early smiled and pronounced premature
judgment on his new opponent; as he expressed it years later he
was "satisfied that the commander opposed to me was without
enterprise, and possessed an excessive caution which amounted
to timidity."[57]

It was a case of the fly calling the spider a coward. Lee had
been reinforcing Early's army, and some reports had magnified
the number of troops sent to the Valley. Despite the pressures
for quick action, Sheridan did not waver from his opposition to
pointless sacrifice and blundering. He waited. He measured his
opponent, probing constantly with his cavalry and prodding
with infantry reconnaissances. He studied the ground, poring
over maps of the Valley with a topographical engineer named

John Meigs (son of the army quartermaster general) who quickly became a favorite staff officer. He set a few traps, which Early declined to enter.

At first Grant urged caution, then grew restive and decided to visit the Valley to see what was going on. He took with him a plan of attack, intending to share it with his subordinate, but he never got a chance to take it out of his pocket. Sheridan was ready with a detailed, closely analyzed plan that, Grant saw at once, could not fail. He headed back to the Army of the Potomac with a grunt of approval: "Go in."[58]

Sheridan went in across Opequon Creek at dawn on September 19, with an attack that was flawed by an early morning traffic jam, and a slightly skewed advance. At midday the attack had not succeeded, and Jubal Early was congratulating himself on winning what he called "a splendid victory," by which he meant that he had avoided defeat. Meanwhile, Little Phil was incinerating cigars and building a new plan of attack from the wreckage of his old one. He unleashed the new assault —a massive flanking maneuver by his old friend George Crook, combined with one of the largest cavalry charges of the war— at 4 P.M. Within minutes, Jubal Early's victory and his army had disintegrated and were, as Sheridan's prompt telegram to Washington phrased it, "a whirling through Winchester."[59]

After confirming the victory with another at Fisher's Hill three days later, and after running Early's army into the Blue Ridge and taking possession of the Valley as far south as Staunton, Sheridan declared his job done. Grant did not see it that way. For several months, he had wanted the Army of the Shenandoah to do two things: clear out the Confederates, thus closing the Valley as an invasion route to the north and denying the region's abundance of food and forage to Lee's hungry army; then cross the Blue Ridge and destroy railroads. Grant had been unable to destroy Lee's army, but he had succeeded in pinning it down, in its Richmond-Petersburg lines. Now he intended to strangle it, by constricting the iron arteries that supplied it with nourishment.

One of the most important of these was the Orange and Alexandria Railroad between Richmond and Lynchburg. It ran along the eastern edge of the Blue Ridge, northeast from

Lynchburg through Charlottesville to Gordonsville. (Before the war it had continued to Alexandria, but now it was broken up between Gordonsville and Manassas.) At Gordonsville it intersected with the Virginia Central, which ran southeast to Richmond. An additional lifeline to the Army of Northern Virginia was the James River canal, which followed that watercourse northeastward to within fifteen miles of Charlottesville, then turned eastward to Richmond.[60]

Now that Sheridan had accomplished the first objective by clearing the Confederates from the Valley, the next step was obvious to Grant. On September 26, while Sheridan was still chasing Early up the valley after the battle at Fisher's Hill, the general in chief had wired, "If you can possibly subsist your army to the front for a few days more, do it, and make a great effort to destroy the roads around Charlottesville and the canal wherever your cavalry can reach it."[61]

The problem was that business of subsistence. An army of 32,000 men and something like 10,000 horses travels, as Napoleon observed, on its belly, and this was an enormous belly indeed. As Sheridan had already pointedly observed to Grant, Harrisonburg was a hundred miles from the nearest Federal railhead at Martinsburg. That was a long haul, through territory infested with night-riding, hard-hitting partisan guerrillas, for the endless succession of enormous wagon trains required to feed and supply an army of this size. What Grant now wanted Sheridan to do—cross the Blue Ridge and chase Early toward Richmond—would make the supply problems much worse.[62]

It would be impossible to haul the required quantities of food and ammunition all the way up the Valley and then across the Blue Ridge; instead, the Federals would have to repair the Orange and Alexandria Railroad north of Gordonsville, to connect that junction once again with Manassas and Alexandria. It would take an enormous number of men to guard the length of the railroad from the partisans, Sheridan argued, and in addition he would have to leave a large garrison in the Valley to keep it secure. What remained, he wrote later, would be "a wholly inadequate number of fighting men to prosecute a campaign against the city of Richmond."[63]

In Sheridan's view, as explained years later, Grant was "so

pressed by the government and by public opinion at the North," to achieve more victories and to avoid even the appearance of a reverse, that he had accepted a flawed plan. Grant being Grant, he "adhered to this plan with some tenacity," Sheridan remembered with careful understatement, and "considerable correspondence took place between us."[64]

A great deal of it was written on the day Early's troops were slogging through the rain and sleet back to the Valley Pike. Sheridan composed three long telegrams that day—two to Grant, one to Halleck. "The difficulty of transporting this army through the mountain passes onto the railroad at Charlottesville," he told Grant bluntly, "is such that I regard it as impracticable. I think that the best policy will be to let the burning of the crops of the Valley be the end of this campaign, and let some of this army go somewhere else."[65]

On two counts, this was a remarkable proposal. The more astonishing aspect of it was that Sheridan was actually advocating the dismantling of his own command, the reduction of his status and power. This was unheard of. So were the methods of making war that he now proposed to apply to the Shenandoah. He was about to inaugurate—in fact, had already begun—what one anguished Confederate would call the Valley's "Red October."

Grant had ordered the destruction of the Valley's crops and the removal of its livestock three months earlier. It had been an idea born of frustration. He had been unable to find a general who could take and hold the Valley by military force, and it seemed the next best thing would be to strip the Valley of everything valuable to the enemy: the mills that ground and housed the flour and meal to sustain Lee's troops for another winter; the corncribs and granaries and haystacks bulging with provisions to strengthen gaunt horses for another battle in the Shenandoah; the herds and flocks of livestock that could provision a new invasion of the North.

In July Grant had ordered Sheridan's predecessor, General Hunter, to make of the Shenandoah and the nearby little valleys of the Alleghenies "a desert as high up as possible." Grant was specific; "every particle of provisions and stock should be removed, and the people notified to move out." The Federal troops, he wrote, must "eat out Virginia clear and clean as far as they go, so that crows flying over it for the balance of the season will have to carry their provender with them."[66]

Hunter had been run out of the Valley before he could implement these stern instructions. Sheridan had been too busy maneuvering and fighting to turn his attention to them until September 29. On that day, he had flung his cavalry corps across the entire Valley, from the Blue Ridge to North Mountain, and then had drawn the twenty-mile line of troopers slowly northward, with each man instructed to apply the torch to all the "forage, mills, and such other property as might be serviceable to the Rebel army." By the time the rain came two days later, there was hardly a scrap of hay or a morsel of meat left in the four hundred square miles of the Valley between Staunton and Harrisonburg.[67]

The red glow from those fires signaled the dawning of a new and terrible age—the era of total war. There had been foraging aplenty in the past three years of conflict, there had been individual acts of vengeance and rage, and there had been criminal behavior masquerading as military necessity. But never before in this war, if ever in history, had military force on such a scale been applied to the economic resources of civilians.

The distinction is not only blurred today, it seems almost quaint, like the eighteenth-century British officer's protest that to aim one's musket at an individual while firing a volley at an enemy formation would be to commit murder. A world inured to blitzkrieg, scorched-earth and search-and-destroy has difficulty seeing the horror in the burning of some barns and mills. Yet it was an apocalyptic breakdown; until then, despite the bitterness of this fratricidal war, the unwritten rules of "civilized" combat had been honored, with a few inevitable exceptions. The South, with its chivalric traditions and romantic self-image, had been avidly solicitous of noncombatants. Lee's strict orders to his troops during the invasions of the North were held up as examples of gentlemanly restraint in the enemy's country. With less polish but equal good-heartedness, most Federal commanders, up to and including the president, had been careful to prohibit the mistreatment of civilians.

Confederates contrasted Lee's grace with the depredations of

"Black Dave" Hunter—so named by his own men—the demented scion of an old Virginia family who had taken up the cause of the Union and the Negro with a crazed fanaticism. He was glad, he said once, that Virginians participated in John Brown's ill-fated uprising, because that justified the destruction of the state. Hunter had seemed to take that destruction as his personal mission; on virtually every day of his service in the Valley he had found a reason to burn someone's home, frequently that of a relative or family friend. A military failure, Hunter sank rapidly into obscurity after leaving the Valley, and the legacy of hatred he left behind was transferred to the better-known name of Sheridan. This was understandable but unjust; in retrospect it can be seen that what Hunter indulged in, contrary to standing and specific orders, was pyromania, while Sheridan, in executing the specific and detailed orders of his chief, was practicing war—albeit of a new and ugly kind.[68]

He had ordered the burning of September 29 in anticipation of winning his argument with Grant; it was the beginning of the retrograde movement that had not yet been authorized by the general in chief. Sheridan had halted the army just south of Harrisonburg in order to conduct his argument by telegraph. He had no doubt he would prevail—doubt was not one of Little Phil's afflictions—and sure enough, on October 5 Grant relented. He had not given up his designs on the Confederate railroads, but he would not overrule the commander on the scene. Sheridan could withdraw as far as Strasburg, and then they would see.

On the morning of the 6th the army moved out, burning its way toward Cedar Creek.

Chapter 3

Fanny and Tex:
October 6, 1864

On Thursday, the sixth day of the Valley's Red October, the burning resumed in earnest. While the dense, miles-long columns of Federal infantry, limbered guns and wagons trudged and rumbled northward along the Valley Pike (Sheridan in the back of a two-seat wagon, his feet propped up on the front seat, a cigar clamped jauntily in his teeth), the horsemen brought Apocalypse to the Valley behind. To do their work, the blueclad riders formed a line extending twenty-five miles from North Mountain eastward to the Blue Ridge.[1]

Over and over again an awful scene was repeated. Into a farmyard where none but family and friends had ever come the soldiers would ride, hard-eyed, carbines ready and torches guttering. That they were not there to kill, or to destroy homes, was hardly a comfort; they had come to destroy what a lifetime of labor had built up, and that was as hard as death.

The barn—raised in a long-ago year of hope and peace by a flock of laughing neighbors—would be the first to go, responding to the torch with an ugly bloom of crimson heat and roiling smoke. The cows or pigs or sheep—markers of a family's treasure, nursed through years of birthings and injuries and illness—were driven off, squalling. If there was a haystack or a corncrib—containing a harvest clawed from the earth by those considered unfit for war, whose thin bodies had been barely equal to the weight of the half-filled pitchfork and the bushel basket —it, too, soon gushed its contribution into the darkening sky. Through the smoke and the horror, anguished grandfathers and fearful women could see their next visitor, black-mounted Famine, coming with the winter.

Sheridan the bookkeeper reported with satisfaction that by the time his army reached Woodstock, thirty-five miles down the Valley from Harrisonburg, his men had burned "over 2,000 barns filled with wheat, hay, and farming implements; over 70 mills filled with flour and wheat; have driven in front of the army over 4,000 head of stock, and have killed and issued to the army not less than 3,000 sheep."[2]

The Confederate view of these events was clouded not merely by smoke but by consuming, mostly impotent, rage. General Early's adjutant general, Major Henry Kyd Douglas (whose home was just across the Potomac River from the Valley's Shepherdstown), was shaken anew by his memories when he set them down on paper years later. "I try to restrain my bitterness," he wrote, but he could not. He told of riding north behind the Federal cavalry, "beneath great columns of smoke which almost shut out the sun by day, and in the red glare of bonfires which, all across the Valley, poured out flames and sparks heavenward and crackled mockingly in the night air; and I saw mothers and maidens tearing their hair and shrieking to Heaven in their fright and despair, and little children, voiceless and tearless in their pitiable terror.

"I saw a beautiful girl, the daughter of a clergyman, standing in the front door of her home while its stable and outbuildings were burning, tearing the yellow tresses from her head, taking up and repeating the oaths of passing skirmishers and shrieking with wild laughter, for the horrors of the night had driven her mad."[3]

Old Jube's infantry could only watch, and trail behind, and wait for a chance at retribution. The men of the Second Corps, most especially the Valley men in the proud Stonewall Brigade, stored up their anguish, saving it for a day of reckoning. They moved out at dawn on October 6, thinking to lash into Sheridan at Harrisonburg, punish him and hold him there, away from the beleaguered Lee. But their infantry advance met only silence, found only empty campgrounds; the enemy, oblivious to the danger, had by chance moved away from it. The foot-soldiers could do nothing for the time being but follow the "smoky trail of desolation" as one of their number put it, "of the devil's inspector-general."[4]

The cavalry might do something, but neither Early nor the infantry expected much. Fitzhugh Lee's division was without its leader; the young giant had been wounded at the battle of Winchester, and the next in line, Brigadier General Williams Carter Wickham, had decided to resign from the army and take his long-held seat in the Confederate Congress. The other cavalry division, under Fitz Lee's close friend and former West Point classmate Lunsford Lomax, was a discouraged, worn-down, ragtag lot consisting of the five small brigades that had been fighting in and around the Valley, alone or in various combinations, all year. Lomax, a smooth-faced, twenty-nine-year-old West Pointer, had taken over the command in August, and although he was a capable officer, there had been no way to withstand the rampaging Federal horsemen at Winchester or Fisher's Hill.[5]

Afterward the infantry was contemptuous of the cavalry. "For some cause known only to their whimsical philosophy," wrote Captain V. E. Turner of the 23rd North Carolina, "Imboden's cavalry was an especial object of their disesteem. By way of derision they called it 'Jimboden's' cavalry." The footsoldiers did not think much of their general, either, to hear Turner tell it. He remembered seeing, during the retreat from Fisher's Hill, "a ragged, dejected, unkempt 'Confed' crouched over a little fire, regarding naught, absorbed alone in warming numbed fingers and toes, for the day was chilly. As he crouched and shivered he droned a song in whose tone disgust, despair and disdain all strove for mastery. The song, which must have been rich, was lost except the following stanzas caught as a group of officers rode by: 'Ole Jimboden's gone up the spout, / And Old Jube Early's about played out.' 'Gone up the spout' was war lingo for passed into nothingness."[6]

On Wednesday evening, October 5, the Laurel Brigade of cavalry had joined the Army of the Valley after a long, hard ride from Petersburg. Their eyes were hollow and their horses skeletal, but their anger sustained them as they took their place in the line that morning. Most of them were Valley men who ached with special ardor to chastise the barnburners.[7]

At the beginning of the war, far too disorganized to be called a brigade, the group had been known simply as Turner Ashby's cavalry, and had fought in Stonewall Jackson's legendary Valley Campaign of 1862. After Ashby's death they had been converted slowly from a tribe to an organized military unit, chiefly through the efforts of Brigadier General William E. "Grumble" Jones (a near duplicate, in appearance and asperity, of Jubal Early). In its two years under Jones, the brigade—the 7th, 11th, and 12th Regiments of Virginia cavalry, along with the smaller 35th Battalion—had gone along on both invasions of the North and often had defended Richmond. But its usual place had been in the Valley, the men fighting for what their Scots comrade and historian Captain William McDonald called "their native heath."[8]

Never before had it gone this hard on the Valley. While Lomax's division followed the Federals down the Valley Pike, Rosser's moved along the Back Road, a sinuous track across the eastern shoulders of North Mountain. "The sight of the burning barns and stack-yards," Captain McDonald recalled, "banished everything from their minds but the thought of vengeance. The fires of destruction were partly visible. Clouds of smoke hung across the Valley, extending from the Blue Ridge to North Mountain, hiding the movements of the incendiaries but clearly showing the fiendish character of their work."[9]

The Laurel Brigade's commander for the past year, the twenty-seven-year-old Brigadier General Thomas Lafayette Rosser, had on arrival taken over Fitz Lee's division. He was not from the Valley, and did not feel as keenly as did his men the agony of its destruction. He was fired up, and anxious to fight, and he rode their passion as he would ride a feisty horse —they would "run over everything in the Valley," he boasted prematurely—but he was driven by a lighter anger born of frustration. Tom Rosser had felt frustrated about one thing and another through much of the war: promotions had come too slowly; Jeb Stuart, the great cavalry chief whom Rosser tried in every way to emulate, had mistreated him; Wade Hampton, Stuart's successor, had persecuted him; Robert E. Lee was incompetent; and Jubal Early was a "miserable old rascal."[10]

There was only one man in the world for whom Tom Rosser

maintained a lasting affection, from boyhood days at West
Point, through the war, into later years. Like Rosser, he was a
young brigadier general just promoted to divisional command,
and like Rosser was on the Back Road that afternoon. But his
uniform was neither gray nor butternut, and when at midday
Rosser ordered his raging brigades to attack and destroy Sheridan's Third Division of cavalry he was zestfully ordering the
destruction of his best and oldest friend—George Armstrong
Custer.

There was anger in the Federal ranks as well that day. They,
too, felt their enemy had gone beyond the bounds of ordinary
warfare, and they thirsted for vengeance. The feeling had been
building for some time, but had been focused and intensified by
what had happened three days before.

After a fine October Sunday it had rained all day again on
Monday, October 3. Toward evening the downpour intensified,
and no one saw the need for John Meigs to make the four-mile
ride from Sheridan's headquarters in Harrisonburg to Dayton.
But Meigs, an immensely popular young lieutenant only a year
out of West Point, was conscientious to a fault about his work
as the army's topographical engineer, especially now that he
had a commanding general who valued what he did, who studied his maps and appreciated his advice. Meigs had surveying
work to do in the Dayton area the next day, and insisted he
would spend the night at the headquarters of the Third Cavalry
Division, which had just been put under the command of the
notorious Boy General, George Custer. The ride was relatively
short, after all, and was miles behind the Federal picket line,
with the enemy army long gone. And so Meigs floundered into
his smelly rubber raincoat, mounted his drenched horse, leaned
into the downpour and, followed by two unfortunate orderlies,
headed out. There are two versions of what happened next.[11]

As Meigs and his men splashed along the Middle Road toward Dayton, they overtook another small group of horsemen,
similarly hunched against the downpour, obviously a detachment from the Third Cavalry. Half-blinded by the pelting rain,
Meigs and his two companions slowly drew even with the other
riders, who suddenly swept back their blue overcoats, jabbed

pistols out at point-blank range, and fired. Meigs fell to the mud, obviously dead. One orderly was never heard from again and was presumed dead or captured; the other, his horse shot from under him, fell with it into some brush and hid there, escaping later to tell his story at Sheridan's headquarters.[12]

When Jubal Early heard the account, after the war, he pronounced it to be nonsense. Meigs had run into a Confederate cavalry patrol, he said, which in the rain had penetrated the lightly guarded Federal lines. The three Southern troopers—in uniform, but perhaps wearing captured Federal overcoats—had surprised the Federal party, had demanded surrender, and had seen all three raise their hands. As Meigs was removing his weapons, he fired from under his cape, wounding Private George W. Martin of the 4th Virginia Cavalry. Martin fired back reflexively, killing Meigs. The detachment then captured one of the Federal orderlies and helped Martin, who was thought to be mortally wounded, back to camp. (Martin lived, although he never recovered completely; and after the war he spent years in hiding in Missouri, the object of a $1,000 reward offered by Meigs's father, Montgomery, quartermaster-general of the U.S. Army.) It had been, said Early, a fair fight.[13]

Sheridan did not think so. He believed Meigs had been murdered by cowardly bushwhackers wearing Federal uniforms, criminals beyond the pale of civilized warfare. It was another depredation, in his view, of the same kind as Mosby's ceaseless harassments farther north; the work of skulking, cowardly nightriders who shot people in the back and with the coming of day blended back into a civilian population that obligingly hid them, fed them, supplied them and made their murdering possible. The ever-ready Irish temper welled up, and Sheridan went into a black rage. He called Custer to him and pronounced sentence on those he judged guilty of participation—or at least complicity—in Meigs's death: burn Dayton to the ground, he said, and with it every house within five miles of the accursed place. Let the people of the Valley know the price of assisting bushwhackers.[14]

It was an outrageous order, even assuming the story told by Meigs's orderly was accurate. As Sheridan must have known, given his habitual attention to the locality in which he operated, the inhabitants of Dayton and its environs were Mennonites, devout pacifists who would not fight for their own lives, let alone for the good of Lee or Lincoln. The able-bodied men on these Valley farms, who made Sheridan think darkly of ambushers and partisans, were people who refused to bear arms of any kind, for any purpose. But they were Sheridan's enemies now, and to Sheridan, enemies were to be obliterated. In this he had a perfectly suited lieutenant in George Custer, who wasted not a second reflecting on the order he had been given, but shouted happily, "Look out for smoke," and hopped into the saddle to light some fires.[15]

But Sheridan was, after all, no Black Dave Hunter. Only a few houses had been burned when he countermanded the order, collared the Boy General once again, and allowed a simmering quiet to return to the area. But anger was in the air, thick and acrid as smoke. Not the straightforward passion of war that stiffened men to the business of killing each other for a cause in a stand-up fight; but a rancorous, malodorous rage born of bushwhackings and throat-slittings and hangings of and by people who were spying, disguised as friends, behind the lines, ignoring the rules of what the punctilious like to call "civilized warfare"—rules, in other words, that stipulated the proper etiquette for mass butchery. These proprieties were regarded as so important that violations not only called for but demanded retributions of the most savage kind.

One such chain of outrage, in which Custer may or may not have been involved, earned him a wide and lasting reputation as a brute. After a September 25 skirmish in the Luray Valley with some of Mosby's Rangers, Federal cavalrymen became convinced that one of their officers had been robbed and murdered after surrendering to the partisans. In a rage, they made a barbaric display of executing six of Mosby's men in and around Front Royal. It was reported to Mosby—and widely believed then and afterwards—that Custer had ordered the executions. No one who was involved talked or wrote much about this shameful incident, but the few references to it that survive indicate that Custer had nothing to do with these killings, although at the time he never denied the accusations, probably approved of the action and most likely enjoyed the additional notoriety.

In November Mosby would order an equivalent number of prisoners from Custer's command marched down the Berryville Road to within a few miles of Sheridan's headquarters and there executed. In a coldly formal letter to Sheridan, Mosby would then demand that the hangings stop. They did.[16]

Many were troubled by such increasingly frequent descents into barbarity, but George Armstrong Custer was not one of them. As Sheridan was a hard-edged Grant, reflecting the aggressiveness cherished by the general in chief without the tempering of intellect or larger responsibility, so Custer was distilled Sheridan—concentrated combativeness with all traces of temperance removed.

Killing his fellow men never bothered Custer, not even the first time. Initiation to the taking of human life usually sobered the most fervent patriot and matured the most callow youth; one could not help but be aware that by such an act, whatever the cause, one crossed a primeval line into country dangerous for one's soul. One shielded mother and sister from such things, and was reticent about the subject in decent company. Custer, on the other hand, reported his first kill to his family with all the zest of an Ohio schoolboy who had bagged his first squirrel.

It happened in August of 1862, during the Peninsular Campaign. Custer was serving on General in Chief George B. McClellan's staff, but on this day had decided to ride along with his old regiment, the 5th U.S. Cavalry, while it ran off a Confederate detachment. Custer wrote home later that he happily galloped along in the chase, finding it to be "the most exciting sport I ever engaged in." He spotted an enemy officer fleeing "on a splendid horse," fired at him on the run, missed, and fired again, whereupon the officer "reeled and fell to the ground."

Custer galloped on, but avidly passed on the further report of a lieutenant who saw, Custer wrote, that the stricken Confederate "rose to his feet, turned around, threw up his hands and fell to the ground with a stream of blood gushing from his mouth. I had either shot him in the neck or the body," Custer noted with satisfaction. "In either case, the wound must have been fatal." Custer not only relished the man's death but later enjoyed his splendid horse and treasured his heavy sword. It was a knightly trophy, just right for the occasion; its long, straight blade was inscribed in Spanish with the admonition, "Draw me not without reason; sheathe me not without honor."[17]

Two years later, Custer had made himself one of the most famous Federal officers in the war. He was by that time the youngest general in the Union armies, having been promoted to that rank in June of 1863, at the age of twenty-three, while a first lieutenant (acting as captain). He relentlessly called attention to himself with outlandish dress, grooming and behavior. He was a fearless practitioner of that most showy of battlefield maneuvers, the cavalry charge, and was so good at it that he consistently excited admiration, envy and hatred among both his comrades and his enemies. Such a man was not subjected to many dispassionate assessments. Captain George B. Sanford, in 1864 serving on the headquarters staff of the Army of the Shenandoah's cavalry corps, offered one of the few.

"He was scarcely more than a boy in years," Sanford wrote, "but was a man of tremendous energy and immense physical power. His great height and striking countenance made him a very imposing figure. His blue eyes, blond mustache and great mass of blond curling hair falling almost to his waist [Sanford exaggerates here; to the shoulders, yes, but not the waist] gave him the appearance of one of the Vikings of old, and his fancy for startling effects was still further indicated by his dress." The uniform was indeed a marvel. As it first appeared—Custer had moderated it a good deal by the fall of 1864—it consisted of riding breeches of dark brown velveteen, piped in gold and tucked into "immensely long cavalry boots;" a dark brown velveteen jacket, sleeves encrusted with the enormous gold filigrees (known as Hungarian knots) of the European and Confederate officer's dress uniform; a crimson sailor's shirt with an enormous collar turned over the top of the jacket; the whole being topped by "an immensely broad 'slouch' hat," and, around the neck, a "long flowing ribbon or cravat of brilliant red cashmere or silk. This streamed behind him as he rode, and made him a marked man a mile away.

"Although this all sounds a little farcical and was at all events scarcely in good taste, it would be a great mistake to suppose that Custer was a braggadocio or anything of the kind. In the first place, he was but a boy in years and feelings when the war commenced, and full of youthful extravagances. He had been brought up in a little Western country village and had seen little or nothing of life until his graduation from the Military Academy, simultaneously with the beginning of the war, opened for him a career of wonderful brilliancy and made him the recipient of such boundless adulation as would certainly have turned a weaker head. Custer was a man of boundless confidence in himself and great faith in his lucky star."[18]

For a Yale man, who had been raised among Connecticut's granitic and proper New Englanders, Sanford saw Custer with remarkably clear eyes (except, perhaps, for his assumption that what one experiences in "a little Western country village" is not life). That Custer was a showman and a barbarian obscured but did not alter the main point: that he was a consummate warrior.

He had been, however, one of the poorest students of war to pass through the ranks of West Point. Like Jubal Early, he had repeatedly accumulated far more demerits than the maximum allowed (often being cited for long hair and unauthorized ornaments), only to have some unknown authority forgive them. Like Phil Sheridan, he had little aptitude for formal learning. But Custer had brought to his studies neither the natural intelligence of Young Jube nor the grinding obstinacy of Little Phil, and had remained at rock bottom in virtually every ranking of his class. "My career as a cadet had but little to commend it to the study of those who came after me," he recalled cheerfully, "unless as an example to be carefully avoided."[19]

It was an odd performance for a young man who had set out to be a teacher, had in fact worked briefly as a headmaster, then had contracted a passion for soldiering and changed his course. One searches his record in vain for some sense of commitment to his new career. Instead, at every turn there is indifference: "It was all right with him whether he knew his lesson or not," a roommate remembered, "he did not allow it to trouble him."[20]

Custer had grown up as a middle member of a large and boisterous Ohio family. The father, Emmanuel, was a blacksmith who bequeathed to young George a lean, well-muscled frame that never seemed to tire. It must have been the mother, Maria Ward Fitzpatrick, who conveyed the blond curls and fine, Teutonic features that earned her son the appalling academy nickname of "Fanny." There had been six older stepbrothers and stepsisters, three younger brothers and a younger sister. The whole family had been fond of loud fun, especially practical jokes. Custer took away with him a broad sense of humor and a penchant for crowded rowdiness that was long remembered at West Point and in the army—Custer's headquarters was always the location of the loudest and longest parties. (That may have been one reason why young Meigs rode through the rain to his death that night; the Boy General had just changed commands, and there was sure to be a celebration on.)[21]

Yet there was something odd in that fun-loving family; something not ordinary about the fact that after the age of ten, young George—"Autie" to the female family members, "Armstrong" to brothers and male friends—spent much of his time living with his married stepsister Lydia in Monroe, Michigan.

Where others might express themselves through their intellect or emotions, George Custer was a physical person. His enthusiasms were untainted by analysis or by any shading of feeling other than the plain exuberance of action. It was a typical, adolescent phase of life, one shared by many comrades at West Point (most of whom, unlike Custer, would grow out of it), but especially by another coltish young man named Tom Rosser.

Rosser was a beefy, six-foot-two-inch, swarthy lad whose black hair and slab-sided facial parts—high cheekbones, prominent nose, squared jaw—suggested Indian blood. When one learned that his middle name was Lafayette and that he came from alligator country, just across the Sabine River into Texas from Louisiana, one thought of Creoles or Cajuns. But Rosser, soon given the rather perfunctory nickname of Tex, had moved to Texas as a boy, having been born in Virginia to a father descended from French Huguenots. In Texas Tom's father had claimed one of the worst pieces of ground in that very large state, and spent his declining years trying in vain to get it to produce.

Rosser had little in common, it would seem, with Custer; he was three years older, a head taller and in a senior class. (After

a brief experiment with five-year classes, the academy returned
in 1861 to the four-year system; thus two classes graduated that
summer, Rosser's in May, Custer's in June.) One was dark and
coarse-featured, one was fair, freckled and finely wrought, one
was South and one was North, yet for all their differences
Fanny and Tex were a match. They were Westerners after all,
hard-muscled sons of a blacksmith and a hardscrabble farmer,
equally thoughtless and feckless and rebellious. They wrestled
and raced, fenced and fought, rode and drank, with the endless,
rambunctious competitiveness of young horses. They collected
demerits together, in equal measure for much the same reasons,
they went to Benny Havens's—the unofficial West Point bar—
together, and stayed together at or near the bottom of their
respective classes in the formal rankings. They were remembered by their peers, however, as being among the best riders
and strongest physical specimens of the entire student body.

The dark passions that rent their country while they pranced
across the playing fields of the Academy seemed to touch them
hardly at all. They intended to go to war on opposite sides, not
so much because they believed differently, if they believed anything at all, but because that was the way it was. The awesome,
blood-soaked conflict looming just over the horizon would be
merely a continuation of their friendly rivalry, a convenient
backdrop against which Fanny and Tex could play out their
games of glory.

The question that concerned Tom Rosser, as secession began
and 1861 drew on, was how to make his move most advanta-
geously. As a presumptuous preliminary, the unknown cadet
wrote to offer his warrior services first to Texas governor Sam
Houston (a Union man, whose brusque reply was that Mr.
Rosser should go back to his studies), then twice to Confederate President Jefferson Davis (who apparently did not reply at
all). Undaunted by this official disinterest, and anxious lest
events move so rapidly that he could not ride their crest, Rosser
took irrevocable action on April 22. He and his roommate John
Pelham resigned and headed south.

Pelham was a slim, dewy-eyed, Byronically pretty young
man who despite his quiet ways and superior academic abilities
had run with Rosser and Custer, and had held his own with

them, especially when it came to horsemanship. Remarkably, Pelham was liked, even as he excelled; as a classmate wrote years later, "he was one of the best of us." The two lads had an adventurous time, as they told it later, making their way south through a country seething with angry mobs on the lookout for traitors. When they finally gained the capital of the Confederacy at Montgomery, Alabama, they were given commissions at once.[22]

There were horsemen and marksmen aplenty for the swelling armies, in fact hundreds were being turned away because hard-pressed officers simply could not fit them in. But these boys possessed something that was badly needed—training in the use of artillery. Pelham was assigned (briefly) to Alburtis's Virginia Battery and Rosser joined the Washington Artillery of New Orleans. By July 17 Rosser was camped with his battalion in the rolling country along Bull Run, near Manassas, Virginia.[23]

A few days later, Custer arrived on the other side of that stream, having taken much longer to make a shorter journey. While Rosser had left the academy before his scheduled class graduation in May, Custer had remained at West Point even after his class departed, in June. The problem was yet another infraction—failure to stop a fight between two other cadets while serving as officer of the guard—that brought a court-martial and reprimand. Despite this, and his poor standing overall, which would ordinarily have consigned him to the infantry, Custer was given command of a company of the 2nd (later 5th) U.S. Cavalry. What with one delay and another, he did not join his regiment until July 20, 1861.

The next day brought the first full-scale battle of the war, in which Custer the indifferent cadet immediately proved to be an inspired combat leader. In the ghastly panic of that shattering afternoon, the young lieutenant displayed extraordinary coolness and presence of mind. He kept his men well in hand, took them off the field in good order after most of the other Federal units had run for their lives, and during the retreat he calmly cleared a bridge that had become jammed with panic-stricken fugitives. His performance was remarkable, and it was noticed. Tom Rosser, meanwhile, had been sent with Dick Ewell's brigade on a wild-goose chase toward Fairfax Court House and had missed the battle. The pattern—Custer in the thick of things, Rosser somehow drawn off to one side of events—would reappear.[24]

What often followed when a young officer showed that he could function in battle now happened to Custer; he was selected for a general's staff. The most frequent and acute need felt by a Civil War general was for information. He needed people who could tell him what was happening, in the noise and smoke and confusion and dying, and he needed the best information precisely when most men were worst at seeing and speaking clearly—when under fire and in mortal danger. Custer obviously flourished under such dire stress, and the first of many generals to grasp his services was the formidable Brigadier General Philip Kearny.

It was a brief assignment—General-in-Chief McClellan soon ordained that regular officers would not be permitted to serve on the staffs of volunteer generals. Custer spent the winter of 1861–62 back in Monroe, Michigan, on sick leave for an illness whose nature was not recorded. On at least one occasion he suffered from another, identifiable illness: he drank so much that on the way home he made a public disgrace of himself in sight of a neighbor girl, a judge's daughter whom he especially wanted to impress, and in front of his stepsister Lydia, who gave him a tongue-lashing. Custer, mortified, vowed never to drink alcohol again.[25]

Custer was back with the 2nd Cavalry when the Peninsular Campaign got under way in the spring of 1862, but was soon detached for more staff work, this time as an engineer's assistant. Here his courage was subjected to a new test; he was required to step into the wicker baskets of Professor Thaddeus Lowe's hot-air balloon and allow himself to be lofted hundreds of feet in the air to observe enemy dispositions. (The previous September, near Centreville, Professor Lowe had learned that his aeronauts were not quite so safe from enemy fire as he had supposed when Tom Rosser dug in the trail of a gun to get the necessary elevation and opened fire with harrowing effect.)[26]

Custer was attached for a time to the staff of Brigadier General Winfield Scott Hancock, who commanded a brigade at the battle of Williamsburg in May of 1862. There, where Jubal

Early earned a name and a wound with a wild charge, Custer joined Hancock's final, victorious push, on horseback, and snatched what turned out to be the first battle standard captured by the Army of the Potomac. His remarkable talent for such exploits forced Custer to the attention of McClellan himself, and got him assigned to army headquarters, temporarily a captain.[27]

It was during this time that he slipped away to kill his first Confederate, yet it was not a good year; too little combat, not nearly enough rank or glory. Then, in November, things went from bad to awful. McClellan was relieved of command, and Custer, along with a great many officers of the Army of the Potomac, was wild with indignation. He was also temporarily without assignment, and went home on leave. There he decided to pay court to the neighbor girl, she who had witnessed his last drunk, but her father slammed the door to that opportunity firmly shut. Her father was a judge; George Custer's father was a blacksmith.

As the spring of 1863 brought campaigning weather, Custer, tired of being a messenger, itched for a command. He had applied to the governor of his adoptive state of Michigan for the colonelcy of the just-organized 7th Michigan Cavalry, but had not been chosen. Instead, he drew another staff assignment, this time with Brigadier General Alfred Pleasonton, the commander of a division in what was now the Cavalry Corps of the Army of the Potomac. In desperation, Custer spent a few days with the 5th Michigan Cavalry, campaigning like a city council candidate for the position of colonel. Shamelessly, he tried to convince the officers of this regiment, who had never even seen him before, to sign a petition to the governor requesting Custer's appointment as their commander. They thought him an upstart, and did no such thing. The war was entering its third year, and Custer's career was stalled.

By that time Tex Rosser had been a full colonel for almost a year, but he, too, was convinced that he was going nowhere. In the desultory sparring that had followed First Manassas in 1861, Rosser had handled his battery with enough vigor to come to the attention of the hard-riding Jeb Stuart. He did so again in the spring of 1862, especially at that small but star-crossed affair at Williamsburg. The following month was a big one for Rosser. He was promoted to lieutenant colonel of artillery on June 10; transferred to the cavalry—Jeb Stuart's brigade—on June 23; and on June 24 was promoted to colonel and given command of the just-organized 5th Virginia Cavalry.

Rosser took firm control of his raw and untrained regiment, and handled it well in the Second Manassas Campaign in August, and in the subsequent invasion of Maryland. But the main chance, the conspicuous role in a full battle, eluded him. The Confederate cavalrymen sat their horses while the infantry made bloody history along Antietam Creek near Sharpsburg on September 17, and remained in winter quarters when the foot-soldiers slugged it out again, three months later, at Fredericksburg.

Stuart had been watching his young protégé closely, and in January of 1863 declared him ready for higher command. (The only other young officer on whom Stuart lavished such favorable attention was his artillery commander, Major John Pelham.) Rosser, wrote Stuart, "possesses to an extraordinary degree the talent to command and the skill to lead with coolness and decision of character." Rosser should be made a general, Stuart told the authorities in Richmond, "I wish to have the valuable assistance of such a brigadier in my sphere of action."[28]

Rosser agreed absolutely. He wrote a friend in the Confederate Congress to see what was delaying his promotion. He explored the possibility of getting ahead faster by transferring to the infantry. He grumbled. The approach of campaigning weather in 1863 found him, as it did his favorite enemy George Custer, fretful and frustrated. They lusted for more combat, more rank, more fame, and at their first chance—Rosser's came at Kelly's Ford in March, Custer's at Brandy Station in June—they reached for the brass ring with everything they had. Meanwhile, powerful changes were taking place in their respective armies.

One of the first signs of a difference in the Federal cavalry was seen on March 17, in a portentous little affair at Kelly's Ford on the Rappahannock River, upstream from Fredericksburg. There was little point to the fight, which was started by a

sophomoric challenge from Fitz Lee to his old West Point
chum William Averell, now brigadier general of Federal cavalry. Averell brought 2,100 troopers across the river that day,
and Fitz Lee rode to meet him, outnumbered almost three to
one but confident the odds were about right. Rosser's 5th Virginia Cavalry led the advance while Fitz Lee brought the rest of
the brigade—and some unusual reinforcements.

Jeb Stuart happened to be in the area, testifying at a court-
martial involving charges brought by Rosser against one of his
subordinates. And young John Pelham—known ever since
Fredericksburg, where Lee had admired his extraordinary
courage, as "the gallant Pelham"—was visiting one of his many
lady friends nearby. At Averell's approach, both Confederate
officers immediately rode to help Fitz Lee meet the danger.

When the hopelessly outnumbered Rosser not only confronted but charged them, the Federals halted and went over to
the defensive, dismounting behind a stone fence. Fitz Lee came
up and ordered a stronger charge. The men galloped up to the
stone wall and then along it to the left, blazing away with their
pistols and looking for a way through. Pelham, who as an artillery officer had no business doing so but was probably overcome by the excitement of it all, galloped diagonally across the
field to join the fight. As he did so, an explosive round burst
over his head and a tiny shell fragment arrowed into his brain.
He was found lying paralyzed on the ground, his eyes open, his
expression pleasant. He died the next day.[29]

To the surprise of the Confederates, Averell's men kept fighting. It was unusual; when driven back they counterattacked,
and when hardest pressed they charged. The riders chased and
sabered and shot each other throughout the long afternoon.
Rosser was among the wounded, but stayed in the saddle until
sundown, at which time Averell "deemed it proper to withdraw." For the first time, Federal cavalrymen had stayed on the
field with Stuart's Invincibles for a creditable length of time,
and had withdrawn of their own volition.

That ominous fact escaped attention as the entire Southland
went into paroxysms of grief over the death of the gallant Pelham. The twenty-five-year-old major, with his almost feminine
grace and fierce courage, had embodied the ideal of Southern

chivalry, and his martyrdom unleashed extravagant sorrows. A weeping Stuart was described as snipping a lock of the dead youth's hair, dripping a tear on the corpse's cheek and murmuring, "Farewell." (Stuart vowed that his next child would bear the gallant name; it turned out to be a girl, born on October 9, duly christened Virginia Pelham Stuart.)[30]

Rosser joined in the grieving, of course, and like Stuart decided to give Pelham's name to his first child. This was premature—Rosser was not yet married—but during the two months it took him to recover from his wound, he took care of that. According to family tradition, Rosser had passed the imposing home of his future lady love early in the war, saying casually to a young man sitting on a fence, "Little fellow, if you bring me a drink of water, I'll come back and marry your sister." A year later, stopping by chance at the same house to borrow a pen, Rosser met the aforementioned sister and from then on was a frequent visitor. On May 28, 1863, he and Betty Barbara Winston were married.[31]

Rosser did his best, at the wedding, to maintain the role of wounded war hero and bridegroom despite nettlesome drawbacks; he had just missed the glorious victory at Chancellorsville, he missed the gallant Pelham, who was to have been his best man, and especially he missed his promotion to brigadier general. He assured his bride, who could not have been enchanted by his brooding about rank, that he only wanted the promotion for her sake. He also vowed to become a better person; he would drink less, would even become a Christian and join her church. Meanwhile, he wanted her to know that their marriage, by clearing his mind of romantic confusions and doubts, would make him a better soldier.[32]

The South needed better soldiers, especially in the cavalry, and most especially on the 9th of June 1863 (by which time Rosser, his mind properly cleared, was back on duty). Out of the fog at dawn, with a blond-haired dervish named Custer galloping in the van (an odd place for a staff officer to be), came the Federal cavalry to confirm the promise of Kelly's Ford—that it was now and would henceforward be a force to be reckoned with. The 11,000 Federals, including some infantry, surprised Stuart near Brandy Station and in a long day of savage

fighting gave the Confederate cavalry its worst beating of the
war in the largest cavalry fight ever seen on the continent.
Rosser missed it; he had been sent toward Warrenton on picket
duty.

Custer, on the other hand, was there with a vengeance, albeit
merely as a representative of General Pleasonton, now the commander of the cavalry corps. When the colonel of the 8th New
York Cavalry was killed during the fighting, Captain Custer
took command of the faltering regiment; when the 8th Illinois
and 3rd Indiana lost their commanders, Custer took them over
as well. Having given himself a battlefield promotion to brigade
commander, Custer pulled the confused regiments together despite the roaring chaos of the battle, organized a saber charge
and brought his adopted men out of their peril in good order.[33]

Stuart's badly shaken command still held the field at the end
of the day, but barely. He was humiliated by the outcome, and
came under rare public attack. The Richmond *Examiner* wrote
darkly of "negligence and bad management." The war, it
pointed out, was after all not "a tournament, invented and supported for the pleasure of a few vain and weakheaded officers."[34]

Things were changing. It was a fine thing to have an ostrich
feather in the hat, a blooded horse between the knees and a
knightly reputation, but now most troopers would rather have
a Spencer seven-shot carbine, or a fifteen-round Henry, the gun
the awestruck Confederates said you loaded on Sunday and
fired all week. "Beauty," as Jeb Stuart was known to some, was
becoming obsolete in his own time. The victories were beginning to go to colorless but careful managers, who got all their
men into the fight at the right time and place, who concentrated their firepower and marshalled their resources for maximum power. These were hard lessons, and now Fanny and Tex
began to learn them together, on the same battlefields.

Lee headed north, through the Shenandoah toward Gettysburg, and sent his cavalry (hot to redeem their honor) east of
the Blue Ridge to screen the movement. The Federal riders,
fired up by their near-victory, were ordered to find out where
Lee was going. The opposing cavalries met in the Loudoun

Valley, between the Blue Ridge and the slighter Bull Run (or Catoctin) Mountain to the east.

On the afternoon of June 17, a Federal brigade commanded by Rosser's former West Point classmate Judson Kilpatrick rode west through a gap in Bull Run Mountain. George Custer, still a staff officer, was along for the ride, sniffing the wind for action. By now his incessant refrain— "I'll be a general before this is over, you'll see!"—had become a kind of standing joke among his fellow staff officers. It was obvious he did not intend to make rank through fastidiousness; he rode with his overly long curls jouncing from under a seedy straw hat.[35]

At 4 P.M. near the village of Aldie, the Federals confronted the pickets of Fitz Lee's brigade, sent to stop them. Fitz Lee was ill, his command taken temporarily by Colonel Thomas Munford, who was Tom Rosser's special (and, as it turned out, lifelong) rival. When the Federals drove in Munford's pickets, Rosser's regiment responded with a headlong charge. Kilpatrick was a jug-eared, lantern-jawed, comical-looking bird, but he was one of the hell-for-leather new breed of Federal riders, and he knew only one response to a charge—a countercharge.[36]

The Confederates shot down the colonel of the leading Federal regiment, then Kilpatrick's horse. The leaderless charge began to falter, but suddenly where Kilpatrick had been there was Custer, waving his Crusader's sword, howling and riding into the enemy. Quite literally; horse or man or both were so carried away by the moment that they plunged into the mass of the now-retreating Confederates, far ahead of the rest of the Federals. Realizing just before his enemies did that he was surrounded, Custer wheeled toward safety, cut down an enemy trooper who took a fatal second too long to react, and rode back unharmed.

Only chance prevented Custer and Rosser from coming saber-to-saber during the melee. Rosser was also in the thick of things, hacking furiously, trying to retain the momentum. He slashed one Massachusetts cavalryman from the saddle with a vicious cut across the face—leaving the man, Henry Lee Higginson of Boston, alive but scarred for life.

Custer attributed his escape to his hat, which he described as "a large broadbrim, exactly like that worn by the rebels." The lesson was an interesting one, especially perhaps to one who did not like uniformity. Had Custer been wearing a regulation kepi or dark officer's hat, as were virtually all of his comrades that day, the Confederates most likely would have shot him down reflexively. But the straw hat, at home among the motley collection of headgear worn by the disheveled Southerners, scrambled the signal of the blue uniform, and Custer had just enough time to save himself.[37]

Kilpatrick's people, with their remounted commander back in the lead, eventually pushed Munford's brigade into the Loudoun Valley, toward Middleburg. They skirmished for five days, during which time the Federals never managed to penetrate the screen, but did push Stuart back to the very crest of the Blue Ridge, and in clash after clash bested their Confederate counterparts.[38]

Meanwhile, the war moved past and away. The day of the clash at Aldie, the Army of Northern Virginia was marching into Maryland, headed for the high-water mark of the Confederacy. On June 23 Jeb Stuart galloped off with most of his cavalry to harass the Federal army as it pursued Lee north. It was the kind of dashing, hearty thing that had won Stuart effusive praise before, and he needed a dose of praise now, for the ostrich plume was showing signs of wilt. Stuart badgered the reluctant Lee for permission, then ignored the qualifications in his orders, and made his bold cavalier's ride clear around the enemy army. As a result, Lee went into the greatest battle of the war blind—bereft of the intelligence, mobility and protection that only the cavalry could have given him.

Three days after Stuart disappeared, the Federal cavalry was dogging the several parts of Lee's divided army northward, trying to figure out what they intended to do. On the rainy night of June 26, Pleasonton's men camped near Frederick, Maryland; it was Custer's chore to place the sentinels for the corps, and it was late when he got back to the headquarters mess. He was in no mood for the mocking salutes and the sarcastic greetings—"Hello, General!" and, "Gentlemen, General Custer!"—of his fellow staff officers. Custer flared into his ritual statement: "Laugh as long as you please, but I will be a general yet, for all your chaff. You see if I don't, that's all."

Then, shrieking with laughter, they gave him the envelope. It was an official one, and it was addressed to Brigadier General George A. Custer.[39]

It was a remarkable leap, from first lieutenant (acting captain) to brigadier general of volunteers. Especially for a twenty-three-year-old. The freckle-faced Boy General sat down and tried to keep from crying in front of his cheering comrades.

Custer was not the only one to feel the vertigo of sudden elevation that day. Alfred Pleasonton was determined to make something of the cavalry corps. He had brought them a long way, but needed bolder leaders who were not shackled to the old, limiting ideas about cavalry. He had identified, and had promoted to brigadier general, three young men from his staff who had the headlong spirit required—Custer, Captain Wesley Merritt and Captain Elon J. Farnsworth. Farnsworth had only days to live—he would die in a suicidal charge at Gettysburg. Merritt, at thirty years of age the eldest of the three, looked younger even than Custer, and made no effort to compensate for his gangly, fresh-faced youth. He let his steely steadiness in battle speak for him.

Custer, on the other hand, felt a need to change his appearance. And so, before taking command of the Michigan Brigade (which included both of the Michigan regiments he had previously pleaded in vain to command), he decked himself out in the velveteen, gold-braided, sailor-shirted, scarf-bedecked ensemble that Colonel Sanford described. The getup may have been straightforward flamboyance, and it may have been something far cannier than that; a realization that changed clothing alters perceptions, that people who are talking about an outlandish style are not talking about youth, or inexperience, or lack of substance.

Determined to make his mark as a general without delay, Custer hurried to join his brigade—at Abbottstown, Pennsylvania, fifteen miles northeast of Gettysburg—on June 29. He did not make the mistake of trying to be liked by his men; if he did, he explained later, "I should soon have them clapping me on the back and giving me advice." Instead, Custer the offhand soldier and collector of demerits suddenly became Custer the martinet, demanding spit and polish, ramrod salutes, everything by the book. For the next two days Custer bedazzled his command like a lion tamer, holding up his rank to fend off attack, popping the whip of military regulation now here, now there, preventing concentration.[40]

He wanted a battle, to show his mettle, but got only skirmishing. Jeb Stuart was coming in from the east, after his long jaunt, and his scouts kept running into the Federal detachments that were between him and Lee's farflung army. Fitz Lee, back in command of his brigade, tried to shove the Michigan Brigade out of the way in a confrontation near Hanover. Rosser was in Fitz Lee's battle line, of course, but saw little action and could not have known yet that his former playmate was directing the pugnacious response that persuaded Fitz Lee to shy away, thus delaying Stuart's reunion with Robert E. Lee for yet another day.[41]

On July 1 the men of the Federal Third Cavalry Division (now commanded by Judson Kilpatrick) heard the muted rumble of battle off to the southwest, around Gettysburg. It went on all day, but they received no orders until the next day, by which time it was clear that what had started as an accidental meeting engagement would be a decisive battle. The Third Division was called in to do the traditional cavalry work of guarding a flank; serious fighting, in the view of the new commander of the Army of the Potomac, George Meade, was infantry business.

Late in the afternoon Kilpatrick's division was sent off to the Federal right, near Hunterstown, to watch for any turning movement. It was nearly sundown when Custer's brigade, in the advance, spotted enemy skirmishers ahead. Almost immediately—almost—the eager Custer galloped to the head of a company of the 6th Michigan and led it in a charge. Inspired as they were supposed to be by their gallant leader, the 60 horsemen galloped over a rise—and straight into 600 troopers from Wade Hampton's division, who shot the little band of Federals to pieces and countercharged. His horse killed under him, Custer found himself on foot, facing a mounted charge, and looking down the barrel of one enemy rifle in particular. Just before history changed, a Union private shot the Confederate who was squeezing the trigger and gave the Boy General an undignified but appreciated lift to safety. People began to talk about Custer's Luck.

The charge had misfired, but a worse debacle had been prevented because Custer had made some careful dispositions in the few minutes before attacking. Hampton's countercharge nearly bagged Custer, and did wipe out half of the company that had made the charge, but then ran into a solid wall of fire from carefully placed lines of dismounted troopers and Custer's highly competent Battery M, 2nd U.S. Artillery, the whole backed by a mounted reserve. Hampton was stopped cold. He had run into more than a showboater, and both sides knew it.

The next day, the long-lost Jeb Stuart finally joined the fighting around Gettysburg. His mission was to punch around the Federal right into the enemy rear, creating havoc there while the ringleted General George E. Pickett threw the massed weight of Lee's infantry against the Federal center. In the early afternoon of July 3, Stuart deployed his 6,300 men and prepared to bull his way past the 4,500 Federal riders in his path. (Kilpatrick's division had been moved to the Federal left, but Custer's brigade had stayed with David McM. Gregg's two 2nd Division brigades on the right.)[42]

At 1 P.M., four miles to the south, 150 Confederate guns opened the heaviest bombardment in American history. For an hour the cavalrymen waited, the earth trembling under the feet of their nervous horses. Then while George Pickett sent his doomed infantry charge sweeping up the flank of Cemetery Ridge, Stuart's skirmishers moved out toward Gregg's line. Custer's dismounted 5th Michigan, in the center, drove off the first assault but ran out of ammunition when the Confederates returned, 2,000 strong. As the 5th Michigan fell back to its main line, the 7th Michigan came careening in from the flank, George Custer in the lead yelling "Come on, you Wolverines!" and smashed into the enemy.[43]

They also smashed into a stone wall, with a wood fence atop it, a barrier that stopped the charge and set the men to milling about while Confederates on the other side of the wall shot them down. Some of the troopers finally tore a hole in the structure with bare hands and the Federals surged through, but were twice driven back by heavy fire from behind other fences beyond. Stuart launched two more Virginia regiments in a charge against the 7th Michigan's left, but just in time Custer led his men dashing back to the main line and his artillery protection.

There was a pause. Then at 4 P.M. Stuart unleashed his reserves in the kind of roundhouse punch that had won many decisions for him. With imposing pomp and parade-ground precision, eight full regiments—a long, narrow column of squadrons with sabers up and glittering in the hot July sun—emerged from the trees on the Federal right. Among them rode Tom Rosser and the 5th Virginia Cavalry. At their head rode the Arthurian Wade Hampton and the bearlike Fitzhugh Lee, unflinching under a murderous, slicing rain of canister from the Federal batteries, trotting implacably toward the Federal center.[44]

Only one fresh regiment—the 1st Michigan—stood in the path of these eight, and General Gregg ordered it to charge. It was suicide, but the Confederate attack had to be blunted before it split the cavalry line and opened a path to the rear of the Federal army, with incalculable effect on the battle raging on Cemetery Ridge. In a flash there was Custer again, howling, "Come on, you Wolverines," four lengths ahead of everybody when the hopelessly outnumbered regiment crashed into Wade Hampton's division-sized attack with the sound, one cavalryman remembered, of "falling timber. So violent was the collision that many horses were turned end over end and crushed their riders beneath them."[45]

Custer later described the effect. "For a moment, but only for a moment, the long, heavy column stood its ground; then, unable to withstand the impetuosity of our attack, it gave way in a disorderly rout, leaving vast numbers of dead in our possession." Typically, Custer recalls the scene as if he were alone in it, but while he charged, so did Gregg's two brigades, one angling in on the Confederate column from each side, severing the gray formation and pursuing its pieces.[46]

Only as far as the original Confederate line. Thus Stuart could maintain, as he did, that he had lost no ground and thus had not been defeated. But there was no doubt, and no resorting to technicalities, on the Federal side. They had met the

Invincibles and had driven them back, more decisively than at
Kelly's Ford or Brandy Station or Aldie. The Federal horsemen
were getting better, and George Custer, by his own estimation,
was the best of them. The stupid mistakes of his first and second charges were forgot; the third had worked. "I challenge the
annals of warfare," he said modestly, "to produce a more brilliant or successful charge of cavalry."[47]

Just as Pickett's shattered division crawled down from Cemetery Ridge, Stuart's mauled brigades rode away from Cress's
Ridge, headed south again, away from the Confederacy's high-
water mark. Custer's weary men were given no rest but followed the retreat, and although held back by Meade's inertia
they harried and punished Lee's army at its two crossing points
on the Potomac—Williamsport and Falling Waters. At the latter place Custer made an unthinkable charge against entrenched infantry, breaking the line and taking more prisoners
than he had men. Meade, incredulous, had the report read to
him slowly a second time before he reluctantly approved it.

As a bright comet seems to dim the stars, so Custer painted
himself in vivid colors against the dull blue tones of his fellow
generals. He was deliberately and provocatively outrageous, not
only in his daredevil tactics in battle but in his every move. He
capered about in his improbable outfit, he acquired a comely
black cook named Eliza (and triggered persistent, dark rumors
about his relationship with her) and adopted a waif to be his
personal valet. He assembled a band to play loud music in
accompaniment of his loud habits, and he required his musi-
cians to play with special enthusiasm during his battles. At the
same time, quietly and craftily, he learned his trade. He did not
repeat his mistakes. He repeated his successes.

And for this reason his men did not laugh; they smiled. Soon
they were out scrounging up red scarves to wear in imitation of
him. They learned to like the music, to respond automatically
to the strains of "Yankee Doodle" or "Garryowen." As one
officer remembered, "At Yankee Doodle every man's hand
went to his sabre. It was always the signal for a charge." Above
all, they learned to follow him. Anywhere.[48]

Tom Rosser emerged from the Gettysburg campaign un-
scathed but bitter. He thought Robert E. Lee had blundered

repeatedly, by failing to concentrate his army, attacking piece-meal and exerting scant control over his subordinates. Rosser's opinions were far from unfounded, but he made no friends in the Confederacy by expounding on them. Rather, he earned the enmity, then and in later years, of the likes of Wade Hampton, Tom Munford, and Jubal Early.[49]

But what really galled Rosser as he rode away from Pennsylvania was the fact that he was still a colonel. By then he was probably aware of the spectacular advance in Custer's career, and he most certainly was soured by the stagnancy of his own. He was especially irate after being passed over in a major reorganization of the cavalry that saw Wade Hampton and Fitz Lee made major generals and several colonels promoted to brigadier general (including one Lunsford L. Lomax, whose brigade now included the 5th Virginia and its seething Colonel Rosser, and Williams Carter Wickham, promoted over the equally disconsolate Colonel Munford).

Disappointment turned Rosser ugly. He vilified Stuart (but only in private), raging in a letter to Betty, "He has been as false to *me* as he has ever been to his country and his *wife*. I will leave him in his glory." All the while, Stuart had been campaigning tirelessly for Rosser's advancement. The inconsolable Rosser decided to leave the cavalry altogether—"the Yankee cavalry can manage our cavalry so easily that they can ride over our country whenever they choose," he wrote to Betty. He would take a post as chief of artillery with Ewell's corps, where promotion was more likely; that would show them. He drank, he whined that he could not spend enough time with his new wife, he let his regiment fall apart, and generally made an ass of himself.[50]

But in October the long-awaited promotion came through. Jeb Stuart, tired of being harangued by the acerbic "Grumble" Jones, brought him up on charges and sent him packing. Jones's replacement was Tom Rosser, who instantly was transformed. With the wreath of a brigadier general on his collar, riding at the head of Turner Ashby's legendary brigade, he was once again the gay cavalier. The change in both his mood and his fortunes was breathtaking; within a few days it seemed as though the old days had returned, that cavalry battles were once again mere exercises for Southern horseflesh, resembling foxhunts more than any contest of equals. This proved especially true where Rosser and Custer next met, a place called Buckland Mills.[51]

After Gettysburg the eastern armies returned to central Virginia, Lee's to Culpeper and Meade's to a blocking position north of Bull Run. There were frequent cavalry skirmishes between the armies, and on October 18, Jeb Stuart (commanding Wade Hampton's division while Hampton recovered from a saber wound received at Gettysburg) chased a Federal force north beyond Manassas, then fell back toward safety. But that evening he was caught and attacked by enemy cavalry in such apparent strength that he thought Pleasonton's entire corps had caught him, and feared for the survival of his division. As night fell he took up a strong defensive position on the south bank of Broad Run, where it crossed the Gainesville-Warrenton road at Buckland Mills.[52]

The attacking force was Kilpatrick's division, with Custer's Michigan Brigade taking the lead as usual. The relationship between the two former schoolmates had become uneasy, a fact that had an odd but profound influence on the engagement about to open. Despite his doltish countenance, Kilpatrick had been given the grim sobriquet of "Kill Cavalry." This was not so much for the enemy troopers he had killed, although his courage in battle verged on the suicidal, but for his willingness to sacrifice his men in battle and his horses on the march— survivors of his campaigns often had to walk home.

On the morning of October 19, Custer probed Stuart's position. Despite the formidable defensive ground, Stuart soon retreated; at about that time Kilpatrick arrived with the rest of the division and prepared to give chase. He ordered Custer to come along. Oddly, Custer demurred, insisting to the point of insubordination that his men must have breakfast before continuing. James Kidd thought it completely out of character; Custer seemed to be avoiding a fight. Kilpatrick gave in and told Custer to follow as soon as possible. Custer let his men take a three-hour breakfast, then at last mounted them up to follow Kilpatrick.[53]

Kidd thought Custer sensed something, that his behavior

that morning was a demonstration of an uncanny prescience in combat situations that would be repeated often in the months to come. For as it turned out, Kilpatrick's thoughtless advance had put the division in great danger. Fitz Lee, whose Confederate division was a few miles away to the east, and Stuart had devised a trap. Stuart was deliberately drawing the Federals after him while Lee raced to take up a position behind the enemy's left flank. The idea was to lull the Federals into overconfidence, then hit them with a simultaneous attack front and rear.

The timing was extremely difficult, yet Stuart led Kilpatrick on at just the right pace, then hid his command in a ravine which the enemy horsemen approached just as Fitz Lee signaled that he was ready. The ambush was so fierce and unexpected that the Federals did not even try to resist, but simply turned and ran their horses up the Warrenton Turnpike as fast at they could go.

They might have been destroyed completely, had they found themselves cut off from the ford at Buckland Mills, but Fitz Lee had not surprised Custer. One of Major Kidd's troopers had spotted a lone rider, off to the east, circling his horse. That was the Confederate signal for sighting the enemy, and that bit of carelessness forewarned Custer. He fended off Fitz Lee's attack and held the ford while the rest of the cavalry got away. Kilpatrick had to leave behind their wagon train, however, and among the losses, much to Rosser's delight, was Custer's headquarters wagon. Some of Custer's private letters to a female friend were not only circulated among the Confederate cavalry, but were published in the Richmond papers, and as one of Stuart's officers put it they "afforded some spicy reading."[54]

The two rivals had faced each other on the same battlefield three times in 1863, and had written remarkably similar records of performance. Both had become brigadier generals, both had gained reputations for courage and competence in battle. Custer's path was arcing a little higher and flaring considerably brighter than Rosser's, but the story was far from over. As winter approached and campaigning slowed, the two went separate ways.

In December Rosser's brigade was sent to the Shenandoah

Valley. It was a first visit for Rosser, but his brigade of course had been back to its home heath many times before. Now Jubal Early was there, having a terrible time trying to pin down a Federal cavalry raid, and Rosser was to help. He got there in time to take part in the lathered riding to and fro that constituted that brief and unhappy campaign, but too late to do any good. Rosser moved Betty to Staunton, where he could see her more often, and thus earned Jubal Early's profound contempt. The sour feelings were reciprocated; it was then that Rosser described him as "a miserable old rascal."

Despite the conflict and the harsh winter campaigning, Rosser seemed to be having a good time. He was more or less on his own, the people of the Valley included him in the affection they automatically extended to Ashby's cavalry, and especially in January and February of 1864 he was given the kind of assignment beloved of the Southern cavaliers—a raid. This was the work that Turner Ashby and Jeb Stuart had shown how to do, the very essence of cavalry work and heroics; you got in the enemy's rear, rode hard, destroyed what you found and brought off what you could and above all you kept moving, never letting the enemy bring you to battle. The longer the ride and the more embarrassing the damage done to the enemy, the greater the honors that accrued, as Jeb Stuart had demonstrated more than once. Never mind that there were growing questions about the strategic value of such dashes, as for example the one Stuart had indulged in just before Gettysburg; they were great for the image, terrific for morale, and Tom Rosser was determined to achieve that kind of renown.

In January he began to earn his ostrich feather. On the 29th he went with Jubal Early, a brigade of infantry and some partisan rangers to Moorefield, West Virginia. They were foraging for food for the desperately hungry Army of Northern Virginia, and when they heard that a heavily laden Federal wagon train was moving up the next valley to westward, Old Jube sent Rosser out to get it.

Jeb Stuart could not have done it better. Rosser got his men over a frozen mountain, found the 95-wagon train, defeated and drove off its 800 defenders, and sent back to Old Jube a cornucopia of bacon, coffee, sugar, rice and such exotic treasures as brandied cherries and pickled oysters. Then Rosser went on to Petersburg, where he gathered up 13,000 Federal cartridges, destroyed some B and O Railroad bridges and damaged a lock of the Chesapeake and Ohio Canal. In later dispatches to Richmond, Jubal Early pronounced Tom Rosser a good man, and for once kept to himself such qualifications as "for a cavalryman," and "for a married man."[55]

Another who approved was Jeb Stuart himself, who used his favorite adjectives—"bold and successful"—to describe Rosser's raid. The enterprise, he wrote in his official report, "furnishes additional proofs of General Rosser's merit as a commander, and adds fresh laurels to that veteran brigade so signalized for valor already." Rosser, on returning to the Valley, issued a congratulatory general order in which he proclaimed that henceforward his command would be known as the "Laurel Brigade," and his men would wear laurel leaves in their hats.[56]

Confederate brigades and divisions were known officially by the name of their commander; thus Ashby's cavalry had become Jones's Brigade and then Rosser's Brigade (by this time Federal brigades were numbered, as were divisions and corps). Nicknames for individuals and units were of course common, as were distinctive bits of ornamentation. But Tom Rosser did not seem to understand that the nicknames were not bestowed from above, by fiat, but from below, by shared experiences and general agreement on the qualities of a leader or an organization. The Stonewall Brigade was not so known because General Jackson had ordered it, but because private soldiers were honored to serve in that storied outfit. Men of the Michigan Brigade had not taken to wearing crimson ties because they were directed to do so, but because they were moved by the breathtaking courage of their chief to try to emulate him. Rosser's attempt to graft a bit of glory onto his outfit was regarded as arrogant by his fellow officers and was—at least at first—largely ignored by his men.

While Rosser had gone raiding in the Shenandoah, George Custer had embarked on a personal campaign whose objective was Libby Bacon, the judge's daughter back in Monroe, Michigan. Now that he was not merely a blacksmith's son but a general, he found the going easier. Judge Bacon had decided it would be all right, after all, if Custer "communicated" with his daughter. Custer had been doing so for some time, calling on her whenever he was in Monroe and between times sending fervid letters to a mutual friend who was supposed to relay their sugary contents.

In one of these letters, for example, the twenty-five-year-old general reflected on the difficulties of life and found that he had conquered them: "Knowing my duty, all that is then requisite to insure success is honesty of purpose and fixed intentions, or, to express the same meaning in different language, I have only to adopt the well known motto: 'First be sure you're right, then go ahead.' To this simple rule, framed though it be in humble language, I can attribute more than to any other my success in life."[57]

Against a man armed with such insights neither Judge Bacon nor his daughter stood a chance; the wedding was set for February 9, 1864. For this occasion Custer abandoned gaudiness. He showed up with his hair cut and polished, his demeanor sober and dignified, his uniform strictly regulation. He stands stiffly in their wedding portrait (taken at Mathew Brady's New York gallery six days later), one arm clamped behind his back, the other placed tentatively on the back of her chair. And there sits the exquisite Libby, those large, intelligent eyes appraising something off to the left of the camera, a serene smile lightening the finely featured face while the hands rest relaxed on the billows of her gown. It is probably only hindsight that makes one presume to see, in that arched back and level gaze, a hint of the steel that would take this lady through civil war to the western frontier and onto the pages of history as one of the most formidable and loyal military wives of history.[58]

Their life together began as a tempestuous and self-conscious adventure. They relished and nurtured his fame, which she now shared, played to the hilt their roles as hero and heroine in a Sir Walter Scott novel, and basked in the general approval of their performances. They engaged in a correspondence that is often embarrassing to read—gushing and vainglorious on his part, cloying and fawning on hers—but that for all its excessiveness seems rooted in real affection. On their honeymoon, a trip to

Cleveland, New York, Baltimore and Washington, they met General Grant on his way to Washington to accept a fourth star and a historic assignment. Libby reported wonderingly that on her account, when the bulldog victor of Shiloh, Vicksburg and Chattanooga wanted to smoke a cigar he courteously stepped outside onto the car's platform. In Washington they met Lincoln, who grasped her hand and said, "So this is the young woman whose husband goes into a charge with a whoop and a shout. Well, I'm told he won't do so any more." She hoped he would, said Libby, and the president replied, his attempt at jocularity slipping hideously awry, "Oh, then you want to be a widow, I see." There was hollow laughter.[59]

When the Federal armies surged into motion in the dark spring of 1864, Custer finally ended an extended, much-interrupted honeymoon, rejoined the Wolverines, and trotted south under new commanders, Grant and Sheridan. Meanwhile Rosser brought the Laurel Brigade east from its wintering grounds around Lexington, in the uppermost reaches of the Shenandoah. They took a prisoner near the Wilderness in May who provided a strange prophecy. The Virginians observed that after crossing the Rapidan, the Federals had not left any pontoon bridges in place. When asked how Grant's army intended to recross the river without pontoons, the prisoner provided an unwitting but perfect reflection of the new Union commander's quiet, flinty spirit: "Grant says that all of his men who go back over the river can cross on a log."[60]

Driven by the slow gaze of the implacable lieutenant general, the blue columns pushed south, were bloodied in the Wilderness but pushed south again, around to the left to Spotsylvania, where they were punished again but kept on again, around to the left toward the South Anna River, and they started calling Grant "the left-handed." In some puzzlement Jeb Stuart wrote to his wife, "We have beaten the enemy badly but he is not yet in full retreat."[61]

The war was changing fast, the cavalry faster. This transformation was embodied by Phil Sheridan and rammed home with the raid that had its climax at Yellow Tavern. As that confrontation assumed its shape, as Sheridan and Stuart looked each other over and the tension mounted, Custer decided he could not stand by and let a Confederate battery continue to bang away at his boys from the left of Stuart's line. And he proceeded to demonstrate, as dramatically as only he knew how, that he was no longer the hothead who had charged the stone wall in Pennsylvania; but that he was precisely the kind of hothead that Sheridan wanted.

Having made the impetuous decision to charge the battery, Custer made meticulous preparations, taking well over an hour to prepare a secondary attack and arrange for support on both flanks. Then he took the 1st Michigan, 1,000 strong, forward toward the spitting guns. They faced Wickham's and Lomax's brigades, the latter including Tom Rosser's old regiment, the 5th Virginia. Rosser's luck—a peculiar inverse of Custer's—had separated him from the action yet again; he and the Laurels had been left behind with the infantry.[62]

Sheridan was profoundly impressed to see the Wolverines begin their charge at a *walk,* with bugles blaring and the band playing "Yankee Doodle." There were five fences in the way; at each the column stopped while details calmly carried away the fence rails, then moved unhurriedly to the next while the earth heaved and erupted under the onslaught of shells. They trotted to within two hundred yards of the waiting Invincibles, then leapt to the gallop with a roar and, wrote a watching staff officer, "rode boot to boot into what seemed the very jaws of death." They took the guns, broke the line, and later it was a Wolverine's bullet—exactly whose remained forever a subject of controversy—that claimed the life of Jeb Stuart.[63]

The death of Beauty and the rise of the unattractive Little Phil certified the ascendancy of the Union cavalry. The Southern cavaliers were gone, and so were the Northern shopkeepers on plow-horses. The days of romping about in search of the enemy, then standing aside for the infantry, were over. Now the relentless Federal horsemen were probing constantly for weak points, and when they found one were dismounting to unlimber their Spencers with fearful force.

Meanwhile the Confederate cavalry was deteriorating. There were no new weapons, except those captured from the enemy, and hence no corresponding change in tactics (except that those armed with superior British Enfield rifles were sometimes organized as sharpshooters). In fact, the cavalry carbines being supplied were so inferior in quality that most had to be discarded and replaced with infantry rifles—so oversized and heavy that many a trooper heaved his into the nearest bush.[64]

Moreover, it was becoming impossible to find horses. A Southern cavalryman (or infantry officer) provided his own mount, and if it were shot or broken down he was expected to replace it. While the Federal bureaucracy was shipping 200 horses a day to Grant's cavalry, Lee's men had to scrounge around, in a region that had been a battlefield for three years, trying to buy scarecrow mounts at inflated prices. Then there was the matter of feeding the animals. A Federal horse enjoyed an average ration of ten pounds of feed per day; the Confederate counterpart was lucky to get one pound.[65]

Yet even with its troubles, even after losing Jeb Stuart at Yellow Tavern, even after Phil Sheridan had won his independence from Meade and was using his troopers in the new way, the Confederate cavalry could hold its own. The courtly and competent South Carolina planter Wade Hampton, the senior cavalry commander after Jeb Stuart, understood the new rules and was suited to them; he was a careful, pragmatic man who saw a battle as a problem of applying force, not a stage providing the opportunity for drama.

Generals Custer and Rosser, of course, still thought in terms of show, Rosser striving with every fiber of his being to emulate —to become—Jeb Stuart, and Custer writing his own role as he went along. With new tactics and weapons to back him up, and with hard new commanders to guide him, Custer had abundant advantages. But he was far from immune to defeat, and Rosser was capable of handing it to him, as was demonstrated at Trevilian Station in June of 1864.

With two divisions, 6,000 men, Sheridan had headed west along the North Anna River for about fifty miles, then had turned south to strike the Virginia Central Railroad at Trevilian Station. Wade Hampton led the Confederate cavalry in pursuit, and reached Trevilian Station ahead of the Federals, who were still three miles to the north. On the morning of June 11, before all of his 4,700 men were in position, he ordered an advance along two roads that converged at the Federal camp.

The Confederates moved early, but Sheridan had started first. At 6:30 A.M., before Fitz Lee's Confederates could get on the field, Sheridan attacked Hampton just north of Trevilian. Custer was given a special assignment; swing around to the left and get in the enemy's rear.

On confusing trails through thickly wooded terrain, Custer's Michigan Brigade got badly strung out, but managed to slide through the closing gap between Hampton's right and the approaching Fitz Lee, emerging behind Hampton's division and on top of its wagon train. One regiment—the 5th Michigan—captured the wagons and guards, then went on to attack Hampton's horseholders, claiming later to have captured 1,500 horses and 800 men.[66]

If Sheridan had expected Wade Hampton to break when attacked from the rear, he had underestimated his opponent. Hampton had kept Rosser and the Laurels in reserve, and he now unleashed them on the Wolverines. Rosser smashed into the badly exposed 5th Michigan and drove it back to where Custer was trying to form the rest of the brigade. "I was too quick and too strong for him," Rosser boasted afterward, stressing that Custer was a worthy opponent: "He made a gallant and manly effort to resist me. Sitting on his horse in the midst of the advancing platoons, and near enough to be easily recognized by me, he encouraged and inspired his men by appeal as well as example." It is difficult to remember, reading Rosser's sporting account, that men were dying in agony all around him.[67]

It was beginning to dawn on Custer that this was serious. With Rosser's men assailing his front and right flank, Fitz Lee's division appeared out of the woods behind to strike Custer's left and rear. The Wolverines were caught in the open, badly outnumbered, and surrounded.[68]

Custer was momentarily stunned by the gravity of his predicament. When the badly frightened commander of the brigade's wagon train rode up to plead for permission to take the wagons to the rear, Custer agreed—"Yes, by all means!"—but he was so distracted that he had not really considered the request. As the officer galloped away (to make a senseless run for it, delivering into Rosser's hands all the brigade's reserve ammunition

and supplies, including Custer's headquarters wagon), Custer
shook himself, surveyed his contracting horizon, and bellowed,
"Where in hell is the rear?"[69]

It was Custer's first last stand. There was nothing to do but
hunker down and take the punishment, banging away with the
Spencers in all directions while converging fire cut the brigade
to pieces. Half the 5th Michigan had been taken prisoner. Custer's color-bearer was mortally wounded ("by Major Conrad of
my staff," crowed Rosser. "Custer grabbed the staff to save the
flag, but the death grip of the sergeant would not release it; so
with a quick jerk, Custer tore the flag from its staff"). Half of
Custer's staff officers and escort went down dead or hurt; his
men were lying on the field in hundreds.[70]

All the while Wesley Merritt, commanding the Reserve Brigade of regular cavalry, had been hammering Hampton's center
slowly back through dense forest until the Federals could
glimpse Custer's dusty, smoking circle beyond; they saw the
swallow-tailed flag go down and hollered for permission to
charge. Sheridan had kept his head in the confusion and,
guided mostly by sound, organized a concerted attack on
Hampton's center that, just in time, punched through to Custer
and wedged the two Confederate divisions apart again as nightfall ended the fighting.

The two forces had fought savagely, and had inflicted approximately equal punishment on each other, but Hampton
was forced to withdraw from the field and reorganize, thus
yielding a technical victory to Sheridan. But Hampton withdrew to the west, threw up entrenchments, and was there waiting the next day when Sheridan tried to get on with his job.
This time it was Sheridan who withdrew, heading back to the
Army of the Potomac.

Rosser, whose leg had been broken by a Union bullet before
the affair at Trevilian Station ended, was strident in declaring a
glorious Southern victory. "Sheridan displayed no skill in maneuvering," he insisted, and had been "not only whipped but
routed." Using reasoning identical to that which Early would
apply to the battle of Winchester in September, Rosser claimed
that "if Sheridan had been even a tolerably fair general he

would have taken advantage of the scattered condition of Hampton's command and destroyed him.[71]

But Rosser was strident about everything that summer and fall. It was not the course of the war that concerned him, the condition of the cavalry or even his wound, but his promotion to major general. He was sure that Hampton's elevation to overall command of the cavalry, which everyone regarded as imminent, would result in his being given command of Hampton's division. Hampton's promotion came through on August 11, but Rosser's did not. Hampton named his fellow South Carolinian M. Calbraith Butler to the command Rosser coveted, and Tex immediately branded Hampton a faithless turncoat.[72]

Betty Rosser gave birth to a daughter on August 17. Tom Rosser returned to his command a week later, although his leg was not yet fully healed, and continued to brood. He considered taking more sick leave. He contemplated transferring out west, to get away from the treacherous Hampton. He knew Betty would not like that, and admonished her not to interfere with his interests. He wanted to know why she seemed unhappy.[73]

There were rumors that the Laurels might be sent to the Valley to help Jubal Early. He did not want to go there, Rosser told Betty, but "I want to get out of this mess. I begin to fear that there is no chance for my immediate promotion."[74]

As it happened, Custer got to the Valley first. While Rosser had been recovering in a Richmond hospital, Custer had been languishing in the Petersburg area, on sick leave, the illness again unspecified. He recovered in time to ride west with Sheridan to the Shenandoah. He led the Wolverines through a hard six weeks of skirmishing and probing, confirming anew his remarkable battle instincts. He took vigorous part in the charge, led by Merritt and Averell, that brought to a thundering end the Confederate defense of Winchester on September 19. And he participated in Torbert's failure to get up the Luray Valley to cut off the Confederate retreat from Fisher's Hill on the 21st. Torbert's career survived, but Averell's ended when he failed to chase the Confederates that night, and in the succeeding reorganization Custer was separated from the Wolverines and put

in command of the Third Division. A few days later, Rosser
rode into the Valley to assume command of Fitz Lee's division.
Their personal game was on again.

Eastward through Brock's Gap, which is notched into North
Mountain like a gunsight, trickles the North Fork of the Shenandoah River. Late on the afternoon of October 6, the wild
Laurels led Rosser's division in a thrust at Custer's rear guard,
on the south side of the river. The Federals did their best to
fend off the surprisingly fierce onslaught, but with their Third
Division strung out across the Valley as it was, they could not
hope for much help and had to fall back across the river, leaving some of their wagons, including a forge, behind. A battery
sent racing back by Custer deployed on a hill there and helped
keep the Confederates back until dark. Then the Federal rear
guard joined the rest of the division and continued the work of
the Burning.[75]

"During the whole night the work of destruction went on,"
wrote Captain McDonald of the Laurel Brigade. "The burning
parties distributed across the Shenandoah swept it with the fire
of desolation. Every home was visited, the proud mansion and
the humble cottage feeling alike the blasting and savage hand of
war." He wrote contemptuously of the Federals' unwillingness
to fight the avengers; the fact was that the Federals had no
orders to fight. They were to retire, burning the Valley's provisions as they went, and that is what they did, merely fending off
Rosser long enough to get the job done and move on.[76]

With the first light Rosser's men were in the saddle, frantic
to find a way to bring the arsonists to battle. But the Federals
had been on the move all night, still were not disposed to fight,
and it was three in the afternoon before Rosser could catch up
with a force that would not slip away from him. It was on the
opposite bank of Mill Creek, west of Mount Jackson, "in force
and strongly posted," as Captain McDonald recorded.[77]

Lieutenant Colonel Richard H. Dulany, now commanding
the Laurel Brigade, took part of it downstream to a lower ford.
Custer sent a detachment dashing to hold it, but the Laurels
got across first and met the Federals on their own side of the
river. With an odd, corkscrew charge that veered off to the left

and then snaked back in to take the confused Federals in the
flank, the Virginians drove the Federals back to their main
force, then charged the main force. Meanwhile the rest of the
brigade, followed by the rest of the division, surged across the
ford.[78]

"The Confederates, eager to get within sword range of the
detested barn-burners, rode at them furiously," wrote Captain
McDonald. "The Federals fought bravely, but could not withstand men who were seeking vengeance rather than victory."
They edged away, rallied, then edged away again until night
fell, at which time they edged farther away. By noon the next
day Rosser had caught up with them again and resumed the
harassment, cutting and slashing at the Federals as they worked
their way north along the Back Road until they were north of
Woodstock, and had crossed a stream called Toms Brook.[79]

Annoyed, Custer drew his men together and led them off to
the east, toward the Valley Pike. When he had gone a mile or
so, he turned south and rushed for Rosser's rear. In their enthusiasm, the Confederates had outdistanced their infantry support by some twenty-five miles, and Custer aimed to cut them
off and destroy them. But Rosser was watching his old friend
closely, just as he had during their wrestling bouts at the Point,
and he instantly faded back, got his men in front of Custer's
turning movement, met it with a saber charge and stopped it.
On the evening of October 8 the Confederates crossed to the
south side of Toms Brook and camped.

They could see the lights of the Federal cavalry camp not far
to the north and beyond it the fires of Sheridan's infantry,
countless as fireflies. Ardor was one thing but this was another;
they were too far from help. Now the Valley men who had been
on fire for revenge came to Rosser in the night and suggested,
as emphatically as their dignity would permit, that they get the
hell out of there. But Tex had been having the better of his
tussle with Fanny for two days, and he was not about to quit.
He would play it out.[80]

Custer was beside himself. He could not stand not to fight,
especially when the opponent was Rosser. The Confederate riders had decked themselves out with laurel branches, and Rosser
was being called—possibly at his own insistence—the Savior of

the Valley. Custer had more men, better weapons and superior horses, and he knew he could whip Rosser, but Torbert was adamant; his orders were to retire down the Valley, they said nothing about fighting, and the cavalry was to keep moving. Only the rear guard was to engage the enemy. Merritt was having similar troubles while moving north along the Valley Pike, although he was not being pushed by Lomax as hard as Custer was being bedeviled by Rosser. Toward evening on the 8th, Merritt had sent two brigades over to help Custer's rear guard send Rosser back across Toms Brook.[81]

There had been a lot of gunfire that Saturday afternoon, and when evening came Phil Sheridan rode back to find out what it was all about. What he learned put him in one of his incandescent rages. He expected a commander to have fire in his belly, to look for excuses to maul the enemy. What he had been getting from his cavalry generals—with the notable exception of Custer and Merritt—was excuses. Averell had failed to pursue the enemy after the crushing victories of Winchester and Fisher's Hill—he had actually made camp and let the infantry chase Early, ineffectually, up the Valley Pike—and Sheridan had sacked Averell. Wilson had not been warrior enough for Sheridan, either, and probably would have met Averell's fate had he not been transferred out west. Torbert had been sent up the Luray Valley to get behind Early's army and cut it off so that it could be destroyed; instead, Torbert had been stopped by an enemy force whose size was a mere fraction of his own. Torbert's career was hanging by a thread. He followed orders; he did his duty; he was brave and competent; that was not good enough.

And so, when Sheridan found his two favorite generals, Custer and Merritt, snorting with rage at the pummeling they had been taking for two days, stamping with eagerness to chastise the enemy but with their warrior lust curbed by Torbert, well, Little Phil went looking for Torbert. According to one account, it was the cavalry chief's further misfortune—as if he needed any more bad luck—to be found not under canvas, in the spare, soldierly sort of camp that Sheridan preferred, but in a mansion near Strasburg, where he and his staff had just feasted on a twenty-five pound wild turkey.

Sheridan arrived like a thunderstorm. He blew open the door, stomped into the room, and roared, "Well, I'll be damned! If you ain't sitting here stuffing yourselves, general, staff and all, while the rebels are riding into our camp! Having a party, while Rosser is carrying off your guns! Got on your nice clothes and clean shirts! Torbert, mount quicker than hell will scorch a feather!" Apparently there was more in this vein back at Sheridan's headquarters. Staff officers were standing well clear at this point, and poor Torbert, the only one to hear the monologue, never felt like discussing it afterward. Captain George Sanford did hear Sheridan's ringing conclusion (given the volume with which it was delivered, Tom Rosser might have heard it): "I WANT YOU TO GO OUT THERE IN THE MORN- ING AND WHIP THAT REBEL CAVALRY OR GET WHIPPED YOURSELF!"[82]

Thus unleashed, Custer and Merritt headed their commands south and approached the enemy at first light. Merritt's divi- sion outweighed Lomax's 1,500 men by roughly two to one along the Valley Pike. But Rosser had something like 3,000 troopers facing Custer's slightly larger force, and was ready to fight. On the ridge that formed the south bank of Toms Brook he had deployed three lines: one of dismounted troopers at the base, behind the cover of stone fences and fence-rail barricades; a second and stronger dismounted line, similarly protected, near the top; and his mounted reserve and six guns on the crest. It was a formidable position, as Custer saw immediately when he drove in the Confederate skirmishers from the vicinity of Mount Olive.[83]

For their part, the Confederates had grown used to dealing with the rear guard, and were awed by the numbers of Federals who suddenly appeared. "Every opening disclosed moving masses of bluecoats," Captain McDonald wrote, "and soon they advanced, covering the hill slopes and blocking the roads with apparently countless squadrons." Rosser's cannon, under the direction of Early's artillery chief, the capable Colonel Thomas H. Carter, opened a deadly, plunging fire on the "dense swarms" of bluecoats while his sharpshooters banged away at Custer's skirmishers, who were "pressing on with con- fidence."[84]

It was a new confidence. Under James Wilson, the Third Division had been a lackluster organization, its troopers envious of the First Division's fire and dash, which had emanated from the Michigan Brigade. Now the Third was awakening. "Wilson was universally considered to be an unlucky man," wrote Sergeant Roger Hannaford of the Second Ohio Cavalry. "We never went into a fight but that we expected to be beat." Already, under Custer, "we never began but we felt sure of victory."[85]

Custer ordered his guns to begin counterbattery fire, but to his intense annoyance the gunners had been issued some defective ammunition and could do little damage. He deployed a three-regiment line of mounted skirmishers to press Rosser's line, but first he did an amazing thing. Out in front of his lines he galloped, well into the open ground before the creek, where all the men who were about to fight and die could see him. Effortlessly holding his prancing horse in place, he swept his hat from his head and down to arm's length, bowing in the saddle in the direction of his foemen. "See that officer down there?" said Rosser to his staff. "That's General Custer, the Yanks are so proud of, and I intend to give him the best whipping today that he ever got. See if I don't."[86]

Some saw Custer's little dance as another bit of flamboyance, more stage-acting in his private, Romantic epic; others thought it a touching salute to his old friend Rosser; and no doubt there was something of both in his gesture. But those who knew Old Curly well knew he was doing something else—taking a last, close look at the enemy position. Ever since his men had smacked into the stone wall at Gettysburg, Custer had looked before he charged.[87]

Now, having spotted the weakness in Rosser's position—its left was in the air, there were neither men nor natural obstacles there to prevent Federal riders from getting around it into the Confederate rear—and having sent three regiments to exploit it, Custer was ready to charge. Just then he saw blueclad horsemen trotting toward his left. Merritt was deploying; he had sent Colonel Charles Russell Lowell's brigade (the Regular Reserve Brigade plus Lowell's own 2nd Massachusetts Cavalry) around the Confederate right, which was also in the air, and he had

sent another brigade to his own right to make contact with
Custer. On seeing the riders' red neckties, Custer raised his
trumpet voice: "There is my old Michigan Brigade on the
flank!" Down came the sword until it was leveled straight at
Tom Rosser. "Now go for it!"[88]

The bugles sounded, the band played "Yankee Doodle," the
eight regiments went from the walk to the trot and then the
gallop, but it looked as though the wave of blue must break
against that hill bristling with lead and iron. Rosser's dismounted men were working their pieces with a will, feeling
reasonably solid, until they heard the firing and the yelling
behind them, to the left. A glance showed masses of bluecoats
coming in the rear. There was no worse word in the soldier's
vocabulary than the shout of "Flanked!" and it was especially
horrifying to a dismounted cavalryman. Without his horse he
was just a footsoldier, with no hope of escape. In increasing
numbers, Rosser's men on the left ran back to the horseholders,
mounted and looked for a way out.[89]

The same thing was happening to Lomax's right under the
assault of Lowell's regulars. Both Confederate divisions were
holding in the center, but their opposite flanks were caving in.
Rosser had to abandon his magnificent position or suffer a
double envelopment. There were Federals so far in his rear by
this time that getting out did not mean a dignified withdrawal
—it meant a flat-out, neck-stretching, pounding race to the
rear. Once started, such a run is almost impossible to stop, but
Rosser did it, re-forming part of his command two miles back
and bringing the pursuit to a shuddering halt. Then it was
Rosser's turn to charge, and he drove Custer's two brigades
back half a mile.[90]

"Now was Rosser's time to fight," wrote the newspaper artist
James Taylor, who watched the fight with Sheridan from
Round Top, "and now was the time he missed it." All the
combatants were mounted now, and had moved away from the
creek into open, gently rolling country that had been largely
stripped of fences and obstructions. Rosser's only chance was
to rely on speed and the saber, but instead he went over to the
defensive, posted men and guns in a strip of woods, and gave

Custer the initiative. Custer knew what to do with it; quickly he assembled his entire division for another grand charge.[91]

More than two hours had passed. Lomax had been giving ground, stubbornly but continuously, along the Valley Pike. A charge by Lowell's brigade had broken Lomax loose at about the same time that Custer had driven Rosser, and now Captain Sanford of Merritt's staff came loping up to Old Curly to inform him of developments on the left. Sanford's mission was legitimate—Torbert had ordered it—but the Boy General and the boyish Merritt were about as friendly as two young stallions in the same pasture, and Sanford worked for Merritt. The 1st Division had taken five guns, Sanford bragged, and he wondered had Custer got any? "All right, hold on a minute," barked Custer, "and I'll show you six."[92]

Away went the charge, and there stood Rosser to receive it. The momentum was entirely on the side of the howling Yankees. The excitement was still on Custer when he wrote his official report four days later: "Before this irresistible advance the enemy found it impossible to stand. Once more he was compelled to trust his safety to the fleetness of his steed rather than the metal of his saber. His retreat soon became a demoralized rout. Vainly did the most gallant of this affrighted herd endeavor to rally a few supports around their standards and stay the advance of their eager and exultant pursuers, who, in one overwhelming current, were bearing down everything before them. Never since the opening of this war had there been witnessed such a complete and decisive overthrow of the enemy's cavalry."[93]

It was true. Always before, at Brandy Station, Yellow Tavern, Buckland Mills and Trevilian Station, it had been the Federal cavalry who left the field, however badly they first had mangled the Confederates. But now the remnants of Ashby's proud cavalry, along with the entire mounted arm of the vaunted Second Corps, was running. "The pursuit was kept up vigorously for nearly 20 miles," exulted Custer, and not only dispersed the enemy force but overran the Confederate guns— the six Custer had promised Sanford—and wagon trains, including "the headquarters wagons, desks and papers of the rebel General Rosser." Up the Valley past Woodstock, past

Edinburg and Mount Jackson the humiliated Confederates ran,
Lomax up the Pike and Rosser on the Back Road, in a debacle
that would immediately become famous as "The Woodstock
Races."

Tom Munford—still a colonel in Fitz Lee's division—blamed
the defeat on his old rival Rosser, for giving battle in a hopeless
situation: "Rosser's head seemed to be completely turned by
our success, and in consequence of his rashness, and ignorance
of their numbers, we suffered the greatest disaster that had ever
befallen our command, and utterly destroyed the confidence of
the officers of my brigade in his judgement—they knew that he
would fight and was full of it, but he did not know when to
stop, or when to retire."[94]

That night Rosser took the nastiest cut of all from the de-
spised Old Jube: "I say, Rosser, your brigade had better take
the grape leaf for a badge. The laurel is a running vine."[95]

Rosser turned surly again. His letters to Betty became a litany of woes: his wound was bothering him; he would take sick
leave but there was no one to replace him; he had arrested
regimental commanders for cowardice and worried about his
popularity with the men; there was not enough food. She suggested he resign. Forget it, he answered, they would just make
him serve as an enlisted man.[96]

The next day Custer clumped around his camp wearing Rosser's captured dress-uniform coat and hat, the garments gro-
tesquely large on Custer's spare frame. The men laughed de-
lightedly at the oafish clowning of their new general, and the
clown must have got a brighter glitter in his eye when he saw
what they were doing as they laughed: rounding up and putting
on red neckties. All in all, Custer sighed in a letter to his Libby,
it had been "a glorious day for your Boy."[97]

The letter was written from the new Federal camp on the
banks of Cedar Creek, and as it was written Jubal Early's army
was advancing again.

Chapter 4

The *Chevalier* and
Uncle George:
October 13, 1864

Thirty years after the Valley Campaign of 1864, John B. Gordon began writing his memoir of the great conflict. His point of view is interesting because he was a volunteer officer with no formal military training who rose rapidly and deservedly to the rank of major general. Only four other Confederate generals became corps commanders without the benefit of either intensive schooling at a military academy or long experience as a regular army officer.[1]

Gordon was no stranger to soldiering, however; his family was steeped in a military tradition both longer and deeper than that of any American army. Warriors of the Scots Clan Gordon had been striding through the battles of European history for seven centuries when the Civil War began; and the transplanted Gordons of Virginia and South Carolina had fought for American Independence, most notably at the battle of King's Mountain. The Gordons embodied the deeply held American belief that professional armies were unnecessary and dangerous when ordinary men could grab their muskets, form up, and deal with any military emergency that might confront the country.[2]

With the departure from the Valley of John C. Breckinridge after the battle of Winchester, Gordon had become the senior division commander in the Army of the Valley. His recollections were gracefully written, modest, a little flowery for modern tastes perhaps but far less so than the usual flights of nineteenth-century writers moved by thoughts of Cause and Honor. Even when describing how it felt to be shot five times, in the firestorm at Antietam Creek, or to be unhorsed at a critical juncture of the fight along the Monocacy, Gordon maintained a detached and ironic point of view, and stressed repeatedly the devotion and courage shown by Federals and Confederates alike; the enemies he faced in mortal combat were almost invariably brave men led by gallant officers. These sentiments no doubt came easier later in life, after the passage of three decades and a distinguished career in politics. They read easily, too, and his account is one of the most frequently quoted of the period. It is passing strange, then, that he makes no mention whatever of the events of October 13.

Major General George Crook, a first-class Indian fighter from Ohio who in the fall of 1864 was not only one of Phil Sheridan's three top infantry commanders, but his best friend, also wrote a memoir. When he was finished, he put it in his attic and forgot about it. Years later his widow gave it to a family friend, the friend's widow eventually gave it to the Army War College, a researcher found it there in 1949 and prepared it for publication.

George Crook was cursed with a bright mind and a slow mouth, and even when he wrote he was introverted. His unschooled phrases stamped about, as blunt and rough-hewn as the man, knocking over the army's crockery and gouging spur tracks across some carefully polished reputations. Crook hated posturing, incompetence, bureaucracy and politics. And he, too, had nothing to say about October 13.[3]

What happened on that day was what the mountain men of George Crook's proud little Army of West Virginia liked to call a "right smart little fight." It was a nasty and unexpected skirmish that for a time showed signs of becoming a full-scale engagement. The casualties were high for a skirmish; it cost the Federals 209 men, including one of Crook's most able brigade commanders, and took a similar toll of Confederates. Yet Crook wrote no report on the affair, he merely forwarded the terse account of one of the colonels involved. Gordon apparently did not even do that much. No official report from him is on record; perhaps it succumbed to the same sinister force that (he would hint darkly) vaporized his report on later events.[4]

Gordon and Crook had so much to say about other matters —especially how they either won, or could have won, the war's pivotal battles despite the incompetence of their superior officers—that their silence on this subject is arresting. They went on at length about the events of October 19, and rightly so; their commands would be the most heavily engaged on that morning, and their individual contributions would be decisive in the early hours of the battle. After Cedar Creek, each would have accusations to refute, each would have a bitter brief against his commanding officer to present to the court of history—or, in Crook's case, to his attic. October 13, apparently, was not worth discussing.

It was an easy day for the Federal Army of the Shenandoah. The weather was clear and cool, with a sharp wind snapping the colors and flapping the tent walls. There was no marching to be done, and the enemy, supposedly, was nowhere near. The infantry had completed the move back to its familiar camping ground north of Strasburg, along the east bank of Cedar Creek, on the 10th, the day after the cavalry battle at Toms Brook.

The dismantling of the army began at once. Three hard months after leaving the Army of the Potomac to lend a hand with the emergency at Washington, VI Corps marched away on the 12th, headed back to the trenches at Petersburg. Meanwhile, Sheridan resumed his wrangling with Washington and City Point about what to do next, and the men still with him— the cavalry, the two XIX Corps divisions, and Crook's infantry —took a break.

No one knew what to call Crook's command, and that included Crook himself. The original nucleus of the force had come from VIII Corps, the umbrella organization for all troops assigned to the Middle Department, and some clung to that name. But since its reorganization and assignment to the Department of West Virginia, it was listed in the official reports as the Army of West Virginia. This was a correct, but grand, title for an outfit whose 4,000-man strength was hardly that of an 1864 division, and whose two brigade-sized divisions were commanded by colonels. Crook once snarled that it was little more than a large raiding party, at other times he slipped and called it a division. By whatever name, this was a fiercely independent bunch of Westerners from Ohio and West Virginia, whose relations with the Easterners of VI and XIX Corps were never easy, and were not improved by what happened at Cedar Creek.[5]

The infantry was camped near the Valley Pike between the village of Strasburg, which lay snug against the northwest tip of Massanutten Mountain, and the hamlet of Middletown five miles to the northeast. Those who did not consult a compass thought of Middletown as straight north of Strasburg, because it is straight down the middle of the Valley; directions tend to get skewed because of the oblique trend of the enclosing mountains. Another source of confusion is that Cedar Creek's course across the Valley, from a gap in North Mountain to the Shenandoah River just downstream from Strasburg, is actually not easterly, but due south.

A traveler on the Valley Pike, heading northeast from Strasburg, first would cross the shoulder of Hupp's Hill, just outside of town; would veer to eastward, descend to Cedar Creek and cross it on a modest bridge; then would turn back to the northeast while climbing the rather abrupt rise on the east side of the creek. There the traveler would find that the pike followed the crest of a long ridge that fell away gently to westward but in more abrupt, rugged slopes to the east, and would there be greeted, if the date were October 13, 1864, by an awe-inspiring panorama of thousands of white tents.

On the left of the road, in the gently rolling fields undulating away to the Valley's mountain walls, sprawled the camps of the two XIX Corps divisions, and dimly seen beyond that, a white fleece on the brown October hills, the cavalry camps. Crook's men were close at hand, camped on two hills to the right of the pike. Colonel Joseph Thoburn's First Division had the forward position, on a hill about one-half mile south of where the pike crossed the creek. The Second Division under Colonel Rutherford Hayes was on another hill a half mile to the northeast. There was more cavalry posted out to the east, guarding the flank.[6]

A Captain Willard of the 34th Massachusetts, part of a bri-

gade in Thoburn's division, recalled the scene on that relaxed
Thursday as he and some comrades sought shelter from the
wind in order to pursue a favorite recreation: "About noon
might have been seen five pairs of heels protruding from a shelter tent near the center of the line of the 34th, the owners of
which were deeply engaged in a game of cards, although an
indifferent spectator might have supposed from their position
that they were trying to swim on dry land. The bugles had just
sounded the call to dinner.

"Boom! Boom! suddenly broke upon our ears. Hallo, says
one, there goes a salute! We must have been licking the
graybacks again!

"Boom! Boom! This time accompanied by the whizzing of a
shell which struck the ground midway between the tents and
regimental headquarters. Nice kind of salute that, thought we,
as scrambling out we got on our feet and looked around to see
what it all meant." The surprise was universal. "From General
Crook on down," recalled Lieutenant Colonel William C. Starr
of Crook's staff, "it was as unlooked for as lightning out of a
clear sky, for not a mother's son of us dreamed of the enemy
being within 50 miles of Cedar Creek."[7]

Nevertheless, there they were, on Hupp's Hill straight west
of Thoburn's camp. When the Federals had recovered from
their shock, they decided that the enemy force was not much of
a threat. "A couple of batteries only," wrote Captain Willard,
"with a small supporting force of infantry." At least, that was
all the infantry that could be seen, and it was partially hidden
by the woods on the hill. Crook presumed it to be a reconnaissance intended to stir up some shooting and thus reveal the
Federal strength and positions. This was a standard gambit, to
which Crook made the standard response; he sent out two brigades—a force that seemed large enough to brush away the
enemy threat while revealing as little as possible.[8]

These were orthodox maneuvers, yet there were puzzling as-
pects. Jubal Early had a signal station atop Shenandoah Peak
(the southernmost and highest eminence on Three-Top, or
Massanutten, Mountain), seventeen hundred feet above the
Valley floor, from which his spotters could see every detail of
the Federal dispositions, as later events would confirm. More-

over, he had been in close contact with Sheridan's army since August, had been engaged with it three times during the past thirty days and had seen it take up almost identical positions along Cedar Creek before; it is difficult to see the need for another test of strength. Firing on the Federals gave away Early's biggest advantage—that of total surprise.

It may be that Early did not intend to do any shooting that day. He was observing Thoburn's Federals, he wrote later, "without displaying any of my force except a small body of cavalry," when to the commanding general's apparent surprise "a battery of artillery was run out suddenly and opened on this division, scattering it in great confusion." One would expect Old Jube to have a great deal to say about a battery commander taking the bit in his teeth at such a critical juncture. His reticence suggests that the whole thing was an embarrassment to him.[9]

Thoburn hastily formed his First Brigade, under the dependable and well-liked Colonel George D. Wells, along with Colonel Thomas M. Harris's Third Brigade, and sent them forward. Captain Willard was in Colonel Wells's 34th Massachusetts: "In our front, and between us and the creek, there was a piece of low open ground, about two hundred yards wide, which must be crossed." Off they went, veterans doing an offhand bit of work, moving in column a quarter of a mile to the right, across the creek toward the Valley Pike, while the shells screeched in among them. Then, under cover of some woods, they swung crisply into the familiar line of battle, the four regiments under Wells south of the pike and Harris's five to the north, a two-hundred yard interval between the brigades.[10]

As far as any Federal could see, this was more than enough force—nearly 2,000 men—to deal with the insolent little bunch on Hupp's Hill. In fact, it might well be enough to capture the guns. (The Federals had been taking so many guns from Jubal Early lately that at least one replacement cannon sent out from Richmond, according to John Gordon, had been labeled by some disgusted Confederate functionary, "Respectfully consigned to General Sheridan through General Early.") What the Federals could not see was that just over the crest of the hill and in the woods were nearly 7,000 Confederate infantry, with 5,000 more in supporting distance.[11]

Across the open ground to the creek the Federals marched, rifles shouldered, here and there a man or group of men falling, shattered by a cannon shell, the survivors trying to ignore the fire and concentrate on the chances of taking a significant prize. As the two brigades climbed, they found themselves gradually separated by the crest of a ridge they were following toward the main hill, and then further isolated from each other by a belt of woods between them, along the top of the ridge. Wells's brigade continued on the left of the ridge, bearing a little to the left, while Harris's men pushed forward along the right slope of the ridge, veering a bit to their right.

Meanwhile the Confederates, unseen as yet by their opponents, were rushing into line of battle to meet the sudden advance. Kershaw's division was south of the pike and Gordon's north of it, with Wharton coming up on Gordon's left. Kershaw's old brigade, now under Brigadier General James Conner, led the way toward contact with Wells's Federal brigade, which was now struggling blindly up the hill through thick underbrush.[12]

As the lines were closing to rifle range, the Federals came upon one of a soldier's best friends—a stone wall. They dashed to it, took cover, and opened fire. One of the first rounds fired shattered General Conner's knee, a wound that would require later amputation of the leg. Minutes later, the senior colonel of Conner's brigade was just getting his bearings on succeeding to command when he was mortally wounded. The highest ranking officer in the brigade was now a major.[13]

The Federals were taking severe punishment as well. Their stone wall turned out to be a low one, offering scant protection from the continuing cannon fire and musketry from the hillside above. Captain Willard was not unduly worried, just impatient for the order to advance and get it over with, when he saw an astonishing thing.

"Believing that the Second Brigade was quite near, on our right," he wrote later (mistakenly referring to the Third Brigade as the Second, which was on detached duty elsewhere), "I had paid but little attention to my flank, although I was on the extreme right of our regiment and brigade; nor did I dream of danger from that quarter." Then one of his men shouted and pointed at the woods to the right; a scattering of men in gray and butternut, advancing against the brigade's flank. Captain Willard wheeled some of his men into line at right angles to the stone wall and drove the enemy off with a few volleys. Then, thinking it must have been some kind of a fluke, he returned his men to the original line.[14]

But the Confederates came back at him from the right flank, and this time there were more of them. Now two companies changed front, the firing increased in intensity, Willard sent a warning to Colonel Wells, and the men began to wonder: what had happened to the Second Brigade? Just how many Confederates were they up against? What was going on?

No one knew, then or later. Colonel Harris claimed that his brigade formed on the right of Wells and was soon "fiercely engaged with the enemy's infantry," which in his case was Gordon's division, a far larger force than the Federals had expected. Worse, Wharton's division was coming up on Gordon's left, and Harris now saw that the Confederate line extended far beyond his own. It was at this point, Harris said later, that he received an order from Colonel Thoburn to withdraw. The Third Brigade pulled back, hard-pressed by the enemy, but Wells did not get the order—Harris said the courier's horse was killed—and the First Brigade was left unsupported on the field, with neither brigade aware of what the other was doing.[15]

Colonel Starr had a different impression of things. He reported that when the two brigades became separated during their advance, the enemy took advantage of the First Brigade's isolation and "hurled his main force again Wells." When Harris saw how badly things were going for Wells, according to Colonel Starr, Harris "wisely withdrew ere suffering much damage."[16]

However it happened, Wells's brigade ended up alone on Hupp's Hill, under fierce attack from two sides by an overwhelmingly superior force. "We had, in reality, lost no ground," Captain Willard insisted, when the order to withdraw finally reached the brigade. It had been difficult enough for Colonel Wells to retain control of his heavily besieged men;

now he was going to have to keep them together while retreating under fire. Wells could have done it—he knew what he was doing and the men respected him—but he did not get the chance. Moments before the order reached him, a rifle ball struck him in the middle of his chest and punched through his body.[17]

As he slid helplessly to the ground, his staff grabbed his horse and prepared to carry him to the rear. "It is of no use, gentlemen," he yelled through the din of battle. "I cannot live. Let me lie here. Take my money and watch, and save yourselves." He insisted, and the grieving staff left him alone with one obstinate aide who sat mutely nearby, determined to escort the colonel to his fate. Moments later Captain Willard, taking his men to the rear, saw his wounded commander lying near the stone wall and tried to help, but Wells ordered him to keep moving. Willard hesitated just a little too long; screaming Confederates came pouring over the wall and took him prisoner. Now under guard, he helped carry Wells up the hill toward the still-firing Confederate batteries.[18]

General Early rode over, looked down at the stricken Wells, and asked his name. Then Old Jube wanted to know if this was the Colonel Wells who had commanded the infantry expedition up the Valley the previous December. Told that it was, Early summoned an ambulance, but Wells died as he was being put into it. Captain Willard started the long walk to Richmond's Libby Prison. The Federals, having suffered 209 casualties—159 in the First Brigade—re-formed on their side of Cedar Creek, posted a strong picket line and thought things over. About midnight they probed the hill again, but by then the Confederates were gone.[19]

It had been a minor engagement but a heavy skirmish, and it had been a Confederate victory. Coming as it did after a string of humiliating losses, and containing as it did the opportunity for further embarrassing Jubal Early, it is remarkable indeed that Gordon did not tell the story in his recollections. He missed few opportunities for taking a shot at Old Jube.

John Gordon was a preacher's son with no particular profession, but a courtly man of archetypal Southern charm nonetheless, a thin, hawk-faced six-footer who was always careful about his grooming, and who always turned so that photographs would not show the left side of his face, ruined by an enemy bullet at Antietam. He was a master of gentle language, noble sentiments and self-deprecating humor, but he had a hard streak in him. In combat this savage side of his nature took over, suffusing his spare frame with martial fervor, glittering from his eyes, transforming his voice to a trumpet ringing clear over the roar. "He dressed for battle as others would dress for a ball," one of his soldiers recalled. And when the fight started, an electric charge ran through him, and into his men; "His face grew white in battle, and the scar on his cheek grew red or purple, his eyes blazed, and Gordon's Brigade stood ready to die in their tracks."[20]

Those who remembered him in battle reached for literary allusions to express their admiration. "Pure as Sir Galahad, knightly as King Arthur, he was as brave as Sir Lancelot and gentle as the dawn," wrote one veteran. Another equated him with the *Chevalier Bayard,* he who was *sans peur et sans reproche.* But it was an artless, unstudied tribute that truly measured the man. Robert Stiles once asked a badly wounded young soldier, who had just endured a grueling train journey and was lying in his stretcher on the platform, the name of his commander. "I belong to Gordon's old brigade, Cap'n," said the youth, who then heaved himself painfully up on one elbow. "Did you ever seen the Gin'ral in battle?" he asked eagerly. "He's most the prettiest thing you ever did see on a field of fight. Why, it'ud put fight into a whipped chicken just to look at him!"[21]

Then and later, on the battlefield and on paper, John Gordon took his military avocation very seriously. One sees the glint of steel among his velvet words whenever it is even remotely necessary to defend his generalship; or whenever the name of Jubal Early comes up for discussion. Like most people, Gordon had a good memory—that is to say, he remembered what made him look good, and forgot the rest. In his detailed account of the battle of Monocacy, for example, in which his 2nd Corps did most of the fighting and won the day for the Confederates, Gordon described his central role in rich detail, with becoming modesty but with unmistakable emphasis—he deployed his division, he saw the difficulties, he gave the orders, he overcame misfortune and achieved the victory. The picture seems complete until one looks at it through the eyes of Glenn Worthington, then a terrified boy in the basement of a farm home near the thick of the fighting, later a historian of the battle. Then, and only then, one sees another figure—that of the equally impressive General Breckinridge, Early's second-in-command and Gordon's superior officer—sharing the dangers, the decisions and the achievements.[22]

Gordon had no such reticence about Jubal Early. On three different occasions, according to Gordon, the two men had battlefield confrontations in which Gordon advocated bold action leading to certain victory, but either largely or entirely because of Early was ignored, the glorious opportunity consequently lost. In October of 1864 two of those confrontations—one at Gettysburg, one in the Wilderness—had taken place. The third, and most bitter, was just a few days in the future.

The year before, Gordon's Georgia Brigade—then part of Early's division of Ewell's Second Corps—had come swinging into the vicinity of Gettysburg at mid-afternoon of July 1, about four hours after the beginning of full-scale fighting (despite the best efforts of generals Lee and Meade to avoid an engagement just then). The Second Corps had been almost to Harrisburg, northeast of Gettysburg, when recalled, and their route brought them onto the battlefield to the rear of the Federal right flank.

The enemy was advancing, Gordon wrote. "A few moments more and the day's battle might have been ended by the complete turning of Lee's flank. I was ordered to move at once to the aid of the heavily pressed Confederates. With a ringing yell, my command rushed upon the line posted to protect the Union right. Here occurred a hand-to-hand struggle." The Federal line broke and began to flee. Soon the plain north of Gettysburg and the town itself were thick with fleeing Federal soldiers, all running for the heights of Cemetery and Culp's hills south of town.[23]

"As far down the line as my eye could reach the Union troops were in retreat," Gordon wrote, the heat of battle in him again as he remembered, more than thirty years later. "In less than half an hour my troops would have swept up and over those hills, the possession of which was of such momentous consequence." He was, in other words, about to win the war when, to his dismay, he was ordered to halt. At first he disobeyed and continued the attack, he wrote, but when told that General Lee did not want to bring on a general engagement he grudgingly complied.[24]

John Gordon fought courageously and well at Gettysburg as elsewhere, and it is no reflection on either his valor or his honesty to say that his memories were inexact. The image he presents is one of *his* troops breaking the Union flank, of *his* command poised to drive to Cemetery Hill and of his acceding to General Lee's wishes. The correct perspective is to see Gordon's brigade advancing along with the three other brigades of Early's division and, on breaking the Federal line, joining with the four brigades of Rodes's division and coming once again under the command of the corps commander, General Ewell.

In fact, both Jubal Early and Robert E. Lee (who had just arrived on the battlefield and was not far to the west) saw the same potential for victory that Gordon did, and Lee urged General Ewell to follow it up. Gordon claims that Ewell and Early were too far from the battlefield to make proper decisions, but the problem was with Ewell, whose inertia on July 1 was only part of the story of uncharacteristic failures that crippled the Confederate effort at Gettysburg. Gordon is correct when he says that an opportunity was lost on that afternoon; but he overstates his personal potential for having grasped it.

In the Wilderness ten months later, according to Gordon, there was committed a similar and "even greater blunder." There, on the morning of the second day (May 6, 1864) of the first slugging match between Lee and Grant, Gordon's scouts reported a remarkable happenstance. The previous night, after a day of confused fighting while the two armies groped for each other through the dense tangles of brush, Ewell's Second Corps had gone into line on the Confederate left, opposite the Federal VI Corps, with Gordon's brigade on the extreme left. At dawn his patrols reported that fully half of the brigade extended beyond the end of the Federal line. What is more, the Federal flank had been left in the air, completely unprotected to its right and rear, no reserves nearby, the men on the line oblivious to the proximity of the enemy.[25]

It was hardly creditable that the Federals would make the same mistake that had lost the battle of Chancellorsville exactly a year before, just a few miles away. Gordon had other scouts check the report, and when they confirmed it, he went out and looked himself. It was true. Gordon could wheel half of his brigade to the right, put the unprepared enemy in a sudden, horrendous crossfire between the flanking force and the main Confederate line, and roll up VI Corps—perhaps the entire Army of the Potomac—like a rug.

On fire with the possibilities, Gordon went to Ewell's headquarters, where he ran full tilt into Jubal Early. The plan was foolhardy, said Old Jube, for two reasons: according to his information, the entire Federal IX Corps was lurking little more than a mile away behind the VI Corps right, and would annihilate any Confederate turning movement; besides which, any such attack would have to be made without reserves, which meant that if anything went wrong, the entire left wing of the Confederate army would be in mortal peril. Gordon protested that he had been out there, and that there was no sign of IX Corps. Old Jube, who disliked getting advice from subordinates, got testy. Ewell, as he had at Gettysburg, temporized. He would take a look himself, later. He might do something, but it would be later.

All day Gordon listened, fuming, to the battle raging three miles to the south while only the occasional spatter of firing, never enough to alert either side to the true situation, disturbed the Federal right. Then, as Gordon remembered it, at about half past five in the afternoon General Lee came riding over to ask, "Cannot something be done on this flank to relieve the pressure upon our right?" Gordon says Ewell and Early could not think of anything until he reminded them of his plan, whereupon General Lee ordered it done immediately. "His words were few," Gordon recalled with satisfaction, "but his silence and grim looks while the reasons for that long delay were being given, and his prompt order to me to move at once to the attack, revealed his thought almost as plainly as words could have done.[26]

Finally, with only minutes of daylight left, Gordon unleashed his men on the VI Corps flank just as Stonewall Jackson had leaped out of the woods at XI Corps the previous May. The Confederates "struck the Union flank and with thrilling yells rushed upon it and along the Union works, shattering regiments and brigades, and throwing them into wildest confusion and panic. There was practically no resistance." The entire VI Corps was coming apart, but Gordon had to stop his men; in the darkness the troops on the main Confederate line, unable to distinguish the advancing Georgians from defending Federals, were firing into their comrades. Gordon reckoned that half of his sixty casualties were inflicted by friendly fire.[27]

Once again, the reality seems to have been somewhat less dramatic, and less centered on John Gordon, than Gordon remembers. Jubal Early's information that Burnside's corps was behind the Federal right was correct when he received it, the previous evening. That Burnside had marched on to the other end of the Union line had not been reported when Gordon proposed his attack. The record indicates that Ewell did in fact look the situation over and that he had already decided, when Lee appeared that afternoon, to make the attack, although after a lengthy and unnecessary delay. Gordon's account of Lee's intervention, hinting as it does at Lee's displeasure with Ewell and Early, and indicating that Lee gave Gordon the order to attack, is unsupported by other evidence. It is also at odds with Lee's renowned delicacy toward his lieutenants and his unwillingness to go outside of the chain of command.

In any case, by the time Gordon became Jubal Early's second-in-command in September of 1864, the two had crossed swords twice. But the thing that irritated Jubal Early most often about Gordon was neither the younger man's growing fame nor his pushiness in giving advice to his seniors nor the growing rivalry between them. It was Mrs. Gordon.

John and Fanny Gordon were deeply, romantically, in love. Aside from her insistence on staying with him throughout the war, they were not ostentatious about their affection for each other, but it was unmistakable. She, too, came from a family with a military tradition; her father had been a general of Georgia militia and her grandfather a soldier of the Revolution. She understood when, upon the fall of Fort Sumter, her husband had to go to war. But she had no intention of being left behind. She turned her two children, aged four and six, over to Gordon's mother, climbed into a buggy, and with one of the family slaves driving she followed her man.[28]

They had been married in September of 1854, when Fanny Rebecca Haralson was a mere seventeen years old and he was twenty-two. He had been trying to make his mark as a lawyer in the burgeoning railroad town and newly designated county seat of Atlanta, and she was the sister of a senior partner in his firm. He saw her standing in her brother's yard, a gardenia in her hair, and was forever smitten. As that ubiquitous observer John Wise reported years later, she was a beautiful young thing with a "tall, willowy form" and "gazelle eyes, lighted with love and patriotic fire." Three weeks later, John Gordon rode the seventy miles to her home, started arguing his case, and would not stop talking until she had agreed to marry him and her father had consented.[29]

Despite apparent gifts of oratory, Gordon did not succeed as a lawyer and soon left the Atlanta firm. He experimented inconclusively with newspaper reporting, gave up, and then went to work for his father. Zachariah Gordon, a Baptist preacher with a keen eye for things material, had developed a successful resort in northwest Georgia. There Zachariah had befriended a vacationer named Mark Cooper, industrialist and owner of the gigantic Etowah Iron Works, who introduced the preacher to the glories of coal. Cooper's blast furnaces needed it, northwest Georgia had it, and before long Zachariah was in the coal-mining business. He flourished, and in the spring of 1856 offered his floundering son a supervisory job.[30]

John moved to Dade County, and did the work required, and made good money at it, but it was not the future he had envisioned. His marriage was passionate, his family was growing, his future, it seemed, was ordained. But it must have galled him, living in his father's shadow, stepping in his father's tracks. One cannot escape the thought that he turned to the passions that led to war with more relief than reluctance.

In the spring of 1861 the Gordons lived in Alabama, got their mail in nearby Tennessee and worked in Georgia. It was rough country, and in the rush to join the Confederate army that followed Lincoln's call for 75,000 Federal volunteers, Gordon was thrown together with some of the country's rougher people. Miners and mountain men, hunters and hard-scrabble farmers, they were hardy and unkempt and independent. It is a tribute to both him and them that they elected the ramrod lawyer sporting the bottle-green militia coat their captain, and shuffled along happily in his impeccable footsteps; but the only uniformity they would adopt in their clothing or behavior was the coonskin cap each man wore with pride. The men insisted on being called the Raccoon Roughs.[31]

Fanny Gordon stayed with her husband for the duration. She lived with him in camp while, as colonel of the 6th Alabama, he distinguished himself in the Peninsular Campaign of 1862. She nursed him back to health from his awful wounds at Antietam. Then when he took over the Georgia Brigade and was promoted to brigadier general, she and her servant followed him in their buggy from Chancellorsville to Gettysburg, through the Wilderness to Petersburg and back to the Valley.

She drove Old Jube to distraction. It was bad enough that John Breckinridge and Tom Rosser brought their wives to the Valley when things were quiet, and that the fierce young division commander Dodson Ramseur was mooning over a new bride left behind, but these were occasional irritations; Mrs. Gordon was there all the time, and something about her beauty, her devotion to her husband and his affection for her was sand in Old Jube's soul. "I wish the Yankees would capture Mrs. Gordon," he is supposed to have said once, "and hold her till this war is over!"[32]

She heard about his tirade, and was amused. When she got the chance, at a rare camp dinner to which wives were invited, she asked him about it, no doubt to watch him squirm. Squirm he did, but General Early had secret resources of graciousness that could take one's breath away: "Mrs. Gordon," he finally said, "General Gordon is a better soldier when you are close by him than when you are away, and so hereafter, when I issue orders that officers' wives must go to the rear, you may know that you are excepted." His staff gave him a round of applause.[33]

John Gordon also relished a remark Early made one night when the advancing army's wagons were going into park near Winchester. Dimly seen in the gathering darkness, one of the first vehicles to clatter to a stop was a buggy of some sort, distinctly out of place among the heavy wagons and ambulances. "What's that?" barked Early; "Mrs. Gordon's carriage, sir," came the answer; "Well, I'll be damned," snorted Old Jube. "If my men would keep up as she does, I'd never issue another order against straggling."[34]

Thus, on several counts, the relationship between Jubal Early and John Gordon was, in mid-October of 1864, an itchy one. Its prospects were not improved by the fact that Gordon decided, on October 17, that he was "not entirely satisfied" with Old Jube's plans for the next move.

That move had to be made quickly. All of the army's supplies were being hauled down the Valley from above Staunton, beyond the reach of Sheridan's destruction, and the Confederates did not have the wagons or the horses to sustain that supply effort. As Early put it, he had to attack or retreat. He would not retreat.[35]

There appeared to be only one way to get at Sheridan's position. His left, near the river below Massanutten Mountain, was inaccessible. The mountain was jammed up against the south bank of the river, and the Federals controlled the heights on the north side. But the Federal right, off to the north and west, tapered away in the broad fields of the Valley where there was room to maneuver an army and a chance to turn a flank. There were drawbacks, of course. In order to assail the Federal infantry, the Confederates would have to cross Cedar Creek under fire and storm the rugged heights and formidable earthworks opposite. Meanwhile, the open fields that gave Early room to maneuver offered the same advantage to the Federal cavalry. But flaws or not, it was the only thing to do, and Early ordered preparations made.

As they went forward, Gordon became uneasy. The plan was too ordinary, too much the expected thing, to have a chance against Sheridan's superior weight of numbers and guns. That weight was even greater now, for as the signal station on Shenandoah Peak reported, immediately after the skirmish of the 13th the Federal VI Corps had marched back from the east and had gone into camp to the northwest of XIX Corps.

The blustery weather of the 13th had ushered in one of those prolonged periods of crisp, clear weather during which the Valley air is scrubbed clean of its customary summer haze by brisk northerly breezes. This was ideal observation weather for the signal corps station, and on Monday the 17th, Gordon was sent to have a look at the situation from that vantage point. (Early, stooped and in pain, could not go himself.) He took with him Jed Hotchkiss, the careful diarist and superb mapmaker who had charted Stonewall Jackson's Valley Campaign; Brigadier General Clement A. Evans, the dependable Georgian who was in command of Gordon's old brigade; and Major Robert W. Hunter, Gordon's chief of staff (and a relative of "Black Dave" Hunter, the vindictive Union general).[36]

It was a rugged climb, requiring hours of torturous clambering, Gordon recalled, "through tangled underbrush and over giant boulders and jutting cliffs." The reward, however, was proportionate to the effort. "It was," said Gordon, "an inspiring panorama." There, spread out below them like toy soldiers on an exquisitely modeled miniature field, lay the Union army. With his field glasses Gordon could see not only the lay of the land and the position of the enemy, but every detail. "I could count, and did count, the number of his guns. I could see distinctly the three colors of trimmings on the jackets respectively of infantry, artillery and cavalry, and locate each, while the number of flags gave a basis for estimating approximately the forces with which we were to contend in the proposed attack."[37]

Of course, this information had been available all along to the signal corps spotters manning the station. But now two battle-wise generals and an expert topographical engineer were scrutinizing the entire situation. Not surprisingly, they immediately saw a magnificent opportunity. The Federal left was in the air; the cavalry division that had been guarding it was gone, leaving, Gordon wrote, "a very small detachment of cavalry on the left bank of the river, with vedettes on their horses in the middle of the stream." Sheridan's cavalry was now massed on his right, "where he supposed, as all others had supposed, that General Early must come, if he came with any hope of success. As to his left flank—well, that needed no defense; the impassable Massanutten, with the Shenandoah River at its base, was the sufficient protecting fortress.[38]

"It required, therefore, no transcendent military genius to decide quickly and unequivocally upon the movement which the conditions invited." An attack on that unprotected flank, even by an outnumbered force, could do incalculable damage. If Old Jube would accept his plan, "the destruction of Sheridan's army was inevitable." Gordon was so sure of the result, he said to his companions, that should the attack be approved, and fail, he would take the responsibility. This was the same assurance he had given when recommending the attack in the Wilderness, and it bordered on the fatuous; as Gordon very well knew, no commander could avoid official and public censure for a failure by protesting that a subordinate officer had agreed to take the responsibility.[39]

In fact, as Gordon left his mountaintop he was undoubtedly inspired by what he saw, but he had no plan. His thinking ran along the lines of the hungry man's lament: if we had some ham, we could have some ham and eggs, if we had some eggs. Similarly, Gordon had determined that if they could attack the Federal left, they could have a great victory, if they could somehow get at the Federal left. A road and a railroad track ran east from Strasburg, crossed to the south side of the Shenandoah a mile out of town, then continued to Front Royal ten miles away. Three-quarters of a mile east of the bridge the road forked, with a branch leading north across the river at a ford and then onward beyond the left and into the rear of the Federal army. But no armed force could move along the road between Strasburg and the ford without being detected by Federal pickets north of the river. For the whole distance either the river or the road were snugged tight against the precipitous and heavily wooded flanks of Massanutten Mountain.

Notwithstanding the gaping hole in their tactics, Gordon and Hotchkiss recommended to Early that he change his approach and mount an attack on the Federal left. To his enormous credit, given his reputed unwillingness to listen to advice and his experiences with Gordon, Old Jube was receptive. No doubt it helped enormously that Hotchkiss was not only in favor of the plan, but was able to produce a detailed map of the entire situation. Early listened carefully, then said that if they could find a way to get into position, he would order the attack made as they recommended.

On the 18th Gordon and Hotchkiss went prowling the woods and ridges of the Shenandoah's right bank looking for the key —the route to the ford. About midday they found it; a narrow trail, along which only one man could walk at a time, threading the ridges south of the river until it reached the Front Royal road just east of the bridge. When they got to the vicinity, they appropriated some rough work clothes and corn knives from a farmhouse and went into a field near the river to cut corn and spot Union pickets. Gordon calculated that if the infantry started marching single file from Fisher's Hill at sundown, all three divisions of the Second Corps could be in position to attack by daylight. Early agreed and issued orders for a night of complex movements by the entire army, followed by a dawn attack.[40]

In view of the later controversy, an obvious point should be stressed here; the moment Jubal Early approved of the planned movement of his army, the plan became his. A general is not expected to have all the good ideas, but he is expected to recognize them, and if Early is to be criticized for failing to recognize a good plan in the Wilderness, then by the same standard he deserves praise for recognizing a good one at Cedar Creek.

By sundown on the 18th, the plan was in place. Gordon would take temporary command of the Second Corps divisions —Ramseur's, Pegram's, and his own under Evans—and make the night flanking movement. Tom Rosser would make a demonstration against the Federal right, where the attack was expected. Early would supervise Kershaw's and Wharton's divisions in a frontal attack down the Valley Pike against the Federal center, while Tom Carter's guns pounded away from Hupp's Hill. Lomax's cavalry division, meanwhile, would swing all the way over to Front Royal, then come in behind the Federal left. If the rather complicated plan worked, Sheridan's army would find itself assailed from virtually every point of the compass. The first and heaviest blow would fall on George Crook's Army of West Virginia.[41]

The Crook family, like the Gordons, had come over from Scotland in time to fight for independence along with George Washington, but instead of turning afterward to the pulpit and the bar, had taken up the plow. Thomas Crook had been a tanner in Baltimore until he went west to Ohio in 1814 to start farming—and raising children. There were nine in all, of which George was the eighth. Small wonder he never talked much.[42]

Unlike John Gordon, Crook had neither a special flair for battle nor an electric personality, but he had a solid, kindly professionalism that endeared him to his men. His craggy countenance and lanky, slightly awkward frame gave him an ordinary, friendly look that made one think of Abraham Lincoln, and encouraged his men to call him "Uncle George." This, of course, out of his earshot; he was a very stern, although never harsh, taskmaster and disciplinarian. At the same time he affected, perhaps by way of recalling his Indian-fighting days, an indifference to proper uniform—his dress was "half civil, half military," one soldier remembered—and commemorated his cavalry service in the West by wearing enormous cavalry boots.[43]

Those boots got him in trouble during the first battle of the 1864 campaign. He had been leading an infantry charge—a rare thing for a general to do—at Cloyd's Mountain, near Dublin in far southwest Virginia. The men came to an unexpectedly deep little creek in mid-charge, and Crook's high boots filled with water until he very nearly could not move. The privates, surprised to see him there at all, dragged him out, and a lieutenant cracked later that the only problem with generals leading charges seemed to be that they needed to be helped over water.[44]

By the fall of 1864 George Crook believed, as John Gordon did, that he had come up with some pretty good solutions to combat problems recently; that he had, in fact, shown the way to win some major battles. Crook's problem was not that his ideas had been rejected; they had been acted on and had, in fact, won the battles of Winchester and Fisher's Hill, or so Crook believed. His problem was that he was being denied credit for them, and this by his old friend Phil Sheridan.

"We had known each other as boys before we entered the army, and later as men," Sheridan would write of Crook years later, "and I placed implicit faith in his experience and qualifications as a general." It was awkward and carefully limited praise for a boyhood friend who had shared not only the terrors of Indian fighting and civil war, but the formative terrors of West Point. Weathering those first tests had come easier to the lumbering Crook—described by an earlier schoolmate as "a big Newfoundland dog among a lot of puppies"—than to his incandescent little friend. Where Sheridan had had to strive even to get appointed to the academy, Crook had been sought out.

Congressman Robert P. Schenck of Dayton, whose district included the Crooks' prosperous Miami River farm, recalled that he had been trying without success to think of "a bright lad to nominate" when "I finally remembered that old 'Squire Crook, a fine old Whig farmer, and a friend of mine, had some boys, and I sent word for him to come to town. He came in, and I enquired if he had a spare boy he'd like to send off to West Point. After studying a while he said he didn't know but what he had. I suggested that he send him in. He did so.

"The boy was exceedingly non-communicative. He hadn't a stupid look, but was quiet to reticence. He didn't seem to have the slightest interest or anxiety about my proposal. I explained to him the requirements and labors of the military school, and finally asked him. 'Do you think you can conquer all that?' His monosyllabic reply was, 'I'll try.' And so I sent him, and he came through fairly."[45]

Plebes together, fugitives at Benny Havens's drinking establishment together and graduates together, Crook and Sheridan were both sent to do their military apprenticeship in the West Coast Indian wars. They served there until the war broke out, their paths crossing frequently, their opinions about Indians and duty hardening along diametrically opposed lines. Sheridan scoffed at the miserable savages who had somehow got it into their heads "that they could successfully resist the pressure of

civilization." He regarded them with all the tenderness of an
attack dog dealing with an intruder.[46]

Crook, on the other hand, grieved for the people he was
required to fight and raged over the lawlessness of the white
miners and prospectors. "The country was over-run by people
from all nations in search of the mighty dollar," Crook wrote,
"greed was almost unrestrained." Indians who got in the way
were shot or raped, and "such a thing as a white man being
punished for outraging an Indian was unheard of." The army
had no power to correct these injustices, Crook said, but when
the natives "were pushed beyond endurance and would go on
the war path we had to fight, when our sympathies were with
the Indians."[47]

Ironically, Crook had already fought and killed many more
Indians than had Sheridan, and carried a flint arrowhead em-
bedded in his hip as a memento of one particularly terrifying
time. He had been shooting at some Indians from partway
down a steep bluff on one side of a narrow canyon when a flight
of arrows—"the air apparently full of them"—came in from
the rocks on the other side. Crook was hit, jerked the shaft out
of his right hip, and began a desperate climb "through a shower
of arrows. The ascent was so steep that I had to pull myself up
by catching hold of bunches of grass, rocks, and such things as
I could get hold of. In one bunch of grass I caught hold of two
arrows that had been shot at me. The wonder was that I was
not hit oftener. By the time I reached the top the perspiration
stood out on me in large drops, and I was deathly sick." The
surgeons could do nothing for his wound but let it heal; seventeen days later, Crook was back in the saddle, chasing a party
of Indian raiders.[48]

The enduring difference of opinion with Sheridan about the
nature of the Indian would later destroy their friendship and
stifle Crook's career, but in 1864 it was not an issue. Whenever
Sheridan had a slow day, he liked to get together with Crook
and a couple of other veterans of the western wars and talk
about the good old days. At such times Sheridan dropped his
tightly wound reserve and actually became pleasant. "Occa-
sionally," Major Newhall of Sheridan's staff recorded, "when
the old associations come back to the party very strongly, they

lapse into the Indian tongue." The major supposed that this was to permit discussion of things that "if told in plain English, would astonish the audience."[49]

This easy camaraderie had begun to fray after the battle at Winchester in September. During the frightful stalemate of that endless afternoon, when the men of VI and XIX Corps, attacking toward Winchester from the east with XIX Corps on the right, had been hammered to a standstill by the outnumbered but desperately fighting divisions of Dodson Ramseur and John Gordon, Sheridan had changed his battle plan. Crook's original orders had been to swing to the south and across the Valley Pike, thus cutting the Confederate line of retreat and making possible the destruction of Early's army. When, thanks largely to Gordon's timely arrival and vigorous fight on the Confederate left, Early showed no signs of retreating, Sheridan gave Crook new instructions, which were to become a point of contention between them.

According to Crook, his orders were to "go in on the right and rear of the Nineteenth Corps." But Crook decided, he says, to do things a little differently. "I felt morally sure," he wrote later, "that if the enemy were to resume their attack on the Nineteenth Corps and succeed in driving them back, they would carry me with them. So I left one division, Thoburn's, on the right of the Nineteenth Corps while I took the other division in person and felt my way around the enemy's left, intending, if possible, to turn his flank."[50]

Crook and his men floundered around the end of the enemy line through terrain so swampy that he was told some men drowned trying to get through it. Once on more solid ground, he groped for his bearings, finding to his consternation at one point that he and a few staff officers had somehow ridden well to the rear of an enemy line of battle. But he got his division squared away, charged, broke the Confederate left and won the battle of Winchester. So he remembered it. "We captured over 1,000 prisoners," he wrote. "Just then our cavalry came up on a charge and gobbled up all the prisoners and afterwards turned them in and was allowed credit for them. I complained of this to General Sheridan, who asked me to say nothing about it in my report, but that he saw the whole affair, and would give me credit for it." A month later, Crook was still waiting for credit.[51]

It was nothing new to him. As he tells it, he was surrounded by incompetents from the very start of his army career. Most of the officers he encountered in the Pacific Northwest, he wrote, "had been in command of small posts so long that their habits and minds had narrowed down to their surroundings, and woe be unto the young officer if his ideas should get above their level and wish to expand." For much of the war Crook had been left on his own, with small, independent commands, to apply the lessons of the Indian wars to rooting out bushwhackers from the hollows and ridges of the Kanawha River valley, in what soon became West Virginia. In times of need, however, he and his small command would be pulled east, or marched west, to help. He always did the job, then returned to the West Virginia mountains, apparently (if his memoirs reflect at all his state of mind at the time) to brood about the inferiority of his colleagues.[52]

In the fall of 1862 he and his men were called east to plunge into the maelstrom along Antietam Creek. They were deployed in the fields south and east of the town of Antietam when a courier brought orders to "take the bridge." Puzzled, Crook asked him what bridge. "He said he didn't know. I asked him where the stream was, but he didn't know." It turned out to be the soon-to-become-infamous stone bridge where Burnside's full division had been repulsed that morning with a loss of 600 men. Crook said later that "such imbecility and incompetency was simply criminal," adding that "it was galling to have to serve under such people." He had little to say, however, about the fact that even when he had found the bridge he had been unable to take it.[53]

After a time back in the Kanawha, Crook and his brigade were sent west to join the Army of the Cumberland in Tennessee. His old friend Sheridan was by that time famous for his hard charging at Perryville and Stones River, but Crook did not include that in his recollections. During the summer of 1863 Crook was transferred to the cavalry, and by fall he was commanding a division of the army's cavalry corps, in time to distinguish himself at the battle of Chickamauga. At one point during the fighting a panicky infantry general who had completely lost control of himself and his troops begged Crook for help. Having straightened the mess out and gone on his way, Crook was astonished after the battle to hear the general bragging about "the valorous deeds of his command. It was humiliating to see persons wearing the uniforms of general officers to be so contemptible."[54]

Crook's own conduct could be less than acceptable, but in these cases his memory lacked clarity. In October of 1863, while the army was under a state of partial siege in Chattanooga, Crook's cavalry was guarding the fords of the Tennessee River between that city and Knoxville. They drove off and gave chase to a large enemy raiding party that had been heading for the Federal rear, and Crook organized an ambush; he would attack with most of his command while a brigade led by Colonel Robert Horatio George Minty attacked from a different direction. "By some mistake," Crook wrote disingenuously, "Minty's brigade did not move out of camp in the morning, saying he had no orders, etc., so failed to be at the junction of the two roads as directed, and we failed to accomplish the results to which we were entitled." Crook did not tell the rest of the story: that he had Minty arrested and tried for disobedience, but that the colonel was acquitted when Crook had to admit that he had forgot to give his brigade commander any orders.[55]

In January of 1864 Crook was returned to the Kanawha, according to him as a result of petitions from the residents. He had been in line for command of the cavalry corps of the Army of the Cumberland, and did not want to leave, but General Grant had been impressed by Crook's performance in the west and had important work for him to do.

Under Grant the department commander in West Virginia would not be simply scouring the hollows for bushwhackers; Grant was already zeroing in on the all-important railroad connections between Richmond and the West; especially the Virginia and Tennessee line that passed through southwest Virginia not far south of the Kanawha Valley. Crook's first assignment on his return—and Grant called him east to give him the orders in person—was to march southwest from the

Kanawha with a combined force of infantry and cavalry, destroy the bridge that carried the Virginia and Tennessee Railroad over the New River, then push northeast to Staunton and join forces with General Franz Sigel.[56]

John Breckinridge had to divide a tiny Confederate force to meet both threats, and Crook confronted part of it—a mixed bag of 3,000, including untried militia and home guards—at Cloyd's Mountain on May 9. "They may whip us," Crook opined, "but I guess not." Whereupon he deployed his 6,000 men, ordered a charge, led it in person, and whipped them. Then, after destroying the New River bridge, Crook for some reason decided to abort the rest of his mission and retreat back into the mountains. Not until June 8 did he get back to Staunton to meet the army under Sigel's successor David Hunter; and then all Hunter did was march to Lynchburg, take a look, fire a few volleys and retreat into West Virginia yet again. Of course Crook was disgusted by all this incompetence. During the advance, he wrote, he was the only one to make a serious attack; "I had to do all the work as it was, for I got no material assistance from anyone else." And on the retreat Crook had to guard the rear, "and had to do all of the fighting. The lowest of the low fell on me and my division."[57]

When the command straggled back to Harpers Ferry, by way of Charleston, it was just in time to get in on the befuddled, comic-opera chase of Jubal Early just after the Confederate raid on Washington. Crook, with part of his command, got on the east side of the Blue Ridge and on July 17 tried to trap the Confederates between his force and VI Corps. Early slipped between them, crossed the mountain at Snicker's Gap and camped near Berryville. The next day, when Crook's men came down off the mountain and crossed the Shenandoah at its base, Early was waiting with his whole army. When the Federals were partway across the river, and most vulnerable, the Confederates opened fire.[58]

Crook could see from the mountain that his men were in trouble, but General Horatio G. Wright of VI Corps was in command. "I desired to withdraw my troops to our side of the river," wrote Crook, fuming, "but he said no, he would order Gen. Ricketts to cross the river and support me with his division." When General Ricketts saw the strength of the enemy, however, he declared the situation to be untenable and refused, perhaps wisely, to cross the river and attack. This, said Crook, "allowed many of my men to be sacrificed. I lost some vulnerable men here, murdered by incompetency or worse." The survivors retreated across the river, one amused VI Corps soldier recalled, "in intense disgust."[59]

Early, having bloodied his pursuers' noses, continued his retreat southward with Crook leading the chase. The Federals assumed Early was leaving the Valley, and VI Corps, having done its duty by shooing the enemy away from Washington, did an about face and headed back to the capital. On July 23 Crook was camped just south of Winchester at Kernstown, confidently pausing in the chase so that Early might let down his guard. The previous morning the cavalry had reported enemy approaching, but when Crook went out to look there was nothing there. That morning the cavalry again reported enemy coming, and Crook ignored them. Minutes later Early appeared, with his whole army, attacked and overwhelmed Crook. It was not quite a rout, but it was a rapid retreat that did not end until the little army was back at Harpers Ferry. "Our cavalry was of little or no assistance," Crook grumbled. "Gen. Averell was accused of getting drunk during the fight."[60]

It is difficult to square the surliness of Crook's writings with the great-hearted leader described by his colleagues. He was, according to his artillery chief Henry DuPont, "a notably keen and clear-headed man—genial, patient, low speaking and inclined to reticence, whose equanimity was rarely if ever disturbed even under the most trying circumstances." Other close associates expressed similar admiration. It does not seem likely that a man seething with the resentments that lace his memoirs could have been so pleasant in person. The bitterness, apparently, was retroactive. Perhaps, like a buried arrowhead, the events surrounding Cedar Creek festered and became more painful with the passing of the years.[61]

As the abundant honors heaped on John Gordon in later life seemed to sweeten his memories, so, perhaps, the lack of recognition soured George Crook's. He remembers, for example, being asked during the early stages of the fighting at Winchester

to remonstrate with a Colonel Stephen Thomas, alleged to be
"a damned coward," and "see if I could induce him to fight."
Crook went to where the colonel's regiment—the 9th Vermont,
part of a XIX Corps brigade—was waiting to advance and relayed the accusation of cowardice. "His face had an ashy hue,"
Crook recalled, "and I told him I did not believe it, but now
was the time for him to disprove this soft impeachment. He
said, 'Do you want me to go in without my generals, General
Dwight and General Emory?' Whereupon I explained that this
was no time to be hunting up generals."

Crook left in disgust, and did not see Colonel Thomas until
after the rout of the enemy, when the New Englanders marched
past in what Crook called sarcastically "splendid line." Colonel
Thomas, proud of his men, shouted to Crook, "Who said they
were cowards?" Crook was scornful: "The enemy must have
been at least three miles away, in full retreat."[62]

Whether deliberately or not, this story does a grave injustice
to Colonel Thomas and calls into serious question Crook's
judgment. Colonel Thomas and his New Englanders had been
fighting heroically for several hours when Crook made his visit;
they had withstood the brunt of a Confederate counterattack;
and had suffered substantial casualties. Colonel Thomas had
received a direct order, through his chain of command, to remain in place until he could be properly supported. Brigadier
General William Dwight was his division commander, Emory
his corps commander, and his question to Crook was appropriate; he may have been trying to tell Crook to mind his own
corps' business. When it came time for the brigade to charge,
Colonel Thomas led it with exemplary courage, and was afterward commended by his brigade commander—Brigadier General James W. McMillan—for "gallantry and coolness at all
times." A month later, on the banks of Cedar Creek, he would
win a Congressional Medal of Honor for extraordinary heroism. Never was sarcasm more inappropriate than General
Crook's in this case.[63]

The confusion and ill will over the performance of XIX
Corps in that battle was widespread. Early in the day, when an
oversight in Sheridan's marching orders had opened a gap between VI Corps on the Federal left and XIX Corps on the

right, a fierce Confederate counterattack led by John Gordon had driven back XIX Corps' Second Division. In his official report of the battle, General Dwight, the First Division commander, had condemned the behavior of the Second Division and its commander, Brigadier General Cuvier Grover. Grover retaliated by bringing formal charges against Dwight—alleging seventeen instances of conduct unbecoming an officer, four of neglect of duty on the field of battle, and two of misbehavior in the face of the enemy. Now the thing was out of hand; the latter two charges were serious enough that Dwight had to be placed under arrest until a court could be convened. Meanwhile, General McMillan took over the First Division, and Colonel Thomas succeeded McMillan in brigade command.[64]

By comparison with this unseemly squabble, Crook was merely disgruntled by the lack of credit for his performance at Third Winchester. He would become apoplectic over the aftermath of Fisher's Hill, but only much later; in October of 1864 the anguish to come was only a suspicion. Crook could not have known how Sheridan was going to characterize the decisions made at Winchester and Fisher's Hill in an official report that would not be written until February of 1866.

By that time Sheridan would be remembering his decision making to his own advantage, and would claim that at Winchester he ordered Crook "to act as a turning column, to find the left of the enemy's line and strike it in flank or rear, break it up, and that I would order a left half-wheel of the line of battle to support him." Crook's memory of the instructions were quite different: "the idea of turning the enemy's flank never occurred to him, but I took the responsibility on my own shoulders."[65]

It is not clear from the record whether Crook thought of the maneuver first, or Sheridan did, or whether each thought of it separately at about the same time. But with respect to Fisher's Hill, Crook's contribution was clear. When Sheridan first confronted the formidable Confederate position there the day after Winchester, he was going to attack the enemy's right flank, where it enjoyed the protection of the steepest part of Fisher's Hill. Sheridan may have figured that an army that had just been routed would not mount a serious fight, even in a favorable position. In any case, Crook saw a better way.

Off to the west the country flattened, and was more weakly held by Early's attenuated force. Crook thought he could sneak his command through the patches of woods, moving at night and hiding by day to avoid detection by the enemy signal station on Shenandoah Peak. In this way he could get onto the timbered slope of North Mountain, then descend on the enemy left and rear with devastating effect. Painfully aware of his own lack of eloquence, Crook detailed a subordinate officer to present the case at a meeting at headquarters that evening. The designated speaker, Colonel Rutherford B. Hayes, apparently displayed the persuasive powers that would eventually help make him president of the United States, for Sheridan approved Crook's plan. Crook executed it flawlessly, and rolled Early's army off Fisher's Hill with trifling casualties.

Sheridan later claimed to have thought of the idea himself, but in this case the record is unequivocal. "It was fully understood at the time by everybody at our corps headquarters," wrote Captain DuPont, "that Crook had suggested this movement." Colonel Hayes, in a letter to his uncle written shortly after the battle, before any controversy had arisen, observed with more sadness than anger that "General Sheridan is a whole-souled, brave man, and believes in Crook, his old class and room-mate at West Point. Intellectually he is not General Crook's equal, who is the brains of this army."[66]

It is perhaps not so surprising that Hayes found so much to like in Crook, a fellow Ohioan, but DuPont's support is remarkable. Henry Algernon DuPont—whose father ran the mills that provided a significant portion of the Union armies' gunpowder—was an aristocratic Easterner and a scholarly soldier who was contemptuous of the rustics who were running this war. "My absurd prejudice against volunteers," he wrote home not long before coming under Crook's command, "arises from a very strong feeling I have against having my battery destroyed by the absurdities and gross ignorance which you meet at every turn." Yet Crook he found to be "keen and clear-headed."[67]

The bitterness that would arise over Winchester and Fisher's

Hill had not yet bloomed on October 18, and it is not clear to what extent Crook sensed that things were not as they should be between him and Sheridan. He writes of that time that his command ("my division") was posted "over a mile from any other troops." He carefully points out that Sheridan had removed the cavalry pickets from the area between Crook and the river ("I might say here that all the cavalry reported directly to General Sheridan . . .") and that his force had been reduced by losses and details to "less than three thousand men."[68]

If these things were on Crook's mind on October 18, as his argumentative memoirs indicate, then his errors of that day are mystifying; all the more so when one recalls the similar situation at Kernstown three months before. Crook was a good officer, who had proved himself on many fields to be careful and thorough and brave. He was never anything but brave; but for some reason on October 18 he was anything but careful and thorough.

There had been for several days a great deal of confusion in the Union high command. Grant still wanted to do things differently than Sheridan did, and the defensive duo in Washington —Secretary of War Stanton and Chief of Staff Halleck—was sneakily keeping in play yet a third approach. Before long things were hopelessly snarled.[69]

Grant was gratified that Sheridan had quieted things down in the Valley sufficiently to return VI Corps, which was badly needed at Petersburg. But the general in chief could not let go of his desire to sever Lee's western railroads. He had understood Sheridan's objections and had yielded to his judgment, but still he worried the idea like a terrier with a dead mouse. Unfortunately, he also expressed himself further on the matter in a wire to Halleck. The words are clear enough to a dispassionate reader: "I think Sheridan should keep up as advanced a position as possible toward the Virginia Central Railroad and be prepared with supplies to advance on that road at Gordonsville and Charlottesville at any time the enemy weakens himself to admit of it. The cutting of that road and canal would be of vast importance to us." In other words, Sheridan should keep his eyes open and, should the opportunity present itself, at his discretion, other things being equal, make a raid. That is what Grant meant to convey. That is not what was conveyed.[70]

The previous month, just before Winchester, Grant had made a personal trip to the Valley to discuss his strategy with Sheridan, not trusting his chain of communications. "I knew it was impossible for me to get orders through Washington for Sheridan to make a move," he wrote years later, "because they would be stopped there and such orders as Halleck's caution (and that of the Secretary of War) would suggest would be given instead and would, no doubt, be contradictory to mine." Apparently Grant understood the situation better when he wrote his memoirs than he did at the time, because here he is a few weeks later giving Halleck and Stanton the opportunity to dabble in something about which they felt strongly.[71]

Both elders believed that Grant was playing a dangerous game when he circled south of Richmond and left open the roads to Washington. How on earth Lee could take those roads without food, wagons, horses or any other means of sustaining himself in the North—why he would leave his fortifications and *his* capital, thus placing it and his army at the mercy of Grant's numerous legions—Halleck and Stanton did not know. They just worried about it. More so when it seemed Grant and Sheridan were not going to seal off the Valley.

All along Halleck had been plugging mulishly away at his own design, never minding what the general in chief wanted done. He had a crew under Major General Christopher Columbus Augur at work repairing the Manassas Gap Railroad, the one Sheridan did not want to have to protect with men who could as well be fighting at Petersburg, and they were now at Rectortown, halfway between Manassas and Strasburg. Sheridan thought railroads and forts were more trouble than they were worth, and that the war could be won only by finding and killing the enemy. But Halleck believed that the way to subdue western Virginia—at no risk to Washington—was to build a railroad, then a fort, more railroad and another fort, until there was no room left for rebels. With this in mind, Halleck translated Grant's message before forwarding it to Sheridan on October 12.[72]

"General Grant wishes a position taken far enough south to serve as a base for future operations upon Gordonsville and Charlottesville." So far, so good, although Halleck's "future operations" is a term that weighs more heavily than Grant's "advance on that road." It is what comes next that counts. Grant had been suggesting that Sheridan stay ready for an opportunity and take advantage of it when and if "the enemy weakens himself sufficiently." Halleck, however, left Sheridan no discretion as to the method—the place "must be strongly fortified and provisioned"—or the location— "some point in the vicinity of Manassas Gap would seem best suited for all purposes."[73]

The next morning Sheridan responded curtly that "if any advance is to be made on Gordonsville and Charlottesville," in addition to guarding a railroad and building a fortress, he would need all the men he had; "I have therefore countermanded the order directing the Sixth Corps to march to Alexandria." No doubt the appearance of Confederate infantry on Hupp's Hill that noon made him glad he had done so. But this did nothing, of course, to clear up the matter of the next move. Halleck and Stanton knew they were pushing Sheridan on this point, and probably surmised that the only way they were going to be successful was to keep Sheridan and Grant apart. Now Stanton weighed in, with a wire Sheridan received on the 14th: "If you can come here a consultation on several points is extremely desirable. I propose to visit General Grant, and would like to see you first."[74]

Right behind that wire came another, from Halleck, telling Sheridan what the first wire said, and hinting heavily at the intended outcome of the proposed meeting. "General Grant's wishes about holding a position up the valley as a basis against Gordonsville, etc., and the difficulties of wagoning supplies in the winter, may change your views about the Manassas Gap road." With a sigh, Sheridan abandoned for the moment his plan to attack whatever force Early now had at Fisher's Hill, and made plans to go to Washington. He also arranged, perhaps as a sop to General Grant's feelings, a cavalry raid on Charlottesville to destroy the railroad bridge there. On the 15th all of them rode away, Torbert and the cavalry accompanying

Sheridan as far as Front Royal. There they would push south toward Charlottesville while Sheridan headed for Rectortown and took the train to Washington.[75]

But when the party reached Front Royal on the morning of October 16, it was stopped by an anxious message from General Wright, who had been left in temporary command of the army. There had been a new development that made the situation even more confused, and a great deal more worrisome. Signal Corps clerks had copied and decoded a message being flagged by the Confederate station on Shenandoah Peak. The message was addressed to Jubal Early and signed by the formidable James Longstreet, commander of Lee's First Corps: "Be ready to move as soon as my forces join you, and we will crush Sheridan." General Wright was worried. "I shall hold on here until the enemy's movements are developed, and shall only fear an attack on my right, which I shall make every preparation for guarding against and resisting."[76]

"I first thought it a ruse, and hardly worth attention," Sheridan wrote years later of the Longstreet message, "but on reflection deemed it best to be on the safe side." Early had, after all, been oddly pugnacious three days before; things were quiet at Petersburg, perhaps Lee had dared to send Longstreet sneaking off on a distant mission. Deciding that he had best keep his army together until things were cleared up, Sheridan ordered Merritt's and Custer's cavalry divisions to return to Cedar Creek. Powell's division would stay in the Front Royal area and watch for Longstreet. "Make your position strong," Sheridan told Wright. "Close in Colonel Powell, who will be at this point. If the enemy should make an advance, I know you will defeat him. Look well to your ground and be well prepared."[77]

Sheridan's instincts, as usual, were correct. Old Jube had composed the Longstreet message, and had ordered it sent to himself in full view of the Federal watchers. After all, when presented with a nearly identical situation in August, Sheridan had retreated; perhaps he would do so again and give the Confederates a little room. Early thought his game was a harmless gamble, but as a result of it 6,000 Federal cavalrymen returned to Cedar Creek who otherwise would have been absent when he made his move.[78]

Wright seemed unsure of what he was supposed to do, and perhaps his uncertainty affected Crook. To their credit, it must be remembered that they were suddenly responsible for defending a piece of ground that Sheridan, only two months earlier, had declared undefensible. Back in August, when he had made his first advance up the Valley only to run into rumors that Early had been heavily reinforced (by Longstreet's corps, it was said then, too), Sheridan had declined to stay at Cedar Creek even though retreating was highly embarrassing. He had told Grant then that the position was "a very bad one, as I cannot cover the numerous rivers that lead in on both of my flanks to the rear." And he wrote later that the country miles to the north, near Harpers Ferry, offered the only "really defensive line in the Shenandoah Valley, for at almost any other point the open country and its peculiar topography invites rather than forbids flanking operations."[79]

Wright was an engineer, a thinking soldier from Connecticut who had graduated second in his West Point class and had been in the army for half of his forty-four years. He was a man of classical attributes—an athletic physique, finely molded head, luxuriantly curly locks, and a clear, incisive mind. His performance throughout the war had been so consistently solid that it had attracted little attention. Sheridan, however, had two reasons to be grateful to Wright: the elder general had been a signatory of the famous telegram describing Sheridan as "worth his weight in gold" and recommending his promotion to brigadier general; and although he outranked Sheridan by virtue of his time in grade as a major general, Wright neither protested Sheridan's appointment to command of the Army of the Shenandoah nor withheld his full cooperation. Sheridan later acknowledged his debt to Wright, but where the battle of Cedar Creek was concerned did not honor it.[80]

Wright had the support, in his temporary responsibilities, of another thoroughgoing professional in William Emory of XIX Corps. Emory, at fifty-three the crusty old man of the Federal high command in the Valley, had made a name as a surveyor after graduating from West Point in 1831, and had surveyed the boundary lines of both the northeastern and southwestern United States. Like Wright, Emory had from the beginning of the war set a standard of performance so consistently high that it seemed ordinary.[81]

Yet the response of Sheridan's subordinates to their new situation at Cedar Creek was oddly uneven. Wright was so worried about the right flank that he sent both Custer's and Merritt's cavalry divisions out there on their return from Front Royal to take positions echeloned back from the VI Corps right. But he apparently remained unconcerned about the left and neglected Sheridan's order to "close in Powell." With the exception of a single brigade, Powell's command remained at Front Royal, ten miles away, out of touch with the army.[82]

Wright did something else that seems inexplicable. Despite all the uncertainties of his situation, and contrary to Sheridan's exhortation to "be well prepared," Wright canceled a precautionary order that had been in effect for several days. Under that order, the entire army had been getting up at 2 A.M. and standing to arms, just to make sure they could not be surprised by a pre-dawn attack. Perhaps Wright thought this was excessive caution on Sheridan's part. In any case, Wright cancelled the order for the morning of the 19th.

Crook did send out a reconnaissance on the 18th. A brigade under Colonel Harris, whose performance in the skirmish five days before had been open to two interpretations, marched south, then came back in to report that the enemy was gone from its former camps. Now there occurred a dismaying breakdown in communications. It was assumed by all who heard Harris's report that he meant the enemy was gone from Fisher's Hill, where it always camped when in this part of the Valley. But Harris meant only that the Confederates were no longer on Hupp's Hill, where he had engaged them on the 13th. That, of course, could be seen from the Federal camps, and why Harris thought that to be a legitimate result of a full-scale reconnaissance remains a mystery. One wonders, too, how George Crook was so thoroughly misled.[83]

Not everyone was satisfied with Colonel Harris's report. General Wright, for one, thought something was amiss and ordered the job done again by a brigade from Emory's XIX Corps the next morning. For good measure, he told Torbert to send a brigade of cavalry along the Back Road while the infantry brigade pushed up the Valley Pike, and both commands were to keep going until they found the enemy.

Nor was Wright the only one worried. Various men of varying ranks were sniffing the wind that afternoon and evening, nostrils twitching, trying to confirm vague but urgent messages being sent from deep wells of intuition. General Crook, who had more reason than most to have developed a sixth sense about sneak attacks, seems not to have been among them.

The XIX Corps officer of the day that Tuesday was Colonel Stephen Thomas of the 8th Vermont, he whom Crook had thought cowardly at Winchester. Thomas was conscientious about his responsibility for the security of the corps that day, and kept up a careful, personal watch on the pickets and the nearby ground. During the afternoon, while scanning the terrain across Cedar Creek with his field glasses, Colonel Thomas spotted two civilians. They were dressed as farmers or laborers, but their manner did not fit their dress. Thomas picked up a sense of urgency in their conversation, saw them point now and again to various parts of the Federal line. Were they exhibiting idle curiosity or something more? If there was no enemy army in the area, who could they be? (The evidence that they were, in fact, General John Gordon and Jed Hotchkiss, is circumstantial but intriguing.)[84]

Worried but unsure of his worry, Thomas went to General Emory and reported what he had seen. General Emory, not sure what to make of it, sent the colonel to General Wright to repeat the story. General Wright, whose own worries were focused on the right, not on the left where Thomas had seen the mysterious civilians, thought there was no reason for alarm. In any case, he said, there would be a strong reconnaissance first thing in the morning, and then they would know what was going on.[85]

Another officer who felt twitchy that afternoon was Captain Henry DuPont, who as Crook's chief of artillery had responsibility far beyond his rank. As an artilleryman, DuPont could not stand the thought of losing a gun, and he kept thinking about how two of his three batteries were sitting out on that lonely hill with only Thoburn's little division for company, and a steep ravine between them and the rest of the army. Crook, he says, protested the isolation of the First Division, but was ignored. DuPont kept going around asking who was guarding all that rough country out beyond the left of the line, toward the river and the Massanutten. "The invariable reply was that our left was protected by Powell's cavalry division," DuPont recalled, "which was not at all satisfactory to me as nobody seemed to be informed as to its exact position: I even went so far as to ride out beyond our left to try to locate it but returned after going some distance and seeing nothing."[86]

The signs and portents continued. Lieutenant George H. Putnam (son of the prominent New York publisher) thought the evening was "milder in its temperature than some of the autumn nights that had preceded it. I remember lying out on the turf with a group of comrades," admiring the low profile of the Blue Ridge far to the east and the higher bulk of nearby Massanutten to the southeast. Suddenly, "there came from one of the upper slopes of Massanutten a series of flash-lights that looked for the moment as if a group of shooting stars had been suspended over the tree tops. 'The Rebs are signalling again,' was the word." Putnam and his friends in the 176th New York thought this ominous—forces of considerable size, with missions of some importance, must be on the move if they had to relay signals at night by way of Shenandoah Peak. But the Federal soldiers were not worried; their commanders were surely watching, too, and taking steps.[87]

Colonel Thomas, who had been reassured not at all by General Wright's attitude, stayed in the saddle all evening and into the night, prowling and checking. After making his midnight tour of the pickets, he rode alone out into the empty country, listening and watching. He made his way down into a ravine.

"Surrender, you damned Yankee!" came a sudden bark, and ominous forms materialized in the moon shadows.

"No, sir! It's too early in the morning!" Thomas wheeled his horse, dug in spurs, and the startled animal lunged up the steep bank in a spattering of bullets. Man and beast came unhurt back into their lines. For the moment there was no way to know; had the colonel run into enemy pickets? Or worse?[88]

Meanwhile, Crook's officer of the day was less fortunate. He, too, went outside the lines, to investigate sounds he assumed were made by patrolling Federal cavalry. He was taken prisoner by Confederate infantry. Now he alone among the Federals on Cedar Creek knew what was about to happen, and there was nothing he could do.[89]

Chapter 5

The Firebrand and the Future King: October 18, 1864

"The 18th of October in the Shenandoah Valley," remembered an officer who was there, "was such a day as few have seen who have not spent an autumn in Virginia—crisp and bright and still in the morning; mellow and golden and still at noon; crimson and glorious and still at the sunsetting; just blue enough in the distance to soften without obscuring the outline of the mountains; just hazy enough to render the atmosphere visible without limiting the range of sight."[1]

"As evening closed above the valley," continued Major A. Bayard Nettleton of the Federal 2nd Ohio Cavalry, "the soft pleadings of some homesick soldier's flute floated out through the quiet camp, while around a blazing campfire an impromptu glee club of Ohio boys lightened the hour and their own hearts by singing the songs of home. An unusually large letter-mail arrived that evening and was distributed to the men, which reminds me that the First Connecticut Cavalry, belonging to Custer's division, had a unique and pleasant manner of announcing the arrival of the mail: the regimental trumpeters, constituting a sort of cornet band, would form in front of the colonel's tent and play 'Home, Sweet Home,' sometimes following that immediately with 'The Girl I Left Behind Me.' "[2]

There was no such peace and relaxation in the Confederate camps five miles away. As the mellow afternoon softened into evening on Fisher's Hill, all was bustle and rising tension as

Major General Stephen Dodson Ramseur, looking much older than his twenty-seven years, formed the men of his division into column. They moved with a little more snap than the other Confederate divisions showed; Ramseur was a stickler for precision, a bit of a martinet in fact, but was so earnestly devoted to the Southern cause and oblivious to danger in combat that his men had come to trust and respect him despite his hard, West Point ways. They also had forgot how young he was, which was easy to do, so thoroughly was his age belied by his confident air of command, prematurely balding head, full beard and weary eyes. His men stepped lively.[3]

He told them what they needed to know of the plan he had helped thresh out at a 2 P.M. meeting of Early's commanders and staff officers. Only John Pegram had dissented from the plan advocated by Jed Hotchkiss and John Gordon. Pegram was not flourishing in this war. Although a West Pointer and a division commander, he was still only a brigadier general; despite reputable service as a cavalryman out west under Nathan Bedford Forrest, his reputation was overshadowed—especially since he had insisted on returning to fight in his native Virginia —by that of his young brother William, a brilliant artillerist who had taken the place of John Pelham in the affections of Lee. Pegram had gone out to take a personal look at the Federal lines and had come back in with a plan to turn their right, and had argued his idea persistently until it was clear that Early was committed to assailing the enemy left.

Ramseur knew exactly what was in store for his men on their six-mile march, because along with Gordon and Hotchkiss he had gone over almost the entire route late that afternoon. Ramseur ordered each man issued 60 rounds of ammunition (40 in the cartridge box, 20 more stuffed into pockets), briefed on the need for absolute silence, and stripped of tin cups, canteens and any other nonessentials that might clank or jingle. Then, after a splendid sunset and a long twilight, when the stars finally began to glitter in the crystalline sky, Ramseur's division marched east, across the Valley Pike.

And halted. General Gordon had been summoned to Early's headquarters. There was a problem. General Pegram, after his plan had been rejected that afternoon, had gone up on Shenandoah Peak to take his own look at the enemy positions. Now he had returned to report that the Federals were building new earthworks, extending across the very road Gordon was planning to take around the Federal left. The attack was doomed, said Pegram, it must be abandoned.[4]

It would have been easy to suspect Pegram of raising a self-serving alarm, but what he had seen was real. Crook had ordered the rather perfunctory earthworks fronting the position of his Second Division—that of Rutherford Hayes, behind Thoburn's First Division—continued out to the left. The 9th West Virginia had been detailed to move out three-quarters of a mile and work on this detached new line, which Crook did not intend to man because he lacked the troops, but was building as a precaution.[5]

Early had no way of knowing that what Pegram had seen was only a minor threat to his plan, but he held firm. The movement would continue. He did make one change, however; Kershaw's division, instead of attacking along the Valley Pike, would ease across Cedar Creek farther south, halfway between the pike and the river. Now their first objective would be not the formidable earthworks of XIX Corps but the lesser and more isolated fortifications of Thoburn's division. Thus Kershaw's force would more quickly get within supporting distance of Gordon's, in case what Pegram had seen turned out to be a serious problem. By the time all this was worked out, more than an hour of darkness had passed. At about 8 P.M. the Second Corps finally moved out.

They marched to the southeast, along the foot of Fisher's Hill to the Shenandoah a mile away. They forded the river and, still heading eastward, began to climb a gently rising hollow toward the heights of Massanutten Mountain. On their left, a protruding ridge concealed them from any observer to the north until they gained the cover of the forest higher up, a mile from the river. There, as John Gordon remembered it, "striving to suppress every sound, the long gray line like a great serpent glided noiselessly along the dim pathway above the precipice."[6]

One who made that night-long march, Captain Samuel D. Buck of the 13th Virginia, wrote of it before his memories mellowed quite so much, and called the dim pathway "a pig's path." For two miles they slipped and stumbled and clambered to eastward, over treacherous chunks of shale and fallen logs, through tangles of brambles and saplings, with the Shenandoah sometimes glimmering through the trees a hundred feet and more below them to their left. It was hard going, but it was worse stopping; the night had turned brightly cold, the men had been thoroughly soaked fording the river, and when they were not marching they began to shiver. Warming fires were, of course, out of the question; the town of Strasburg slumbered a little more than a mile to the north, and presumably there were Union pickets just across the water, watching the open fields and the Front Royal road, listening to the murmurings of the clear October night.[7]

"When the head of the column was reaching the Yankee vidette," a captain in the 21st Mississippi recalled, "the line of Rebs, with heads up, hand to ear to catch any sound or order from the front, like a monstrous reptile moved along the foot of the mountain. Not a word was uttered except in a very low tone, and that with mouth to ear. The occasional low croak of a tree frog seemed to admonish us of the impending storm." Few in the column felt the mixed emotions of Captain Buck, who was marching under stern discipline where he had once ambled away the endless days of childhood: "Every tree was familiar to me. I used to hunt squirrels and partridges all over these grounds, but now I was hunting men, and found game plentiful."[8]

There was little to do, even for a major general, but keep walking (leading his horse), and Dodson Ramseur was probably glad to have the time to think; he had much to ponder, a great deal more than the coming roar of guns and chance of dying. He had been a major general for only four months, a time of high adventure during which he had had a disastrous reverse and an exhilarating personal triumph. But his career was not much on his mind that night. Rather it was Nellie, his bride for the past eleven months and three weeks, on whom his thoughts centered.

He had become enamored of Ellen Richmond in the fall of 1862, while recovering from a grave wound received at the battle of Malvern Hill that July. It had been a long, difficult, but nonetheless rewarding convalescence. He had managed to retain possession of his mangled right arm thanks to an enlightened surgeon (who, after Ramseur had been disabled and in pain for months, used his scalpel to remove bits of cloth from the wound rather than the limb itself). In November Ramseur had been promoted to brigadier general and given a brigade in Robert Rodes's division, despite the fact that the Seven Days' battles (of which Malvern Hill was the last) had been his first major combat test as a regimental commander. And as if that were not enough, he had fallen in love.

She lived in Milton, North Carolina, just south of the Virginia border and not far from Danville. That was a long 135 miles northeast of his home in Lincolnton, in the Catawba River Piedmont country northwest of Charlotte. But it was Ramseur's mother's home, and he had visited there from time to time. In November of 1862, while visiting his uncle in Milton, Ramseur came to know Ellen, whom he had doubtless met before, but whom he now saw with different eyes. She was, he soon proclaimed, his "long cherished ideal of womanly perfection." She was also a great deal like him—small, pert, brown haired and bright, with large brown eyes glowing from a delicately formed oval face—and no wonder; she was his cousin. By the time he was strong enough to join his new command, in January of 1863, they were engaged.

He loved her passionately and volubly, which was the way he embraced every enthusiasm of his life. Thus, while still a boy, he had become ardent about his Presbyterian religion, once assuring his sister in a letter from boarding school that he was spending his Sundays "in such a way I think will please my Father in Heaven, and will be beneficial to my never dying soul." Even at that age, Ramseur's passions were neither shallow nor brief. Four years later he was proclaiming his faith to his best friend and future brother-in-law, George Schenk. One did not have to leave happiness or profits behind to become a good Christian, said Ramseur, God wanted His children to be "fervent in spirit, diligent in business, serving the Lord." Schenk should give his heart "completely, unreservedly to God," Ramseur advised. "This alone is peace; this alone is true happiness."[9]

As with God, so with Country. He was determined to serve his beloved United States by going to West Point and becoming an army officer. Although he was the eldest son (second of nine children) of a prominent Lincolnton merchant whose ancestors had prospered in the town for a century, Ramseur's appointment to West Point was not easy to arrange. He was rejected in 1853, and spent two years at Davidson College improving his academic credentials. Thanks to help from a new superintendent of Davidson, former West Pointer Daniel Harvey Hill, he finally got the coveted appointment in 1855, in the first of the new five-year courses. Once there, however, he decided that it was not the whole country he loved, but the South.[10]

He was repelled by the "scheming, cold-hearted North," where people were motivated by love of money and acted toward one another with "cold distrust and mean deceit, which is inbred with the Yankees." Whether or not some of this resentment had to do with the fact that the Northerners had much better schooling, and therefore usually an easier time of it at the academy, is hard to say. But his attitude became more and more entrenched, and when his sister went north to school in Philadelphia, he admonished her that "I would much prefer your intimate friends to be Southerners."[11]

As sectional passions became inflamed, so did Ramseur's. In the summer of 1856, as he observed the presidential election campaign, he became convinced that "an awful crisis is approaching." Northern abolitionists and "black Republican hellhounds" were mounting an assault on the basic, sacred rights of the Southern states. Chief among these, of course, was their right to sanction slavery, "the very source of our existence," wrote Ramseur, whose merchant father owned 20 slaves at the time, "the greatest blessing for both master and slave that could have been bestowed upon us." Even though the abolitionists did not win the presidency in 1856, Ramseur believed that the country had been cut too deeply to heal, and that secession must come "at whatever cost." The South must prepare, he wrote, even as he was preparing, for that "most desperate of all calamities—civil war."[12]

His animosity was further fueled the following year when his father's business partner, a Northerner, defrauded the elder

Ramseur of most of his considerable wealth. Dodson raged, vowed revenge, promised to leave the army soon after graduation so he could earn more money to help the family. He was disabled for a time by severe headaches.

There was considerably more misfortune to come, but Ramseur persevered. He was promoted to cadet sergeant, then demoted for showing favoritism in assigning sentry duty, then in 1859 was promoted again to captain of cadets, the highest rank attainable at the academy. He thought that would be his last year at West Point—the army had decided to abandon its experiment with five-year classes and graduate Ramseur's class in 1859. But to his bitter disappointment, the decision was rescinded, and graduation postponed. In December of that difficult year his mother, to whom he had been exceedingly close, died.

Despite all this, Ramseur retained not only his high academic standing (in the top third of his class) but the high regard of his peers. He was still animated by his boyhood passions—the religion that suffused his life, the love of the South and everything it stood for, along with the corollary hatred of the North and its abolitionists—but they were layered over now with both his natural reserve and a new veneer of gravity imposed by his private griefs. One plebe, no doubt awed by Ramseur's senior rank, always remembered the "dark-eyed, stern, dignified Ramseur of North Carolina."[13]

He had achieved that precarious balance of characteristics that inspires in other men admiration rather than envy. He was deeply religious, yet enjoyed flirting with the girls—even Northern girls, whom he found to be "bold" and "immodest" —and was fond of raising a tankard of rum flip down at Benny Havens's off-limits tavern; thus leavened, his religion became to others an interesting model rather than a stern admonition. He was just as fervent in his political beliefs and his personal loyalties, yet was unfailingly controlled and polite in his expression of them; thus he was listened to, and liked, by those who might otherwise have reviled him.

So it was that as his graduation day finally approached, in the spring of 1860—with the flames of sectional hatred raging in the country and casting their angry red glow into the academy—Ramseur and a handful of classmates were given a nonregulation farewell party. Its location was the infamous Benny Havens's. The hosts were the two wild men, George Custer of Ohio and Tom Rosser of Texas, along with Rosser's roommate John Pelham of Alabama. The guests included Wesley Merritt of Illinois, who thought Ramseur was the most universally beloved member of the class of '60; and probably Henry DuPont of Delaware, a special friend of John Pelham.

It was a long and boisterous night. They drank and laughed and drank and sang, especially the old hymn to the cadets' beloved tavern: "We'll sing our reminiscences of Benny Havens, O." One verse especially, a study in sophomoric irony, would be remembered: "To our comrades who have fallen, one cup before we go, / They poured their life-blood freely out *pro bono publico.* / Tall marble points the stranger to where they rest below; / They lie forgotten far away from Benny Havens, O." In the early hours of the morning, with Fanny Custer's toast—to the finest class ever to go through West Point—reverberating pleasantly in their minds, they weaved laughing out into the darkness, toward graduation and war.[14]

Ramseur was assigned to the artillery, and then to posts at Fort Monroe, Virginia, and Washington City. For a year he watched the country slowly, creakingly break apart. During the first week of April 1861, although North Carolina had not yet decided to join the Confederacy, he could stand it no longer and resigned his commission. A few weeks later he was a major of North Carolina artillery, in command of the prestigious battery named for the governor of the state.[15]

The Ellis Artillery comprised a company of gentlemen who had ambled into the war to see if they couldn't lend a hand without any serious inconvenience to themselves. Ramseur began by ordering them to enlist for the duration of hostilities or get out. Some, aghast at the thought of being ordered about by a social inferior, went home. The rest discovered that their social inferior had only just begun. He drilled them, and schooled them, and then drilled them some more. It went on without end for weeks, then months, until the Raleigh newspapers were debating whether he would ever take his battery to the fighting. It was the spring of 1862 before he joined the embattled forces on the Peninsula, and even then for one reason and another his battery saw virtually no action.[16]

In April a newly organized regiment of North Carolina infantry elected Ramseur its colonel. The delighted young commander joined the men in Raleigh and commenced his drilling program again, but there was little time left for that—the crisis of the Peninsular Campaign was at hand. The 49th North Carolina was summoned to Petersburg, arrived early in June, but beyond a few skirmishes became involved in no serious fighting, even during the six days of grinding, incessant combat that ended that month. July 1, however, was the last of the Seven Days and a different story.

Ramseur's regiment was part of a division commanded by his former teacher and benefactor, Major General Daniel Harvey Hill of North Carolina. Late on that hot July afternoon, in a continuation of the confused bungling that had plagued the Confederate army throughout the Seven Days, Hill led a misguided, ill-timed charge against McClellan's impregnable position on Malvern Hill. "It was not war," General Hill grieved later, "it was murder." Ramseur kept his 500-man regiment in the forefront of the doomed charge; in a few minutes the 49th North Carolina had lost 100 casualties, including Ramseur. In his first significant battle he was met by the bullet that nearly cost him his arm, gained him a wife and won him a general officer's wreath.[17]

When Ramseur was finally able to join his new brigade at Fredericksburg in January (and, reflexively, to begin drilling the men until they dropped) he made two significant new acquaintances. He was still in Stonewall Jackson's Second Corps, but under a different division commander; Harvey Hill had been transferred, his place taken by an impressive, thirty-three-year-old Virginian, Brigadier General Robert E. Rodes. Ramseur took over his brigade from the temporary command of Colonel Bryan Grimes of North Carolina, one of the few planters to do any fighting in the Civil War. (Grimes had led a 500-man regiment into action at Fair Oaks and Seven Pines, in the Peninsular Campaign; afterward only he and 38 enlisted men were still standing.)

On the first of May 1863, when the Army of the Potomac

crossed the Rappahannock River west of Fredericksburg, Ramseur's brigade was in the vanguard of the force that stopped the Federal advance and drove it back to a dusty little crossroads tavern with the outsized name of Chancellorsville. Ramseur's drilling habits more than paid off as he maneuvered his command with polished skill through the tangled terrain. Bryan Grimes remembered Stonewall Jackson watching Ramseur's performance approvingly, muttering, "Press them, Colonel."[18]

The next day, Rodes's division led the way as Jackson took most of Lee's army on a daylight flanking march around the unsuspecting Federals' right. But when Jackson's Second Corps thundered down on the astonished Federal XI Corps and sent it running back toward the Rappahannock, Ramseur was assigned a secondary role. To his intense frustration he was placed in support of a timid and hesitant brigade commander who managed to keep himself, and consequently Ramseur, pretty much out of action all day. But on May 3 Ramseur got all the fighting he wanted.

With Jackson badly wounded and Jeb Stuart in command of the Second Corps, the Confederates attacked the Federal army, which had regrouped and entrenched in front of Chancellorsville. After making some initial headway, the attack stalled. The weary Confederates, shaken by the loss of Jackson and by the Federals' surprisingly strong defense, began to lose not only momentum but cohesion; entire units refused to attack when ordered to do so, and huddled on the ground. The victory was slipping away when Ramseur heard a brigade commander refuse an order to attack, and shouted to the staff officer, "Give me the order and I will charge." Literally walking over their prostrate comrades (Bryan Grimes deliberately stamping on the head of a high-ranking officer), the North Carolinians breasted the waves of enemy fire and rolled over the Federal breastworks facing them. They almost had to fall back for lack of support, but the Stonewall Brigade lent a hand and they held on. The Federals had lost the initiative and would soon retreat across the river.[19]

As the firing slowed, Jeb Stuart ordered the men nearby to cheer Ramseur's North Carolinians. Their commander, said Stuart, should be a major general. Their commander looked around him at the carnage—more than half of his 1,509 men were dead or wounded—and burst into tears. That evening, a shell fragment struck Ramseur a glancing but laming blow on the shin, very nearly adding his name to the casualty list again.[20]

Ramseur was proud of his men and their contribution to the victory at Chancellorsville, but he chafed at the lack of public recognition they—and he—received. At the time he did not know that Jackson, while disabled with the wound that would kill him, had praised Ramseur's performance in a message to Lee, or that Lee had repeated the praise in a letter to the governor of North Carolina. All Ramseur knew at the time was that other troops were getting better treatment in the newspapers.[21]

Ramseur professed not to care about newspaper coverage. Throughout the war he permitted only one photograph to be taken of him because, he said, he was afraid his likeness would be used in unfitting ways. He made a point of telling his friend David Schenck that no newspaper correspondent was ever stabled in Ramseur's tent. Yet in private, especially with Schenck, he checked constantly on what the newspapers were saying and indicated strongly how others might influence them. After Chancellorsville, Ramseur complained to Schenk that the Richmond papers always favored Virginians and would surely not give his brigade its due; urged him to clip all references appearing in North Carolina; and sent him a copy of his official report for reading to "particular friends." It was not for publication, of course; that would be "highly unmilitary."[22]

Ramseur's brigade was the first Confederate unit to cross the Potomac on Lee's second invasion of the North. Rodes's division marched to Carlisle, Pennsylvania, and spent a pleasant couple of days there while Lee worked on a plan. When the army was ordered to concentrate near Gettysburg, Rodes had to march his men to the southeast to get there.

They arrived at mid-afternoon on the first day of fighting. They came on the field to the north of the contending lines, which were then a mile west of the town, with the Federals backed against Seminary Ridge. Rodes moved immediately to attack the enemy right, which was anchored on the north end of the ridge. The Federals refused their flank with a hasty deployment behind a stone wall, and cut to pieces Rodes's first two attacking brigades.

Then Ramseur came up, marshaled the survivors along with his own brigade, and swept the defenders from the stone wall. As the men on that part of the field saw it, that success cracked the Union line and started the rout of XI Corps through the town of Gettysburg. It was reported that Rodes and Ramseur led the chase and were the first Confederates to enter the town.

Ramseur was in a frenzy, but even so did not quite forget his piety. "Damn it," he yelled to an orderly at one point, "tell them to send me a battery! I have sent for one half a dozen times!" Immediately Ramseur threw up his hands, looked imploringly skyward and added, "God Almighty, forgive me for that oath."[23]

From the streets of the town, Ramseur could see the Federals regrouping on Cemetery Hill and wanted to keep the momentum going by attacking them and taking that high ground. But Ewell held back, wanting more men and guns, and the opportunity was lost. When the story is thus told, from Ramseur's point of view, the participation of Jubal Early's division (arriving as it did after Ramseur had attacked the stone wall) is but a footnote. And the role of John Gordon's brigade, which seemed so decisive to him, does not deserve mention.

Remarkably, in the heavy fighting of the next two days that decided the course of the war's most fateful battle, the men of the Second Corps were little more than spectators. They held the left while the right shattered itself against the guns of the Peach Orchard and the Devil's Den and the Round Tops; then retreated angrily, undefeated, hoping that Meade would follow, attack and give them their chance, depressed by the consequences of a defeat in which they had not even been engaged. From the west came news of the fall of Vicksburg; the Union had grasped the Mississippi River, sundering the Confederacy. "I look the thing square in the face," Ramseur wrote Nellie, "and am prepared to undergo dangers and hardships and trials to the end." He no longer spoke of "victory or death," as he had so often; now he thought that if the South could endure, it might achieve "a glorious and honorable peace."[24]

Ramseur had hoped, until the Gettysburg Campaign had intervened, to marry Ellen that summer. Now he named September 17 as the wedding date. This seemed to catch Ellen off guard. A cousin protested on her behalf that she could not be ready in time, to which Ramseur sent the steely response that he insisted on "the immediate consummation of our engagement." Nellie asked for a two-week delay, was granted one week, and was told that she was not sufficiently "impressed with the uncertainties of military life." As it turned out, though, she had plenty of time.[25]

During September and much of October, Lee and Meade probed each other so frequently, looking for an advantage while sending reinforcements out west to grapple for possession of Tennessee, that Ramseur could not leave his command. He wished desperately for a battle to settle the issue, and wrote anguished letters about "cruel, cruel war." Not until October 28 did he achieve the consummation for which he had so devoutly wished.[26]

During his month-long honeymoon, Ramseur missed Jubal Early's humiliation at Rappahannock Bridge, but returned in time for the frustration of the Mine Run Campaign and the long, slow starvation of the winter. He continued to drill his men, whether they had food or not, and made them clean their camps and repair roads and practice regimental and brigade maneuvers—anything to keep them busy. His brigade was not immune to the plague of desertions sweeping the army (those who deserted and were captured Ramseur marched out in front of the brigade and shot), but his men were better off for his stern regimen, and knew it. On January 27 they unanimously reenlisted for the duration of the war "without condition"—a move that stimulated imitation throughout the army and earned more praise from General Lee.[27]

But Ramseur was practically oblivious to both the rigors of the winter and the approval even of the beloved Lee; Nellie joined him in January, and for three months he was with her every night. It was, glowed Ramseur to his friend Schenck, "a cozy, comfortable, *spooney* time." But it was soon over. When April brought its warm breezes, dogwood blooms and rumors of Grant, Nellie left for North Carolina. She did not know it yet, but as she left the killing fields of northern Virginia, she carried within her a budding new life.

Ramseur faced front again, and assessed the military situation. He hoped for a decisive campaign, one that would dismay the North, cause the defeat of Lincoln in the fall elections and make possible peace negotiations between the new president and an independent South. It seemed possible. Ramseur was eager to do his part. "Surely our Father will bless His faithful people."[28]

The decisive campaign that Ramseur had wished for began on the 5th of May when the Federals came across the Rapidan again and the two armies groped into contact with each other in the tangled Wilderness. On that day Ramseur's brigade was in reserve while the brigades of John Gordon and Junius Daniel fended off repeated, ferocious attacks on Ewell's left, and to the right, or south, A. P. Hill's 14,000-man Third Corps held its own against a fearful onslaught by 38,000 Federals. That evening's dispositions left a mile-wide hole between Ewell's right—where Ramseur was in reserve—and Hill's left.

The next morning while the reinforced Federals drove Hill back, only to be repulsed when James Longstreet finally arrived to support Hill, all was quiet on the Confederate left (while Gordon, Early and Ewell argued about Gordon's plan to turn the Federal right) until mid-afternoon. Then the Federal IX Corps commander, Ambrose Burnside, as usual showing up late and in the wrong place, stumbled into the gap between Ewell and Hill.

It was Ramseur who had to meet him, a single brigade against a Federal corps. But under Burnside's leadership, IX Corps was never much of a threat; Burnside was a man of genial, self-admitted incompetence who nevertheless was continually being thrust into positions where he could order the slaughter of thousands. As the unwilling commander of the Army of the Potomac at Fredericksburg, he had piled up his own dead like cordwood, and later he would stack more thousands of sacrifices to his ineptitude at Petersburg's Crater. On this day he was no smarter, but apparently was not in a sacrificial mood. Finding himself poised with his entire corps in front of an enormous gap in the enemy's line, just when the contending armies were at their limits of exertion and had reached the climactic moment of decision, Burnside ran into Ramseur's skirmish line. And retreated.

It was not much of a fight, but Ramseur was in the right place at the right time and stabilized the line. That evening Gordon tried to change the balance with his flank attack on the Federal right, but ran out of daylight. After two days of dreadful carnage—18,000 Federal casualties and about 8,000 Confederate—the two armies grudgingly admitted a draw and sidled off to come to grips again at Spotsylvania.

The Confederates got to that vital crossroads first and by May 9 were building formidable entrenchments in front of it, in the shape of a large hairpin. Ewell's corps manned the horseshoe-shaped northernmost bulge of the line while the First Corps lines angled away to the southwest and those of the Third Corps to the southeast. Ramseur's brigade was placed in the western face of the salient known as the Mule Shoe; behind him, Early's division (under the temporary command of John Gordon while Early ran the Third Corps) formed a secondary line across the throat of the hairpin.[29]

In the misty dawn of May 12, Winfield Scott Hancock's Federal II Corps came smashing into the point of the Mule Shoe, forcing open a potentially disastrous rift between the two wings of Lee's army. John Gordon's division absorbed the terrible momentum of Hancock's blow and, just barely, held together the almost-severed Confederate lines. Rodes had to change front to align with Gordon and counterattack to the north in a desperate attempt to restore the line before Hancock could regroup or be reinforced.[30]

Once again all could see the benefit of Ramseur's ceaseless drilling as he wheeled his brigade into the new line, on Gordon's left, and, looking to one of his officers like "an angel of war," led a charge into what a soldier in an adjoining brigade thought looked like "the very jaws of death." It was nearly so. The counterattack had hardly begun when Ramseur's horse went down and a bullet found his right arm again—this time below the elbow. Bryan Grimes quickly stepped in to keep the men moving, while Ramseur, his bleeding arm hanging useless at his side, found and mounted another horse and tried to keep up with his men.[31]

The brigade gained their old breastworks, but the Federals clung to the other side of them, and for the next twenty hours the two lines lay nearly face-to-face on their respective slopes, butchering one another with an almost-continuous, roaring fusillade that completely severed one twenty-two-inch-thick oak tree. They brained one another with clubbed muskets, skewered one another with bayonets on pieces lofted over the works, even reached out and dragged each other to doom by the hair. During that endless morning, afternoon, and night Ramseur stayed with his men, ignoring his painful but not serious wound. He had two more horses killed under him and felt four more bullets pluck at his uniform. But he and his men endured until notified, long after midnight, that the engineers had completed a new secondary line within the Mule Shoe—known ever afterward as the Bloody Angle—and that they could at last disengage.[32]

Ramseur received the personal thanks of Lee and warm congratulations from Rodes and Ewell, but it was Gordon whose role that day became legendary. Ramseur continued to protest that he did not care for newspaper attention, that he kept no reporters at his headquarters, and so on. But when he found a report in a British newspaper that gave him proper credit and compared his brigade favorably with the legendary Stonewall Brigade, he carefully cut it out and sent it to Nellie. And just as Gordon did not remember Ramseur being on the right of his brigade at Gettysburg, so Ramseur, when he recounted the battle of Spotsylvania in his official report and his letters home, did not recall seeing Gordon there.

He did remember Gordon, however, when telling how a few days later, during a reconnaissance to the right of the army, Ewell's corps had run into trouble and Gordon's men had been driven back in confusion. Ramseur, on Gordon's right, had not only held on but had counterattacked, driving into the enemy line until nearly enveloped, then backing away to form a solid line of resistance.[33]

In the reorganization that followed Spotsylvania, Ramseur was promoted to divisional command. Early took over the Second Corps from the ailing Ewell, Gordon was made a major general and moved to permanent command of Edward Johnson's division, and Ramseur took over Early's old division from Gordon. Ramseur had only a few days to take hold of his new command when he and Old Jube inaugurated their new responsibilities with substantial foulups.

The debacle came on May 30. The Second Corps, with Anderson's in support, was ordered to move rightward again and stop Grant's persistent, sideways advance. They were in flat, swampy country now, where tortuous streams and bands of woods made travel and maneuver very difficult. Ramseur's division was in the lead when Old Jube found the Federals at Bethesda Church, and came under fire from a single enemy cannon in the woods off to their left. Ramseur asked permission to attack. Early held back, then approved. Quickly, Ramseur advanced John Pegram's brigade, with Colonel Edward Willis commanding, in a line of battle. The Federal gunners limbered their piece and galloped away; the Confederates pursued, through the woods and into a field.

There they came under a slaughtering fire from Union batteries massed behind an entrenched line in the next stand of woods. They were up against the Federal V Corps, and they were cut to pieces. A soldier in the 49th Virginia wrote later that the line "melted away as if by magic." Colonel Willis was mortally wounded (in his last moments telling a comrade, "I am no more afraid to die than I was to go into the battle"). It was a debacle, for which both Early and Ramseur were roundly criticized. Ramseur had attacked blindly, said one angry survivor, "without knowing anything about the ground or the force he was fighting," and "ought to be shot for the part he played in it."[34]

Four days later, Ramseur's promotion to major general was announced to the army. Nine days after that the Second Corps marched for the Shenandoah Valley. Ramseur's division scared Hunter's Federals away from Lynchburg, watched John Gordon's men do the bulk of the fighting at the Monocacy on July 9, and did little more than skirmish in front of Fort Stevens at Washington two days later. Until July 19 the new division commander's assignments consisted chiefly of marching. Apparently his men were marching well, however, for about that time Ramseur said in a letter to Nellie, "I may be pardoned for saying that I am making a reputation as Major General."[35]

On that day, the army was camped at Berryville but could not stay. Early had stopped Crook's small force with a surprise attack at the Shenandoah the day before, but four full divisions were right behind Crook, and an additional force of infantry and cavalry was coming down from Harpers Ferry. Early had to go before he was caught in the vise, and as he headed south he sent Ramseur west, with a brigade of mounted infantry commanded by Brigadier General John C. Vaughn, to cover the withdrawal of supplies and wounded men from Winchester.

The Federals approached from the north on the 20th. Ramseur was two miles north of the town with the infantry, while Vaughn ranged farther north, watching for the enemy. When he made contact, Vaughn was little concerned; he sent for a battery, and asked how far he should drive the enemy. But when Ramseur heard gunfire, about 4 P.M., it was coming his way.

The division marched north to meet Vaughn, who still was not worried. He was facing merely a regiment of infantry, another of cavalry, plus a battery, he said. Ramseur formed a line of battle and advanced confidently to eat this Federal force alive. But when the lines of battle made contact, Ramseur's was overlapped on the left by two hundred yards. Before his reserve brigade could extend the line, two threatened regiments on that flank, to everyone's surprise, broke and ran. Almost before Ramseur knew what had happened, his entire division had dissolved in what he fumed later was "perfect and unaccountable panic," and "the most perfect rout I ever saw." A few minutes later the Federals withdrew, taking with them four of Ramseur's guns and 267 prisoners.[36]

Ramseur was humiliated. Like Jubal Early, he knew immediately whom to blame: "My men behaved shamefully," he raged to Nellie, "they ran from the enemy. And for the first time in my life I am deeply mortified by the conduct of troops under my command." He knew his superior officers would understand—as they did, Early remarking only that Ramseur did not take the proper precautions before attacking, and Lee sug-

gesting he had been bested by a superior force—but, raged
Ramseur, "newspaper editors and stay at home croakers will sit
back in safe places and condemn me."[37]

Once again the newspapers that he professed to care so little
about were his main concern. Nellie saw through this, and
wrote a gentle, rare reproach. No one was censuring him, she
said, people "simply express regret that the affair should have
happened." He could not expect to achieve fame in war "without passing through some shadows for a moment, no man ever
did yet. Let us not succumb to the first trial of faith, but act
with firm confidence."[38]

Similar reassurances from friends and fellow officers eventually calmed Ramseur, but he remained fiercely determined to
expiate the reverse. His chance came on the morning of September 19, when Sheridan's VI Corps came ramming up out of
the Berryville Canyon and Ramseur's division was the only
force between the Federals and Winchester. Ramseur and his
men held their ground all morning in desperate fighting, anchored the Confederate right all afternoon, and that evening,
when Crook and the Federal cavalry routed Early's left, Ramseur's division kept its organization and conducted a fighting
retreat to Fisher's Hill. Whatever blot had been on his escutch-
eon was erased.

Nor was it replaced by the rout at Fisher's Hill three days
later; that embarrassment was shared equally by the whole
army. And by this time Ramseur was thinking less about military glory and more about home—about the child that was
about to be born there. "As *the day* approaches," he wrote
Nellie, "I grow more and more anxious to be with you. But
these recent battles and defeats will make it almost impossible
for me to leave this army." Now the hard-charging Ramseur
wanted the campaign to be over so he could take leave and go
home. He may have been a major general, but he was also a
twenty-seven-year-old: "How much do I regret to lose all this
lovely, precious time of our young life," he wrote to Ellen. "To
be separated from you is to lose it all."[39]

Such thoughts must have plagued him on that long night
march along Massanutten Mountain on October 18. And by
now his longing was even worse, for three days before, on Sun-

day, a terse message had come wigwagging down the Massanutten signal stations addressed to him. "The crisis is over," was all it said, "and all is well." He was a father. Nellie was all right. He went immediately to share his news with Bryan Grimes, now a close friend, and an especially sympathetic listener because his wife was also expecting. Ramseur poured out his joy and relief and loneliness for a while, and Grimes left. Minutes later he was back. His message had come. Grimes was a father, too. They sat under an old oak tree and talked for hours. The next day Ramseur wrote home pleading for details and adding, "Oh Me! I want to see you so bad!"[40]

With his division bringing up the rear, Ramseur missed the alarms and adventure experienced by the vanguard. Pioneers had spent the afternoon clearing and smoothing the trail as best they could without attracting attention, and sentries had been posted at various places to make sure the column took the correct turns. This was especially important when the men filed down off the mountain and into the bottom lands, with their network of farm roads. At one deceptive fork, no sentry had been left because a small downed tree lying across one path had offered a clear enough sign that the proper route was the other one. But when Gordon came to the place, saw the tree in the dark shadows and started down the other trail, he sensed something different. It was a vague sensation, but he halted the column with a whispered command sent rippling back along its serpentine length.

The tree was still there. It clearly blocked one path and invited them down the other. But Gordon thought it looked wrong. Precious minutes slid away while he sent staff officers to a home nearby to roust and interrogate an undoubtedly terrified farmer. Yes, he had used the road that day; yes, as a matter of fact, he had moved the tree out of the path he wanted and had thrown it into the other. "On such small things," Gordon wrote later, "sometimes hangs the fate of great battles."[41]

Then there were the enemy sentries. Someone in the advance spotted them and hissed a warning, stopping the column again. There were two of them, standing alongside a rail fence, directly in the Confederates' path. This was serious; shots fired now could ruin everything. A handful of men, led by an experi-

enced scout, would have to try to capture the sentinels without
making a sound. With agonizing care they slithered along the
base of the fence on the side opposite the sentries. Gordon
watched tensely, the Second Corps waited as quietly as it could,
wondering what the holdup was. The precious minutes passed.
At last the attackers were in position. They gathered themselves, leaped to their feet and leveled their muskets—at two
six-foot cedar trees. Forward march.[42]

They were approaching the river now, in good time despite
the delays. In fact, they would have to wait here for perhaps an
hour. There were real Federal cavalry pickets watching the ford
and the road leading from it; there was no way to cross the
river without alerting them. The attack was to begin at 5 A.M.,
and Gordon was to launch it from the Cooley farm about a
mile north of the river. From Shenandoah Peak Gordon had
seen the white farmhouse, shining in the sun like a beacon,
opposite and slightly behind the end of the Federal entrenchments. He reckoned it would take half an hour to reach the
farm, swing the men into a line of battle facing east, and
charge. At 4:30, then, he would unleash Colonel William H.
Payne's skimpy brigade of 300 cavalry to drive off the pickets.
It would be noisy, but there was no help for that. Meanwhile,
the men would wait.

Ramseur came forward now, and as his men filed quietly by
to take their positions near the river and rest in place, he and
Gordon sat on a rock outcrop and talked in muted tones. Ramseur talked about his baby, of course—he did not know yet
whether it was a boy or a girl—and of his ache to see his wife
and child. Whether Gordon knew by now that his own wife
was expecting—their baby would be born amid the awful fires
of April 1865—he did not record. But he liked the young hot-
blood, and no doubt listened with fatherly courtesy as Ramseur
expressed the hope that this battle would be decisive, so that in
its aftermath he could justifiably take leave and go home. He
would do his best to make it so. Then it was time to rejoin his
command. "Well, General," he said quietly, getting to his feet,
"I shall get my furlough today."[43]

The minutes flowed slowly by. Nearly nine thousand men lay
on their weapons or sat in whispering clumps, mere yards from

the tree-lined river. In mid-stream, the sleepy Federal videttes sat their horses, oblivious to the massive force assembled a stone's throw away. The moon had set. Straining Confederate eyes thought they could see a lightening of the eastern horizon. Every few minutes a staff officer would walk to the rear, find some cover, strike a match, read his watch and report back to Gordon.

"In the still starlit night," wrote Gordon, reliving the anxious hour years later, "the only sounds heard were the gentle rustle of leaves by the October wind, the low murmur of the Shenandoah flowing swiftly along its rocky bed and dashing against the limestone cliffs that bordered it, the churning of the water by the feet of the horses on which sat Sheridan's faithful pickets, and the subdued tones of half-whispers of my men as they thoughtfully communed with each other as to the fate which might befall them each in the next hour.[44]

"The whole situation was unspeakably impressive."

At about the time Ramseur's men arrived at the river east of Strasburg, Colonel Charles Russell Lowell of the Federal cavalry emerged from his tent west of Middletown. It was his habit to be up before reveille, which for his brigade was set for 4 A.M., to watch his men mutter and clink their way into readiness. This morning they would have a half hour; they were to ride south before first light and find Jubal Early's army.[45]

The day promised to be a delightful one, for an easy reconnaissance. The scene that confronted Lowell as he cleared the sleep from his head had been surveyed a few hours earlier by a fellow Third Division brigade commander, Colonel James H. Kidd of the Michigan Brigade. Kidd had been uneasy that night, and at 11 P.M. had been pacing his camp—to the right rear of Lowell's Reserve Brigade (with Custer's First Division farther to the northwest)—enjoying the bright October night despite his vague apprehension.

"The moon was full, the air crisp and transparent," Kidd recalled. "A more serene and beautiful scene could not be imagined. The spirit of tranquility seemed to have settled down, at last, upon the troubled Shenandoah. Far away, to the left, lay the army, wrapped in slumber. To the right, the outlines of the

Blue Mountains stood out against the sky and cast dark shadows athwart the Valley. Three-quarters of a mile away the
white tents of Custer's camp looked like weird specters in the
moonlight. Scarcely a sound was heard. A solemn stillness
reigned, broken only by the tread of the single sentry, pacing
his beat in front of headquarters." By the time Lowell got up,
the moon had set and a thick fog had oozed down the hollows
and streambeds to blanket the Valley floor.[46]

Lowell was twenty-nine years of age, slight, and fragile looking; anything but a prepossessing figure. His frame was small,
bony, all sharp angles, a small neck perched on thin shoulders
in support of an angular head. In his portraits, with his wavy
hair, large eyes and wispy mustache, Charlie Lowell had a fey
look about him. Here was no West Pointer, but a Harvard man,
valedictorian at that, with an insatiable appetite for books of
philosophy and poetry; no regular-army type, but an amateur
volunteer who as a Boston Brahmin had the political pull to get
rank fast (yet, oddly, was still a mere colonel); a veteran not of
the Indian wars but of endless tours of Europe; a man who
throughout his sickly youth had never ridden a horse. A cavalry officer whose favorite oath was "By Plato!"

Yet Lowell had been promoted, on his own merits, to the
command of a brigade of cavalry. What is more, this was no
ordinary, volunteer outfit, but was composed mostly of tough
regulars—one of the few regular brigades in the Army of the
Potomac and the only one with the Army of the Shenandoah.
It was, in the estimation of the hard-eyed Phil Sheridan, "one
of the best brigades of the army." And Sheridan's keen glance
had fallen more than once on the brigade commander; had
marked him, in fact, not only for promotion in rank (Lowell
did not know it, but his commission as a brigadier general was
signed and on its way from Washington) but for a much more
responsible command, one that would give "more scope to his
remarkable abilities as a leader of men." Others said later that
Sheridan was thinking of making Lowell chief of cavalry for the
Army of the Shenandoah. Obviously, Lowell was no ordinary
bookworm.[47]

In July, when Jubal Early had made his run at Washington
City, Lowell had been in command of a different, small brigade

posted at Vienna, Virginia, engaged in the arduous and thankless business of trying to protect Federal camps and supply lines from Mosby's Rangers. Until then Lowell's reputation for competence and bravery had been solid; on the day he chased Early's cavalry through Rockville, it began to flare into legend.

With his own 2nd Massachusetts and the two New York regiments of his brigade—the 13th and 16th—Lowell was pressing Early's rear guard, a brigade of cavalry under John McCausland. In the confusion caused by Early's threat, the Federal generals in and around Washington were still falling all over themselves, and Lowell's brigade was virtually alone in giving chase. His presence was a severe vexation to Early, who needed room to get safely across the Potomac at White's Ferry and back into Virginia. When Lowell's command was strung out in the streets of Rockville, where it had no room for maneuver, McCausland's cavalry turned and charged.

With unnerving suddenness the street in front of Lowell filled with straining horses pounding toward him—those of his own advance, running for their lives, and behind them rank after rank of the enemy, sabers up, coming hard. Lowell, a light, buoyant rider who somehow managed to look authoritative in the saddle, barked out an immediate—and incredible—order: "Dismount! And let your horses go!"

To tell a cavalryman to let his horse go in the face of the enemy was the equivalent of asking a seaman to scuttle his own ship in mid-ocean. But Lowell had seen at a glance that despite the advantage of having the new Spencer repeating carbines, his men had no chance if one-quarter of them were to act as horseholders. With all of them in the firing line, there was a chance. Hence the order. His men obeyed instantly.

As their horses stampeded away behind them, they all formed a line across the street, waited until the charging Confederates were almost on top of them, then opened fire. The sustained shock of the massed Spencers battered the charge to a halt. Lowell ran out in front of his men, waving his hat, and led them down the street, firing, driving the superior force of Confederates from the town. The horseless Federals were unable to resume the pursuit of Early, but they were able to return to camp with light casualties and a handsome bag of prisoners. It was a remarkable outcome to what had seemed a certain disaster, and no one doubted who had brought them out of it.[48]

Toward the end of July, Lowell was sent to the Valley to command a provisional brigade made of his 2nd Massachusetts and some other, fragmentary units. When Sheridan arrived a week later and reorganized the cavalry, Lowell's brigade was assigned to Wesley Merritt's First Division. During the long sparring between the armies that preceded pitched battle in the Shenandoah, Lowell's men were at the forefront, and were increasingly in awe of their bantam-rooster colonel.[49]

Horse after horse was shot from under him; he would lose an average of one a week for thirteen weeks. Dr. Oscar DeWolf, surgeon of the 2nd Massachusetts, reported seeing the frail Lowell fresh and cheerful after seventy hours without sleep, teasing his officers for looking bedraggled. For fifteen consecutive days beginning on August 16, Dr. DeWolf wrote, "Lowell's brigade was skirmishing every day, a kind of irregular fighting that no one outside the army immediately around him ever heard of, but which in several instances was very gallant, and always requiring that sleepless anxiety and devotedness for which Colonel Lowell was so remarkable."[50]

The officers and men of his ragtag brigade began to strive for the approval of this steely little colonel, who had something new to show them every day. Dr. DeWolf remembered an occasion when Lowell rode alone to a hilltop to make a reconnaissance, and came under fire from an enemy cannon. Lowell sat his jumpy horse quietly, taking a long look, while solid shot plowed the ground around him, then when he was through he rode slowly back to the column. This was not simple grandstanding, said the surgeon; Lowell wanted his men to understand that artillery fire was much less dangerous than it looked. "Incidentally," the doctor added, "he was educating his horse."[51]

Phil Sheridan witnessed a typical Lowell engagement during this trying period of probing and fending. "The Rebels had rails piled up to form breastworks," Lowell's orderly recalled, and from that excellent cover unleashed a volley at Lowell's four companies as they charged. The unnerved Federals stopped. "The Colonel rode out ahead of them and waved his saber and cheered them; then the men started, and he led them, and he was the first man to jump the rail-pile in to the Rebs; then they broke and ran, and the Colonel captured 67 privates and seven commissioned officers. General Sheridan's orderly told me that when the Colonel jumped the rail-pile, the General said, 'Lowell is a brave man.' "[52]

The respect was mutual. "I like Sheridan immensely," Lowell wrote in a letter home, "whether he succeeds or fails: he is the first general I have seen who puts as much heart and time and thought into his work as if he were doing it for his own exclusive profit. He works like a mill-owner or an iron-master, not like a soldier—never sleeps, never worries, is never cross, but isn't afraid to come down on a man who deserves it." Like most honest tributes, this one precisely described the giver, as well as the recipient.[53]

Lowell was born to a family of mill-owners and iron-masters in Boston on January 2, 1835. He was of the ninth generation of Massachusetts Lowells, who for two centuries had been predominant in the economic, legal, political and cultural affairs of New England. There was no need to look to West Point for an education; the best the country had to offer was available to Charlie Lowell as a matter of course. After attending two preparatory schools he entered Harvard at fifteen years of age, the youngest member of the class of 1854.

"He was unusually boyish in appearance," a classmate recalled, "with a ruddy countenance overflowing with health and *animal spirits,* and a manner somewhat brusque. He did not win popularity at once; but as his powers and character developed, and toned down the rather boisterous life and manner of the body, he came to be proudly acknowledged, without a dissenting voice, as the foremost man of the Class."[54]

On graduation, Lowell began a series of menial jobs designed to prepare him for leadership. It is not clear whose design this was—Lowell's own, his parents', or that of some other member of the family. It seems unlikely that it was his father's plan; the elder Lowell was living out his life in a kind of muted disgrace, having lost a sizable chunk of the family businesses in a financial panic that struck the country in 1837, while *his* father was abroad. No permanent harm had been done the family fortune, but Charles Russell Lowell, Senior, would never hold responsibility again. His life's work from then on was in the private library of the Boston Athenaeum. There he spent his days filling out file cards for the first catalog of that Brahmin institution's 100,000 books. In the sizable body of correspondence accumulated by the younger Lowell, the letters addressed to his father are extremely rare.

It was his mother to whom he wrote about his travels, his readings, his opinions and plans. Anna Cabot Jackson Lowell was the no-nonsense headmistress of a girls' finishing school that she founded and made successful after her husband's failure. She was a member of the Boston aristocracy—the Cabot, Jackson and Lowell families were thoroughly intertwined, she was her husband's third cousin—but she had no time for pretentious students. "Those who give themselves airs on no grounds whatever," she said once, "cannot be taught."

Young Charles went to work first in a commercial counting room in Boston, to learn bookkeeping. "He penetrated the mysteries rapidly," according to his employer, and the next year moved on to work in a Maryland iron mill as a laborer. There he studied the minutiae of handling not only iron, but men. He had not been among laborers before, and while he was a bit disoriented—he tried to organize singing classes to fill their idle hours, and sent home for good novels to improve their minds—his concern and sympathy for their struggles was genuine. He became convinced that the corporation, managed as it was by a paid agent, embodied the wrong approach to commercial affairs. He preferred the English tradition of companies run by managing directors who had a share in the ownership, and were thus inclined to be less rapacious in their methods.[55]

It is not surprising to find such an attitude expressed by a favorite nephew of the poet James Russell Lowell, whose position in the first rank of American letters rested above all on his celebration of the ordinary Yankee farmer; by a young man who counted as a strong influence and a close family friend Ralph Waldo Emerson, the foremost American philosopher of his time, high priest of Transcendentalism and oracle to such other luminaries as Henry David Thoreau. (Emerson's son Edward would become the young Lowell's admiring biographer.)

What is surprising is that the young Lowell seemed determined to live out his beliefs, to exercise and test them without the protection of his family fortune. As Edward Emerson explained it later, "he laid out the plan of his life on large lines, namely, to bring his powers and training to the service of his generation in a working life with those who had had less opportunities." The effort nearly killed him.

In the fall of 1855 Lowell took a head-office job at a rolling mill in Trenton, New Jersey. There he faced death for the first time, when coughing, fevers, weakness and then hemorrhaging lungs announced the onset of industrial New England's so-called "white plague"—tuberculosis. The disease was seldom cured, often fatal, but in this case the death sentence was commuted by a two-year sojourn in New Orleans, the West Indies, and then the Mediterranean. This was recommended by Lowell's doctor (and great-uncle), who further prescribed the absolute avoidance of strenuous activity until after the age of thirty (that would be 1865), and was arranged by another remarkable man, who set out to take a small hand in Lowell's affairs but instead found himself caught in a tremendous attraction.[56]

John Murray Forbes was to American commerce what Emerson was to its philosophy and James Russell Lowell to its literature—a paragon. Forbes had made his first fortune in the China trade by the time he was twenty-two (in 1835) and had then turned to building domestic railroads as well as maintaining his overseas empire. Twenty years later, when he met Lowell, his rails stitched together the farms and factories of the Midwest from Buffalo, New York, westward to Iowa, and from the Great Lakes southward to Hannibal, Missouri. Yet Forbes was renowned fully as much for his character as for his immense wealth and enormous achievement. In an age of rapacity that would be remembered chiefly for the rise of its robber barons, Forbes was a gentle giant. "Mr. Forbes never seemed to me a man of acquisitiveness," wrote a business partner, "but very distinctly one of constructiveness. His wealth was only an incident. I have seen many occasions when much more money might have been made by him in some business transaction, but for this dominant passion for building up things."[57]

He may not have been rapacious, but John Forbes was no pushover; he had bested some of the most powerful men of several countries. Yet he was entranced by young Lowell, and somewhat awed by the effect the boy had on him. He wrote to a business partner who once traveled halfway across the country to try to hire Lowell, "One of the strange things has been how he magnetized you and me at first sight. We are both practical, unsentimental, and perhaps hard, at least externally; yet he captivated me, just as he did you, and I came home and told my wife I had fallen in love; and from that day I never saw anything too good or too high for him."[58]

Lowell recovered his health, although he would always have what he referred to as a "poor" lung. He did not spare himself during his touring—he dismissed his mother's worries by quoting Emerson's fatalistic "I sail with God the seas"—but learned horsemanship and swordsmanship, picked up some French, Italian and Spanish, observed with interest (not a special interest, just the standard, consuming curiosity he applied to whatever came within his view) the maneuvers of the Austrian and French armies. Above all he rode and exercised and rode and rode, as if daring his body to let him down. It did not, instead it browned and hardened and healed, and in July of 1858 Lowell returned to Massachusetts to resume his life.[59]

He took a job as treasurer on Forbes's Burlington and Missouri River Railroad—later the Chicago, Burlington and Quincy—settling down with good humor far from the glittering society of Boston. The rustic little river town of Burlington, Iowa, he wrote, had an "unfledged look, its pin feathers being still very apparent." In charge not only of the road's finances, but of the disposition of its 300,000-acre land grant from the government, Lowell worked tirelessly, often until midnight. (To an earlier warning not to sell himself too cheaply, Lowell had responded: "*Nothing* can repay a man for what he has done well—except the doing of it.") A subordinate who later became president of the road wrote years later that Lowell "left his mark indelibly wherever he went; the affection with which he is remembered by the many, especially working-men, with whom he was brought in contact in his business, is remarkable."[60]

Despite his grinding schedule, Lowell was always careful to

spend a part of each day riding, for the benefit of his constitution, and reading, for the benefit of his mind. His continual correspondence with his mother, with whom he enjoyed a closeness that was intellectual as well as emotional, revolved during this period around the books he was reading, and the sizable shipments of additional volumes to fuel his daily literary half hour.[61]

Otherwise he worked (his one ambition, he wrote Forbes, was to "keep up my old power of work—to be able to 'toil terribly,' as Mr. Emerson says of Sir Walter Raleigh"); kept a quiet household with two other railroad employees on the edge of town; learned to cook ("If architecture is frozen music," he rhapsodized over a successful pea soup, "cooking is melody boiled and roast"); and listened to the agony of his country.[62]

Of course Lowell was an abolitionist, and not merely through his association with such anti-slavery zealots as his uncle James and Emerson. As a boy, he and his pal Henry Lee Higginson had become emotionally involved with the case of Anthony Burns, a black preacher and slave who had escaped from a Virginia master, had been recaptured in Boston, and was returned to Virginia in accordance with the Fugitive Slave Law. Lowell and Higginson tried in vain to see and plead with the judge who heard the case, then saw the unfortunate Burns, guarded by 1,100 militiamen, led down State Street to the wharves for shipment south. "Charlie," said Higginson to his friend's fervent agreement, "it will come to us to set this right." (Another who was deeply moved by that day's events, Walt Whitman, penned the caustic "A Boston Ballad" for later inclusion in his *Leaves of Grass.*)[63]

Lowell's later opposition to slavery was as pragmatic as it was idealistic. There was no question in his mind that slavery was morally wrong, but he did not burn with that issue alone; rather, as Lincoln did, he looked beyond the individual tragedies to the long-term social, political and economic malevolence of the practice. Lowell agreed with the president that the preeminent danger to the Union was secession. "Who cares now about the slavery question?" he wrote in March of 1861. "Secession, and the new Oligarchy built upon it, have crowded it out." Unlike Lincoln, and unlike most of his fellow intellectuals, Lowell thought by then that the time for compromise and deliberation had passed. "Lincoln must *act* soon, or forfeit his claim to our regard."[64]

By that time Lowell had come back east to take a job as ironmaster at a Mount Savage, Maryland works. But he had been there only a few months when the groaning Union splintered, and war became the only remedy. When rebel-minded Marylanders in Baltimore fired on Massachusetts troops headed south to defend Washington, Lowell immediately resigned his post and went to the beleaguered capital to lend a hand where he could with organization and management.

Meanwhile, he waited for a reply to a letter he had sent to Charles Sumner—U.S. senator from Massachusetts, a likeminded Republican and abolitionist—asking for "any appointment in the Army" that might be at Sumner's disposal. It was not the typical such letter of application: "I speak and write English, French, and Italian, and read German and Spanish; knew once enough of mathematics to put me at the head of my class at Harvard, though now I may need a little rubbing up; am a tolerable proficient with the small sword and single-stick; and can ride a horse as far and bring him in as fresh as any other man. I am 26 years of age, and believe that I possess more or less of that moral courage about taking responsibility which seems at present to be found only in Southern officers."[65]

Whether for the quality of the letter, the applicant, his family or his references (James Russell Lowell and John Murray Forbes), the young Lowell received highly unusual consideration. He was commissioned a captain in the regular cavalry and assigned to the crack 3rd U.S. Cavalry under Colonel William H. Emory, whom he would meet again. The summer and fall of 1861 he spent recruiting in the west, and did not see action until the Peninsular Campaign of 1862.

There he did his first fighting against Jeb Stuart's Invincibles, during the Confederate withdrawal from their initial Peninsular line of defense. This was at about the time and very near the place where Jubal Early (on Stuart's left) was wounded during his ill-considered charge on the Federal pursuers; and near the spot where George Custer, whom Lowell was soon to join on McClellan's staff, was making his first kill. Like Early and

Custer, Lowell immediately made himself a reputation for headlong audacity.

His orderly, Frank Robbins, set down an appreciation of Lowell after the war. By that time, as Edward Emerson wrote, "an atmosphere had gathered" around the events, and Robbins's unlettered account "runs as naively as a fairy tale." Yet it was mostly true. On one occasion, Robbins recalled, Lowell was at the head of his squadron of two companies when the rear guard reported a hundred Confederates behind them. Lowell was dismissive: "We are not going backwards, we are going forwards, they will not trouble us." Then the advance guard reported a thousand Confederates ahead. According to Robbins, Lowell's response was, "I would rather fight one thousand fair than one hundred in ambush—we will go and see the thousand." They charged the enemy five times, Lowell leading each time, and drove them off.[66]

Lowell's younger brother James, an infantry captain serving nearby, heard of and recorded another incident during that fight. During a charge, Charles was suddenly confronted by a Confederate trooper about to fire a carbine into his chest. "Drop that!" roared Lowell, and the astounded Confederate involuntarily lowered the muzzle even as he squeezed the trigger, with the result that he blasted Lowell's rolled coat, on the saddle behind him. "You can usually make a man obey you," Lowell commented off-handedly about the episode afterward, "if you speak quickly enough and with authority."[67]

Shortly afterward, the brothers were separated when the cavalry headed back down the peninsula to army headquarters, where Charles was promoted to major and appointed to McClellan's staff. Meanwhile James and the infantry slugged it out with the enemy in the Seven Days' battles. During one of them, at Glendale near the White Oak Swamp, James was mortally wounded. The young man's cool courage, as he was left behind to die in enemy hands, impressed all who saw it. To each of his fellow officers he gave a warm smile, a firm handshake and an unsentimental good-bye, asking only that his sword be kept from the enemy. Of his family he said, "I have written them all. Tell them how it was."[68]

Charles and his mother shared over the death of James a

deep, wholesome, smiling grief. "Your last two letters have told me more about Jimmy than I had learned from his friends here," Charles wrote her. "They seem to bring me very near to him and also to you and Father—nearer than I might ever had been, had the little fellow lived." They shared pleasant memories of the lost son and brother, and shared that intense intimacy that perhaps arises only from such sorrow: "Do, dear Mother, write to me a little oftener," he concluded one letter, "and try and help me to be a little more like what you saw me as a little child."[69]

As a staff officer for McClellan, Lowell missed Second Bull Run and should not have been in action, except as a courier, at Antietam. But like Custer, Lowell could not pass by a combat crisis, even when under orders to do so. During the morning of that terrible September day, he came upon a disorganized remnant of Major General John Sedgwick's division of II Corps, driven back stunned and bleeding from its attack on the Confederate left north of Sharpsburg.

Lowell's strong young voice recalled them to their purpose, the calm presence gave them back their will; they reformed their lines and, with Lowell riding ahead of them indifferent to the storm of lead, they attacked again. Two bullets punched into his horse, one of them shattering the scabbard of his saber on the way, the other lacerating his rolled overcoat on the saddle. When the line was stabilized again, he rode his wounded horse back to his staff duties.

Lowell made no effort to draw attention to what he had done or the dangers he had endured—not in his letters home ("Our loss was very serious," he wrote to Forbes, "I have had my usual luck but shall have to buy a new saber."), not even with a personal collection of trophies. To his orderly's dismay he simply discarded the ruined sword and gave away the punctured overcoat. Still, he was noticed; as questionable as McClellan's generalship had been, and as inconclusive as the outcome of the campaign, there were still 39 captured battle flags to be carried in ceremonial triumph to Washington. This special honor went to Captain Lowell.[70]

He was soon offered another honor, but in this case he was merely irritated. A friend of Forbes, another influential Bostonian working in support of the Union effort, proposed that a unit of cavalry be raised for Lowell to command. Forbes relayed the proposition, which was somewhat garbled by the non-military men who conceived it. Reference was made to recruiting "gentlemen," to which Lowell responded scathingly, "What do you mean by gentlemen? Drivers of gigs?" There was confused talk of a battalion—a unit designation not recognized by the War Department—and of home-guard cavalry, a kind of service Lowell held in contempt. It all smacked of "improper influence," Lowell wrote to his influential friends: "I should merely be exchanging active service for at least temporary inaction, for the sake of getting rank and pay as Major. I want to keep my military record clearer than that."[71]

Apparently, however, the offer was well intentioned. Things were sorted out, Lowell donned the eagles of a colonel and spent the winter of 1862–63 in Boston raising a proper regiment, the 2nd Massachusetts Cavalry. A large portion of his men were Californians—expatriate Massachusetts men gone west for gold and now come back to fight for their home state. But for the rest, Lowell was required to do some scouring. The days of patriotic fervor in the East were long past, and the recruiting offices were now the haunts of bounty jumpers and other malefactors. There might have been some doubt about whether the slight young scholar, who in his leisure time was attending the learned discourses of the famed Saturday Club with Emerson and James Russell Lowell, would have the mettle to deal with the rougher forms of humanity.

Any such doubt was soon dispelled. On his regular morning visit to the recruiting station one day, he found a squad of newly recruited troopers in open mutiny against their sergeant. The sergeant told Lowell he had ordered a troublemaker handcuffed, but the man and his friends were resisting. Lowell turned to the rebels and said, "The order must be obeyed." They began to shout their defiance and their complaints, but Lowell's battlefield voice stilled them: "After it is obeyed, I will hear what you have to say, and will decide the case on its merits, but it *must* be obeyed *first*. God knows, my men, I don't want to kill any of you; but I shall shoot the first man who resists. Sergeant, iron your man."

As the sergeant moved to obey, the mutineers lunged at him. Lowell drew his pistol and shot the leader in his tracks. The mutiny collapsed, the men shocked and in tears. Lowell went immediately to the office of the governor of Massachusetts, strode in, saluted, and said, "I have to report to you, sir, that in the discharge of my duty I have shot a man." He left immediately, and so did not hear the governor say to someone in his office, "I need nothing more. Colonel Lowell is as humane as he is brave." And that was the end of the matter.[72]

That was the winter he suddenly changed his attitude toward his childhood friend Josephine Shaw. She was from far-away Staten Island, and had spent four years in school in Rome and Paris, but they saw each other frequently; her parents were close to the James Russell Lowells, and she was a graduate of Anna Lowell's finishing school. In a sequence of events that coincidentally paralleled Dodson Ramseur's romance, there was an awakening, a whirlwind courtship and an engagement, with the wedding date to be set subject to military necessity.

Recollections of Josephine Shaw do not dwell on her beauty —her facial features were somewhat too generously proportioned for that—but on her spirit and grace. She was nineteen, slender, a superb horsewoman, and had what one friend described as "a thinking, inward-lighted countenance." Her photographs suggest a resemblance to Anna Jackson Lowell. The young William James, whose fame as a philosopher would later rival Emerson's, remembered Josephine as "surely one of our noblest and freest." The twenty-one-year-old James, not yet in the army that spring—indeed, he would never enlist—recalled being affected oddly by his dashing friends at a military parade. Charles Lowell and Josephine Shaw, "then just engaged I think, came whirling up on horseback, and drew up close to where I was standing among the crowd of spectators. I looked back and saw their faces and figures against the evening sky, and they looked so young and victorious, that I, much gnawed by questions as to my own duty of enlisting or not, shrank back —they had not seen me—from being recognized."[73]

The regiment on parade that day was commanded by Josephine's brother Robert; he had volunteered, at considerable risk to his reputation, to command the first regiment of black troops to be raised in a free state (the 54th Massachusetts Infantry). The experiment, which was championed, bankrolled and supervised by John Forbes and a few friends, was very unpopular; most New Englanders were prepared to free the Negro in the South but had no intention of encouraging black aspirations in the North. Passions ran high, for and against, but Charles Lowell did not waste his adrenaline. He heartily approved, and admired Shaw for taking on the unpopular and difficult task, but he was not at all sure how it would turn out. He wrote to his friend, Major Henry Lee Higginson of the Massachusetts Cavalry, that "I am very much *interested* without being at all *sanguine.*" And to his mother he commented, "It is important that it should be started slowly and not spoilt by too much fanaticism. Bob Shaw is not a fanatic."[74]

In the spring of 1863 Lowell had all he could do to get his men ready to function in the field. In May they were sent to Washington City, where they camped on the Capitol grounds and were introduced to horses. Long before the acquaintanceship of men and animals had ripened into friendship, a general named Silas Casey ordered a review; after feverishly rehearsing his awkward riders, Lowell decided they could manage the affair, at a walk, with "successful solemnity." But when General Casey arrived, he wanted to see the maneuvers executed at the gallop.

"I smiled," Lowell confided to Josephine, "I knew I was well mounted and could keep ahead of my Command—I knew I could take round most of my horses and perhaps a few of my men. I smiled, for I thought of Casey's probable fate—one Major General less, dead of a review, ridden over by wild horses. When I made the last turn, I glanced backward, the column was half a mile wide where I could last see it and seemed to stretch *ad infinitum.*" Casey survived, however, and so did the reputation of Lowell's green but rapidly improving regiment. "Don't blush for us," he concluded his account, "we are entirely satisfied with our own appearances."[75]

Lowell's letters to his betrothed have none of the heavy breathing of Ramseur's passionate declarations and remonstrances. In true Yankee fashion he clothed his emotions in more formal attire, or draped them in humor, or gave them a fleeting, backhanded recognition. Also present was the stern Yankee regard for duty: "The Nile would be very pleasant, but we do not own ourselves and have no right to even wish ourselves out of harness."[76]

While the Army of the Potomac was humiliated at Chancellorsville and the Army of Northern Virginia launched its second invasion of the North, Lowell and his men were assigned to the defense of Washington and its environs. First from the vicinity of Fort Stevens in Maryland, then from near Centerville, he and his men chased Mosby and looked for Jeb Stuart through long, frustrating months of hard duty.

Meanwhile Lowell made a contribution of another kind. His friend John Murray Forbes, laboring ceaselessly on behalf of the war effort, was in continual contact with Secretary of War Edwin Stanton, Secretary of the Navy Gideon Wells, Secretary of the Treasury Salmon P. Chase and Massachusetts Governor John Andrew. In these portentous dealings—as for instance when he went to the aid of Charles Francis Adams in England at a moment when that country's unofficial support of the Confederacy had brought the United States to the brink of a declaration of war—Forbes relied for background information on the firsthand perceptions of his sagacious young friend.[77]

And well he might. At Lowell's rank and level of operations, where war seldom made any sense at all, the ordinary observer recorded little more than personal anecdotes and army gossip. But Lowell never lost sight of the larger context of events and was able to evaluate small things against a much larger perspective. As a result some of his observations, casually made at the time, later took on the ring of prophecy.

In September of 1862, for example, Lowell told Henry Lee Higginson that General McClellan was a great strategist and an admirable planner who prepared fully for every contingency. But "when he comes to strike, he doesn't strike in a determined fashion; that is, he prepares very well and then doesn't do the best thing—strike hard." Much later, this would come to be the accepted evaluation of McClellan, but spoken as it was before the bloody confirmation of Antietam, by an amateur and still inexperienced soldier, Lowell's comments have the sheen of clairvoyance.[78]

In May of 1863, ten days before the first Confederate troop movements toward Gettysburg and more than a month before the battle at that town confirmed his thought, Lowell told a fellow officer, "*Lee* will not remain idle if *we* do; he will send a column into Maryland again when the crops are ready: I look for a repetition of what occurred last summer." The next month he commented that "I should not be surprised to see exhibitions of disloyalty in some of our Northern cities." The next week there were draft riots in New York and Boston.[79]

Lowell took an increasing interest in the black troops, partly because his fiancée's brother was involved with them, but also because of their unexpectedly solid performance. He made a point of mentioning his approval to Forbes, and in May of 1863 to Secretary of War Stanton. Not many young colonels had the opportunity to chat about war policy with the imperious Mr. Stanton; but the secretary called the exceedingly well-connected young colonel in to check up on him, see that he was getting everything he needed, that sort of thing.

It was a marvelous opportunity for seeking rank or favor. Lowell asked for nothing. Stanton volunteered, Lowell told Josephine later, to "have all my requisitions filled by preference, and when I said I was ready he would give it the post of honor." Lowell, skeptical but polite, brought up the success of the 54th Massachusetts and left.[80]

In July the 54th was sent south, on Colonel Shaw's insistence that it be given a chance to show what it could do, to help in the siege of Fort Wagner, not far from Fort Sumter in the harbor at Charleston, South Carolina. The regiment was used to spearhead a desperate assault, gained a foothold in the fort, but was eventually driven back with heavy casualties. Robert Shaw was killed. When a party under a flag of truce requested the return of his body, the Confederates, outraged to find themselves under attack by Negroes, responded, "We have thrown him into the ditch under his niggers." The Union dead were buried there together.[81]

Lowell wrote of Shaw's nobility in undertaking the leadership of the black regiments, saying that in so doing Shaw was "fighting for a cause greater than any National one." In comforting Josephine, Lowell said "he had such a single and loyal

and kindly heart. It cannot be so hard for such a man to die."
Two months later, when Charleston fell, Federal authorities
contacted Colonel Shaw's parents and offered to retrieve his
remains from the mass grave. "We wish no search made," responded his parents, "nor is there any monument so worthy of
a soldier as the mound heaped over him by the bodies of his
comrades."[82]

In July Lowell was given command of the 13th and 16th
New York Cavalry regiments in addition to the 2nd Massachusetts Cavalry, and with his small brigade he spent the rest of the
summer and fall harassing and being harassed by the Confederate partisan rangers of northern Virginia—chiefly, of course,
those under the command of Mosby.

On the last day of October 1863—three days after the far-
away wedding of Dodson and Ellen Ramseur—Charles Lowell
and Josephine Shaw were married. Like the Ramseurs south of
the Rapidan, the newly wed Lowells spent a snug and warm
winter in a house in northern Virginia while he took care of the
light duties of winter quarters. When, in the spring, General
Grant lashed the war back to rumbling life, Lowell's duties
were grueling but incidental, involving mostly reconnaissance
and patrol, until July and Old Jube's raid on Washington. Then
came the chase, and the transfer to a different brigade in the
Valley.[83]

Early in September Sheridan gave Lowell command of the
Reserve Brigade—the 1st, 2nd and 5th U.S. Cavalry regiments,
plus Battery D of the 2nd U.S. (regular) Artillery—in addition
to his own 2nd Massachusetts. The temper of these regulars
Lowell was now to lead was demonstrated by an incident during a fight at Smithfield, Virginia a few days before his arrival.
Lieutenant Joseph S. Hoyer of the 1st U.S. Cavalry had ridden
up to his company commander and requested permission to
leave the column. "What for, Mr. Hoyer?" demanded the captain huffily. "Because I am mortally wounded, sir," responded
the poker-faced Hoyer. It was true. With the astonished captain's permission Hoyer rode to the rear, dismounted, lay
down, and a few hours later died. Such men could not have
been pleased at the prospect of being commanded by a wispy
little slip of a volunteer; "I have stepped into a rather trying

position now," Lowell wrote Josephine, "the regular Brigade is hard to run." Much more would be expected of him, he said, and that was especially true on September 19, the day Sheridan stopped sparring and started slugging.[84]

While the infantry struggled through the traffic jam in Berryville Canyon to attack Ramseur's men outside Winchester, Sheridan's cavalry swung wide to the left and right, James Wilson's division to the south, Merritt's and Averell's divisions to the north. Lowell's Reserve Brigade led Merritt's division across Opequon Creek into contact with Breckinridge's infantry on Early's left (Devin's brigade following, while Custer's crossed farther north against even more vigorous opposition).[85]

All day long the Reserve Brigade slugged away, punching into the enemy lines, wheeling back, re-forming, and punching again; or dismounting and charging, gaining an objective, then dashing back to the horseholders to canter forward and do it again. Slowly they forced Breckinridge back, bending inward Early's extended left.

Always Lowell was at the forefront. Sometimes he left so many exhausted horses and confused men behind that he was virtually alone. "At one time he found himself with one captain and four men face to face with a Rebel gun," the surgeon of the 2nd Massachusetts reported. "The piece was discharged, killing both horses and tearing off the captain's arm." (Presumably the four men were dismounted.) "The Colonel quietly mounted the first horse that came up, and the gun was his."[86]

There was little for the cavalry to do at Fisher's Hill; most of it, the Reserve Brigade included, was involved in the failed attempt to get up the Luray Valley and behind Early's army in time to cut it off and destroy it. For two weeks afterward the riders returned to their routine of constant, unremarked skirmishing, with the addition now of the repellant duty of burning out the Valley's farms and mills. Not until October 9 was there another pitched battle, this the all-out cavalry fight at Toms Brook, and the fearful Massachusetts surgeon did not believe that Lowell could survive it.

"He rode up to a corner of a fence where two men of his skirmish-line were crouching to protect themselves from the storm of bullets, and ordered them to advance. I dared not look at him for *I knew he would fall,* and yet he came back steadily and all right, his horse always wounded or killed, and himself never, until I began to feel that he was safe."[87]

Lowell had been doing the job of a brigadier general for a year, yet he gave no indication, in public or private, that he was impatient for promotion. Unlike Custer, who had been promoted before ever doing the work of a general officer, or Ramseur, who had been impatient even while being promoted regularly, Lowell made no move to call attention to his readiness for higher rank. When Forbes—a man who could have got an incompetent raised to general officer with a casual mention— inquired about the appropriateness of Lowell's rank, the younger man was dismissive: "I have no idea of being a brigadier," he responded, "for various reasons." When in October his wife suggested that there might be no point finishing the new colonel's shoulder straps she was making him, he told her to finish the job: "Those eagles will flourish a good while yet. I'm perfectly satisfied, too, now that I have this Brigade."[88]

Nor did Lowell make any move to promote his public reputation. He sent no official reports to friends for circulation in the proper places, wrote no boastful letters home. He was irritated by Custer's posturing, and the excessive praise showered on the Boy General by Custer's pet reporter, E. A. Paul of the *New York Times.* "Custer from the beginning has been the laughing-stock here," Lowell wrote Forbes on October 17, "his absurd newspaper reporter may have caused this." The newspapers were no judge of military merit, Lowell warned Forbes: "The reputation of regiments is made and is known in the Army—comparative merits are *well* known there.[89]

As much as anything, however, Lowell's correspondence concerned the welfare of his horses, with occasional discussions of the prospects for a long war, the effects of government policies, and the importance of reelecting Lincoln in November. About his own role in the fighting Lowell was virtually silent. An October 17 letter to his mother was typical: "We are in glorious company, with fine air to breathe and fine views to enjoy; we are kept very active, and have done a good deal of good work; I have done my share, I think—but there's nothing to make a letter of."[90]

Yet the man who mounted up on the morning of October 19, to ride south in search of the enemy yet again, was in considerable agony. He was no hound of war, addicted like a Custer or a Sheridan to the orgasmic clash of combat; he was a man doing a singularly nasty piece of work for his country. It was the beauty of the Valley that he found glorious, not the war; thus deprived of the stimulants of contrived passion, and cursed with sensitivity and imagination, he paid a terrible price each time he had to nerve himself to face the guns. He did it, every time, but it cost him.

He had begun to write about taking leave, about what he would do when the war was over, about going home. He apparently made no mention in his letters of the fact that Josephine was pregnant, but he must have known, for their child would be born in November. He struggled to maintain his former, jocular tone, but now and again he sounded deep chords of melancholy. "I *do* wish this war was over!" and, a few days later, "I should like to have Sundays quiet."[91]

In one October letter the careful mask slipped even further, and the anguish showed through starkly: "I don't want to be shot until I've had a chance to come home. I have no idea that I shall be hit, but I *want* so much not to now, that it sometimes frightens me."[92]

But when the Reserve Brigade splashed across Cedar Creek on the morning of October 19 and disappeared into the dark fogs of enemy country, Charles Lowell was riding lightly in the lead.

PART II

THE GUNS

Chapter 6

"They Jumped Up Running"

To the east a coppery glow began to lighten the rim of the sky. The massive, rounded shoulders of the Massanutten Mountains loomed against the waning southern stars. Thick tendrils of mist congealed in the pre-dawn chill, oozed along the streambeds, spilled languorously across the lowlands. Soothed by the beauty of their surroundings and the safety of their position, 30,000 Federal soldiers slept. Mere yards outside their lines, 17,000 Confederates tensed for the leap toward death and victory.[1]

Tom Rosser and just over 2,000 men—his Laurel Brigade along with Wickham's brigade, dismounted, under Colonel Thomas H. Owen of the 3rd Virginia Cavalry—waited tensely on the Back Road five miles northwest of Middletown; a few hundred yards east of him, Federal pickets watched the banks of Cedar Creek and a ford near Cupp's Mill. A few thousand yards beyond were the tents of Custer's division, with Merritt's camp just a mile and a half to the southeast—more than 6,000 men in all. Rosser was supposed to attack and hold them.[2]

In the councils of the previous day, Rosser had recommended that he be permitted to follow the infantry attack with a charge up the Valley Pike, thus adding to the shock of the assault and increasing the momentum of any breakthrough. The proposal was admirable for its concentration of applied force and its appropriate use of cavalry. General Early brushed the idea aside; it was his belief that Rosser's small division could hold both Federal cavalry divisions out of the battle by

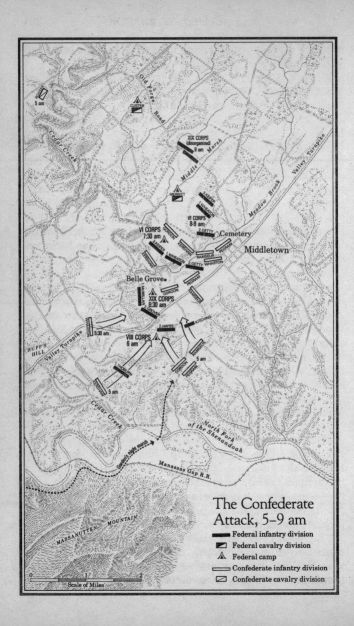

5 am

CUSTER

Old Forge Road

XIX CORPS
(disorganized)
9 am

Middle Marsh

MERRITT

AVERELL
WHARTON

VI CORPS
8-9 am

2 GETTY

Cemetery

VI CORPS
7:30 am

GORDON

AVERELL

KEIFER

Middletown

RAMSEUR

2 GETTY

PEGRAM

PENNINGTON

WHARTON

2 GETTY

WHARTON

Meadow Brook

Valley Turnpike

Cedar Creek

Belle Grove

GORDON

XIX CORPS
6:30 am

McMILLAN

PEGRAM

GROVER

RAMSEUR

5:30 am

KITCHING

2 HAYES

VIII CORPS
6 am

PEGRAM

RAMSEUR

GORDON

PEGRAM

5 am

HUPP'S
HILL

Valley Turnpike

PEGRAM

5 am

Cedar Creek

North Fork of the Shenandoah

Gordon's night march

Manassas Gap R.R.

MASSANUTTEN MOUNTAIN

The Confederate
Attack, 5–9 am

▬▬ Federal infantry division
◪ Federal cavalry division
⚐ Federal camp
▭ Confederate infantry division
▨ Confederate cavalry division

0   1   2
Scale of Miles

making a diversionary attack on their right. It was a belief that would far outlive its usefulness.[3]

Rosser's assignment was all the more daunting because one of his brigades—300 men under Colonel William H. Payne—was off with Gordon's turning force, under orders to make a dash for Belle Grove and try to capture Sheridan. And Lomax's division was miles away to the southeast, confronting Powell's Federal division near Front Royal, under orders to try to gain the Valley Pike behind the Federal infantry. Early had prepared a stunning infantry attack and artillery barrage, but his cavalry forces were dangerously divided, awkwardly placed and had tentative, uncoordinated and unrealistic objectives. Tom Rosser undoubtedly understood this, and felt hobbled by a bad plan. But the riders who had been forced to run for their lives in the Woodstock Races lusted for revenge, and presumably Rosser was ready as always to take on Custer one more time.

(He had demonstrated this willingness two nights before, when he had tried to capture Custer's entire division. The Third Cavalry Division then had been camped farther out toward North Mountain, isolated from the main army to the extent that Early had sanctioned the strange mission. Rosser's two brigades took along an infantry brigade, the foot soldiers riding double with the horsemen on the skinny horses. After an all-night ride they had launched a dawn attack from the rear of the Federal camp, only to find that Custer had moved in toward the army the previous evening.)[4]

Five miles south and a little to the east of Rosser's jumpoff position on the morning of October 19, the 1,400 men of Brigadier General Gabriel C. Wharton's little division stood edgily in column on Hupp's Hill just outside Strasburg. Ahead of them the Valley Pike stretched away to the northeast for a mile, then bent to the east and, before returning to its more northerly course, crossed Cedar Creek under the formidable guns and fortifications of the Federal XIX Corps.

"The enemy's breastworks were built of strong timbers with earth thrown against them," wrote one of the Confederates whose job that dark morning was to assault them, "with a deep trench on the inside, being deeper from the bottom of the trench to the top of the works than the heights of the soldiers when standing. Thus a step of three or four feet was built for the troops to stand on and fire. The breastworks wound in and out with the creek, some places jutting out almost to the very brink; at others, several hundred yards in the rear, a level piece of bottom land intervening. This ridge and plateau were some fifty feet or more above the level of the creek, and gave elegant position for batteries. In front of this breastwork, and from forty to fifty feet in breadth, was an abatis constructed of pine trees, the needles stripped, the limbs cut and pointed five to ten feet from the trunks. These were packed and stacked side by side and on top of each other, being almost impossible for a single man even to pick his way through, and next to impossible for a line of battle to cross over. All along the entire length of the fortifications were built great redoubts of earthwork in the form of squares, the earth being of sufficient thickness to turn any of our cannon balls, while all around was a ditch from twelve to fifteen feet deep—only one opening in the rear large enough to admit the teams drawing the batteries. Field pieces were posted at each angle, the infantry, when needed, filled the space between. These forts were built about two hundred yards apart, others being built in front of the main line. This I believe was one of the most completely fortified positions by nature, as well as by hand, of any line occupied during the war."[5]

There were 9,000 men and 20 guns in the XIX Corps lines west of the pike, more in Thoburn's position to the east; even if surprised, the entrenched Federals could extinguish Wharton's little force in minutes. But, as Early wrote later, he had not ordered Wharton to attack, merely to "move forward, support the artillery when it came up, and send a force to get possession of the bridge on the pike over the creek." It was a limited but important objective. The pike would be not only the army's route of supply and retreat, but its best position on the battlefield, since after crossing the creek it ran along a ridge commanding the entire area. Its possession would be a prerequisite of victory.[6]

The safe and timely arrival of the guns was also essential. They had not been advanced earlier because the rumbling of their wheels would have given away any attempt to sneak them into position. Colonel Tom Carter was waiting a mile and a half behind Wharton, on the pike at the foot of Fisher's Hill, his 40 guns limbered and ready. Carter, a cousin to Robert E. Lee, was one of those rarities in the Confederate armies: a planter who had willingly left his baronial estate to do his part in the war. What is more, that spring Carter had found himself directing the fire of his guns from his own lawn—his King William County plantation was in the path of Grant's rounding of Richmond. Carter, trained in artillery at Virginia Military Institute, was a cool and supremely competent officer, and he waited patiently now, while his gunners and cannoneers strained to hear, over the restless stamping of the horses and jingling of their harness rings, the first crackle of musketry that would call them toward the front.[7]

A mile east of Wharton's position, where a road from Strasburg crossed Cedar Creek—at a ford a half-mile upstream from the Shenandoah—Jubal Early directed the disposition of his largest single division. Major General Joseph Brevard Kershaw's 4,000 men of Longstreet's Corps had spent much of the summer marching, their location a barometer of General Lee's worries about the Valley: In July they had headed west to bolster Early against Federal reinforcement and Sheridan's arrival; two months later, with Grant across the James and hammering at Petersburg, Kershaw's men had returned to the east only to rush west again after the disasters at Winchester and Fisher's Hill. Kershaw was a lawyer and politician from a distinguished South Carolina family. His stature had required that he be given rank in the army; despite this, he had proved to be a competent and reliable officer.

Now his men were to have their first general engagement under Early (although they had taken part in the short, sharp fight on Hupp's Hill on the 13th), and the commanding general was on hand to see to every detail of their preparation. They had moved out from Fisher's Hill about an hour after midnight, and, Early recalled, "we got in sight of the enemy's fires at half-past three o'clock." The moon was still up, and in its light the Federal tents massed on the heights beyond the creek glowed like bleached bone. "The division was halted under cover to await the arrival of the proper time," wrote Early, who then endured what must have been the longest hour of his life.[8]

Now was the time of doubt, the hour of night when the human soul is at its lowest ebb and is most easily overwhelmed by despair. When examined in the dark hours of the morning, dreams wither as if brushed by flame, plans crumble at the slightest touch and dangers swell up in all directions. Courage at such an hour, Napoleon thought, was a soldier's rarest attribute.

Old Jube had bet everything—his army, his career, the Shenandoah Valley, and the trust placed in him by Robert E. Lee—and had flung the dice, which were about to hit the gaming table. His forces, outnumbered nearly two to one, were widely separated in the face of the enemy. If his plan worked, it would be called brilliant, would be compared with Stonewall Jackson's audacious flanking of the Federal army of Chancellorsville. If it did not work, it would be, in the eyes of Extra Billy Smith, the newspapers and commentators of the South and perhaps even Lee himself, an unforgivable waste of lives.

In minutes it would begin. In a few hours it would be decided. "I pointed out to Kershaw and the commander of his leading brigade the enemy's position and described the nature of the ground, and directed them how the attack was to be made and followed up." The moon set, the fog came up, and the hunched gray figure on horseback waited.[9]

Suddenly, from the northeast, came the rumble of heavy wheels in motion. Early, wrenched by strain, cried out: "It's all up with us! We are discovered, and that is the enemy's artillery." Jed Hotchkiss said he did not think so, and in a few moments the sound, receding, proved to be some wagons moving to the Federal rear.[10]

At about 4:30 A.M., with a degree of coordination remarkable for such a complex enterprise, Tom Rosser spurred his horse, John Gordon nodded to Colonel Payne, and Jubal Early leaned forward to whine a command to Kershaw. Rosser's troopers dashed for the ford, Wickham's thousand men running on foot with the Laurel Brigade's thousand following mounted at the trot, setting up an earthen drumroll that must have snapped up the heads of the sleepy 7th Michigan Cavalry pickets just ahead; Payne led his 300 horsemen at the gallop into the Shenandoah River on top of the astonished Federal videttes; and Kershaw unleashed a band of sharpshooters against Thoburn's sentinels at the Cedar Creek ford below Strasburg. The ball had opened.[11]

As the first muzzle flashes stabbed the early gloom near Cupp's Mill, the forward pickets of the 7th Michigan coolly pulled back before Rosser's advance to the east side of Cedar Creek, where they formed a denser line with their reserve. Although Custer's camp was closer to them, the 7th was in Merritt's division, under Colonel Kidd's command. Kidd, who had fallen asleep fully dressed only a few hours before, sprang from his tent at the call of a sentry. He heard "scattering shots," he wrote later. "They were not many, but enough to impel me to a quick resolve." He ordered the Michigan Brigade to prepare to move. "In an incredibly short space of time, the order was executed. The tents were struck, the artillery horses attached to the gun carriages and caissons, and the cavalry horses saddled. No bugle call was sounded.[12]

"The firing grew heavier, and from the hill where Custer was rang out on the air the shrill notes of Foght's bugle, telling us that our old commander had taken the alarm." The call was "To Horse," and in minutes Custer's division was up and mounted, with guns hitched. Meanwhile, Merritt had sent a courier galloping after Lowell's outward-bound Reserve Brigade, which had just reached the picket line, with orders to halt and await developments. Then Merritt sent Colonel Kidd with the Michigan Brigade out to support the pickets.[13]

But as Kidd observed, "the Seventh Michigan had made a gallant stand alone," and hardly needed help. Rosser's men had taken the ford and the mill, but had pushed no farther; Merritt thought their attack "feebly made." Lowell shifted his brigade to the right, coming on on the left of the Michigan Brigade to confront Rosser. "The enemy did not see fit to press the attack," wrote Kidd, "but contented himself with throwing a few shells from the opposite bank, which annoyed us so little that Martin [Captain Joseph W. Martin, commanding the brigade's horse artillery] did not unlimber his guns."[14]

Custer and Merritt, their blood up and their commands

ready, sat their horses on their respective hilltops and sniffed the wind. They smelled feint in the chattering fire to their right; they soon heard a more sinister, deeper-throated roar from the far left. They were ready to go. But they received no orders.

Seven miles to the south, at almost the instant of Rosser's attack, Payne's men had galloped whooping across the river while behind them the proud remnants of the Stonewall Brigade led Gordon's infantry forward. "Well do I remember how we plunged into the icy waters of the Shenandoah as day was beginning to dawn," wrote Isaac G. Bradwell of the 31st Georgia, "the struggle to reach the other side, and the efforts to reach the high embankment, now made slick by our wet clothing; how some comrade jostled me just as I reached the top and I slid back into the cold water and had to try all over again." Another soldier, in the 31st Virginia, remembered with a shudder that the water was so cold "it felt like cutting the legs at the top water line."[15]

Now General Wright's failure to "close up Powell," as Sheridan had directed, had a small but painful additional effect on Federal fortunes. Powell's camp and divisional headquarters were located near Front Royal, to the east; naturally, his pickets reacted to the overwhelming attack by falling back in that direction—away from the threatened army. A brief rattle of small-arms fire was the only warning Crook's divisions had of the approach of Gordon's 9,000 men. The Confederate turning force now marched to the northeast at the double quick, passing a mile to the east of Thoburn's massive breastworks, angling closer to the eastern, unprotected edge of Hayes's camp.[16]

Meanwhile Kershaw's sharpshooters had had similar good luck at their ford. It was being guarded by Thoburn's 54th New York Heavy Artillery (employed as infantry), and according to the VI Corps assistant adjutant general, Major Hazard Stevens, the pickets were "badly posted and negligent." Kershaw's sharpshooters simply rose up and ran over the New Yorkers, overwhelming them without firing a shot. Captain D. Augustus Dickert of the 3rd South Carolina (part of Kershaw's old brigade) wrote that there was "a flash, a report or two, and the enemy's outpost at this point was ours." Of the 5th New York's 349 men, 309 were taken prisoner.[17]

Now the Confederates pushed north across the ford as fast as they could in the fog and the gloom and began to deploy from column of fours into line of battle under Thoburn's fortifications. Kershaw put no skirmishers out; he was going to hit the enemy with the main line of battle, no warning first. As they formed up, a litter was carried past the column to the rear, bearing a sharpshooter, one of the first men down that day. "Nothing but a low, deep groan was heard," Dickert remembered, "which told too plainly that his last battle had been fought."[18]

Inside the Federal lines, alarm was flaring up but would not take hold. Captain Henry DuPont, commanding Crook's artillery brigade, heard the scattered shots in front of Thoburn's line. Two of DuPont's batteries were posted in the fortifications, facing south; the third was across a ravine on another ridge to the rear, trained westward to cover the pike where it crossed Cedar Creek. The artillery camp, caissons, wagons and horses were in the steep ravine that curled in behind Thoburn's hill, separating it from the Second Division camp. "Not being yet fully awake," DuPont recalled, "my first impression was that our pickets were chopping wood to make fires, the night being quite cool, but as the firing did not cease I jumped up, put on my clothes, ordered my horse, called the chief bugler and directed him to sound the 'reveille.'"[19]

DuPont was going to have "Boots and Saddles" sounded, so the men would harness the teams, hitch the batteries and prepare for action. "But upon reflecting that under orders from army headquarters we had stood to arms at 2:00 A.M. for three or four nights previously, and that no such instructions had been given for the past night (presumably for some good reason), I concluded that 'boots and saddles' might needlessly alarm our infantry; and then, too, a surprise seemed unlikely, as it was generally known that a brigade of the Nineteenth Corps was ordered to make a reconnaissance in force at daybreak to feel the enemy." DuPont's battery commanders went ahead with the regular morning roll call.[20]

Lieutenant Colonel Thomas F. Wildes, commanding Thoburn's First Brigade since the death of Colonel Wells, had had no comforting second thoughts. When he heard the shoot-

ing, he sent his wagons to the rear, his men into the works and
his skirmishers forward; they "soon met the enemy advancing
silently through the woods." Having issued these orders,
Wildes rode with some of his staff over to Colonel Harris's
Third Brigade on his right, "which we found," he recalled dis-
gustedly, "in their beds." The brigade that had failed to distinguish itself on the day Colonel Wells had been killed was not
particularly anxious, it seemed, to redeem itself. "Some good,
vigorous efforts were made to arouse them. There stood the
guns of the battery with only a sentinel over them, and only a
man now and then of the infantry or artillery could be roused
up enough to ask 'What's up?' or, 'Who the hell are you?'"
Captain H. L. Carr of Wildes's staff found Colonel Harris
asleep in an ambulance a half-mile from his lines and told him
of the danger. "He raised himself slightly in his bed," reported
the disgusted Carr, "and answered, 'That cannot be.'" Colonel
Wildes and his officers returned angrily to their regiment,
"which we had scarcely reached before the storm burst in front
and on both flanks."[21]

At exactly 5 A.M., by Early's recollection, Kershaw launched
his attack, *en echelon* from the right by brigades. "Nearer and
nearer came the roll of battle as each succeeding brigade was
put in action," wrote Captain Dickert, whose brigade was on
the left of the line and the last to advance. Then, "we were
moving forward at the double quick," climbing the fifty-foot
incline to the plateau above. "Now the thunder of their guns is
upon us; the brigade on our right plunges through the thicket
and throw themselves upon the abatis in front of the works and
pick their way over them."[22]

Major D. A. Grimsley of Payne's cavalry, who was riding
north from Gordon's crossing point and was more than a mile
east of Kershaw's attack, was astounded by the abrupt savagery
of its opening volley. "It was not ushered in by a few preliminary shots, as was generally the case," he wrote later, "but it
was a prolonged roll, without cessation, for apparently five
minutes. After the volley was over the echo of it seemed to roll
back and forth over the Valley a half dozen or more times.
When it had once died away it would return to you again from
another direction."[23]

Dickert's brigade emerged into the open to find a broad field between it and the Federal line. "We could see the enemy in great commotion, but soon the works were filled with half-dressed troops and they opened a galling fire upon us. The distance was too great in this open space to take the works by a regular advance in line of battle, so the men began to call for orders to 'charge.' Whether the order was given or not, the troops with one impulse sprang forward." Above the crashing of the rifles rose the hair-raising ululations of the Rebel yell.

Near the center of the field, in a depression in the ground, they came upon the abatis, impossible to cross under concentrated fire. But the Federal shooting was panicky. "Those behind the works would raise their bare heads above the trenches, fire away, regardless of aim or direction, then fall to the bottom to reload," wrote Dickert. "This did not continue long, for all down the line from our extreme right the line gave way, and was pushed back to the rear and towards our left, our troops mounting their works and following them as they fled in wild disorder. 'Over the works, cross over,' was the command now given, and we closed in with a dash to the abatis—over it and down in the trenches—before the enemy realized their position." Some of the Confederates were screaming in derision, "Another Union victory!"[24]

"The mist and fog was so heavy that you could hardly see the length of a regiment," Colonel Wildes remembered. His brigade held its own for a few minutes, only to see its efforts doomed by the feeble performance of Harris's brigade. Wildes's 4th Massachusetts on the right of the brigade did its best, he wrote, but "they were struck so suddenly and heavily on the flank that they broke, and becoming involved with the utterly stampeded and broken masses of the surprised brigade and battery on their right, fell back in confusion."[25]

Captain DuPont had by this time reached his Regular battery (Light Battery B, 5th U.S. Artillery) on the extreme right of the line. Battery D of the 1st Pennsylvania Light Artillery, four hundred yards to the left, was being overwhelmed, the men "bayoneted or struck down with clubbed muskets at their pieces, the sounds of the conflict being plainly audible for quite a distance." Lieutenant Henry F. Brewerton, commanding the

Regular battery, yelled to DuPont that his six guns were loaded with canister but he could see no enemy below the ramparts on account of the fog. Open fire anyway, said DuPont: "To Brewerton's inquiry, 'At what shall I fire?' I replied, 'Fire to the left in the direction of the sound,' and he opened at once with his two center pieces." The pounding roar of DuPont's cannon, added to the swelling clatter of the rifle fire and answered at once by some of the Pennsylvania guns (now captured by the enemy and wrestled around to open on the fleeing Federals) rolled over the Shenandoah Valley and announced to any who still doubted that a general engagement was under way.[26]

DuPont knew there was no time to get teams up the hill and hitched to the limbers of these guns before they were overrun. He ordered Brewerton to "hold his ground until he could see the forms of the enemy approaching," and then "run the pieces down the hill by hand, abandoning the limbers." DuPont plunged his horse down into the ravine, where in the growing roar of the battle the enlisted men of the Regular battery were struggling to hitch their excited teams. They were to unlimber and abandon the caissons, DuPont shouted, and take the hitched limbers to the foot of the hill to receive the guns being rolled down by hand. He galloped up the other ridge to where Battery L of the 1st Ohio Light Artillery was posted, and from there saw Wharton's Confederate skirmish line coming down the pike toward the creek. DuPont ordered two of his guns to open fire on the skirmishers while the rest moved five hundred yards back to the left and rear, along the ridge parallel to the pike, to take a covering position.[27]

Meanwhile Brewerton turned his guns on the breached Federal line to his left, firing along the trenches into the Confederates pouring into them. He stood fast until enemy soldiers materialized in the dense fog twenty-five yards away, then sent his men scrambling down the hill in a barely controlled avalanche of 6 one-ton cannons. One gun wobbled into a tangle of bushes and had to be spiked and abandoned. While following the last piece down, Brewerton was overtaken and captured.[28]

Captain Dickert leaped onto the Federal breastworks and surveyed the exhilarating scene. The fog had not obscured the higher elevations, and the light was growing stronger. "For a mile or more in every direction towards the rear was a vast plain or broken plateau, with not a tree or shrub in sight. Tents whitened the field from one end to the other for a hundred paces in rear of the line, while the country behind was one living sea of men and horses—all fleeing for life and safety. Down to our left we could see men leaving the trenches, while others huddled close up to the side of the wall, displaying a white flag."[29]

The First Division of the Army of West Virginia had lost most of its organization and was offering little resistance to the triumphant enemy. "Men, shoeless and hatless, went flying like mad to the rear, some with and some without their guns," Dickert recalled. "Here and there loose horses galloped at will, some bridleless, others with traces whipping their flanks to a foam. Such confusion, such a panic, was never witnessed before by the troops." Beyond Dickert's view Colonel Wildes had two of his regiments, the 116th and 123rd Ohio, in hand as they backed down into the ravine, then up the other side toward Hayes's position. Somewhere in the maelstrom, roaring and swinging his sword, Colonel Thoburn was laboring to stop the river of running men when a bullet found him, pierced his upper body, and he fell dying to the ground.[30]

The Federals were given a momentary respite by what they had left behind them in their camps: Captain Dickert remembered "costly blankets, overcoats, dress uniforms, hats, caps, boots and shoes all thrown in wild confusion over the face of the earth." Others were transfixed by the food, in amounts such as they had not seen for months. "Good gracious, what a feast we had," recalled a captain in the 17th Mississippi. Edibles of every kind and in great abundance were there. "Five- and ten-gallon camp kettles on the fire were full of boiling coffee." According to Dickert, "All this fabulous wealth of provisions and clothing looked to the half-fed, half-clothed Confederates like the wealth of the Indes. The soldiers broke overall order and discipline for a moment or two and helped themselves." The breakdown was, apparently, a brief one, after which "a partial line of battle was formed and the pursuit taken up." Or as the Mississippian put it, "We got some of the good things, filled our tin cups with the coffee, and moved on after the Yankees, eating, drinking, and feeling big and brave."[31]

General Early wrote that he saw Wharton's attack off, then "rode as rapidly as possible to the position on Hupp's Hill to which Wharton and the artillery had been ordered. I found the artillery just arriving," thundering up through the sleeping town to the crest, the six-horse teams wheeling, the men scrambling to get their pieces unlimbered and into action. "Wharton had advanced his skirmishers to the creek, capturing some prisoners, but the enemy still held the works on our left of the Pike, commanding that road and the bridge, and opened with his artillery on us." That would have been DuPont's Ohio battery.[32]

In minutes that battery, and the ravine into which the Regular battery had executed its iron avalanche, were "practically surrounded," Captain DuPont recalled. "Our people were making superhuman efforts to escape." Thanks to the fog, and Kershaw's pause to realign, and the general confusion, all five remaining guns of Battery B were hustled out of the ravine, westward onto the pike and toward the rear. The escape, said DuPont, "seemed absolutely miraculous."[33]

DuPont was also surprised to see Wharton's men across Cedar Creek come to a halt under the fire of only two guns; only one section of the Ohio battery was firing on Wharton, while the other galloped back to higher ground about five hundred yards to the left rear. DuPont, perhaps forgetting the formidable strength of the XIX Corps earthworks just across the pike from him, thought the Confederates should have disregarded the cannon fire and pushed forward.[34]

But DuPont soon found he had trouble enough. The section he had sent to the high ground came thundering down again, "having found itself almost face to face" with advancing Confederates. Until then DuPont had not realized "the extensive scale upon which the Confederate turning movement was being carried out nor the vigor with which it was being pressed." DuPont and his gunners ran for their lives, north to the pike and along it to Hayes's line, where they went into battery again.[35]

The roar of the battle had sounded an urgent reveille for the

Lieutenant General Jubal A. Early (*Cook Collection/Valentine Museum*)

Major General Philip H. Sheridan (*National Archives*)

Brigadier General Thomas L. Rosser (*Cook Collection/Valentine Museum*)

Major General John B. Gordon (*Cook Collection/Valentine Museum*)

Major General Stephen Dodson Ramseur (*The Western Reserve Historical Society*)

Brigadier General George Armstrong Custer (*National Archives*)

Major General George Crook (*National Archives*)

Colonel Charles Russell Lowell (*The Western Reserve Historical Society*)

General Sheridan and his corps commanders leaving their headquarters at Belle Grove House during the Union occupation of the Cedar Creek line in August. (*The Western Reserve Historical Society*)

General Custer doffs his hat to his old friend Tom Rosser before unleashing the Third Cavalry Division against Rosser's Laurel Brigade at Toms Brook on October 9. (*The Western Reserve Historical Society*)

Sheridan orders George Crook to lead his corps to the right of the Union line during the Third Battle of Winchester on September 19, 1864. (*The Western Reserve Historical Society*)

General Gordon and Jed Hotchkiss survey the position and strength of Sheridan's army from Signal Knob, the northernmost prominence of Massnutten Mountain, on October 18, 1864. (*The Western Reserve Historical Society*)

Coming upon a knot of retreating soldiers, Sheridan hauls his horse Rienzi to a halt and yells, "Boys, if I had been with you this morning this thing would not have happened!" (*The Western Reserve Historical Society*)

A distraught General Gordon (left) pleads with the dismissive General Early for reinforcements on the left, toward the end of the long midday pause in the Battle of Cedar Creek. (*The Western Reserve Historical Society*)

The Union Sixth Corps (left) moves forward at the onset of the late-afternoon Federal counterattack. (*The Western Reserve Historical Society*)

Leading his men in a charge on the Confederate lines in Middletown, Colonel Charles Russell Lowell is shot from the saddle by a sharpshooter. (*The Western Reserve Historical Society*)

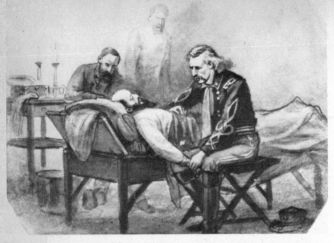

General Custer says farewell to his West Point friend and Civil War enemy, the dying General Ramseur, in Belle Grove House. (*The Western Reserve Historical Society*)

Elizabeth Bacon Custer representing her husband, George, presents the flags captured at Cedar Creek to the War Department. (*The Western Reserve Historical Society*)

rest of the Federal army. "I was awakened at the first signs of day by a terrific clap of thunder," recalled Captain S. E. Howard of the 8th Vermont, "and sprang into a sitting position and listened." He placed the commotion at Crook's camp and assumed an enemy probe was being repulsed. "I listened for the yell of our men, but alas, it never came; instead, the Yi Yi Yi! of the Confederates—it seemed to me as if our whole left were enveloped, enfolded, by this cry. It was like the howls of the wolves around the wagon train in the early days on the great prairies."[36]

Captain John W. DeForest of Emory's staff was at breakfast with the XIX Corps' Second Division commander, Brigadier General Cuvier Grover, when over to the left the "shrill prolonged wail of musketry broke forth, followed by scream on scream of the Rebel yell." In the "unexpected and astounding clamor," the two officers "silently exchanged a glance of surprise and comprehension," as DeForest remembered it. Then General Grover turned to an aide to say, "in his usual gentle, monotonous voice, 'Tell the brigade commanders to move their men into the trenches.' " It was the Second Division that was to have conducted that morning's reconnaissance; they were up and ready, and in minutes were on the firesteps.[37]

Captain DeForest galloped to General Emory's XIX Corps headquarters near Belle Grove and found his chief "just up, coatless and hatless and uncombed, shouting for his horse and his orderlies. He was more excited and alarmed than would have seemed necessary to an ignoramus in warlike matters." Emory sent DeForest on to Wright's headquarters to report that Crook had been assaulted in force. "As I rode away I heard him grumbling, 'I said so; I knew that if we were attacked, it would be there.' " General Wright, although in command of the army, was not at army headquarters but at his own, in the VI Corps camp a half-mile to the north. He was preparing to mount as DeForest rode up to him, and was considerably more calm than Emory. "He knew what I had to tell him, but he listened to my brief message patiently and replied with the formal courtesy of the regular army, 'Give my compliments to General Emory and say that I will be with him shortly.' "[38]

Meanwhile, a mile south of Belle Grove and half a mile northeast of Thoburn's shattered division, Colonel Hayes was forming his command—about 2,000 men of the Second Division, temporarily augmented by a provisional division comprising a thousand raw recruits under Colonel John Howard Kitching. Hayes and his two brigade commanders quickly got the 1,500 men in their camp—one regiment was on picket duty and another (the 9th West Virginia) was camped a half-mile to the southeast, where they had been working on the new entrenchments—up and into a line of battle parallel to the Valley Pike, facing south and east. Kitching did likewise, extending the line to the left. An officer from Thoburn's staff galloped in to report that the First Division was being driven from its works. Hayes soon had more supervisory help than he needed; General Crook, who had been staying at Belle Grove, arrived with his staff, and so did generals Wright and Emory.[39]

Minutes passed. Hayes ordered his men to lie down and wait. DuPont and the Ohio battery rumbled into position between his division and Kitching's men. Nothing could be seen in the fog-cloaked hollow in front of the camp, but the eerie keening of the Rebel yell and "the firing in our front and both on our right and left flanks," Hayes reported later, "told plainly enough that the rebels were rapidly advancing." The question was where they would hit.[40]

The generals were concerned but confident. They had a strong line, plenty of manpower and enough time to deploy. The weak spot was the open hinge between Hayes's northeast-southwest line and XIX Corps' entrenchments, which began on the other side of the pike and ran to the northwest. Emory now ordered Colonel Stephen Thomas's brigade, in reserve on the right of XIX Corps, to shift left and fill that gap, while Wright sent orders for two VI Corps divisions to follow. They could be there, he reckoned, in twenty minutes. General Wright reported later that he "felt every confidence that the enemy would be promptly repulsed."[41]

For the men, however, it was a nerve-stretching wait. Something was coming at them from the slowly roiling fog. DuPont's battery and some of the XIX Corps guns were pounding Wharton's Confederates on the pike near the Cedar Creek bridge, and the Confederate cannon, having thundered through Strasburg onto Hupp's Hill, were opening counter-battery fire. In the dense fog, Major Stevens recalled, "nothing could be seen, nothing could be fixed except that pandemonium on the left. And soon crowds of scattered men came issuing out of the dense veil of fog, some running, most walking fast, but all intent on putting ground between themselves and the fight. And now wagon after wagon, with here and there an ambulance, came bumping over the fields, the drivers urging their teams and casting scared looks behind." Something awful was coming.[42]

Hayes rode his line, steadying the men, showing his calm presence. He especially wanted to bolster Kitching's recruits, who were about to face a severe first test. Colonel Kitching was a veteran of the Peninsula and the Wilderness, but he was a mere twenty-five years old, and Hayes thought he was a good deal more confident than he should have been. "I shall have no trouble," Kitching said. "This is a good position, and I can hold on here if you can hold on down there." Nerves were raw, and Hayes did not expect to be addressed as if he were the junior officer. "You need not feel afraid of my line," he snapped. "I will guarantee that my line will stand there."[43]

Then Hayes turned his horse and saw rising up from the fog in a screaming tidal wave 9,000 fresh Confederate troops, coming not from the southwest where everything was in readiness but from the east, into his left flank. They came on howling, not firing, driving in the skirmishers and saving their bullets for the main line. Long before they closed, the main line began to run.[44]

It was Gordon's three-division turning force. While Kershaw had hit Thoburn's line, Gordon had rapidly deployed his line of battle on the Cooley farm—his own division under Clement Evans on the left, Dodson Ramseur's on the right, Pegram's in reserve behind Evans. They had swept forward, rolling over the isolated camp of the 9th West Virginia before the Federals knew what was happening. "They jumped up running," recalled Private G. W. Nichols of the 61st Georgia, "and did not take time to put on their clothing, but fled in their night clothes, without their guns, hats or shoes." Driving the terrified West Virginians like sheep, the battle line had driven on to the northwest, a rugged half-mile to go.[45]

On the flat behind the new earthworks was an enormous wagon camp, apparently placed there because the left flank had been considered so much safer than anywhere else. "As we were forming in the gray dawn," said Bradwell of the 31st Georgia, "we could see fires kindling in these camps to burn the great collection of army supplies of every kind collected." Sweeping through the burning wagons, the charging Confederates came to the steep ravine and, as Bradwell recalled, "found the whole force which we had been fighting lying down at the bottom of it to escape our fire. Poor fellows! It looked like murder to kill them huddled up there where they could not defend themselves, while we had nothing to do but load and shoot. At the first volley most of those who were not killed or wounded began a scramble to ascend the steep side of the ravine, catching to bushes and any object that offered help. Their knapsacks on their backs presented a conspicuous target for our rifles, and I was surprised as I crossed the ravine to see how few of them were killed."[46]

Meanwhile, behind the Federal lines generals Wright and Emory had moved along the pike to the dangerous opening between the IX Corps entrenchments and Hayes's position. There they met Colonel Wildes coming in from the south with his two battered Ohio regiments—all that was left of the First Division. He had tried to bear east, toward the Second Division, but had run repeatedly into enemy troops on his flank, even behind him. They had driven him from the ridge onto the pike. Unable to get to his own commander, General Crook, Wildes reported to Emory, telling him "what was coming, and of the situation of affairs on his left. The enemy now filled the woods behind us, not over 300 yards from where we struck the Pike." Confederates in force were approaching the gap between the two wings of the Federal army.[47]

The Federals had to have more time, and the Ohio regiments were the only men who could buy it. Emory's order to Colonel Wildes was immediate: charge the woods. The response was just as quick: the 116th and 123d Ohio formed a line of battle again and headed back into the storm. "Every officer and man in our little band knew he was going to meet overwhelming numbers in those woods," Colonel Wildes wrote later, "but they never hesitated. Fixing bayonets, we started on the way back down the hill from the pike, and as we started to ascend to the woods raised the old yell and dashed forward. Just after we started, General Wright rode out in our front and most gallantly led the charge."[48]

This was an extraordinary and not very sensible thing for an army commander to do. It was also a radical departure from Wright's usual cool professionalism. Apparently the desperation and confusion of the moment overwhelmed his judgment, and he impulsively offered his own life in an attempt to rally the two disintegrating corps. "We advanced close to the edge of the woods," Colonel Wildes recorded, "where we met with a terrible fire and a counter charge from ten times our number, which swept us back again to the pike. General Wright was wounded in the face, and came back bleeding freely. He displayed great personal courage, but gallant as he and the men who followed him were, they were obliged to give way before the awful fire they met at the edge of the woods. Falling back again to the pike, we found the 19th Corps changing front to the rear along down the pike." Colonel Stephen Thomas's brigade of XIX Corps was deploying across the pike between the fortifications and Hayes's right.[49]

But even as Thomas closed the gap, the left wing was collapsing. Gordon's howling Confederates struck Hayes's line, according to Major Stevens of VI Corps, "at its weakest point, its left, where stood Kitching's raw men with their left in the air. They broke and fled, with scarcely a show of resistance." Colonel Kitching was shot in the foot as he rode up and down trying to rally his men, but despite great pain and loss of blood, he continued the work, reluctantly following them off the field. (His wound would prove intractable, causing the loss first of his lower leg and then, in January of 1865, of his life.) As his men fell back from their line, Stevens wrote, "Hayes' division, bewildered in the fog and smoke and din, shaken by the rush of fugitives through and past them, with the serried rebel lines smashing their left and advancing toward their rear, gave way."[50]

The stalwart 1st Ohio Light Battery limbered up again and rolled down the pike looking for a new position. DuPont remembered that his bugler, riding just behind him, "had his forage cap shot off his head by a Confederate bullet, whereupon he coolly got off his horse, picked up his cap which the impact of the projectile had carried a number of yards to the rear, and replaced it on his head." About eight hundred yards to the north the Ohioans went into battery again and resumed firing.[51]

The fleeing infantry left Colonel Hayes behind, sitting on his horse dumbfounded and in mortal peril. He wheeled his mount to the rear and spurred it to a gallop, apparently planning to get ahead of his men again, so he could try to rally them. He had gone only a few yards when a bullet tore into the horse, killing it instantly. In the sudden, heavy fall, Hayes was knocked momentarily unconscious, and when he came to had a searing pain in one ankle. He struggled to his feet and saw the enemy battle line rolling toward him, "too near for me to escape unless I used a good deal of strategy and a good deal of speed." Finding to his relief that he could walk on the injured leg, Hayes started hobbling for the rear, only to hear a shouted, profane demand that he halt and surrender. The Confederates had caught up with him.[52]

Hayes forgot the pain, and ran. He dodged into a grove of trees, eluding the charging enemy soldiers for the moment, and kept running. A spent bullet came spinning down out of the roaring air and slammed him on the head; he staggered, stunned, but kept running. Eventually he caught up with his staff, commandeered a horse, remounted, and started looking for a way to stop the rout.[53]

The swelling flow of men, the Army of West Virginia melting away from a shock it could not stand, moved northward across the fields of Belle Grove. The soldiers were not frantic, reported Captain Howard, "only stolidly, doggedly determined to go to the rear. Many of them were only partly dressed, some wearing only underclothing, but they generally carried their muskets. An officer wearing his cap and carrying his naked sword was attired in a shirt, drawers and shoes. The flash of a musket showed him to be a man of forty with a full beard, and I think I should recognize his face today. They passed around us, through our ranks, and almost over us, insistent, determined. They heeded none of our cries to 'Turn back!' 'Make a stand!' but streamed to the rear."[54]

Captain DeForest came across a crowd of stragglers "trudging tranquilly rearward like a crowd hastening home from a circus. 'Captain, what *does* this mean?' I said to the first officer whom I met. 'Why, I suppose it means that we are retreating,' he replied with a bitter smile and a satirical emphasis on the final word." DeForest reflected later that "the chief trouble with them seems to be that they have got out of their places in the military machine. If one of them finds his own company, he will probably rejoin it; he will also join another company of the same regiment; but another regiment he has no use for. An officer who loses his command appears similarly bewildered. He rarely attempts to rally any but his own men and wanders about in search of them, letting the battle go."[55]

Major H. M. Pollard and another divisional staff officer from XIX Corps were "picking our way through these stragglers and trying to ascertain from them what was the matter, when the bridles of both our horses were seized and we were ordered to surrender." The pursuing Confederates were so intermingled with "the fleeing mob" of Federals as to be indistinguishable, and the two men had ridden into the enemy forces. Pollard spurred his horse, which jerked its bridle free and galloped away while "the bullets came like hail, the din was fearful, and the company altogether disagreeable." Pollard's horse was hit twice, but not seriously hurt, and he escaped; his companion was taken prisoner.[56]

The direct line of retreat took most of Harris's First Division stragglers northeastward down the pike, while many of Hayes's men headed northwest, cross-country to Belle Grove. There, Crook and Hayes managed to put together a semblance of a formation again. Hearing of its existence, Colonel Wildes guided his Ohio regiments there.[57]

The men of XIX Corps would be the next to face the onslaught, and they knew it. "The fog was so dense we could not see the enemy in front of us," recalled Major Elias P. Pellett of the 114th New York; "but the rapid and incessant discharge of small arms and cannon, the bursting of shells, and the whizzing of the bullets, mingling into a sound like that of the moaning wind, and thinning our ranks, told us unmistakably of his presence." Early's 40 guns were pounding the line from the other side of the creek; Wharton's division was across the bridge and moving against the left; the sounds of disaster floated in weirdly from the fog-cloaked hills and hollows to the left and rear. The men had formidable breastworks to protect them, and more time than Crook's unfortunate divisions to prepare themselves —but that was also more time for the fear to build.[58]

The interval between Emory's and Crook's forces, into which Thomas's XIX Corps brigade had been moved, was suddenly the left flank of the Federal army. Colonel Thomas, the man who had been interfered with and slandered by General Crook at Winchester, and who had narrowly escaped capture just before the opening of battle, had four New England regiments in his command—the 12th Connecticut, 160th New York, 47th Pennsylvania and 8th Vermont. They were in the path of Jubal Early's entire army; Kershaw's division followed by Wharton's was approaching from the right, Gordon's three divisions from the left.[59]

It now seemed probable to the Federal high command that they were going to have to abandon their entrenchments. If they could do so in a controlled manner they could make a fighting retreat to a new position farther north and hold there. But they had to keep XIX Corps under control; any further loss of organization in the face of an advancing enemy could run through the entire army and lead to its annihilation. "It required much shouting and gesticulating to prevent the worried troops from dissolving into swarms of runaways," said Captain DeForest, and it was frequently a very near thing; "One brigade went rearward at double-quick until the line began to fluctuate ominously, when the officers sprang to the front with drawn swords and beat back the panic, after which the men moved on at the ordinary marching step and in good order." But an orderly withdrawal required time; the momentum of the enemy attack must be spiked. Thomas's brigade would have to be sacrificed. It fell to General Emory to instruct his subordinate and friend to launch a hopeless attack across the pike. Emory said years later, "I never gave an order in my life that cost me so much pain."[60]

Knowing full well what he faced, Thomas formed his brigade and advanced it across the pike toward an enemy-infested wood on the other side, climbing what a *Harper's* correspondent called "this horrible hill of sacrifice, where it offered itself up for the salvation of the army." Private Herbert E. Hill of the 8th Vermont wrote later that "as the great drops of rain and hail precede the hurricane, so now the leaden hail filled the air, seemingly from all directions, while bursting shell from the enemy's cannon on the opposite hill created havoc on our only flank not yet exposed to the rebel infantry."[61]

There was time for a single volley; then, wrote Hill, a "sudden rush of the enemy from every direction, in their yellowish suits, breaking through even the short intervals between the commands, forced each regiment to fight its own battle as the swarming enemy broke upon it with almost resistless fury.

"Suddenly a mass of rebels confronted the flags, and with hoarse shouts demanded their surrender. Defiant shouts went back. 'Never! Never!' And then, amid tremendous excitement, commenced one of the most desperate and ugly hand-to-hand conflicts over the flags that has ever been recorded. Men seemed more like demons than human beings, as they struck fiercely at each other with clubbed muskets and bayonets."

The scenes of frenzy must have seared themselves into Private Hill's mind, for he later reconstructed a remarkably detailed account: "A rebel of powerful build, but short in stature, attempted to bayonet Corporal Worden of the color-guard. Worden, a tall, sinewy man, who had no bayonet on his musket, parried his enemy's thrusts until some one, I think Sergeant Brown, shot the rebel dead. A rebel soldier then levelled his musket and shot Corporal Petre, who held the colors, in the thigh—a terrible wound, from which he died that night. He cried out: 'Boys, leave me; take care of yourselves and the flag!' But in that vortex of hell men did not forget the colors; and as Petre fell and crawled away to die, they were instantly seized and borne aloft by Corporal Perham, and were as quickly demanded again, by a rebel who eagerly attempted to grasp them; but Sergeant Shores of the guard placed his musket at the man's breast and fired, instantly killing him. But now another flash, and a cruel bullet from the dead rebel's companion killed Corporal Perham, and the colors fell to the earth. Once more, amid terrific yells, the colors went up, this time held by Corporal Blanchard; and the carnage went on."[62]

And on and on: "As the enemy crowded on, a hundred rebels took the place of the dozen grasping for the flags." A sergeant, flailing mightily around him with the butt of his rifle, was surrounded and "forced into the enemy's ranks, but refused to surrender, when a side shot tore away his belt, cartridge box, and the flesh to his backbone, which crippled him to the ground (later, when Gordon's men swept by the spot, some of them wearing blue coats picked up in Crook's camps, the sergeant got up and charged with them, firing into the air, until he could slip into his own lines again).

"Over one half the regiment was wounded or killed when the third color-bearer, Corporal Blanchard, was also killed, and the silken colors, their soft folds pierced with bullets, and their third bearer weltering in his blood, bowed low to the earth amidst triumphant yells of the enemy; but to their chagrin in a few seconds it was again flaunting in their faces. Bleeding, stunned, and being literally cut to pieces, but refusing to surrender colors or men, falling back only to prevent being completely encircled, the noble regiment had accomplished its mission." It had bought the required time, at a fearful price; of the 164 men engaged (half the regiment had been on picket duty and was cut off across the creek until later in the day) 110 had been killed or wounded.[63]

The other two regiments had fought as savagely and had been punished as severely—about half the brigade was down— and now they had done all they could do. "It was useless to stand against such fearful odds," wrote Hill, "neither could such frightful butchery be endured longer; and the regiment, now almost completely surrounded by dense masses of rebel infantry, was for a few moments tossed about as a leaf in the small, fitful circle of a whirlwind, and then by a mighty gust lifted from the ground and swept from the field, but not without the flags."

Captain Howard of the 8th Vermont said that everyone

seemed to know when it was time to go, and then it was "every man for himself and the enemy on every hand." Howard was racing along behind Private Robert Sturgeon when "a tall bearded fellow in gray bounded out of the mist and ordered him to halt. They were not twenty feet apart. Sturgeon's gun was empty and his bayonet lost. He cast a startled glance over his shoulder and ran at the top of his speed. The Confederate's long legs took tremendous strides—he sprang forward with a rush and gave a vicious lunge with his bayonet." The thrust went through Sturgeon's clothes, just grazing his side, whereupon the private stopped and threw up his hands. "The stalwart in gray was reaching out as if to take him by the collar, when presto! one in blue, pausing in his hot haste for scarcely one second, placed the muzzle of his gun hardly a foot from the Confederate's head, fired, blowing the head to fragments, and without a word was gone."[64]

The brigade rallied two hundred yards back. But as Captain DeForest (who was with General Emory's staff, not in the fight with his comrades of the 12th Connecticut) reported later, "this second stand was too near a victorious and advancing enemy to result in anything but a little more useless bloodshed. A semicircle of dropping musketry converged on the new position, for Early's reserve under Wharton had just got within range, and its skirmishers were raking us from the south. Our men were apparently bewildered, and did not know which way to face, and could not be brought to fire." The dazed survivors were ordered to retreat northward along the pike.[65]

During Thomas's struggle, Emory had sent Colonel Daniel Macauley's brigade into position on the extreme left of the XIX Corps earthworks, with the 176th New York and part of the 156th New York thrown out at right angles behind the works in an attempt to refuse the flank. Emory ordered Macauley to "stand fast," and sent word to Colonel Edward L. Molineux, whose brigade was next to Macauley's on the right, to "put his men on the reverse side of his rifle-pits. General McMillan, commanding the First Division, promptly placed his First Brigade in the same position, and with excellent judgement, as it was now evident that the enemy's force was coming in upon our left and rear in overwhelming numbers."[66]

It was a very confusing situation; while Kershaw's men slammed into the XIX Corps' left and Ramseur's division came onto the high ground overlooking the Federal rear, Captain DeForest remembered that some of the corps "continued for the present at the breastworks, guarding against an expected attack in force from the south; for none of us could yet believe that Early's main body was in our rear and that our fortified plateau had become a trap, sure to ruin us if we did not skip out of it."[67]

The left regiments had barely time to get into their new positions before they saw the enemy line—Kershaw's—coming at them out of the fog, at right angles to the useless breastworks. "The troops were coming across the pike in masses," recalled Lieutenant Putnam of the 176th New York, "and were so sure of their advance that they could even afford in part to disregard the portion of our line that was most immediately to be reached, and to press their way northward with the view of occupying the pike and of cutting off the retreat of our division."[68]

But the Confederates soon came under a murderous bombardment from a battery—Battery D of the 1st Rhode Island Artillery—that had been placed on the left of the New Yorkers. "A desperate hand-to-hand fight ensued on the left of the brigade line," reported Lieutenant Colonel Alfred Neafie of the 156th New York. "The enemy had planted their colors on our works and were fighting desperately across them, meeting with a stubborn resistance, while they swarmed like bees around the battery on our left and rear. The enemy rushed upon, seized, and attempted to capture the colors of the 156th and 176th New York."[69]

Sergeant Philip Decker of the 156th New York saw his regiment's color-bearer shot down and leaped forward to grab the flag. He came face-to-face with two Confederates, one of them the color-bearer of Kershaw's 53d Georgia, and for a few seconds the three men wrestled each other for possession of the two flags. One of the Confederates was shot down, and so many of the nearby Federals that the regiments began to give way behind Sergeant Decker, who, afraid he was going to lose the flag, ripped it from the standard and started for the rear. A bullet shattered his elbow, but he kept on as long as he could, and when he fell from loss of blood he handed the colors on to an officer, who saved them from the melee. The flag of the 176th New York was brought off in similar fashion.

While the New Yorkers were being hammered northward away from the XIX Corps trenches, personnel at corps headquarters were laboring to get the heavy supply wagons and ambulances away on what DeForest called a "wretched country road" to Winchester. "The general ammunition wagons had scarcely begun to file out of the park when one of Payne's troopers dashed up shouting, 'Here! Bring that train this way.' 'What the hell have you to do with this train?' replied a guard, and sent a bullet through the bold adventurer.[70]

"Patrick, one of the Negro waiters at Emory's quarters, made a gallant attempt to save the staff cow, but was obliged to take to his heels across lots, leaving his charge mortally wounded. At a little stone house nearby, a reporter of the New York *Herald* was yelling for his blanket roll and getting it thrust out to him through a half-opened door, which was immediately slammed in his face to keep out random bullets. The occupants of this dwelling, a poor widow and her children, remained shut up in it all day, cowering below the level of the windows for safety."[71]

Emory ordered the rest of the corps to abandon the breastworks, "fall back and establish a new line of resistance." As DeForest put it, "Our camp, overlooked as it now was by the enemy, had been changed from a fortress to a slaughter pen." Yet to his amazement, DeForest saw very few enemy soldiers: "We were being peppered and demoralized and beaten by an undiscoverable enemy."[72]

As the men of XIX Corps retreated, they passed what was left of Crook's Army of West Virginia, now the size of a brigade, gathered in front of Belle Grove. "Here were Crook and his staff, Hayes and his staff, and a large number of officers," wrote Colonel Wildes, "striving with might and main to stem the tide of disaster." Meanwhile frantic clerks and staff officers were flying in and out of the great house, flinging the papers, maps and records of Sheridan's headquarters into wagons while others packed the camp and prepared the headquarters wagons for flight. Similar efforts were going on in the nearby tents of Torbert's cavalry command, in an orchard toward the pike. They were all in acute danger of being overrun by the oncoming tide of Confederates, which was now across the pike and on the plain in front of the house.[73]

Captain Sanford of Torbert's staff was trying to help get the camp struck and the wagons away when he "noticed with some surprise" that his own tent, which he shared with an Irish-born infantry officer, Captain John J. Coppinger, "was still standing though everything else in the headquarters was down. I had just called Sergeant Tully to 'get that tent down' when Gen. Torbert dashed up and asked what the tent was standing there for. The sergeant, who had been in to the tent to see, came out and saluting the General said, 'Captain Coppinger is taking his bawth, sir!' I thought Torbert would ride him down as he screamed, 'Cut those tent ropes. Cut the ropes, I say.' It seemed that my gallant tent mate had concluded that things were not particularly desperate, and that at all events the rebels would not be so ungentlemanly as to interfere with his toilet."[74]

While most of XIX Corps filed to the rear past Belle Grove, Crook's men advanced. "We checked the advance of the enemy, and pushed him back a short distance," said Wildes, "and I think the very hardest and most stubborn fighting of the day took place here. We were fighting Kershaw's and Wharton's rebel divisions." He thought perhaps 1,500 Federals were in this makeshift line, with a very high proportion—"fully one-fourth"—of them being officers. "A great many line and staff officers took muskets and lay down in the ranks of the men, while all mounted officers used their holster revolvers." One of these was Crook's adjutant, the quiet and studious Captain Phil Bier, transformed into a tiger now, raging up and down just behind the desperate line, unfortunately on a white horse that marked him and drew the bullets that before long struck him down and claimed his life. But, said Wildes, "the position was held for over half an hour, which gave time for the trains to move out of the way."[75]

Off to Crook's right, a brigade of XIX Corps had faced about and conducted a similar holding action. To his left rear the incredible Colonel Thomas, seeing that the headquarters train was having difficulty getting across Meadow Run, halted his battered regiments and faced them toward the enemy yet again. Into his line he dragooned the passing stragglers from Crook's divisions. General Crook rode up, approved what Thomas was doing with a curt "All right," and then "rode away as he came," Private Hill noted, "unattended by even an orderly." Thus several units, each thinking it was alone, fought vicious little holding actions, but these were merely eddies in the remorseless tide of men moving to the rear.[76]

General Torbert had galloped north from Belle Grove to Merritt's camp, and in Sanford's words had "found our own troops in beautiful order." But they had nothing to do. Rosser's attacking force was seized of a curious lassitude, entirely out of character for the Laurel Brigade and their hard-charging commander. They seemed content to hold their position at the ford and pop away at the two brigades (Lowell's and Kidd's) confronting them. It was true that the Federal cavalry was not interfering with Early's attack, and perhaps Rosser chose to declare this mission accomplished. But in fact the Federal troopers were being kept from the fighting not by Rosser but by lack of orders.[77]

Colonel A. Bayard Nettleton of the 2nd Ohio Cavalry remembered that awful time of waiting while "the rattle of musketry in front of the infantry increased to heavy volleys, the volleys thickened into a continuous roar; and now, as day began to dawn, the deep bass of the artillery came in to complete the grand but terrible chorus of battle.

"Awaiting orders! That is the time that tries the courage of the bravest. Once in the heat and hurry and inspiration of the battle, the average soldier forgets fear in the excitement of the hour; but to stand at a safe distance, though within easy sight and hearing of the conflict, ready, expectant, every nerve strung, awaiting the word of command to march into a hailstorm of death, that is the crucial test. It is at such a time that all the mental struggle involved in a soldier's death is undergone, leaving nothing but the mere physical pang of sudden dying to complete the sacrifice."[78]

An hour went by. Another. Still the cavalry sat their horses, waiting. Merritt deployed his headquarters escort—the 5th

U. S. Cavalry—along with his divisional staff officers and orderlies in a line across the fields north of Middletown to stop stragglers. They had only limited success, although they beat on the stubbornly fleeing men with their sabers and even opened fire on them.[79]

It was about 7:30 A.M. Captain Dickert of Kershaw's brigade, which was now northwest of Belle Grove, turned to look back at the overrun Federal camps and headquarters: "What a sight! Here came stragglers, who looked like half the army, laden with every imaginable kind of plunder—some with an eye to comfort had loaded themselves with new tent cloths, nice blankets, overcoats, or pants, while others, who looked more to actual gain in dollars and cents, had invaded the sutlers' tents and were fairly laden down with such articles as they could find the readiest sale for," especially frying pans and tin cups. "I saw one man with a stack of wool hats on his head, one pressed in the other, until it reached more than an arm's length above his head."[80]

Not far to the north, Captain DeForest trudged away, behind the sullenly retreating XIX Corps. "Random bullets tossed up whiffets of dust from the hard-trodden earth, and their quick, spiteful *whit-whit* sang through an air acrid with the smoke of gunpowder. Here and there were splashes of blood, and zigzag trails of blood, and bodies of men and horses. I never on any other battlefield saw so much blood as on this of Cedar Creek. The firm limestone soil would not receive it, and there was no pitying summer grass to hide it."[81]

DeForest heard a straggler, loping to the rear through the ranks of men who were still uncertainly facing the enemy, bellow cheerfully to a retreating comrade, "The bloody Sixth is going in. *They'll* stop these blasted cusses. They say that, by Jesus, *they'll* hold 'em."[82]

Chapter 7

The Fatal Pause

The men of VI Corps, in their reserve position well away from the point of impact of the surprise attack, had plenty of time to prepare for the onslaught. "Although the call to battle was sudden," wrote Lieutenant Colonel Moses M. Granger of the 122d Ohio, these veterans "knew how to answer it"—coolly, methodically, fatalistically. "Without coat or hat, Adjutant Wheeler hurried to each first sergeant with the orders—'Pack up—send to the rear every thing not needed in a fight; form lines, stack arms and then do what *can* be done about break-fast.' There was no disorder; no hesitation. The first brigade order, 'Be ready to move at a moment's notice,' found us so ready we could have moved *then.*"[1]

The men dressed, rolled their shelter halves in their blankets, folded the tents, packed their knapsacks if they had them and formed up while the crashing waves of gunfire lapped ever closer, as storm waves mount a beach. Orders reached the ranks smoothly despite the ripple of command changes caused by Sheridan's absence; with Wright commanding the army, Brigadier General James B. Ricketts of the Third Division had the corps, and Colonel J. Warren Keifer succeeded Ricketts. Through this chain came Wright's summons for two divisions —the Third and the First—to advance to the threatened hinge between Crook and Emory.[2]

"Fall in, men, fall in!" yelled the officers of Keifer's Third. The troops ran into ranks, stood to attention, dressed their alignment, counted off and faced right or left. But as Colonel

Granger recorded, this was still the army, and for all their hurry the men were not moved out immediately. "With prudent prevision we used the short interval of delay for packing rations in the inner man. Our hasty meal was ending when, 'Form line; follow the 110th Ohio,' set us in motion." Feeling its way south through the murky, pre-dawn light toward the thunder of battle ahead and to the left, the column tramped and clinked across its campground plateau, then down into the fog-choked ravine of Meadow Brook toward Belle Grove.[3]

During this descent, with no enemy visible and the fighting still ahead somewhere in the formless fog, the battle reached out for them. "Just as we neared the creek, Lieutenant Hilliard of Company I, sat suddenly down, and to my question, 'Are you hit, Ned?' in quiet tones replied, 'Yes, Colonel.' Compelled to move on with the regiment, I left him, but could not help noticing the composure with which he spoke. His wound proved to be a mortal one."[4]

Colonel Granger led his men up onto a field just west of Belle Grove. There the brigade was broken up and borne back—not by the enemy but by the relentless press of fleeing XIX Corps soldiers—and he saw immediately that there was no point in trying to stay. To Granger's left a wagon train was pounding toward Middletown, while beyond it a "thin line of blue, facing southeast, was firing at clumps of men in gray east of the turnpike." The thin line may well have been Colonel Thomas's New Englanders. Colonel Granger took his regiment back across the creek in search of a better position.[5]

It was exceedingly difficult to know what to do. "Unable to see the ground for over a hundred yards, unable to fix the position of other troops, each command was in a measure isolated," recalled Major Hazard Stevens. Meanwhile "the heavy and continuous firing, the rebel yells, the swarms of fugitives, the whizzing musket balls, the roar of the enemy's guns (which, having crossed the creek after Wharton, were now opening along the pike) and the shriek and burst of their shells told only of disaster."[6]

Yet to a remarkable degree, everyone kept his head. When XIX Corps gave way, Wright ordered Ricketts to get VI Corps moving to the left, to try to get in front of the attack. Despite the fog and the confusion, these orders were promptly obeyed, and in the meanwhile the division, brigade and regimental officers, who had been through the fire many times before, reflexively attempted to do the right things: maintain contact with one another, keep their men calm and under control, and find a defensible line.

The VI Corps artillery now went into action "in a huddle, almost as they stood in camp," said Stevens, 24 guns firing whenever they had an opening through the masses of fleeing wagons and comrades. The gunners had no targets, they merely discharged their pieces "into the fog and at the noise." The Third and First Divisions, in some confusion and with much mixing of units, formed in support of the guns.[7]

Colonel Granger found the Third Division in line to the right of the guns, facing south, as he came back across Meadow Brook; followed by the 67th Pennsylvania he deployed his men on the right of the position. But, he wrote later, "it was at once apparent that the line was wrongly placed. The ground sloped upward from us to the edge of the plateau. The enemy ascending from the run (which turning southwest separated us from Belle Grove) could lie down and use that edge as a breastwork from which to fire at us in open ground. So I, at once, ordered my two regiments forward."[8]

At the crest of the ridge Granger's men collided with a portion of Kershaw's division, which came swarming over the top. After a sharp struggle Kershaw's men fell back down the slope toward Belle Grove to regroup. For a time the Federals had a breather; Granger could see an enemy column probing off to the right, under fire from the rest of his brigade, and he watched "straggling clumps of rebels moving north along and near the pike," off to his left, firing as they went. But for the moment, "no enemy was in sight upon my front." General Wright galloped up, his beard matted with blood. He questioned Colonel Granger about the situation and then rode away, looking "serious, but not discouraged."[9]

Meanwhile, VI Corps' First Division had followed the Third only a short distance southward before it got orders to head east, toward Middletown, and take position to the left of the guns. With the enemy already well beyond it to the east and

even the north, the division took up a line along the crest of
Meadow Brook's north bank, on a road running parallel to, and
a half-mile west of, the Valley Pike.[10]

"The first gray light of dawn began to show," a soldier in the
121st New York remembered, "and up from the fog in our
front came men moving rapidly toward us, the continued noise
and tumult of conflict growing nearer all the time." These were
not enemy troops, yet, but they were almost as demoralizing;
"a disorderly mass of men, officers and privates, as helpless and
panic-stricken a crowd as ever was seen. Our officers made
strenuous efforts to check and compose them, but without
avail. They were simply insane with fear, and so cursing them,
we permitted them to continue their flight."[11]

A short distance to the east, Captain Benjamin W. Crowninshield of Sheridan's staff was struggling to rally the stragglers,
who were utterly impervious to his efforts. "Although not running, the men poured steadily to the rear, officers and men
alike, and no efforts of mine could stop one." But he was finally
able to snag two guns that came rumbling out of the fog. He
placed them "in battery in an excellent position on the crest of
the hill, and looked about for supports. I got a regimental color,
about two hundred men, and finally a major; formed a line, and
put him in command, expecting great things. I then went after
more men to support, and found and brought them back only
to find guns, colors, men and major gone."[12]

While the First Division braced itself, the Second crossed to
eastward behind it, "endeavoring to reach the high ground on
the pike near Middletown," as Major Aldace F. Walker recalled it. General Getty apparently began this movement even
before receiving Wright's orders. Like Wright, Getty understood immediately that if the Federals could not stabilize their
left and get a grip on the Valley Pike, they faced destruction. As
the men of the Second marched toward the vital road through
the lightening gloom, Major Walker could see to his right, in
the declivity of Meadow Brook behind Belle Grove and along
the rising ground between the brook and the pike, a scene of
"universal confusion and dismay.

"Wagons and ambulances lumbering hither and thither in
disorder; pack horses led by frightened bummers, or wandering

at their own free will; crowds of officers and men, some shod and some barefoot, many of them coatless and hatless, few without their rifles, but all rushing wildly to the rear; oaths and blows alike powerless to halt them; a cavalry regiment stretched across the field, unable to stem the torrent; and added to the confusion and consternation the frequent sight of blood —ambulances, wagons, men, stained and dripping—with here and there a corpse; while the whistling bullets and the shrieking shell told that the enemy knew their advantage and their ground."[13]

The Second Division came under fire from Confederate skirmishers already in the woods just across Meadow Brook, and General Getty put his men into line along the creek, to the left and rear of the First Division. He then ordered his skirmishers forward to clear the woods. This they did, and as Walker put it, "for the first time during the day the enemy was opposed by the regular formation of a skirmish line masking a line of battle." The din was awesome, Major Stevens recalled; "the crash and crackle of musketry, the boom of guns and burst of shells, mingled yells and cheers." Yet the Federals felt a new confidence that "now at last surely the rebel onslaught could be repulsed and hurled back."[14]

With remarkable speed given the circumstances, the corps had managed to fling together a more-or-less contiguous line extending a mile and a half to the west from Getty's left, which was about three hundred yards from the pike and about a half-mile south of Middletown. Lieutenant Theodore Vaill, adjutant of the 2nd Connecticut Heavy Artillery (fighting as infantry), took a moment to look around at the First Division line. "General Wright, bareheaded, and with blood trickling from his beard, sat on his horse nearby, as if bewildered, or in a brown study." (This characterization by a junior officer, based on a glance, is unfair; Wright had a great deal on his mind, but as the constant stream of his orders throughout the battle attests, he was far from bewildered.) "The newly risen sun, huge and bloody, was on their side in more senses than one. Our line faced directly to the east, and we could see nothing but that enormous disc, rising out of the fog, while *they* could see every man in our line, and could take good aim."[15]

The Confederate situation was somewhat confused, but extremely satisfying to John Gordon. "A little after sunrise we had captured nearly all of the Union artillery," he wrote; "we had scattered in veriest rout two thirds of the Union army; while less than one third of the Confederate forces had been under fire, and that third intact and jubilant. Only the Sixth Corps of Sheridan's entire force held its ground." This, of course, was a problem: "It stood like a granite breakwater built to beat back the oncoming flood; but it was also doomed unless some marvelous intervention should check the Confederate concentration which was forming against it."[16]

At about 7:30 A.M., from a vantage point on the heights traversed by the Valley Pike east of Belle Grove, Gordon kept his concentration moving. Kershaw, while not technically under Gordon's command, moved eagerly forward with the Second Corps. Colonel Carter, whose guns were arriving on the heights from Hupp's Hill, rode up to Gordon. Carter was not under the Georgian's command either, but, like Kershaw, was unconcerned with protocol; Gordon was rolling and all Carter wanted to know was how far he was going to go before regrouping. Carter knew there would have to be a stop somewhere, soon; the men had been up all night, marching for much of it, and had been fighting for more than two hours. The formations were becoming ragged. But Gordon was not ready to rest them yet; "I am going through the town," he told Carter, "and stop beyond it."[17]

Colonel Carter was more than ready; "General, you will need no infantry," he said. "With enfilade fire from my batteries I will destroy that corps in twenty minutes." Gordon knew better. He appreciated what Carter's guns could do from the high ground along the pike, and of course he wanted them there, but if he was going through Middletown, he was going to have to go through VI Corps, and only infantry could do that. All the infantry, in a concentrated attack. He kept the line moving. There was a great deal of confusion and intermixing of commands, but in general it was still Kershaw on the left, advancing against the Third Division, with Evans facing the First Division in the center and Ramseur pressing down the pike into Middletown against the flank of Getty's Second Division.

Pegram was in close support of Ramseur, and Wharton, presumably, was coming up the pike and would be available soon.[18]

The Federals of the 121st New York, in the First Division line to the left of the corps artillery, had just noticed that the flow of stragglers had subsided when Evans's Confederates came at them out of the fog. "The tide of battle was stayed for a while," recalled a New York soldier, "but they poured a withering fire upon our brigade, and Lamb's gunners and our men were falling fast. We maintained our position for nearly half an hour, until the fog lifted and revealed our position to be perilous in the extreme."[19]

Over on the right, the Third was being hit hard by Kershaw. Colonel William Emerson had marched his brigade to the left of that division and had found a place next to Captain James McKnight's Battery M, 5th U.S. Artillery. There Emerson ordered his men to lie down, he reported, while "troops, artillery and wagons went pouring through our lines. It being quite foggy, it was difficult to tell when our troops were through and the enemy commencing to come. As soon as satisfied on that point the brigade commenced firing."[20]

So did the battery. "Captain McKnight ordered us to open with case," Corporal Augustus Buell recalled, "but there was such a jam of wagons and other debris in our immediate front that we had to wait for them to clear the way, and when we did open, the enemy was pretty close to us." And coming hard. Emerson's line was trembling under the force of the onslaught when it suddenly came under severe enfilading fire from the right—where minutes before there had been Union troops. "I ordered up support from the second line," said Colonel Emerson, "but the fire was so heavy the men could not be held there."[21]

The Second Division, to the left rear of the First, was the last to breast the surging waves of gray. Down in Meadow Brook hollow in front of them the fog persisted, and Getty's skirmishers also hesitated to fire for fear of hitting their own men. "At last a scattered line was dimly seen approaching through the mist," wrote Walker, "which felt no such hesitation, giving us a volley which at once convinced us that the skirmishers of the

enemy were upon us. Their progress was stopped without difficulty, but a double line of infantry was soon made out moving
forward in perfect array, the front line firing heavily as they
came."[22]

These were Ramseur's men—Battle's and Grimes's brigades,
for a time separated from his other two brigades which had
crossed the grounds at Belle Grove and were advancing with
Kershaw—who thus far had had a walkover and were primed
for a fight. Ramseur, characteristically, was intoxicated by
combat. Mounted on a flashy bay, impeccably uniformed, a
flower in his lapel to commemorate the birth of his child, he
ranged his lines, urging his men on. One of his brigade commanders described Ramseur's "presence and manner" at such
times "electrical." At about this time Major Henry Kyd Douglas of Early's staff saw Ramseur "leading his men and driving
the enemy. He was greatly excited, pleased, and laughingly
cried, 'Let's drive 'em, Douglas, for I must get a furlough to see
my little wife and new baby!' "[23]

Meanwhile the pugnacious Getty had ordered his division to
attack into the teeth of Ramseur's advance, and at the same
time to wheel right to gain the pike and turn the flank of the
Confederates assaulting the First and Third Divisions. "Getty
bestrode his horse just in front of the right of his line," Major
Stevens, remembered. "His staff officers galloped back to him
and reported that the brigade commanders were all ready to
advance, and he turned to give the final order, when the troops
on his right were seen to break and fly in the utmost confusion.
As far down the line as could be seen in the fog, the men were
breaking successively, file after file, like a row of toppling bricks
set up in play by some sportive urchin. We could see the break
run along the line until it came to the last man next to the
division, and he, too, sprang from his place and ran back after
the others."[24]

As the Third Division had begun to give way over on the
right, Major Stevens reported, "instantly the swarming rebel
infantry was among the guns, and captured three of Captain
James McKnight's." But the next battery in line slewed a gun
around and "belched canister" into the Confederates; the 10th
Vermont and the 6th Maryland mounted a desperate counter-

charge, and in hand-to-hand fighting cleared the enemy from the battery again. But by this time the Third Division right had been hammered back, and the First had begun to abandon its line. It had lost nearly half its officers and one-third of its men in thirty minutes.[25]

Colonel Ranald Mackenzie's 2nd Connecticut Heavy Artillery was still clinging to its position when a First Division staff officer brought orders to "move directly to the rear by right of companies." The horrified Mackenzie yelled, "My God! I cannot! This line will break if I do!" The officer had no time to argue. "Well," he shouted as he turned his plunging horse toward the rear, "there goes the 65th [New York], and the First Brigade is gone." Moments later, Lieutenant Vaill reported, Mackenzie's horse "was struck square in the head and after spinning around two or three times on his hind legs went down —dead as a stone; and the Colonel, who had previously got a shot through the heel, went off over his head. The fog had now thinned off somewhat, and a firm rebel line, with colors full high advanced, came rolling over a knoll just in front of our left, not more than three hundred yards distant. 'Rise up! Retreat!' said Mackenzie, and the battalion began to move back."[26]

McKnight's battery was now fearfully exposed. "The enemy came up out of a ravine to our left and fired a scattering volley," wrote cannoneer Buell. "This killed George Appleton. He was standing close to me, and his blood spouted in jets as he fell, staining my jacket and trousers from the breast to the knee." The guns were nearly enveloped, and McKnight finally ordered a retreat. More Confederates appeared from the ravine, said Buell, "and, as we were limbering up, fired a volley which downed every driver and team on No. 2 gun of the left section, and they also reached far enough around our left flank to get in on our rear and cripple two of the caissons of the left section. But we got off with the other five guns and four caissons, and fell rapidly back."[27]

Behind the breaking Federal formations rose a second, slightly higher ridge—actually the southern end of a half-mile-wide plateau that rose just west of Middletown and stretched away to the northeast. For some time fleeing masses of men had been flowing to either side of this promontory like floodwaters, XIX Corps refugees along its western flank, Crook's men mostly on the eastern side, where the pike was. Now as VI Corps backed away from the onslaught, the Third and First Divisions headed along the western side of the ridge, carrying with them generals Ricketts and Wright. Ricketts was down with his sixth wound of the war. He had been shot full in the chest, and although he would survive and serve out the war, he would never fully recover.

On the way the Third Division tried to rally. Joseph Tennant of the 106th New York stopped behind a rail fence and was plugging intently away at the howling Rebels when his Company B was again flanked, and again fell back. Tennant did not notice the movement at first, and when he did he had to jump up and race after his comrades to avoid being left behind. "The bullets were flying as thick as hail," Tennant recalled. "I could hear the crack of the bullets as they struck the knapsacks of the men ahead of me. The rebels kept up a continuous cry of 'Halt, halt!' but I said to myself, 'Legs, do your duty.' "[28]

"The enemy pushed so furiously that he seemed to arrive at every place we wished to occupy," recalled Captain John K. Bucklyn of the 1st Rhode Island Artillery. "Positions changed so rapidly that staff officers could not report, and commanders could not wait. Guns were limbered up and brought away when the enemy was already within the battery." The VI Corps artillery brigade had lost 6 guns, more than 100 men killed and wounded—25 percent of its strength—and a like number of horses. It was in retreat, but it was still fighting, and the Confederate pursuit was beginning to weaken.[29]

Getty, surprised by what seemed to him to be an unwarranted retreat by the other divisions, reluctantly joined the rearward movement. But he backed only a few hundred yards up the ridge and took position on its southeastern crest. There the Second was joined by McKnight's battery, and Moore's brigade of cavalry. The troopers, after having been driven from the Shenandoah River fords by Gordon's advance, had circled around behind Middletown, had ridden back toward the sound of the guns, and now dismounted and went into line, along with Brigadier General Thomas C. Devin's cavalry brigade, on Getty's left. They were next to General Bidwell's Third Brigade, which was formed north of the cemetery facing southeast toward Middletown; McKnight's guns went into battery just south of the cemetery; the Vermont Brigade had the curving center, overlooking the ground just yielded; and Warner's First Brigade was on the right, facing southwest toward Belle Grove.[30]

As Corporal Buell grudgingly admitted afterward, "the fact is that even the Sixth Corps was in some little confusion there, which is saying a great deal. The enemy himself appeared to be in a good deal of confusion, and took some time to rally— perhaps half an hour—on the ground which we had occupied at first." There was no doubt, however, that Jubal Early's victorious army was coming on, and that Getty's division was now the only organized Federal infantry unit remaining on the field. "So we loaded canister double," Buell remembered, "and braced ourselves for business of a pressing nature."[31]

It was about 8 A.M. The red October sun had been above the horizon for two hours, and was burning the last of the fog from the protected hollows. Jubal Early was making his way leisurely northward along the Valley Pike, apparently content to remain a spectator for nearly two hours after the collapse of the XIX Corps left had uncovered the Valley Pike bridge across Cedar Creek, thus admitting him to the field. He surveyed the litter of a routed army, the rolling billows of smoke and the contesting lines of men, all etched unforgettably by the brilliant morning light, and his heart soared. Couriers from Gordon brought confirmation of the smashing of every Federal attempt at resistance so far.

Old Jube's face "became radiant with joy," a staff officer recorded, and well it might; he had bested the "timid" Sheridan at last, he had redeemed his reputation as a commander from the humiliations of Winchester and Fisher's Hill, he had handed the Confederacy a new lease on life. History had recorded few such stunning successes, but in thinking of his West Point studies, Early remembered how Napoleon had used the fog to best a superior army at Austerlitz, then had greeted the sun that rose on his victory. "Ah," Old Jube intoned, mocking his own pretension even as he thought of it, "the Sun of Middletown! The Sun of Middletown!"[32]

Kershaw and Gordon had executed the attack plan flawlessly, and now it was time for Old Jube to take the reins back into his own hands. It was time to demonstrate that he was, indeed, equal to his own intellect. Early and his staff rode up to General Gordon on the pike just south of Middletown. According to General Gordon's passionate but muddled account of the meeting, Old Jube was in high good humor, and greeted his subordinate commander as if their work were done: "Well, Gordon, this is glory enough for one day. This is the 19th. Precisely one month ago today we were going in the opposite direction." He was recalling Winchester, a battle that he had declared a victory at midday.

"It is very well so far, General," Gordon remembered saying; "but we have one more blow to strike, and then there will not be left an organized company of infantry in Sheridan's army." Gordon formally relinquished command of the Second Corps, noting as he did so that he had just committed Pegram's division. He expressed his confidence that if Early continued to strike with everything he had, the entire VI Corps could be destroyed or captured. As Gordon remembered it, he was horrified to hear Early's smiling, relaxed response: "No use in that; they will all go too directly."

It was as if Sheridan had never come, as if there had been no change in the earlier Federal temerity in the Valley, as if Winchester and Fisher's Hill had never happened. "That is the Sixth Corps, General," said Gordon, appalled. "It will not go unless we drive it from the field."

"Yes, it will go, directly." Early was convinced that the Federals were beaten and could do nothing now but retreat; consequently, there was little left for the Confederate to do but clean up, no need for further sacrifice.[33]

Gordon's narrative was hopelessly vague about the time and place of this exchange, and was perhaps overdrawn. Early made no sudden change when he resumed command of the corps, but as he put it in his own memoir "rode forward on the Pike to ascertain the position of the enemy, in order to continue the attack." Much of the army was badly fagged out and beginning to straggle. They were nearing the spot where Gordon had already said he intended to stop. As usual, Gordon overemphasized what he might have done and undervalued what was done. But when he rode away to resume command of his division, his clear vision of the battlefield was replaced by a limited, badly flawed one; and his fierce, implacable drive was replaced by a certain temerity.[34]

Whether because of the weariness and confusion of the troops, or because of Early's orders, the succeeding attacks were piecemeal. First, part of Kershaw's division struck the Vermont brigade and a portion of Warner's to the right. "Getty's veterans coolly held their fire until the enemy was close upon them," reported Major Stevens, "then delivered it in their very faces, and tumbled the shattered ranks down the hill, pursued to the foot by Warner's two right regiments." Meanwhile, the Confederate guns rolled into position farther forward along the pike, unlimbered one after the other and opened fire, their shells screeching onto the ridge with ever-increasing frequency. Warner's men scrambled back to their positions, and the Confederates re-formed their line.[35]

The next blow fell to the left of center, on the Vermont Brigade again but also heavily on Bidwell's, and McKnight's battery between them. "On the rebels came, through the woods," said Walker, "with a vigor that promised success." These were mostly Ramseur's men—Battle's and Grimes's brigades, along with some of Pegram's troops who had moved forward into the gap opened when Ramseur's brigades diverged—advancing with a heavy skirmish line out, followed by the line of battle. The keening of the Rebel yell rose among the roaring of the guns. Corporal Buell, now an acting gunner, fired his piece at point blank range: "I kept her muzzle down, so that every round threw dirt in their faces, but there was no stopping them."[36]

Skirmishers were supposed to fall back to the main line of battle when contact was made, but these just kept coming. "I could not believe they were actually going to close with us," wrote the astonished Buell, "until the men on the remaining gun of our left section abandoned it and retreated toward the old graveyard wall. Their front line was not in order, but there was an officer leading them, and I distinctly heard him shout: 'Rally on the Battery! Rally on the Battery!' Our section and the right stood firm. Pat Hunt drove home his last double canisters when their leading men were within 40 feet of him, and as our No. 4—sturdy Jake Gabriel—fell shot through the head in the act of 'hooking on' I took the lanyard as it slipped through his nerveless fingers and yanked it right in their teeth, almost, but they were right on top of us, and as Kershaw's [and Ramseur's] Rebel veterans understood this kind of business they 'opened out,' so that the charge did not hit any of them, as I could see." Buell wanted to run, but when he saw the men around him draw their revolvers, determined to make a stand, "I did not see how I could consistently desert them, and so I pulled, too, and began shooting at the Johnnies coming up out of the ravine." In seconds, "they were amongst us, amid smoke, fog, wreck, yells, clash and confusion which no pen can depict and no pencil portray. It was now man to man, hand to hand, with bayonet and musket butt on their side and revolvers, rammer heads and handspikes on ours!"[37]

About 75 Confederate skirmishers were among the Federal guns, which were by now manned by only about 30 artillerymen, many of whom were unarmed. Buell fired his last bullet into the head of a Confederate lieutenant, at such close range that "my flash singed his eyelashes and blew his left cheek full of powder." The officer went down, saved from a mortal wound by a wad of paper he had stuffed in his overlarge hat to make it fit better. "A wiry cuss, bareheaded and wearing a red shirt, lunged at me with his bayonet as the lieutenant was falling." Buell parried with his arm, and felt the bayonet pierce him as he fell over backward. "Just as I was falling I saw a bright bayonet and rifle barrel thrust almost under my nose, with a blinding flash and report, and down came Rebel, musket and all, on top of me. Thinking that he had only stumbled, I quickly disengaged myself, and, rising on my left hand and knee, struck him over the left ear with my pistol barrel, reaching for him with every muscle in my arm. This sagged him a little to one side, and then I noticed that he was 'clawing gravel' with his fingers (the convulsive grasping at the grass and dirt which a man dying of a gunshot wound will always do)."[38]

The sergeant from the Vermont Brigade who had saved Buell's life lifted him to his feet, and they returned to the fight. Buell now saw that "80 or 100 of the Vermonters" had charged in and were driving the Confederates "out of the battery at the point of the bayonet." In seconds, however, the main enemy line would be upon them. "Lieutenant Baldwin desperately attempted to limber the remaining guns to the rear. As the limbers wheeled in for this purpose they got a fierce volley from the enemy's main line about 200 feet from us, and nearly every driver and horse in the five teams fell." Corporal Buell and a handful of survivors—there were no officers left—ran to the guns and tried to wrestle them away by hand through the carnage.[39]

The Confederate artillery, seeing the skirmish line fall back, resumed fire on the battery. A man next to Buell, struck in the neck by a shell fragment, "threw his arms around my neck and asked me to carry him away or save him or something of that sort. But being busy trying to limber up the gun, and having no orders to assist the wounded, it was necessary for me to shake him off." Now Buell's left sleeve and side, in addition to his uniform front, was soaked with gore: "I was literally bloody as a butcher." Somehow the remaining men got two of the guns away, leaving the rest behind. Buell glanced behind and saw "the unconquerable Vermonters" battling the enemy's main line "with bayonet and musket butt right among the guns we had abandoned." Later in the day, "19 dead men were found within the battery front—artillerymen, Vermonters and Rebels —all mixed up and piled across one another in some instances, and of these five showed no marks but those of the cold steel!"[40]

Bidwell's Brigade to the left of the battery and Grant's Vermonters to the right were unable to withstand the overwhelming weight of the attack. But instead of breaking, or retreating to a selected line, they began to yield with excruciating slowness, giving up ground one dogged, backward step at a time. They were at the uttermost limits of exertion, teetering on the edge of disintegration. "A panic for a moment seemed to threaten the Sixth and Eleventh Vermont," Major Walker recalled, "but the bravery of the officers at once restored the courage of the men, and they gave and took without further flinching, though the struggle was deadly. At this critical juncture a shell struck General Bidwell as he sat on his horse holding his men to their work; he was a man of remarkably large frame, and the missile tore through his shoulders and lungs, bringing him heavily to ground."[41]

Although very nearly eviscerated by the shell, Bidwell was still conscious when the surgeon rushed up. "Doctor, I suppose there is no hope for recovery." The surgeon told him there was none. "Oh, my poor wife," said Bidwell. Then, "Doctor, see that my record is right at home. Tell them I died at my post doing my duty." As the surgeon later reported, "a few hours of intense suffering and the brave man was relieved by death."[42]

With their well-liked commander down mortally wounded, and the savage enemy attack coming on unabated, it seemed certain that the Third Brigade would now break. But Bidwell's successor, Lieutenant Colonel Winsor B. French, yelled an inspired command: "Don't run till the Vermonters do!" The result was what Major Walker called "a cheer of desperation" and a charge; Major Stevens reported that "the troops sprang to their feet, dressed their line, fixed bayonets, moved forward a few paces to and over the crest, and met the enemy at 30 yards with so well-aimed a volley, so thundering a cheer and so suddenly and spontaneous a rush forward that he fell back in great confusion."[43]

General Early learned of this repulse from generals Ramseur and Pegram, whom he found in the streets of Middletown. The commanders told Early they needed more weight on the right if they were going to force the determined Federals from their strong new position. Wharton's division was nearby, having done little more than accompany the guns along the pike. "I ordered Wharton's division forward at once," wrote Early, "and directed Generals Ramseur and Pegram to put it where it was required."[44]

This contrasted sharply with Gordon's strong hand; Early seemed unsure of where to put one of his divisions, and delegated the decision to not one but two subordinates. In fact, he seemed not to know where the Federal positions were, exactly —"I was endeavoring to discover the enemy's lines through the obscurity," he wrote. And he seemed somewhat uncertain about where his own men were; "Gordon had got on the left," he reported later, sounding mystified as to how that had happened.[45]

It was confusing. Gordon's division had slashed obliquely across the field from its jumpoff position until it intercepted Kershaw's; when they sorted themselves out and pressed the attack on Getty's second position, Gordon was on the extreme left of the line. Meanwhile, Pegram had come up from reserve into the line among Ramseur's brigades, and one of Kershaw's brigades—Brigadier General William T. Wofford's—had got over on the right with Wharton's division, which had started the day on the extreme left.

While the Confederates tried to retain organization and keep moving, Getty's battered division waited alertly, confidently, on its smoking ridge. The men had battered back three Confederate divisions and were about to take on a fourth without a sign of flinching. With Warner bending his line back on the right to refuse Kershaw's probes, and Bidwell and the dismounted troopers adjusting their line to keep their faces toward the enemy on the pike, the line had been hammered into a horseshoe shape, the Vermonters in the bend. When a courier galloped in with word that General Ricketts was down, seriously wounded, and that Getty must take command of the corps, Getty hardly lifted his gaze from the enemy; he knew there was no VI Corps to command here, only the Second Division. He went through the formality of placing General Lewis Grant of the Vermont Brigade in command of the division, sent word to the other two divisions to conform to his movements if they could, and for the moment left it at that.[46]

Cannoneer Buell was impressed by Lewis Grant's immaculate calm. As McKnight's men were struggling away from the wreck of their battery, the general—whose prim and fussy air had got him tagged with the nickname "Aunt Liddy"—rode up to ask politely whether they had any ammunition left. On being told they did, Grant led them to a position on Bidwell's left, overlooking Meadow Brook and the village. The location was under "a terrific musketry fire" from the pike and the edge of the town, and "a heavy fire of case" from a four-gun battery. General Grant sat his horse imperturbably, and in "a natural and pleasant tone of voice" said to the artillerymen, "Go in battery here and attend to those folks coming out of the village; the men on your right will support you. Now, boys, give 'em the best you've got." Then the "benevolent-looking" general walked his horse back to the center of the division.[47]

The folks coming out of the village were Wharton's men— fresh, unbloodied, coming into action for the first time this day, undoubtedly fired up by the success of the attack and anxious to do their part. A vigorous blow was about to fall on a mauled, outnumbered brigade—Bidwell's, now under French, on the left.[48]

The procedure had become almost routine. Once again the skirmishers came up over the crest to warn of the approach of yet another enemy battle line. "Again the troops rose to their feet, dressed their ranks and gripped their muskets, with bayonets fixed," recalled Stevens. "And again, at the critical moment, just as the charging line, straining up the hill, gained the summit, the steady veterans countered upon it with a terrific threefold blow, a sudden, deadly volley, a fierce charge and a mighty shout, and dashed it in pieces down the ridge."[49]

"Wharton's division came back in some confusion," General Early remembered, "and General Wharton informed me that his division had been driven back by the 6th corps, which, he said, was advancing. He pointed out the direction from which he said the enemy was advancing, and some pieces of artillery which had come up were brought into action. The fog soon rose sufficiently for us to see the enemy's position, and it was discovered to be a strong one." Early ordered Colonel Carter to concentrate the fire of every available gun on the Federal position. Then General Early looked to the right, across the pike to the north. Judging by his reaction, what he saw there struck raw fear into the old lion's heart.[50]

All this time the Federal cavalry had been waiting. Merritt's camp was in the path of those refugees who headed around the western edge of the plateau west of Middletown, and as the hours passed Merritt and Torbert watched in dismay as the torrent of men continued and increased. Of Merritt's three brigades, only Devin's was present; it deployed between the camp and the pike, across the plateau behind Getty's division, and labored to halt stragglers. It was necessary, Devin reported later, "in several instances to fire on the crowds retiring, and to use the saber frequently." Kidd's Michigan Brigade and Lowell's Reserve Brigade were still out confronting Rosser. Custer's entire division remained mounted, poised—and in camp. Thus passed more than three hours.[51]

After Getty's desperate fight was well under way, Captain Crowninshield rode north through Middletown and was appalled to see "rebel cavalry there, and not a Union soldier in sight on the pike." At the north end of town Crowninshield rode west and found Devin's brigade, which was being overseen by both Merritt and Torbert. "Recognizing me as one of the headquarters staff," Crowninshield wrote later, "General Torbert rode out to meet me and asked if I brought him orders. I said no and asked if it were possible he had no orders; and then I learned with astonishment that he neither had received orders, nor did he know fully of the disaster of the early morning."[52]

Apparently General Wright, in his desperation to slow down the enemy flanking movement and patch together his shattered infantry formations, simply did not think about his idle cavalry divisions. It may have been only when he personally reached Merritt's camp with the retreating First and Third Divisions of VI Corps that he remembered the horsemen. At any rate it was after 9 A.M. when he ordered both cavalry divisions to ride to the left and secure the Valley Pike.

"This I was opposed to," Torbert said in his official report, since taking every man east would leave Rosser uninhibited on the army's right. Having noticed the obvious, Torbert then did the obvious, belaboring his point by claiming that he saved the lives of thousands of stragglers by leaving, "on my own responsibility," three of Custer's regiments to resist Rosser. But most of the Federal cavalry officers—including those who were on the line in contact with Rosser, three miles from Torbert's headquarters—were already chafing to get to the left, where the trouble was, and away from the right, where nothing was happening.[53]

This was remarkable. After the first feeble push across

Cupp's Ford, Rosser had stopped fighting. This was contrary to his orders and contrary to his nature—not only was the enemy in front of him, but Fanny Custer, just a mile or so away. Yet Rosser sat on his hands; the Laurels and Wickham's brigade stood around with nothing to do; the Federal cavalry that they were supposed to pin down had no reason to stay.

Except that they had no orders to go. At about the time Wright finally remembered the cavalry, Colonel Lowell rode restlessly over to Colonel Kidd's position at Cupp's Mill to talk about leaving their outpost and heading for the main battle. That is not what he said, of course; in Kidd's account they sound like two schoolboys thinking about playing hooky, each unwilling to say so first. Lowell observed pointedly that his orders were to support the Michigan men, if they needed support. Kidd responded to his cue by stating the obvious: that no help was needed. "The enemy had been easily checked," he recalled, "and, at the moment, had become so quiet as to give rise to the suspicion that they had withdrawn from our front, as indeed they had."[54]

Meanwhile, to the southeast, near the divisional camp they had left hours before, "a great battle was raging." Kidd commented that judging by the sound, the army was retreating. Lowell said he thought so, too. There was a pause. Then, abruptly, Lowell made up his mind: "I shall return." He was turning his horse to head his men toward the sound of the guns when Kidd appealed to him: "Colonel, what would you do if you were in my place?"

Kidd was the junior colonel, having taken over his command only seventeen days before, when Custer had been given the Third Division. Custer had wasted no time when he heard the news, said Kidd, but "hastily summoning me, went away, taking his staff and colors with him. I was obliged while yet on the march to form a staff of officers as inexperienced as myself. It was an unsought and an unwelcome responsibility." Now he was contemplating moving his brigade toward what appeared to be a major battle, without orders. He was far from comfortable.

Lowell's inclination was always to ride toward the guns, and in two months of hard fighting he had learned that no one got in trouble with Sheridan for doing so. The presence of Rosser's force was a problem, but for some reason the Confederate cavalry was at the moment inert, and it was obvious from the sounds that there was a far worse problem on the left. "I think you should go too," Lowell said, thinking intently, then turned in his saddle and added, "Yes, I will take the responsibility to give you the order."[55]

The two brigades headed out to the east-southeast, navigating by the sounds of battle so as to come in behind the infantry's lines. They made their way onto the large plateau a mile or so behind Getty. From this high ground Kidd saw "the full scope of the calamity which had befallen our arms burst suddenly into view. The valley and intervening slopes, the fields and woods, were alive with infantry, moving singly and in squads. Some entire regiments were hurrying to the rear, while the Confederate artillery was raining shot and shell and spherical case among them to accelerate their speed." Kidd, too, was struck by the odd mood of the stragglers. "It did not look like a frightened or panic stricken army, but like a disorganized mass that had simply lost the power of cohesion. They were chagrined, mortified, mad at their officers and themselves—demoralized; but after all, more to be pitied than blamed."[56]

Lowell led the troopers across the front of the First Division of XIX Corps, which was intact, in line and waiting, to Getty's right. General Dwight, still under arrest, remembered being deeply impressed by the demeanor of the riders: "They moved past me, that splendid cavalry; if they reached the Pike, I felt secure. Lowell got by me before I could speak, but I looked after him for a long distance. Exquisitely mounted, the picture of a soldier, erect, confident, defiant, he moved at the head of the finest body of cavalry that today scorns the earth it treads."[57]

Into the terrific cannonade of Colonel Carter's guns the horsemen rode unflinching. "One shell took an entire set of fours out of the Sixth Michigan," Kidd recalled. "Not a man left the ranks. The next set closed up the gap." Ahead of them they could see Devin's New Yorkers, now in position across the pike north of the town, with Custer's Third Division forming behind Devin's left. Merritt's orders now reached Lowell and

Kidd to continue across the pike and join the rest of the cavalry there.[58]

Jubal Early saw them starting to assemble there just after Wharton's repulse, and that is when the dread began to grow in him. "A force of cavalry was advancing along the Pike," he wrote later, "and through the fields on the right of Middletown, thus placing our right and rear in great danger." The danger was greatly amplified by Early's lack of cavalry with which to counter (he had with him only "Payne's very small brigade," which had taken some prisoners and sown some additional confusion among the Federals, but had failed to penetrate to Belle Grove ahead of the infantry), and by his misreading of the battlefield situation (he thought he was facing the entire VI Corps, not just Getty's division, on that hill).[59]

Yet the man who had snarled that "the laurel is a running vine" after Toms Brook, where the cavalry had fought an honest fight, was oddly forgiving of his horsemen in his later analysis of Cedar Creek, where they did not. "Rosser had attacked the enemy promptly at the appointed time," Early wrote, seizing on the one thing Tom Rosser did right that day, "but he had not been able to surprise him. There was now one division of cavalry threatening my right flank and two were on the left, near the Back Road, held in check by Rosser. The force of the latter was too weak to make an impression on the enemy's cavalry, and all he could do was watch it."[60]

Old Jube had lost count of the enemy's cavalry divisions. There were not three, but two, and they were no longer on the left, because Rosser had not held them in check; those two would shortly be massed on Early's right. Meanwhile, Lunsford Lomax, with the other half of Early's cavalry, was turning in a performance fully as desultory as Rosser's. "I received a message from him," Early wrote of Lomax, "informing me that he had crossed the river after some delay from a cavalry force guarding it."[61]

The delay must have been a mental problem; the force was Powell's diminutive division, which in the absence of Moore's brigade consisted of a single brigade. Powell later reported no contact with the enemy until he started to fall back, at Torbert's order, around 9 A.M. Then, Powell reported, "the enemy charged my picket line, but were repulsed with a loss of four men killed." For the next several hours, Powell conducted a leisurely retreat northward eight miles to the intersection of the White Post, Newtown and Winchester roads, then to Newtown, from which he advanced back to the crossroads. All this time, he reported, Lomax's cavalry force was merely "following at a respectful distance."[62]

Thus after unjustly accusing the cavalry of letting him down over and over again—the previous winter, and at Winchester, and most especially and bitterly at Fisher's Hill and Toms Brook—Jubal Early found that when he needed horsemen worse than he had ever needed them before, they let him down. And after years of exhibiting contempt for cavalry, after refusing to consider what it was or how it should work, he found in the decisive moments at Cedar Creek that it was not the enemy's guns, nor the vaunted VI Corps, but the blueclad riders, that touched him with fear.

Jubal Early's next move, after seeing the blueclad horsemen massing on his right, was defensive.

He sent Wharton's division, along with Wofford's brigade of Kershaw's, to deploy east of the pike with Payne and hold off the Federal cavalry. With more than 2,000 fresh troops thus subtracted from the assaulting force, Early decided, or as he put it discovered, that Getty's position "could not be attacked with advantage on its left flank." Gordon and Kershaw would have to attack the Federal right, after Carter's cannonade.[63]

What followed was, by Early's account, an extraordinary bit of staff work. He sent his orders to Gordon with a Captain Powell, of Gordon's staff; "Captain Powell said he did not know where General Gordon was, and expressed some doubt about finding him." Old Jube apparently had some doubts of his own about a staff officer who did not know the location of his own headquarters, and sent the orders again with Lieutenant Page of his own staff. This young worthy soon returned to say, as Early wrote it later, "that he delivered my order to General Kershaw, but the latter informed him that his division was not in a condition to make the attack, as it was very much scattered, and there was a strong force confronting it in front." Gordon's division, behind Kershaw's, "was also much scattered"—small wonder, given what those two divisions had accomplished that morning—and Lieutenant Page announced "that he had not delivered the order to General Gordon, because he saw that neither his division nor Kershaw's was in a condition to execute it." When writing the narrative, Early was apparently so grateful for this opportunity to take a gratuitous swipe at Gordon that it did not occur to him to comment on the monumental presumption of this staff officer's decision not to deliver an order.[64]

In any case, as Major Stevens recorded, both Gordon and Kershaw did advance again (perhaps Captain Powell was not so lax after all). Early's later disparagement of the two Confederate divisions made even Stevens, who spent the day fighting them, indignant: "Oblivious or regardless of the fact that no troops could make such a long and heroic charge and overcome such determined resistance without suffering heavy losses and becoming more or less disordered, he expected them instantly to make a new attack, and begrudged them the time necessary to re-form, and more discreditable yet, he ever afterwards persisted in reproaching these brave soldiers with ill-founded charges of disorder and delay."[65]

All this time, Colonel Carter's guns had been pounding away at Getty's infantry. Major Walker wrote that they "concentrated a terrible fire of artillery upon our position, and shell from thirty guns flew, screaming devilishly, over and among us." But as so often was the case, the damage done by the cannons was not in proportion to the noise they made. "The men hugged the ground, being somewhat covered by the hill, and the loss, as General Getty says, 'was lighter than could have been expected.' After a cannonade lasting for half an hour, our skirmishers announced another charge and the men stood, or rather knelt, to their guns."[66]

But this was not, as might have been expected, another savage punch from the relatively fresh divisions of Wharton and Pegram. Instead, it was a rather ragged push by the exhausted troops of Gordon and Kershaw. "Some scattering musketry was heard on the right flank," Stevens wrote, "and Colonel Warner reported that the Confederates were driving back his skirmishers on that flank, and pushing a column past it." Feeble as it was, the attack succeeded where the others had failed. "Getty had not a man in reserve. He had not a gun. His entire force in one thin line barely sufficed to fill the position. Nothing remained but to get out, and that quickly."[67]

It would be said later that artillery alone drove VI Corps from its second position, but that was not the case. "Their whole army was now up," recalled Major Walker. "We could see heavy columns marching upon the cavalry on our left, while Warner was struck upon his unprotected flank, and a line of rebels even came upon his rear." Early had enough men on the line now, Walker thought, "to bag our stubborn little division entire if we longer maintained our stubbornness." Getty sent Lewis Grant a laconic order to "withdraw, unless he saw some especial reason for remaining."[68]

With cool aplomb the brigades went into column and marched away from their bloodsoaked ridge. A half-mile to the north across the open fields they came to Old Forge Road, which led from the edge of Middletown toward the northwest, where Merritt's and Custer's campsites were. "Here they halted and faced about," Stevens reported; "the lines were readjusted, skirmishers were thrown out and the cartridge boxes filled. The enemy, unconscious of the movement, was still shelling the abandoned crest. By this time the fog had disappeared and given way to a bright sunny day."[69]

Not far to Getty's right, where the Old Forge Road climbed a ridge that commanded a view of VI Corps' former camp, was the First Division of XIX Corps, which had backed its way there from position to indefensible position throughout the morning. Captain Crowinshield, continuing his personal inspection of the battlefield, now rode up to observe that General Emory had had enough, and wanted his troops to know it: "he was telling them emphatically that he would not retreat any further, that there he would stand and fight; and his men were making breastworks of rails, and even digging a little. I stayed there quite a while, watching his preparations and the advance of the rebels—Gordon's and Kershaw's divisions, who were slowly and in fine order coming up the slope, their guns throwing solid shot up the hill at Emory's corps."[70]

Meanwhile, the rest of Merritt's division filed to the left, across the Valley Pike, to confront the slowing enemy advance and secure the pike. Lowell rode in with his proud brigade and took position to the left of Devin; Kidd followed, going to Lowell's left, crossing in front of Custer's division and spotting Old Curly "riding along the front of Custer's division and spotting Old Curly "riding along the front of his command, chafing like a caged lion, eager for the fray." That put more than 6,000 troopers in a dark mass in the corner of Old Jube's eye.[71]

Ramseur and Pegram, realizing that Getty was gone, advanced to and a little beyond the Union position on the crest of the plateau. General Early rode into the town, he reported, "to make provisions against the enemy cavalry, and discovered a large body of it seriously threatening that flank, which was very much exposed." Wharton, Wofford and Payne were not enough protection; Early ordered Pegram, too, to "move to the north of Middletown, and take position across the Pike against the cavalry." His orders were not to attack the cavalry, but to take position against it. Pegram obliqued to the right and Ramseur came into line on Pegram's left, connecting with Kershaw and Gordon on his left.[72]

Getty, meanwhile, had decided he did not like his new location. He could see no infantry near him, he was in a low spot and too far from the pike. And so, Major Stevens recalled, he "moved his division by the flank to the left and rear, soon reached the highway and took up another position three quarters of a mile north of Middletown. The troops set to work piling up rude breastworks of rails, rocks and earth, and although expecting an attack at any moment, all drew a long sigh of relief, feeling that now the Pike was secure the worst was over." Getty was not fond of this position either—there was higher ground to his front and left—but he wanted to stay within supporting distance of the cavalry east of the pike. And, like Emory, Getty was no doubt sick of retreating. It went against his grain.[73]

Now the battered and angry Union infantry began to reassemble. Part of the Third Division, VI Corps, came into line on Getty's right, and there, too, appeared Colonel Rutherford B. Hayes, still hanging on to 60 men from his division of Crook's force (Crook was trying to reassemble the others farther down the pike, behind Getty's left). Captain Crowninshield recorded that while he was talking with the fuming commander of XIX Corps, "an aid of General Wright rode up and gave General Emory orders to retire" and conform with Getty's line. At about the same time Stevens saw Wright—his lower face "swollen and bloody"—join Getty.[74]

Wright had ordered VI and XIX Corps, which had been halted in line along the Old Forge Road, to fall back farther and form on Getty, but now an error interfered with his design. As the VI Corps' Third Division came back across the rolling country and random patches of woods, its easternmost brigade, the Second, spotted the Second Division's line, halted, did an about face and obliqued into place. But Colonel Emerson's First Brigade of the Third, a little farther to the west, was in woods at the time and missed the maneuver, marching on to the north. The First Division of VI Corps, and beyond that the two XIX Corps divisions, guided on Emerson and also missed the connection. It was a small error, one that would soon be corrected, but it would have an impact on Wright's record.[75]

Despite the confusion, the continuing fluidity of the situation and his own wound, General Wright knew where everyone was and by dint of a steady stream of orders was gradually carving order out of chaos. Every division commander's recollection of the battle is punctuated with offhand references to the arrival of Wright, or a courier from Wright, making observations and giving instructions. He held the army together, but for some reason his rock-hard courage did not inspire, his presence did not encourage and his stubborn professionalism did not reassure.

Instead, as Colonel A. Bayard Nettleton of the 2nd Ohio Cavalry recalled, "the universal thought was, 'Oh for one hour of Sheridan.'" The cavalry especially longed for the man who had made them special. They missed "the amazing quickness and precision with which he formed new plans on the field, and his thunderbolt method of executing each design; his success in imparting to his infantry much of the mobility and dash of cavalry, and to his cavalry much of the coherency and steadiness of infantry; all these had combined, in spite of not a few unheroic personal traits, to give his army unbounded faith in his leadership and enthusiasm for the man. But Sheridan was 20 miles away."[76]

The tide of battle, which since dawn had been a flood tide running in favor of the Confederates, had begun to slow when Jubal Early started to think and act defensively; it slowed even more when the Federals got a grip on the Valley Pike; and now it began to show signs of turning as the Federal cavalry arrived in force. Superbly led, eager to fight, full of confidence, with every man alive to the crucial importance of stemming the enemy advance and holding on to the Valley Pike, Merritt's unleashed horsemen began to hammer away.

"Orders were sent to each brigade to press the enemy warmly," Merritt reported. "Never did troops fight more elegantly than at this time; not a man shirked his duty, not a soldier who did not conduct himself like a hero." They began to punish Wharton's advancing skirmishers with short, sharp, punching charges; a gallop, a sharp clash with pistols and sabers, then a return dash to re-form and charge again. General Early savored the memory of the return dashes, which he mistook for retreats: "Several charges of the enemy's cavalry were repulsed." But as General Merritt reported, his line "advanced nearly to Middletown, driving the enemy before it through the open country."[77]

And once again, at center front, "the gallant Lowell, as usual, with his noble command forcing from the enemy every available inch of ground." Wharton's troops, the freshest Early had, were trying to get a line of battle established north of the village. Colonel Carter's guns were turned now on the Federal cavalry, which could only stand and take the fearful barrage, for they had no cover, and there was no such thing as retreat. Again and again Lowell's regulars gathered themselves and charged, wheeled, returned, and charged again. The third time in, a bullet felled Lowell's horse, the thirteenth killed under him in as many weeks. He grabbed another, steadied it, steadied his men.[78]

This was no time for headlong charges or attempted breakthroughs; "This advance," said Merritt, "was intended more as an offensive-defensive movement than one looking to a final victory." The troopers understood and remained under tight control. When Getty's men pulled back from Old Forge Road, the cavalry was exposed to "a murderous fire" from the flank, wrote Merritt; "but there was no movement on the part of the men save that demanded by superior judgement for a fresh disposition to meet the contingency; no running, no confusion."[79]

Lowell, far in advance of the rest of the cavalry, dismounted his men behind a stone wall on the outskirts of the town. There they unlimbered their Spencers and banged away at Wharton's and Wofford's skirmishers, who advanced repeatedly, now on the left, now the right, again in the center. In addition to the constant probes of the skirmish lines, the Reserve Brigade had to endure a constant, deadly fire from sharpshooters on the roofs and in the second-story windows of Middletown; and the continual screeching plunge of shellfire from 30 guns. The artillery fire, wrote Merritt, was "truly terrific; it has seldom been equalled for accuracy of aim and excellence of ammunition." The Federal horse artillery and what was left of the corps batteries tried to mount counterbattery fire, but "were overpowered at times by weight of metal and superior ammunition." (The quality and quantity of the Confederate ammunition expended at Cedar Creek was remarkable given the extraordinary difficulties of manufacture and supply faced by the beleaguered Confederacy.)[80]

Even to the right rear, where Colonel Kidd held his Michigan Brigade mounted and ready, the fire was ferocious. Kidd was conferring with an artillery captain when a bullet fired by a sharpshooter in the town zipped past the captain and disabled Kidd's horse. He appropriated another and held his position: "For perhaps an hour we stood in line inviting attack. But the enemy, strongly posted behind fences and piles of logs, with two ravines and fences separating us, seemed anxious to let well enough alone."[81]

Colonel Wildes, whose 116th Ohio of Crook's First Division had been mauled in Kershaw's first assault, was, with "the remnant of our little corps still clinging to the left," well behind Getty. "We could see the cavalry driving back the rebel hordes," he wrote, "which was the first ray of hope and grain of encouragement we had received during the morning. But the day was lost, as all felt, and the army directed its attention to saving its trains and preventing the enemy from getting complete possession of the Pike and cutting us off from Winchester." But strange as it seemed to Wildes, "the enemy appeared content with his victory, and was now making no attempts to force us further back."[82]

"The battle and the day wore on together," wrote Colonel Nettleton, who with Custer's division had yet to see action. "The sulphurous cloud that overhung the field, and the dense volumes of dust that rose behind the wheeling batteries and the charging troops, contrasted grimly with the sweet light of that perfect October day as it could be seen beyond the limits of the battlefield."[83]

General Early, in his report to General Lee written two days later, described the situation as he saw it a little after 10 A.M. "It was now apparent that it would not do to push my troops further. They had been up all night and were much jaded. So many of our men had stopped in the camp to plunder (in which I am sorry to say that officers participated), the country was so open, and the enemy's cavalry so strong, that I did not deem it prudent to press farther, especially as Lomax did not come up. I determined, therefore, to content myself with trying to hold the advantages I had gained until all my troops had come up and the captured property was secured."[84]

He had 1,300 prisoners and 24 Union guns. He had won a great victory, and all that remained was for Sheridan to recognize the act by withdrawing from the field. It was not an unreasonable conclusion; it was shared by Colonel Wildes and a large proportion of the officers and men of both armies.[85]

Not General Gordon. He remained forever bitter that his intended concentration against Getty's second position "was stopped; the blow was not delivered. We halted, we hesitated, we dallied, firing a few shots here, attacking with a brigade or a division there, and before such feeble assaults the superb Union corps retired at intervals and by short stages."[86]

Now, with the army in line along Old Forge Road on the north edge of Middletown and the Federal army slowly regrouping along a parallel line a mile and a quarter to the north and east, even the piecemeal attacks ceased. "We waited,"

Gordon fumed, "waited for weary hours. Waited till the routed men in blue found that no foe was pursuing them and until they had time to recover their normal composure and courage; waited till Confederate officers lost hope and the fires had gone out in the hearts of the privates."[87]

It was ever Jubal Early's saving grace that he did not spare himself the sting of his caustic humor. And so, in a later, unguarded moment when he was not conscious of testifying to Robert E. Lee or the court of history, he let slip his dread tongue and skewered himself, more effectively than anyone else could have. "The Yankees got whipped," he drawled. "And we got scared."[88]

Chapter 8

Sheridan's Ride

Phil Sheridan had had a maddening three days. In the first place, he had not wanted to leave the army. Although he believed the intercepted message about Longstreet joining Early to be counterfeit, the thing nagged at him. It could be partly true: perhaps Longstreet was coming out to relieve Early and take command for some new initiative; maybe part of Longstreet's corps was coming to the Valley. Even if it was nothing more than a trick, what was its purpose?

Such thoughts had dogged him as he had ridden eastward on Sunday, the 16th. The Sheridan temper must have been smoldering very close to the surface. He had been whipsawed for more than two weeks between Grant's plans and Halleck's plans, when Sheridan knew perfectly well what needed to be done. Now he was being dragged away from his army when something was up—something he could smell in the wind but could not name—in order to have a long chat with some politicians. His mood could not have been improved when he reached Rectortown, about twenty miles east of Front Royal, and met the crew that was repairing the Manassas Gap Railroad—in furtherance of Halleck's tenaciously held plan to create a railhead fortress in the Valley as a base for operations against the railroads farther south. Sheridan did not want to do this; Grant did not want it done; but there was the crew, doggedly working away. The crew had an open telegraph line to Washington, and Sheridan immediately used it to ask for any corroborating information about Longstreet's whereabouts.

Characteristically, Halleck's response confused the situation even more: "General Grant says that Longstreet brought with him no troops from Richmond," the chief of staff reported enigmatically. (So Longstreet had in fact joined Early, then? Without troops?) "But," came the infuriating qualification, "I have no confidence in the information collected at his headquarters. If you can leave your command with safety, come to Washington, as I wish to give you the views of the authorities here."[1]

In another, apparently unanswered wire, Sheridan said unconvincingly, "I would like to see you," then asked, "Is it best for me to go see you?" It was unavoidable. Escorted by a regiment of cavalry, Sheridan rode east with four of his staff officers—Lieutenant Colonel James W. Forsyth, chief of staff, along with a favorite aide, Major George A. (Sandy) Forsyth, Captain Joseph O'Keeffe and, lastly named in Sheridan's account, "Captain Michael V. Sheridan." On the other side of Bull Run Mountain, in the vicinity of Haymarket, they found the terminus of the rebuilt railroad, boarded a train with their horses, dismissed the cavalry escort and hung on as their conveyance lurched off toward Alexandria.[2]

The trip took all night. Around 8 A.M. Monday, Sheridan grabbed a quick breakfast with his officers at Willard's Hotel and then hurried up Pennsylvania Avenue to the War Department. The first thing he did on arriving was to ask Secretary Stanton to order a special Baltimore and Ohio train prepared to take him back to Martinsburg. He wanted to leave at noon, Sheridan said, "I must get back to my army as quickly as possible." When Stanton had complied, the meeting began.[3]

Afterward, the participants did not discuss their conversation in any detail. The evidence indicates, however, that Stanton and Halleck were soon disabused of the notion that Sheridan was there to hear the "views of the authorities." There was a three-hour wrangle in which Sheridan seems not to have been much affected by memories of how "Old Brains" had been his mentor early in the war, or of how Stanton had seemed so daunting earlier in the year. All Sheridan wrote about it later was that the meeting concerned "my operating east of the Blue

Ridge. The upshot was that my views against such a plan were practically agreed to."

Sheridan came out of the meeting intent first on getting back to his army; then on withdrawing it from the exposed Cedar Creek location to a more defensible line from which the Valley could be guarded by Crook's little Army of West Virginia while the rest of the men joined Grant at Petersburg. Halleck, on the other hand, still was not ready to give up on his cherished Manassas Gap fortress idea; he reported to Grant that "General Sheridan has just been here. He has not yet fully decided about the Manassas road, but will do so in a day or two. He has gone back, with Colonels Alexander and Thom, to make a further reconnaissance."[4]

The colonels to whom Halleck referred represented one more weight hung around Sheridan's neck; although he had never demonstrated that he needed help in selecting ground, Halleck now burdened him with two engineers who were to survey the Valley and give their advice on a defensive line. Sheridan must have felt as if he were wading in cold molasses as he collected the engineers, collected his aides (and a quick lunch) at the Willard, found his train, boarded the horses, and set out for Martinsburg. They arrived there at dark, and had to spend the night.[5]

Sheridan felt sure he would be back with the army on Tuesday, the 18th, but it was not to be. The cavalryman whose speed and mobility had become legendary was hobbled by the engineers: "Colonel Alexander was a man of enormous weight, and Colonel Thom correspondingly light, and as both were unaccustomed to riding we had to go slowly, losing so much time, in fact, that we did not reach Winchester till between 3 and 4 o'clock in the afternoon, though the distance is but twenty-eight miles." Then the colonels had to plod over the terrain around Winchester—terrain that Sheridan by that time knew as well as any man alive—and discuss at great length its suitability for a line of defense.[6]

Before embarking on this expedition Sheridan dispatched a courier to General Wright asking for a report. The mild October day was melting into chilly, glittering night, and the fuming Sheridan was just returning from his pointless ramble with the saddlesore engineers, when Wright's answer was brought to him: the enemy was quiet at Fisher's Hill, and Wright would probe them in the morning with a reconnaissance in force. "Greatly relieved" that nothing untoward had happened in his absence, "and expecting to rejoin my headquarters at my leisure next day," Sheridan turned in. He was staying at Lloyd Logan's pleasant frame house occupied by Colonel Oliver Edwards, commanding the brigade from VI Corps' First Division that was on garrison duty in Winchester.[7]

Sheridan planned to sleep late the next morning, but the knock on his door came shortly after 6 A.M. It was the officer of the day, bringing a report from the picket line south of the town. Heavy firing, including cannon, could be heard to the south. Sheridan's immediate question was about the artillery fire; was it continuous or intermittent? Irregular, the officer thought, fitful. It was all right then, Sheridan pronounced, only the reconnaissance feeling the enemy.[8]

"I tried to go to sleep again," Sheridan recalled, "but grew so restless I could not, and soon got up and dressed myself." The guard commander came back to report that the firing was still going on. Asked if it sounded like a battle, however, he said he did not think so. Once again Sheridan convinced himself that it was "Grover's division banging away at the enemy simply to find out what he was up to." But he ordered the horses saddled and breakfast rushed.[9]

Still, it was nearly 9 A.M. before he mounted and led his three staff officers south. The 300-man cavalry escort had camped a mile south of town along Abraham's Creek, also called Mill Creek, and fell in behind as Sheridan passed. By this time, Sandy Forsyth recalled, they could hear the sound of the guns, and "the general was becoming anxious. He leaned forward and listened intently, and once he dismounted and placed his ear near the ground, seeming somewhat disconcerted as he rose again and remounted." So he was. He had concluded, Sheridan wrote later, "that the travel of the sound was increasing too rapidly to be accounted for by my own rate of motion, and that therefore my army must be falling back."[10]

A mile farther on, Sandy Forsyth wrote later, they topped a rise to see a large supply train stopped on the pike. It had been

on its way to the army, but was now halted, "in great confusion. Part of the wagons faced one way, part the other; others
were half turned round, in position to swing either way, but
were huddled together, completely blocking the road." On
Sheridan's order the aide galloped forward to find out what was
going on.[11]

In minutes he was back to report that an officer had come
down the pike from the front and had warned the quartermaster in charge of the train to go back; the army had been attacked, defeated, and was being driven down the Valley. Sheridan made no exclamations, asked for no more information. In
fact, for a few minutes he did nothing but continue to walk his
horse past the jammed-up wagon train, thinking hard, bristling
with rising energy.

"My first thought," he recalled, "was to stop the army in the
suburbs of Winchester as it came back, form a new line, and
fight there." That would be the orthodox, obvious thing to do.
It did not satisfy him. He let Rienzi amble on, let his anxious
staff officers wait. It is unlikely that he spent any time worrying
about what would happen to his career if he were to preside
over yet another defeat in the Valley of Humiliation; unlikely,
too, that he wasted any of his concern on Lincoln's chances for
reelection should the Confederates reclaim the Shenandoah.
Sheridan was neither a conniver nor a politician, he was a war
dog with the scent of powder in his nostrils. He thought about
winning. You did not win battles by falling back and defending.[12]

"I was sure the troops had confidence in me, for heretofore
we had been successful; and as at other times they had seen me
present at the slightest sign of trouble or distress, I felt that I
ought to try now to restore their broken ranks." Writing twenty
years later, occupying a more exalted position and no doubt
cognizant of higher expectations on the part of his public and
his wife, Sheridan felt compelled to append to that honest sentence a rhetorical flourish: "or, failing in that, to share their
fate because of what they had done hitherto."[13]

The time for meditation was over. He began to rap out orders. To Sandy Forsyth: "Pick out 50 of the best-mounted men
from the escort." To chief of staff James Forsyth: deploy Colo-

nel Edwards's brigade across the pike near Mill Creek and stop
any stragglers. To Sandy Forsyth: "You and Captain O'Keeffe
will go with me." Along with the general's orderly, of course,
who kept the swallow-tailed flag fluttering at Sheridan's heels
no matter what.[14]

As Sandy Forsyth watched, Sheridan "turned his horse's
head southward, tightening the reins of his bridle, and with a
slight touch of the spur he dashed up the turnpike and was off.
A yard in rear, and side by side, Captain O'Keeffe and myself
swept after him, while the escort, breaking from the trot to a
gallop, came thundering on behind." One of the most dramatic
rides in military history had begun.[15]

Sandy Forsyth's exhilarating sense of being at the center of
great events was intensified by the great beauty of his surroundings. "It was a golden sunny day that had succeeded a densely
foggy October morning. The turnpike stretched away, a white,
dusty line, over hill and through dale, bordered by fenceless
fields, and past farmhouses and empty barns and straggling
orchards. Now and then it ran through a woody copse, with
here and there a tiny stream of water crossing it, or meandering
by its side, so clear and limpid that it seemed to invite us to
pause and slake our thirst as we sped along our dusty way. On
either side we saw, through the Indian-summer haze, the distant hills covered with woods and fairly ablaze with foliage;
and over all was the deep blue of a cloudless Southern sky,
making it a day on which one's blood ran riot and he was glad
of health and life."[16]

They encountered two more wagon trains that had been on
the way to Cedar Creek and had turned back. Sheridan ordered
the wagons parked where they stood and the wagon guards to
prepare to arrest and return to the front all stragglers. Then
onward, with the big black Rienzi eating the ground with what
Forsyth called "his long swinging gallop, almost a run, which
he seemed to maintain so easily and endlessly—a most distress-
ing gait for those who had to follow far."[17]

So far they had seen only supply trains returning to the rear
area. Now they topped another rise and "came suddenly upon
indubitable evidence of battle and retreat." The road and fields
for a mile in front of them were clotted with the first refugees

from the army; headquarters trains escorted by details of enlisted men, sutlers' wagons, officers' servants, battery forges
and cooks. It was "the first driftwood of a flood just beyond."
Sheridan left the crowded road and loped on through the fields.
Behind him, Forsyth noted, rose "an echoing cheer from the
enlisted men and servants, who recognized the general, and
shouted and swung their hats in glee."[18]

As the horsemen pounded onward, the sound of the guns
grew ever louder, the flood of wreckage on the pike became
ever more grim. Forsyth began to see, in addition to the civilians and rear-area detachments, troops scorched by battle;
"now and then a wounded officer or enlisted man on horseback
or plodding along on foot, with groups of straggling soldiers
here and there among the wagon-trains, or in the fields, or
sometimes sitting or lying down to rest by the side of the road,
while others were making coffee in their tin cups by tiny campfires."[19]

Sheridan would not stop, but he did not ignore these men. As
Rienzi threaded his way among the knots of wagons and men,
"the general would wave his hat to the men and point to the
front, never lessening his speed as he pressed forward. It was
enough; one glance at the eager face and familiar black horse
and they knew him, and starting to their feet they swung their
caps around their heads and broke into cheers as he passed
beyond them; and then, gathering up their belongings and
shouldering their arms, they started after him for the front,
shouting to their comrades further out in the fields, 'Sheridan!
Sheridan!' "[20]

With each stride the road became more closely packed with
stragglers and the wounded. Sheridan pulled up to talk with an
officer he knew, and recalled being told that "everything was
gone, my headquarters captured, and the troops dispersed." A
few miles farther on he paused to interrogate some stragglers,
who told him, with the "peculiar indifference" of the overwhelmed, that "the army was broken up, in full retreat, and
that all was lost."[21]

Now there was no more stopping. "As he galloped on, his
features gradually grew set, as though carved in stone," recalled the awed Forsyth, "and the same dull red glint I had

seen in his piercing black eyes when on other occasions the battle was going against us, was there now."[22]

About the ears of the fleeing men their general's rasping voice crackled like lightning, sent not to chastise them but to light their way back to glory. The poet Thomas Buchanan Read attributed to Sheridan at this time "a mighty oath," an allegation that later bothered the churchly, and apparently rankled the upright Mrs. Sheridan. "I said nothing," the aging general wrote, somewhat defensively, "except to remark as I rode, 'If I had been with you this morning this disaster would not have happened. We must face the other way; we will go back and recover our camp.' "[23]

Such "remarks" could hardly have had much of an impact on a demoralized army. And indeed, others remembered them quite differently. Sergeant L. L. Bell of the 110th Ohio, for example, heard the general howling from the saddle, "Come on back, boys! Give 'em hell, God damn 'em! We'll make coffee out of Cedar Creek tonight!" The way Rutherford Hayes heard it was, "Boys turn back; face the other way. I am going to sleep in that camp tonight or in hell."[24]

They had almost reached the army. Suddenly they came upon a field hospital set up in a farmhouse. The pike nearby was jammed with ambulances, litter-bearers were hurrying into and out of the house with their inert, bloodsoaked burdens, and the surrounding fields were strewn with wounded men. One of them was Captain Howard of the 8th Vermont, who recalled that "the ghastly scenes of a field hospital after a great battle were present in all their horror. The surgeons were covered with blood, the operating tables were loaded." As always, the most common operation was the amputation of limbs whose bones had been shattered by the heavy bullets: "The great pile of arms and legs was constantly growing higher." Outside the farmhouse door along the path to the road lay a neat row of corpses. One look, reported Forsyth, and Sheridan gave the place a wide berth. "We passed through a fringe of woods, up a slight eminence in the road, and in a flash we were in full view of the battlefield.[25]

"In our immediate front the road and adjacent fields were filled with sections of artillery, caissons, ammunition trains, ambulances, battery-wagons, squads of mounted men, led horses, wounded soldiers, broken wagons, stragglers and stretcher-bearers—in fact all that appertains to and is part of the rear of an army in action." Just ahead of this chaos, to the right of the pike, "its standards flying, and evidently well in hand," was Getty's division in line of battle.[26]

There the men were waiting, Major Aldace Walker reported, "sulkily and it is to be feared profanely growling over the defeat in detail which we had experienced." They had been waiting for another Confederate charge, and when it did not come they took the opportunity "to rest, and even to breakfast roughly, in a sort of dogged gloom." Then they became aware of a new sound wafting over the battlefield from the north, a sound so incredible they raised their downcast eyes and looked at each other in frank amazement. "There we stood, driven four miles already, quietly waiting for what might be further and immediate disaster, while far in the rear we heard the stragglers and hospital bummers, and the gunless artillerymen actually cheering as though a victory had been won. We could hardly believe our ears."[27]

For the second time within six hours something strange and nameless was coming into the Army of the Shenandoah. At dawn it had been death and panic rising from the fog; now it was new life billowing among clouds of gray dust along the Valley Pike from the north. Whatever was coming now, observed the artist James Taylor (who happened to be on the pike behind Getty's position), sent before it "murmurs like the breaking of a surge on a far off shore. Nearer it grew. Grew louder and swelled to a tumult. Cheers—the cheers of the stragglers."[28]

"Now the big, black, white-fetlocked Rienzi, bearing the general, thunders by like a whirlwind," Taylor recalled. Knowing that he was a witness to history, and that he would later sketch the scene, Taylor scrutinized the grim little man streaking by. "He is braced well back in his saddle, his body forward bent and his feet in the hooded stirrups are on a line with the animal's breast, that being the only position in which his short legs could insure his seat on the rough Racker. Sheridan, whom I marked closely, wore a beard, a regulation cap with two silver stars within a golden wreath ornamenting its front—his only visible insignia of rank, he being enveloped in a great blue overcoat of the common soldier." For some reason, perhaps because of his visit to Washington, Sheridan on this fateful day was not wearing his usual porkpie hat.[29]

Yet the men had no trouble recognizing their chief. As Rienzi loped past an open-sided ambulance that was lurching to the rear bearing two wounded officers, Taylor recalled, one of them "lifted his hand feebly in salute while attempting a cheer."[30]

Major Stevens, with Getty's staff behind the line of battle, happened to turn and look down the pike in time to see Sheridan "come tearing at full gallop across the roll of ground." Veering off the pike to westward, Sheridan approached the VI Corps commander, "reined up his panting, smoking steed, and hastily demanded to know the state of things." Getty reported briskly.[31]

Without comment Sheridan wheeled his horse, spurred it over the fence-rail barricade the men had thrown together, and rode out in front of the line of battle. In a voice "surcharged with passion and confidence," Major Stevens recalled, Sheridan cried out, "Men, by God, we'll whip them yet. We'll sleep in our old camps tonight!" The men jumped to their feet and cheered. "Instantly," wrote Stevens, "a mighty revulsion of feeling took place. Hope and confidence returned at a bound. No longer did we merely hope the worst was over, that we could hold our ground until night, or at worst make good an orderly retreat to Winchester. Now we all burned to attack the enemy, to drive him back, to retrieve our honor and sleep in our old camps that night. And every man knew that Sheridan would do it."[32]

Lieutenant Colonel Amasa S. Tracy of the 8th Vermont in Lewis Grant's brigade (with Sheridan's return, the temporary commanders would now be shunted down again; Wright to VI Corps command, Getty to Second Division, Grant to Second Brigade) rode up to Sheridan, his hat in his hand, to say with feeling, "General, we're glad to see you." Sheridan was exuberant: "Well, by God, I'm glad to be here! What troops are these?" The answer came as a roar from the ranks: "Sixth

Corps! Vermont Brigade!" And Sheridan hollered back delight-
edly, "All right! We're all right! We'll have our camps by
night!" And then, wrote Captain Walker, "he galloped on."[33]

The thing that Lewis Grant remembered most about Sheridan's arrival was a determined youth who was invisible in
most other accounts. Grant noted that the well-mounted cavalry escort had been unable to keep pace with the formidable
Rienzi and were strung out behind the general when he came
whirling in. "But close at the heels of Sheridan's horse rode his
orderly, a little fellow scarcely more than a boy. His animal was
small, and how he managed to keep up with his chief the entire
distance is something remarkable." When Sheridan brought his
horse to a plunging halt the young orderly "turned with him
and halted almost simultaneously at the proper distance behind. A general cheer went up by those who saw the incident
and our men shouted as much for the little orderly as they did
for Sheridan."[34]

Sheridan then rode to the east again, behind Getty's division,
and remembered that "as I came behind it a line of regimental
flags rose up out of the ground, it seemed, to welcome me. They
were mostly the colors of Crook's troops, who had been stampeded and scattered in the surprise of the morning. The line
with the colors was largely composed of officers, among whom
I recognized Colonel R. B. Hayes." Hayes protested later that
just to the rear of those colors, lying behind a makeshift barrier
in line between the Second and Third Divisions of VI Corps, he
had more than a thousand of Crook's men ready to fight. Apparently unaware of their presence, Sheridan continued across
the pike, to where Crook was trying to reassemble the rest of
his shattered divisions, but recorded not a word about his emotional reunion with his oldest and closest friend.[35]

Others were moved by it. Crook was in the middle of a conversation with General Wright when Sheridan rode up on his
foam-flecked horse. Crook's orderly, M. O. Perkins, grabbed
Rienzi's sweat-soaked reins and held the horse as Sheridan dismounted and exclaimed to Crook, "What are you doing way
back here?" Perkins recalled that "he then threw his arms
around General Crook, for he loved Crook and took him into
his council at all times. I have seen evidences of their confi-

dence and love being reciprocated at all times, even in the field of battle. After the embrace of the two men I thought I saw moisture in the eyes of both."[36]

Sheridan turned and gripped Wright's hand. "Well, we've done the best we could," said Wright, looking pale above his blood-encrusted beard. "That's all right," Sheridan responded kindly. But Sheridan's good humor evaporated instantly when the unfortunate General Emory rode over a minute later to report his corps ready to cover the army's retreat. "Retreat, hell!" Sheridan flared, "We'll be back in our camps tonight."[37]

Sheridan then returned to the west of the pike, crossed Meadow Brook (which turned and ran due north behind Getty's line) and on a commanding hillside established his headquarters. As his generals and staff officers began to ride up, he stripped off his coat, had Rienzi unsaddled and replaced with his gray spare horse, Breckinridge (named for its former owner, who had lost the mount at Third Winchester), and went to work. In the first place, another attack appeared to be imminent, and the army had to be formed in a single line of battle to receive it; second, as Sheridan put it, "I had already decided to attack the enemy from that line as soon as I could get matters in shape."[38]

That was going to take some time, Sheridan thought, and the enemy was looking particularly aggressive east of the pike, where Lowell's dismounted brigade could be seen in action. On his arrival, Sheridan had dispatched Sandy Forsyth to see what the situation was there. When Forsyth found Lowell and told him that Sheridan was up, the colonel breathed a fervent, "Thank goodness for that!" At that moment, sitting their horses in the continuing deadly shower of case shot and sharpshooters' rounds, they were interrupted by a Mr. Stillson, a correspondent for a New York newspaper, who demanded to know what Sheridan was going to do, and who, on being told, pronounced a successful Union counterattack impossible and then ambled off among the whistling projectiles to find more news.[39]

Forsyth and Lowell rode the Reserve Brigade's line, watching the Confederates—Wharton's division—forming for what promised to be a major attack. "Can you hold on here forty minutes?" asked Forsyth. Lowell was firm: "Yes." Asked if he could make it sixty minutes, Lowell said, "It depends; you see what they are doing. I will if I can." Forsyth, who had had the good fortune to run into his orderly who was leading a spare horse, galloped back to Sheridan's new headquarters and reported.[40]

"I can see him before me now as I write, erect, looking intently in my eyes, his left hand resting, clinched savagely, on the top of the hilt of his saber, his right nervously stroking his chin, his eyes with that strange red gleam in them, and his attenuated features set as if cast in bronze. He stood mute and absolutely still for more than ten seconds; then, throwing up his head, he said: 'Go to the right and find the other two divisions of the Sixth Corps, and also General Emory's command. Bring them up, and order them to take position on the right of Getty. Lose no time.' And as I turned to mount, he called out: 'Stay! I'll go with you!' And springing on his horse, we set off together, followed by the staff." Sheridan had already ordered Custer's division returned to the army's right flank. And he had directed that General Dwight be released from arrest and restored to the command of XIX Corps' First Division.[41]

Sheridan carried the orders personally because he wanted to impress on the division commanders that they had to move quickly. The victorious enemy army was in an "immensely strong" position, Major Stevens wrote, that overlapped both Federal flanks, was backed by 40 well-placed guns, and was anchored "by the heavy stone walls which lined the old furnace [forge] road and bordered the fields, and by a stone mill at the crossing of the road and brook. Open ground, which must be crossed by an attacking force without cover, extended in front. There was every reason to expect, and Sheridan did expect, that Early, with his victorious troops rested and re-formed and deployed and united in one strong battalia, would move onward to the attack at any moment."[42]

Meanwhile, Colonel Lowell, keenly aware of the need to hold his position, was riding up and down, intently watching the enemy from behind his line at the stone fence, while shot and shell rained in around him. Now he decided to ride forward and have a closer look at the enemy dispositions. For some reason, Colonel Stephen H. Hastings of Kidd's 5th Michigan Cavalry was there and went along. Somewhere a puff of smoke blossomed from a sharpshooter's rifle; before the thud of the muzzleloader could be heard, Lowell was flung backward on his horse, twisting to his left, struck full in the chest.[43]

Colonel Hastings grabbed him, eased him to the ground, dismounted and bent over the prostrate form. Lowell could not speak, but gestured to his chest. Hastings opened his uniform coat to inspect what both men wordlessly agreed was a mortal wound. But as he folded aside the coat, a flattened and distorted Minié ball tumbled out; the round had struck something, perhaps the stone fence, and had ricocheted into Lowell. It had not penetrated the skin.

Still, it had been a stunning blow, and directly over lungs that had been ravaged by tuberculosis. Lowell could not ride, could not even stand, and could speak only in a whisper. He began to cough blood. He refused to leave the field, agreed only to be laid behind some cover and draped with a staff officer's coat. He would return to the saddle shortly, he croaked, in time for the counterattack he knew was coming. The wound was not as bad as it looked: "It is only my *poor* lung."[44]

Meanwhile Custer, whose body by this time must have been ravaged by excess adrenaline, was obediently trotting his command back to the right without yet having engaged the enemy. There he found that Rosser, six hours after his initial push across Cupp's Ford, had finally bestirred himself and was advancing his division against Colonel Wells's three regiments. Once again it was a timid advance—apparently Rosser still thought Sheridan's entire cavalry corps was in front of him— and had not yet gone a mile. Colonel Wells was demonstrating defiantly, but was prudently falling back whenever pushed, as Custer approached.

Before coming on the scene, Custer reported, he "opened communications" with Colonel Wells; in other words, he found out where the enemy was, something Rosser might profitably have done hours before. With more than two miles of rolling country between Rosser's men and Gordon's infantry, Custer had all the room he needed to come in on Rosser's right flank. Reaching undiscovered a position "almost in rear of and overlooking the ground upon which the enemy had massed his command," reported Custer, "I caused my battery to open suddenly at short range; at the same time charged with about three regiments."[45]

"Of course great confusion ensued," recalled Captain William McDonald of Rosser's Laurel Brigade, "and there was mounting in hot haste." The brigade had been resting from its labors again, in what McDonald admitted was "careless security." Indeed so; they had let an enemy battery get right on top of them, and now as Colonel Funsten of the Laurels tried to get his men out "the shrieking bombs were bursting in his half-formed column, and a number of the men broke ranks."[46]

There is no indication that Rosser was near this threatened point or gave orders to deal with the crisis; but his apparent lassitude on this day was not shared by all the members of this proud and battle-tested outfit. The commander of the 11th Virginia Cavalry, Major E. H. McDonald, gathered about 50 of his men and charged the oncoming Federals. "It looked as if this small Confederate band was inviting destruction," recalled Captain William McDonald. "Behind them was the division falling back, before them a force of the enemy ten times their number, actually encouraging them with shouts to 'Come on!' so confident were they of capturing them."[47]

A little too confident, perhaps. In the sudden release of their pent-up eagerness to fight, Custer's men got strung out, a few of the hotspurs getting far in advance of the main body. On seeing Major McDonald's compact little detachment heading for them, the leaders pulled up to wait. But the rest of the Federals, seeing their leaders halt, halted. Thus they were spread out and at a standstill when the 11th Virginia's desperate charge hit them. "The Federals turned and fled," reported William McDonald, "and were chased back over the hill upon which was planted their artillery." But they were hardly defeated, and in all probability were merely re-forming their line. "Rosser now withdrew the greater part of his division across Cedar Creek."[48]

Rosser was back at Cupp's Ford, where he had started that morning and had spent most of the day thus far. "This enabled me to contract my line," Custer reported with satisfaction, "and collect my command preparatory to further movements."

He first established a two-mile line along the Old Forge Road, just north of his camp of that morning, from Cedar Creek southeast to the right flank of XIX Corps. Then, in response to Sheridan's order to get the division ready "to participate in the attack about to be made," Custer "began massing on the level plain in rear of the ridge which overlooks Cupp's Ford."[49]

It was about noon—the sun of Middletown was near its zenith—and still the expected Confederate attack had not come. Now the Federal infantry was in a compact, continuous line along the Old Forge Road, from Crook's remnants on the left through VI Corps in the center to XIX Corps on the right, with a division of cavalry on each flank. Sheridan began to breathe easier. Let the blow fall now, he was ready.

Sandy Forsyth approached his chief with an idea. In riding up and down the line, Forsyth had found that there were those who did not know, or did not believe, that Sheridan was back. The general should ride the line, Forsyth said, "that all the men might see him. At first he demurred, but I was most urgent." Probably Sheridan did not demur very energetically, for this was the kind of thing he normally did anyway. In any case, he made his ride, yelling, "I'll get a twist on these people yet! We'll raise them out of their boots before the day is over!"[50]

As intended, he triggered a repeat of his earlier welcome. "The sight of that little man instantly inspired confidence in the men," recalled a XIX Corps assistant surgeon, "and threw them into a perfect frenzy of enthusiasm." Major Walker wrote that "Cheers seemed to come from throats of brass, and caps were thrown to the tops of the scattering oaks; but beneath and yet superior to these noisy demonstrations, there was in every heart a revulsion of feeling, and a pressure of emotion, beyond description. No more doubt or chance for doubt existed; we were safe, perfectly and unconditionally safe, and every man knew it."[51]

Sheridan left Sandy Forsyth with XIX Corps to act as liaison to General Emory. Now that the line was formed and skirmishers were out, "the troops were ordered to lie down; an order gladly obeyed, for they had been on their feet since daylight, fighting and without food." But for XIX Corps, the rest was a brief one. The main line was along the northern edge of a thick woods. From those woods, wrote Forsyth, there now arose "the low rustling murmur that presages the advance of a line of battle." Quickly the men formed up. "A pattering fire in front, and our skirmishers came quickly back through the woods, and were absorbed in the line; then there was a momentary lull, followed by a rustling, crunching sound as the enemy's line pressed forward, trampling the bushes under foot, and crowding through bits of underbrush."[52]

"The Confederate soldier, at that period of the war, knew as much about what was going on as did the general officers," wrote Major D. A. Grimsley of Payne's cavalry brigade. "He knew the number against him, and when he was able to withstand and when he was not. He knew the country about Middletown, that it was an open country; that it gave no protection to the weaker against the stronger. It afforded no secure means of guarding and protecting the flanks of the army. He was apprehensive that if the battle was fully joined in this open country the cavalry of the enemy would sweep around the flanks and gobble all up, and he concluded that he had better retreat to a place of safety while there was time. All day long you could hear comment among the soldiers on the halt and the delay in retreating."[53]

Or advancing. Colonel Carter later wrote to General Gordon that at about this time the artillery commander had gone to General Early and "explained that the troops were eager to go ahead, and I had been questioned all along the line to know the cause of the delay. Every practical fighting man in our war knows that troops scattered and panic-stricken cannot be rallied in the face of hot and vigorous pursuit."[54]

As General Wharton had deployed his division on the Confederate right, he wrote later, "I supposed we were arranging for a general movement to the front, and expected every minute orders to advance; but no orders came, and there we stood—no enemy in our front for hours, except some troops moving about in the woodland on a hill nearly a mile in our front. I have never been able to understand why General Early did not advance, or why he remained in line for four or five hours after the brilliant victory of the morning."[55]

Of the three options open to Early's army at midday—press the attack, retreat to a defensible position such as Fisher's Hill, or stay in place in the open, flanks in the air, backs to Cedar Creek—only the last-named made no sense at all to Early's officers and men. That is the one he chose.

In the years-long controversy afterward about why he made such a choice, Old Jube made several arguments. Of these, the saddest was that, as he told General Lee two days later, he was immobilized partly because so many of his men and officers had stopped in the camp to plunder. Early did not say that the plundering was the sole cause of his halt, and the prominence he assigned to it varied in various accounts; but he seemed to believe, after the fact at least, that his army had virtually dissolved in an orgy of looting.[56]

That there was looting of the Federal camps is undeniable. In fact, any claim that some 20,000 famished, ill-clad men could cross acres and acres of land strewn with abandoned food and clothing without touching any of it would be on its face incredible. Captain Dickert of Kershaw's division saw men snatching up treasures even in the heat of the first assault, and when the army was later halted the temptations would have been overwhelming. Not only were the camps gone over, but many dead Union soldiers were stripped of their equipment and clothing.

The difficult question is the extent to which the looting broke down the discipline of the line units and affected the execution of orders. In his official report Early, paraphrasing the information brought him by the remarkable Lieutenant Page, said that Gordon and Kershaw had been unable to advance against Getty's second position because "their ranks were so depleted by the number of men who had stopped in the camps to plunder." (Yet in his later memoir he quoted Page as reporting only that the divisions were "much scattered.") Early had seen looters in the Federal camps as he rode up the pike, and he had dispatched a battalion of Wharton's men to stop them. He had been told later that the plundering was still going on, and sent "all my staff officers who could be spared to stop it if possible, and orders were sent to the division commanders to send for their men."[57]

Early's characterization of this problem made John Gordon,

for one, bitterly angry to the end of his days. His pen hand must have quivered with rage as the elderly senator prepared his rebuttal: "This charge so directly, so vitally concerns the reputation, the honor, the character of Southern soldiers (it concerns all American soldiers, for these men were Americans of purest blood) as to demand the most exhaustive examination. Let the fiercest search-light of historical scrutiny be turned upon those men."[58]

With all the passion appropriate to a Georgia lawyer defending Southern manhood, Gordon made his case and made it well. He quoted General Evans as saying that as soon as the army halted, Evans "had small details sent over the ground we had traversed in order to bring up every man who had fallen out for any cause except for wounds. My command was not straggling or plundering." General Battle said he saw no plundering at all, General Grimes reported very little, and Colonel John Winston of Grimes's brigade said, "I heard of but one man who stopped to pick up a thing. He got a hat, and has charges preferred against him."[59]

General Wharton, who of course was with Early as they came up the pike in the morning, minimized the looting they had seen. In a letter to Gordon, Wharton recalled that "I had a pretty fair view of a large part of the field over which you had driven the enemy. It is true that there were parties passing over the field and perhaps pillaging, but most of them were citizens, teamsters and persons attached to the quartermaster's and other departments, and perhaps a few soldiers who had taken the wounded to the rear. No, general; the disaster was not due to the soldiers leaving their commands and pillaging."[60]

A Confederate chaplain, the Reverend A. C. Hopkins, confirmed Wharton's identification of the stragglers. There were many of them, said Hopkins, and they were plundering; "but they were men who in large numbers had been wounded during the summer's campaign, who had come up to the army for medical examination, and who came like a division down the pike behind Wharton, and soon scattered over the field and camps and helped themselves. They were not men with guns."[61]

As for Gordon himself, he wrote that his troops "were not

absent. They were here in line, eager to advance," and were "astounded at any halt whatever."[62]

But here Gordon may have gone too far. He had told Colonel Carter that he had intended to stop after going through Middletown, and that is where the army did stop. Although Early chose to stress the doubtful matter of pillaging, he is far more convincing when he refers to the fact that his men were "much jaded." In the regrettable absence of cavalry to take up the chase, a pause of some duration to re-form the ranks of infantry was imperative. By the time that was accomplished, as Early wrote later, the Federals had also begun to reassemble and, more importantly, an "immense force of cavalry, which remained intact, was threatening both of our flanks in open country."[63]

This was a powerful argument for retreat, but Early simply says he decided to "content myself with trying to hold the advantages I had gained until all my troops had come up and the captured property was secured." Apparently he was looking for Lomax's cavalry—"I did not deem it prudent to press farther, especially as Lomax had not come up"—as a counter to the Federal cavalry on his right. The hours passed. Lomax did not appear. Rosser was stymied. Gordon fumed. Old Jube vacillated. He ordered a retreat, but only of the captured guns and wagons—an order that was either not carried out or carried out far too slowly. And he ordered an attack, but with a timid order whose phrasing denied its own purpose.[64]

"I rode to the left, for the purpose of ordering an advance," Early wrote. He told Gordon to go forward, "for the purpose of driving the enemy from his new position," with Kershaw and Ramseur following. Even in his later account Early does not use the word attack, and he makes it clear that his orders were tentative to the point of being contradictory. For he was unable to rid himself of the haunting fear of the enemy cavalry. He had ridden away from the "large body" of horsemen "seriously threatening" the exposed right, only to find that "the enemy's cavalry on our left was very strong, and had the benefit of an open country to the rear of that flank."[65]

"A repulse at this time would have been disastrous," Early wrote disingenuously, "and I therefore directed General

Gordon, if he found the enemy's line too strong to attack with success, not to make the assault." This was hardly a clarion call to victory. It was, however, the attack that Gordon said he and his men were burning to make. It was not a forceful plan—Gordon's tired division was to edge forward alone and test the mettle of the re-formed and rested Federal lines—but Kershaw and Ramseur were at least ready to wade in if things developed. It was two hours late and at least two divisions light, but it was Gordon's chance. At 1 P.M. he advanced, his men crunching through the woods toward the left of Emory's XIX Corps.[66]

Sheridan saw the enemy line move out and took it for the attack he had been expecting. He alerted General Emory and ordered the Vermont Brigade to withdraw from Getty's line and take up a position in Emory's rear to be available as a reserve.[67]

Sandy Forsyth happened to be at the point of impact. After an interminable few minutes of listening to the unseen enemy's approach through the woods, he reported, "we caught a glimpse of a long gray line stretching away through the woods on either side of us, advancing with waving standards, with here and there a mounted officer in the rear of it. At the same instant the dark blue line at the edge of the woods seemed to burst upon their view, for suddenly they halted, and with a piercing yell poured in a heavy volley, that was almost instantly answered from our side, and then volleys seemed fairly to leap from one end to the other of our line, and a steady roar of musketry from both sides made the woods echo again in every direction." Here and there, Forsyth saw, the Union line wavered, but the nervous men responded to the shouts of the mounted officers behind them: "Steady, men, *steady*!"[68]

The affair was less impressive to Captain DeForest, who was a short distance away behind the XIX Corps center. Soon after the warning from Sheridan arrived, he wrote, "a violent fusillade broke out along our front line, accompanied by battle yells from our second line; though meanwhile I did not hear a hostile bullet, nor did we have a single man hit. The uproar lasted several minutes, and then I was told that the column had retreated." DeForest decided that it had been merely a cautious demonstration.[69]

"That's good! That's good!" bubbled Sheridan when he was told what had happened. "Thank God for that! Now then, tell General Emory if they attack him again to go after them, and to follow them up, and to sock it to them, and to give them the devil." Infectious as his enthusiasm was, it was short-lived in his absence. DeForest reported that the men on the XIX Corps line "were apparently somewhat dismayed at discovering that the enemy showed a willingness to renew the battle; and while the fusillade lasted I noted some ominously gloomy faces. 'They are not going to fight well,' said one of our staff officers sadly, 'They haven't recovered their spirits. They look scared.' "[70]

Sandy Forsyth, on the other hand, had his blood up, and was incredulous that Sheridan had not given orders for an immediate counterattack. Forsyth tried to endure his growing impatience for an hour, then gave up and galloped over to Sheridan's headquarters. To his astonishment, the young captain found the commanding general "half lying down, with his head resting on his right hand, his elbow on the ground." Asked what he wanted, Forsyth blurted out, "It seems to me, general, that we ought to advance; I have come hoping for orders."[71]

Sheridan "half sat up, and the black eyes flashed." Forsyth suddenly realized what he had said, and to whom. Sheridan was not the kind of general who took kindly to being upbraided by junior officers; Forsyth was a favorite aide, but perhaps that would not save him. He stiffened. "But gradually an amused look overshadowed the anxious face, and the chief slowly shook his head. 'Not yet, not yet; go back and wait.' "[72]

Mystified by Sheridan's sudden loss of verve, Forsyth returned to the right and sat down under a tree behind the XIX Corps line. The men were stretched out prone on the ground, "listlessly and sleepily," and as Forsyth watched them he saw one possible reason for delay: "We were steadily growing stronger. Every now and then stragglers—sometimes singly, oftener in groups—came up from the rear, and moving along back of the line, dusty, heavy-footed and tired, found and rejoined their respective companies and regiments, dropping down quietly by the sides of their companions as they came to them, with a gibe or a word or two of greeting on either side, and then they, too, like most of the rest, subsided into an appearance of apathetic indifference." The mood was sour. They had been bested by a smaller army, one they had beaten twice within a month. It was, said Forsyth, "a bitter cud to chew."[73]

Another hour or so passed, and the restless Forsyth rode out in front of the XIX Corps to try to see what the enemy was doing, without success, and went to see Sheridan again. "Not yet, not yet," the reclining commander said, "Go back and wait patiently." Another hour. Forsyth went out to the picket line again, dismounted and walked forward until he could see the Confederates. After probing the Union line, Gordon's, Kershaw's and Ramseur's divisions had posted a strong skirmish line a half-mile in front of their main position along the Old Forge Road. Forsyth watched them working feverishly on their new position, "piling up stones and rails on the prolongation of a line of stone fences, evidently expecting an advance from our side and preparing for it." Once again Forsyth returned to army headquarters, where he found Sheridan transformed.[74]

The problem all along had been Longstreet. On seeing the wreckage of his army, Sheridan had assumed that the intercepted message must have been authentic, and that Longstreet had indeed arrived to help Early "crush Sheridan." In order to ascertain exactly what he was facing, Sheridan had ordered Merritt to scoop up some prisoners by overrunning a Confederate battery east of Middletown; in this way Sheridan learned that only Kershaw's division of Longstreet's corps was present. Much relieved, he was about to order the attack when Sheridan was told—he does not say by whom— "that Longstreet was marching by the Front Royal Pike to strike my rear at Winchester, driving Powell's cavalry in as he advanced. This renewed my uneasiness, and caused me to delay the general attack till after assurances came from Powell denying utterly the reports as to Longstreet."[75]

As the courier who brought this information from Powell rode away, Sandy Forsyth arrived to hear his beaming chief say, "It's all right now!" He asked the time, and when told it was twenty minutes to four, exclaimed, "So late! Why, that's later than I thought!" Then Little Phil rapped out his orders: "Tell General Wright to move forward the Sixth Corps and attack at once, keeping his left on the pike; then tell General Emory to advance at the same time, keeping the left of the Nineteenth Corps well closed on the right of the Sixth Corps; if opportunity offers, swing the right division of the Nineteenth Corps to the left, and drive the enemy towards the pike. I will put what is available of General Crook's forces on the left of the pike and General Merritt's cavalry also, and send Custer well out on Emory's right to cover that flank." Sheridan wanted his entire line to attack at the same time, yet to wheel to the left and effect a flanking movement. It was a scheme that required extraordinary speed of the right flank and unusual control of the left. Major Stevens wrote afterward that he thought it a tactical mistake to make a frontal attack on the strongest part of the enemy line, just west of Middletown, before the flanking movement had had a chance to turn them out of it.[76]

Stevens also recalled that not everything Sheridan said and did that day had a salutary effect. As VI Corps' Second Division was to be the pivot of the wheeling movement, Sheridan rode over to explain his orders carefully to Getty. Perhaps not fully aware of Getty's heroic conduct throughout this very trying day, Sheridan concluded with a patronizing remark: "Do well in this movement, General, and I will see that you are properly recognized." Deeply offended, Getty replied with icy formality. "General Sheridan, I always do well—the best I can, at all events."[77]

General Wright, resting stretched out on the ground when the orders reached him, climbed to his feet, grunted, "Very well," and began issuing his orders, having some difficulty in speaking because of the swelling of his wound. General Emory began his preparations with his usual crisp efficiency. Word of the attack ran down the Union line like flame along a fast-burning fuse. The men jumped to their feet, shook off their depression and made themselves ready.

"Everywhere along the line of battle," Forsyth remembered, "men might be seen to stoop and retie their shoes; to pull their trousers at the ankle tightly together and then draw up their heavy woollen stockings over them; to rebuckle and tighten their waist-belts; to unbutton the lids of their cartridge-boxes and pull them forward rather more to the front; to rearrange their haversacks and canteens, and to shift their rolls of blankets in order to give freer scope to the expansion of shoulders and an easier play to their arms; to set their forage caps tighter on their heads, pulling the vizor well down over their eyes; and then, almost as if by order, there rang from one end of the line to the other the rattle of ramrods and snapping of gunlocks as each man tested for himself the condition of his rifle."[78]

When their ritual of preparation was done, the men grounded and leaned on their rifles, staring toward the enemy and waiting for the order to go forward again. The line officers stood rigidly, with drawn swords. There was a time of quiet; too long, not long enough. Then, crystalline in Sandy Forsyth's memory, came the moment:

" 'Attention!' rings down the line. 'Shoulder arms! Forward! *March!*' And with martial tread and floating flags the line of battle is away."[79]

"The critical and momentous hour had now arrived," wrote Harris Beecher of the 114th New York, "in which the safety and honor of the army, the question of Northern invasion with all its horrors and devastation, and perhaps the fate of the rebellion, was to be decided. As the men jumped up and marched in breathless silence through the autumnal forest, they felt that glory or defeat, the salvation or ruin of the country, depended upon the issues of that moment."[80]

Perhaps. Or they may have felt, as many of them were heard to say as the advance began, that "we may as well whip them tonight: if we don't, we shall have to do it tomorrow. Sheridan will get it out of us some time."[81]

Chapter 9

"We Want Those Guns!"

Major Hazard Stevens thought it was a clumsy beginning. Although the army was to wheel to the left, the left flank advanced first, delivering the first thrust with the case-hardened steel of Getty's division. Each of the other four divisions on the line was to step off as it saw the one on its left go into motion. Getty's Second moved out along the pike in "one thin, blue line," Stevens wrote, steadily tramping forward into the screeching slam of the shells, toward the first, nervous ripples of the enemy's musketry, rifles shouldered, holding fire.[1]

Colonel Kidd had a grand view from the high ground east of the pike, as his Michigan Brigade of cavalry began the advance on the left of the two-mile-long Federal line: "It was a glorious sight to see that magnificent line sweeping onward in the charge. Far, far away to the right it was visible. There were no reserves, no plans for retreat, only one grand, absorbing thought—to drive them back and retake the camps. Heavens, what a din! All along the Confederate line, the cannon volleyed and thundered. The union artillery replied. The roll of musketry became incessant."[2]

The 8th Vermont, down in the declivity of Meadow Brook in the center of the division, lost sight of the cavalry across the pike to the east, and of the other infantry divisions to the west. It felt lonely, Major Walker reported, advancing across open fields against "a very heavy line of the enemy, covered throughout by a series of stone walls." And well it might; they were up against Ramseur's solid division, solidly placed.[3]

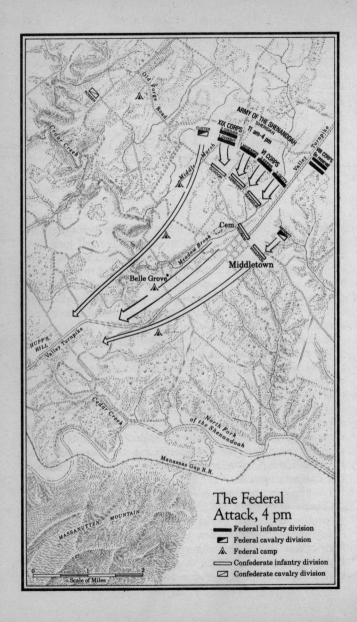

The Federal
Attack, 4 pm

▬▬ Federal infantry division
◤ Federal cavalry division
⚑ Federal camp
▭ Confederate infantry division
▱ Confederate cavalry division

0   1   2
Scale of Miles

Ramseur had put two brigades on the line—his right anchored on Miller's stone mill and outbuildings on Meadow Brook—had held Cox's in reserve and had put Grimes's to the right rear to maintain a tenuous connection with Pegram's division, whose left was some eight hundred yards back, on the Old Forge Road. When he saw the weight of the attack bearing down on him, Ramseur, his horse prancing, his flower still fresh on his lapel and his spirits still high, ordered Cox and Grimes forward to the main line at the double quick.[4]

Across the pike to the east, Merritt's cavalry, moving in three lines of two ranks each, took up the trot as it crossed a ravine and ascended onto a wide plateau where it was pelted with a lethal, leaden rain. The moving lines left behind an obscene litter of horses down and screaming in pain, of men down and writhing, men hobbling away to the rear—and men facedown and still, on the shuddering ground. But the lines closed over the gaps that were constantly being flicked into them, retained their shape and purpose and kept moving. Lowell's riders on the cavalry's right pulled ahead of the plodding infantry to their right, thus coming under savage enfilading fire from Ramseur's men across the pike.[5]

Lowell was in his accustomed place—far out in front. He whose voice had ever been its own bugle, cutting through the pandemonium of battle, had whispered his orders to his aides, and their young voices had yelled them out, deploying the brigade. He who had always bounded into the saddle had needed help this time, but although he rode heavily he rode unassisted, saber up, straight for the enemy—which was arrayed behind a stone wall and firing with the speed of desperation. As ever, he rode as if there were no fear of death, and made his men believe it was so. That is where he was when the bullet found him, the one that arced out from a window on the second floor of the Brinker house in Middletown, lanced him from shoulder to shoulder, severed his spine and dropped him dying to the ground.[6]

The brigade was being shot to pieces in the brutal converging fire and had lost its commander; it was time to re-form. As they had been doing all day, the men wheeled their mounts, galloped back to cover—in this case the ravine to the north of the plateau—and there wheeled again into line, closing up and mustering their strength for another blow. Seeing this tactical maneuver, Kidd and Devin joined in, so that the entire line could be re-formed at once.[7]

The movement exposed the left of Getty's infantry line—the Third Brigade commanded by Colonel Winsor French—to enfilading fire, especially from the Confederate batteries to the east, in front of Middletown. Carter's gunners, the moment they were free of pressure from the cavalry, turned their pieces to the left and began to bombard the infantry across the pike. "The men fell in heaps," wrote Major Hazard, the slaughter made worse by the fact that the division was under orders to advance slowly, so the rest of the army could execute its left half-wheel with the Second as its pivot. But what demoralized the survivors even more than the carnage was the retreat of the cavalry, which they assumed had been repulsed.[8]

Ramseur's rifles, crackling mercilessly from behind the stone wall, completed the unnerving of French's brigade; "which advance was repulsed most gallantly," reported the Confederate Bryan Grimes, "the enemy fleeing in disorder and confusion, throwing down their arms and battle-flags in their retreat." French's men fell back to their starting place.[9]

Meanwhile the Third Division in the center of the VI Corps advance, as Stevens put it, "having become somewhat confused in advancing and guiding on the left, and unable to sustain the destructive fire of the enemy secure behind stone walls, also broke and gave back." They took with them part of Getty's rightmost brigade. But his steadfast Vermont Brigade, along with most of Warner's brigade, would not give ground. According to Captain Walker, it was merely "forced to halt behind a fortunate wall, low, and just long enough to cover our brigade, where we opened fire." The admiring Major Hazard wrote that the Vermonters, "with the utmost coolness, opened so well-sustained and effective a hail of musketry on the gray forms crouching behind the stone walls in front, that their fire visibly slackened."[10]

Similarly, on the VI Corps' right, the First Division had advanced in two lines. The first took severe punishment from the determined Confederate defenders, was battered to a halt, then surged forward when joined by the second line. But they had gained only a little ground when they were forced to stop again by the retreat of the Third Division to their left, and like the Vermonters they could only keep their place and maintain their fire. The VI Corps attack had been stopped, its line bent into the shape of a sine wave.[11]

Meanwhile Merritt's bugles called the regrouped cavalry to the charge again. This time they pressed onward across the deadly plateau, through a second and third ravine, then up the slope toward Wharton's skirmishers deployed behind a rail fence. The Confederate battery that had been punishing the cavalry all afternoon was belching smoke and canister from its forward position on the skirmish line. "Major," howled Merritt as he galloped at the side of Charles Deane, commanding the 6th Michigan, "we want those guns!" The response came just before the leading horses bounded over the rail fence: "All right, we will get them!"[12]

But things were still hopelessly out of synchronization. A glance to the right showed that now the infantry had fallen back, and yet again the cavalry was out in front, its right exposed. As Kidd related it, this posed no particular problem: "The cavalry once more fell back to the nearest ravine, and whirling into line, without orders, was ready instantly for the last supreme effort." But the riders were in a dangerous spot, motionless under converging fire. Fortunately for Merritt's men, the Vermont Brigade never slackened its fire on Grimes's position during the time it took the rest of Getty's division to collect itself.[13]

Colonel French demanded and received from Getty permission to drop the business of advancing slowly; it was no way, French maintained, to cross open ground under heavy fire. That established, the Third Brigade charged at the double quick, came alongside the Vermont Brigade—and kept on going. The Vermonters swarmed out from behind their stone wall and together the brigades stormed the right of Ramseur's line.[14]

Ramseur's men had still been yelling in wild exultation at their repulse of the earlier Federal attack when they had seen trouble developing to their left. Except for an occasional patch of timber and a few depressions in the gently rolling ground, this was the most visible of battlefields, with the contesting lines in clear view along most of their length. Woods obscured the westernmost flank, and clouds of gunsmoke rolled over the contending formations. But looking into the red light of the setting sun, Ramseur and his men could see that something was going wrong. Ramseur reacted instantly. He ordered his brigades back two hundred yards, to another stone fence. The movement started all right, but immediately began to get away from the officers and threatened to degenerate into a rout. Laboring mightily, Ramseur held on to a good portion of his men, re-formed them and settled them down to meet the new onslaught.[15]

Meanwhile the advancing Federals took possession of the mill and its outbuildings. Getty sent staff officers over the rise of ground to his right to make contact with the Third Division. Instead, they made contact with Kershaw's Confederates, still in place on the forward line despite Ramseur's retreat. Once again Getty's men hunkered down, took cover, and resumed shooting. They were under such heavy fire that they could not help their wounded or replenish their ammunition, but there was no thought of retreat.[16]

Over on the Federal right, just before the attack stepped off, Custer had been in the process of massing his command near the XIX Corps flank when he looked to the west and got something of a surprise: "Before this disposition could be completed the mounted skirmishers of the enemy were seen advancing over the ridge." Late in the day, Rosser appeared to have recovered his usual aggressiveness. If so, the consequences for the Union attack could be serious. Custer knew he had to do something, and there was no time for consultation with Sheridan.[17]

"I was compelled, for the time at least," Custer reported, "to break my connection with the infantry on my left, in order to direct my efforts against the force of the enemy now approaching on my right." Custer's division was still spread out; he took a portion of Colonel Alexander C. M. Pennington's First Brigade, along with a battery, forward toward the enemy, leaving orders for the rest of his men to follow. "The skirmishers of the enemy were easily driven from the ridge in front."[18]

Custer galloped onto the crest, to see Rosser's division massed below him. He ordered the battery to open fire and Colonel Pennington to "attack vigorously with three regiments." The gunners "opened a well-directed fire upon the massed squadrons of the enemy and produced the utmost confusion and great wavering in his ranks. Colonel Pennington's charge was completely successful, the enemy being forced back to a position bordering on Cedar Creek. Here the latter opened upon us with four guns, but without effect."[19]

Old Curly was understandably smug about his adversary's puny showing in this fight, but Rosser's belated advance, however tentative, had its effect on the battle. In veering away from XIX Corps to confront Rosser, Custer had left the infantry's right flank not only exposed but overlapped by Gordon's opposing division. The Federal infantry on the right would be advancing into the jaws of a vise.

Gordon, however, had been having his own problems. General Early, thoroughly transfixed by the threat of the Federal cavalry opposite his right, had shifted a great deal of the army's weight to the east of the pike. These dispositions, Gordon claimed later, left "a long gap, with scarcely a vedette to guard it, between my right and the main Confederate line. One after another of my staff was directed to ride with all speed to General Early and apprise him of the hazardous situation. Receiving no satisfactory answer, I myself finally rode to headquarters to urge that he reinforce the left and fill the gap, which would prove a veritable death trap if left open many minutes longer; or else that he concentrate his entire force for desperate defense or immediate withdrawal. He instructed me to stretch out the already weak lines and take a battery of guns to the left. I rode back at a furious gallop to execute these most unpromising movements."[20]

Captain J. S. McNeily of the 21st Mississippi wrote years later that he wondered where Gordon expected Early to get reinforcements, "as our whole force was on the front, and every inch of the line menaced. And how could 'concentration or withdrawal' have been effected in the open country, in the presence of such cavalry? There was nothing to be done but to fight where we stood."[21]

Furthermore, if Gordon is correct in saying that he arrived back at his command after the Federal attack had begun, he damns himself instead of Early. The serious gap in the Confederate line when the Federals hit it was not between Gordon's division and Kershaw's—the maps of both sides show that line closed up, although it may well have been thinly manned; instead, it was between Clement Evans's brigade and the rest of Gordon's division, and thus was Gordon's responsibility. It could have been caused by the execution of an order to extend to the left, but Gordon indicates he did not have time to deliver it. In any case the gap had its positive side, from the Confederate point of view. In the sudden absence of Custer's cavalry, it put Evans beyond the right flank of the advancing XIX Corps.

At the order "Forward march," Emory's troops had tramped stolidly forward through the woods in front of them, and for a few minutes there had been nothing to hear but the shouts of the line officers: "Guide left—*left!*" Sandy Forsyth, riding his horse behind the line, recalled that "now a few scattering bullets come singing through the woods." The orders change to *"Steady,* men!" and "Forward! *Forward!"*[22]

"Soon the woods become less dense," Forsyth wrote, re-creating the scene, "and through the trees I see just beyond us an open field partly covered with small bushes, and several hundred yards away, crowning a slight crest on its further side, a low line of fence-rails and loose stones, which, as we leave the edge of the woods and come into the open, suddenly vomits flame and smoke along its entire length, and a crashing volley tells us we have found the enemy."[23]

"A deep roar broke upon the summer stillness," recalled Dr. Harris Beecher of the 114th New York, "in which the very skies seemed to quake. Then an overpowering torrent of shells, grape and bullets tore through the devoted ranks, with murderous effect, followed by a stifling, acrid cloud of smoke, which hovered over the assailants and dimmed the horrid sight."[24]

The men flinched, the line hesitated, but Gordon's men were shooting high and the damage from the opening volley was slight. "Aim!" roared the Federal officers, and the XIX Corps line bristled with rifles thrown forward and leveled; *"Fire!"* and a shower of lead slammed into Gordon's improvised breastworks. "Pour it into them, men! Let them have it! It's our turn now!" The Union line surged forward again. As Forsyth remembered it, "brute instinct has triumphed, and the savage is uppermost with all of us."[25]

Leading the way across the field of cedars was the Second Brigade of the First Division—the same brigade that Emory had thrown into the breach that dawn and that had wrested its flags from the swarming enemy at so terrible a cost. Colonel Thomas was back with his 8th Vermont—with General Dwight's return to divisional command, General James McMillan had resumed command of the brigade—and the 8th was in the forefront of the charge.[26]

"There was but a short distance to go," Dr. Beecher remembered, "but every inch of it was a bloody one. Scores upon scores dropped from the ranks. There were more lying on the ground than there were survivors running ahead. 'My God,' said Colonel Davis, 'it is all over with us. No mortal man can ever clear that field.' "[27]

The men staggered under Gordon's second volley, but as Private Herbert Hill remembered it, the officers "vied with each other in urging the men on, and the instant the enemy's volley slackened, the regiment swept forward and upon the rebel line." Just as the final rush began, Surgeon Beecher reported, "their bayonets leaped from their scabbards, glistened a moment in the air, and then over the fence they poured in a tumultuous stream." There was a mighty, triumphant shout from Federal throats; "at that instant," wrote Hill, "we realized that the enemy's line was giving way, and we occupied the ground they held a moment before."[28]

There were thick woods to right and left as well as behind. "We were fighting in a jungle," said Hill, "and only by the roar of battle and by the wild shouts and yells which rose above the din of the artillery could we determine the position of the Union and rebel lines to our left." Gordon's men had yielded a little, but had not broken. "Every inch of ground was stubbornly contested." More Confederates began to fall back. "The supreme moment had arrived, and with wild shouts the brigade dashed ahead." In the lead ran the remarkable 8th Vermont, which "pierced the enemy like an arrowhead." Retribution was at hand.[29]

Just then Colonel Thomas's horse plunged to earth, shot. The regiment milled about in momentary confusion. Some distance away, Sandy Forsyth approached, standing in his stirrups, eagerly surveying the break in the enemy line. Vividly he recalled his shock as he heard: *"Crash! Crash!* and from a little bush-covered plateau to our right the enemy sends a couple of rattling volleys on our exposed flank that do us great harm, and I realize that *we are the outflanked!"* It was the Georgia Brigade of Clement Evans, crashing into the XIX Corps' right as it had hit Crook's left that morning.[30]

Once again the 8th Vermont was in mortal peril, caught by the attack from its right rear just as it was plunging forward through the enemy line. "I stood near our regimental colors," wrote Hill, "and shouted to the men to return or the flags would be captured. The sharp firing from the right instantly attracted the attention of the regiment, and in squads and singly, within five minutes most of them returned to the colors."[31]

Farther back, Forsyth was near another color-bearer in the confusion caused by the sudden volley from the flank. Hearing the officers' furious shouts of "Steady! Steady! Right wheel!" the color-bearer ran to the right, "waving his flag defiantly" to show the men the way. After a brief, heated argument, Forsyth persuaded the youth to yield the flag to him so he could brandish it from horseback and make it more visible. "The line catches sight of it, and the left begins to swing slowly round, the men in our immediate vicinity loading and firing as rapidly as they can in the direction from which the enemy is now advancing. The Confederates are giving it to us hot, and we realize that we have lost the continuity of our lines on both flanks."[32]

"Suddenly peal on peal of musketry broke out" from the wheeling Union line, re-forming intact despite its shock and confusion, and a relieved Forsyth saw that "the copse in front of us was fairly bullet-swept by repeated volleys." McMillan's brigade, with Colonel Thomas on foot leading the 8th Vermont in the van, hurled itself against the hidden enemy. "The brigade with shouts and yells charged into the woods," Hill reported, but before they reached the line "the enemy broke in great confusion and ran to the south and west."[33]

The men took "grim satisfaction," said Hill, "in knowing that the swath was being cut through the identical divisions from which we received the combined assault at early dawn." At the sight of the enemy running away, "some of the men jumped up and down, shouted, threw their hats or caps into the air in excitement. Early's left flank (Evans's brigade) was now completely shattered." But there was more hard work to be done, much more. McMillan immediately ordered the brigade to wheel back to the left; they were supposed to be leading the left wheel of the army, but this unexpected problem to the right had delayed them, and they were lagging behind.[34]

This was an assumption; the Federals on the right could see nothing of the rest of the battle because of the intervening woods, although as Forsyth recalled, "the steady roar of artillery and peals of musketry told us that heavy fighting was going on in that part of the field." There was one person, however, who knew where everyone was. "General Sheridan, riding his gray charger Breckinridge, and surrounded by his staff, came out of the woods and dashed up. One glance and he had the situation. 'This is all right! This is all right!' was his sole comment."

But everything was not all right. The entire Federal line was at a standstill, and Custer was not where he was supposed to be. Sheridan told McMillan to close up to the left, restoring the Union line, but to delay any further XIX Corps advance until Custer was in position. Suddenly a lone rider, yellow hair streaming, came pounding up out of the hollow to westward. It was Custer, Sheridan wrote later, "riding at full speed himself to throw his arms around my neck" in delighted greeting. "By the time he had disengaged himself from this embrace," Sheridan recalled with a shudder, "the troops broken by McMillan had gained some little distance to their rear." Custer, who among other things had just assured that his commanding general knew exactly where he was and what he was doing, galloped happily off to lead his belated advance.[35]

Annoyed, but confident Custer would deliver, Sheridan completed his instructions. Dr. Beecher described how the little general impressed his orders on everyone there: "Lie down right where you are, and wait until you see General Custer come down over those hills, and then (he raised himself in the stirrups and made an impulsive gesture with both hands) by God, I want you to *push* the rebels!" Then, Forsyth reported, "the general, followed by his staff, galloped rapidly to the left and rear through the woods, evidently making for the pike, where, judging from the continued roar of the field guns and musketry, the Sixth Corps was having savage work."[36]

Custer, meanwhile, had found himself in a dilemma. He had run Rosser off the ridge overlooking Cupp's Ford just as the XIX Corps' right had collided with the enemy. As Custer sat his horse on the crest, he could see to the right Rosser's division, with its back to Cedar Creek, and to the left the infantry battle. "It was apparent," he said in his official report, "that the wavering in the ranks of the enemy betokened a retreat, and that this retreat might be converted into a rout. For a moment I was undecided." Custer had raised self-promotion to an art form, and his official reports were major literary efforts in the service of that theme; he went on to build suspense and focus the reader's attention on his awesome responsibility. "Upon the right I was confident of my ability to drive the enemy's cavalry with which I was then engaged across the creek; upon the left my chances of success were not so sure, but the advantages to be gained, if successful, overwhelmingly greater; I chose the latter."[37]

His brief struggle with indecision over, Custer moved. He told Pennington to continue the attack on Rosser until the Third Division was under way, then to follow with two regiments, leaving only one in front of Rosser. Thus did Custer express his contempt for Rosser's performance that day. Then the rest of "this entire division," as Custer put it, "was wheeled into column and moved to the left at a gallop."[38]

The thick blue line of nearly 3,000 horsemen pounded into view on the plain between the ridge overlooking Cupp's Ford and the plateau north and west of Middletown now held by the Confederates. The troopers were fresh, eager, confident—and represented a devastating blow aimed at Jubal Early's back. Custer was grandstanding, of course, there was showmanship in everything he did. But behind the grandstanding was tempered steel; never was showmanship more appropriate, more appreciated or better timed.

The 8th Vermont was just resuming their advance after fending off the flank attack by Evans's brigade when the men were granted by circumstance "a rare privilege," as Private Hill put it. "We caught sight for a moment of the dashing Custer, that prince of horsemen, on an opposite eminence toward the setting sun, as he started with his famous division on that fierce charge which did not end till long after dark." Sheridan's confidence had been justified; XIX Corps had not been required to wait for Custer, and now resumed its attack on Early's left flank.[39]

General Gordon was striving with all his usual selfless courage to hold his men to their work. But many of them were tired beyond caring, did not like the spot they were in, had no confidence in Old Jube and now began to fear that they were being flanked by cavalry. In growing numbers they began to express their assessment of the situation with their feet. But even as they began to fall back they turned frequently and lashed out at the enemy, and Colonel Carter's guns continued their outstanding service, isolated batteries and sections blazing away with case and canister in the very faces of the advancing Federals before limbering up, galloping away and stopping a short distance back to open fire again.[40]

Meanwhile, Custer's charge gained momentum. "The design was to gain possession of the pike in rear of the enemy," Custer reported, to retake the Valley Pike bridge over Cedar Creek, along with the nearby fords, and trap the Army of the Valley whole. "Being compelled, however, to advance over an open plain and in full view of the enemy, our intentions were fully and immediately comprehended by him. The effect of our movement, although differing from what we anticipated, was instantaneous and decisive. Seeing so large a force of cavalry bearing rapidly down upon an unprotected flank and their line of retreat in danger of being intercepted, the lines of the enemy, already broken, now gave way in the utmost confusion."[41]

The infantrymen of XIX Corps were plunging ahead almost as fast as the cavalry. "Wounded and dead men marked the enemy's pathway as we rushed over logs, fences, and through thickets," wrote Hill, "till the regiment emerged from the timber and came out on the brow of a hill, in advance of any other Union troops, and in full view of almost the entire rebel army." Despite the confusion and the obscuring woods, McMillan's brigade emerged exactly where it was supposed to be—behind the Confederate left. From there Emory's command, said Forsyth, was able "to pour in a fearful fire on their exposed flank. The enemy was gallantly holding his line behind some stone fences, but flesh that is born of woman could not stand such work as this."[42]

Kershaw's division was now the foremost Confederate unit, still holding along the forward line. It was already taking savage pressure from the front; after the disheartened Third Division of VI Corps had spent three-quarters of an hour firing but not advancing, General Wright had ridden over and given Colonel J. Warren Keifer a peremptory order to charge. As soon as the Third moved forward in response, the waiting First joined it on the right.[43]

Captain Dickert of Kershaw's division recalled with pride that as "the bullets came whizzing over our heads, or battering against the stone wall," his brigade held its own, even after "we noticed away to our right the lines give way." They did not see the left caving in until "someone raised the cry and it was caught up and hurried along like all omens of ill luck, that 'the cavalry is surrounding us.' In a moment our whole line was in one wild confusion, like pandemonium broke loose. If it was a rout in the morning, it was a stampede now. None halted to listen to orders or commands. Like a monster wave struck by the headland, it rolls back, carrying everything before it by its own force and power, or drawing all within its wake."[44]

But the remainder of Ramseur's division was not drawn into Kershaw's wake. Braced for the second onslaught of VI Corps, Ramseur's men clung tenaciously to their stone wall as the army's left folded back behind them. Now Ramseur could see that the right was crumbling, too. For an hour Wharton's and Pegram's divisions had stood firm against the fierce punching of Merritt's cavalry charges and the relentless pounding of Henry DuPont's guns. But Kidd and the Wolverines finally pierced Wharton's right flank and drove past Middletown to the east. Now the Confederate right, too, was flinching away from the prospect of being surrounded by cavalry. Desperately, Jubal Early pleaded with the men around him to emulate what he called later "the gallant stand made by Ramseur with his small party."[45]

Ramseur was determined there would be no more retreating. He had a battle and a furlough to win. Still mounted, he rode up and down behind the wall, oblivious to the blizzard of lead around him, brandishing his sword at the enemy, holding his men in their places with the power of his voice and presence. It was well past five o'clock, the sun was edging down behind the Alleghenies; in another hour it would be fully dark. One more hour and the shooting would stop and the Confederates could repair their line, perhaps fall back to Fisher's Hill, and stabilize things. One more hour.

On Ramseur's left, a fragment of one of Kershaw's brigades was still holding on. "Some one said, 'Look at General Ramseur!'" recalled Captain H. H. Stevens of the 17th Mississippi. "We looked to our rear and saw him sitting his horse, not over 50 yards from us, in plain view of a long line of Yankees advancing and shooting like the mischief."[46]

Ramseur trotted his horse over to the ranking officer, Major George B. Gerald of the 18th Mississippi, to ask if the Mississippians could hold until dark. Gerald thought he could, although the Yankees were pressing from three sides now. Ramseur was loping back to his own command position when his horse fell to earth, shot. Ramseur kept his feet, undismayed, looked around, found himself among Cox's men. He grabbed a horse from one of the brigade couriers, mounted, started to ride on, and that horse tumbled dead to the ground. Horses were getting scarce, and it took him a minute to find another. He had just put a foot to the stirrup to swing up when hot lead punched into his right side, seared through his chest and lodged low in his left side.

Staff officers ran to the fallen general and carried him a short distance to the rear. They turned back to the fighting, leaving Caleb Richmond, Ramseur's brother-in-law and an aide since the organization of the 49th North Carolina, to watch over him. But the men knew immediately that Ramseur was down, and the line began to disintegrate. Despite the gravity of the wound and the agony it might cause him, the staff officers thrust Ramseur back up on a horse and, with an officer running alongside on foot to prop him up, bore their general away from the advancing enemy, toward the pike. There they found an ambulance, laid him in it, and sent it south. Everything was going south.[47]

From his vantage point up on the Federal left, Private Hill watched the spectacle unfolding below him. The ecstasy of the moment gripped him as he wrote years later, "What a sight! Such as our army never beheld before, and never would again; the event of a lifetime!

"We had completed so much of a turn as to face nearly east, and stood on their flank overlooking what then became a great, rushing, turbulent, retreating army, without line or apparent organization, hurrying and crowding on in mad retreat. Back across the sea of half-upturned faces of the enemy we could see the Union flags advancing amid the belt of smoke and flame that half encircled the doomed Confederates, while there was a continual roar of musketry and artillery."[48]

Battered and weary though they must have been, the men of XIX Corps were eager to give chase. But as Forsyth observed, "it was no walkover even then, for the Confederates fought splendidly—desperately even. They tried to take advantage of every stone fence, house or piece of woods on which to rally their men and retard our advance. Their batteries were served gallantly and handled brilliantly, and took up position after position."[49]

Now Emory's corps encountered several threats in rapid succession; one of them from its own comrades. "The Sixth Corps, seeing our men across the skirt of the meadow, mistook them for Confederates and fired upon them before the error was discovered." No sooner had that firing been stopped than a Confederate battery, off to the right of the 8th Vermont, opened up. "The first shot buried itself in the bank below," recalled Hill, "then a second, and a little nearer; while the third plunged underneath us, tearing up the ground and whirling the writer completely about." Two or three men were dead and several badly wounded.[50]

An officer rode over to order Colonel Thomas to charge the battery. Thomas hardly needed to be told: "That's what we are after, sir," he snapped, "I'm only waiting for support." But there was no time for that, and yet again the 8th Vermont was ordered to attack alone. As it started its charge, however, it was joined and followed closely by the 12th Connecticut, and the two regiments made an imposing mass as they ran for the two Confederate guns. "The battery saw us coming, and fired with redoubled energy, but our close proximity and the depression of the ground saved us from loss, and in their confusion the gunners fired wildly, so that most of the storm intended for us fell short or swept just over our heads." At the last possible minute, the Confederates hauled their guns down the opposite slope and got them away.[51]

With VI and XIX Corps now advancing together, scything eastward toward the pike just as Sheridan had planned, with Custer plunging ahead on their right and Merritt punching through on the far left, followed now by a shouting line of Crook's men, Jubal Early at last gave way to dismay. "Every effort to rally the men in the rear having failed," he wrote later, "I had now nothing left for me but to order these troops to retire also. When they commenced to move, the disorder soon extended to them." Captain Crowninshield was amazed at the suddenness with which the Confederate right gave way: "The rebels had here a large number of guns, but when the collapse came, guns and men seemed to vanish as if they had been swallowed up in the ground. Merritt charged with all his cavalry, but they captured no guns on our side of Cedar Creek."[52]

With the fall of Ramseur and the crumbling of the Confederate right, the sustained roar of the battle up to that point dwindled; the artillerists had limbered their pieces and were dashing for the Cedar Creek bridge, the infantrymen were doing well if they persisted in carrying their rifles, let alone firing them. "Did they run us? Yes, they did, and I never will forget it," Captain Benson of Kershaw's Mississippians remembered ruefully. "We ran. Yes, we struck the ground in high places only."[53]

"As the tumult of battle died away," General Gordon wrote, "there came from the north side of the plain a dull, heavy, swelling sound like the roaring of a distant cyclone, the omen of additional disaster." Around each flank of the Confederate army poured the dread horsemen, nearly 3,000 pounding riders on each side, closing a circle of steel and fire around a dissolving and panicky army. The sight and the sound told John Gordon it was all over: "As the sullen roar from the horses' hoofs beating the soft turf of the plain told of the near approach of the cavalry, all effort at orderly retreat was abandoned."[54]

For the infantry, as well, it was now "a race and a chase, not a battle," said one of General Dwight's XIX Corps staff officers, "and the very men who had in the morning so ingloriously fled were now the first in this chase—their legs were always good." Dr. Harris Beecher, assistant surgeon of the 114th New York, was more charitable, observing merely that "those who had the longest wind and the strongest legs were soon far ahead of their comrades in this exciting and exhilarating chase. Yet all moved along in the current, as fast as they could, and every heart pulsated with intense delight. Mounting some elevated spot before them, they observed in the valley a spectacle that caused them to laugh and scream with joy. They saw thousands of rebels indiscriminately mixed together, wearily jogging along, exhibiting nothing but their butternut-colored backs, hurling away their guns and knapsacks in their fright, their courage all oozing out at the ends of their toes, and not daring even to turn around and respond to the fire of the boys." The panting, ecstatic Federals hurled insults as well as bullets: "Johnny Reb, we'll learn you to take a joke!" "Say, you Jeff Davis pimps, how do you like our style?" And, most often, "Surrender, you sons of bitches!"[55]

The flight was so quick that Custer saw he was not going to make it to the Cedar Creek bridge on the pike in time to cut off the Confederate retreat. Instead, he galloped through the old VI Corps camps and struck the creek well upstream. "The rapid pace at which my command had moved had necessarily extended my column," Custer reported, "and upon reaching the vicinity of the creek I had but two regiments available—these were the 1st Vermont and 5th New York; the remainder of the division was coming up at the gallop. With these two regiments, and hidden from the view of the enemy, I crossed

Cedar Creek over a small ford about half a mile above the creek bridge." There the two regiments hurriedly re-formed, counted off, and reloaded their pistols and carbines.[56]

Just south of Custer the Confederates were desperately trying to assemble a line. They were back at their starting place of the morning, but if they could hold here they could save most of their wagons, guns and reputation. Jubal Early was there, hollering and cursing, red-faced, hatless and bedraggled in the dying red of the sun of Middletown. And the thing started to work.

As a pursuing VI Corps soldier, Lieutenant Theodore F. Vaill, described it, "a breastwork of rails was thrown together, colors planted, a nucleus made, and both flanks grew longer and longer, with wonderful rapidity. That growing line began to look *ugly,* and somewhat quenched the ardor of the chase. It began to be a question in many minds whether it would not be a point of wisdom to 'survey the vantage of the ground' before getting much further. But just as we descended into the intervening hollow, a body of cavalry, not large, but compact, was seen scouring along the fields to our right and front, directly toward the left flank of that formidable line on the hill. When we reached the top there was no enemy there!"[57]

It had not been quite so easy as it looked. As Colonel J. W. Bennett of the 1st Vermont Cavalry prepared to lead that compact cavalry charge, he estimated there were 5,000 Confederate infantrymen milling around in front of him, with their officers trying to get them into a line. Tensely, Bennett yelled to Custer, "If I am to charge them it must be at once, for if they re-form they will empty every saddle before I can reach them." Custer stood in his stirrups, surveyed the scene, and agreed: "That is so. When you go, throw in every man you have, and I will take care of you."[58]

Colonel Bennett went. "Seldom have I heard the air more heavily freighted with lead than at that moment," he recalled. "Of the four of us riding abreast," ten or twenty feet ahead of the regiment, "two certainly went down. I cannot recall what became of the third. But I was alone. Then I ordered the charge, and my men, with set faces, leaned forward low on their horses, and putting them to their utmost speed, rushed

upon the enemy (a body sufficiently numerous to have de-
voured all my men, had they been good beef)."[59]

But the utterly demoralized Confederates, finding themselves
yet again flanked by the fearsome Federal cavalry, fired a wild
volley and tried to disperse. "The enemy when we struck them
were in a dense body, covering several acres, and the broken
and disorganized rushed upon those in better order, so that all
were thrown into the confusion. My men with carbines, lying
along the side of their horses' necks, fired point blank upon this
mass. At one point some of the enemy fell and others fell over
them until the ground for the distance of nearly half an acre
was covered with a struggling mass of fallen men."[60]

Captain Henry DuPont, meanwhile, had galloped his nine
guns up the pike from Middletown to the high ground overlooking the Cedar Creek bridge from just in front of the XIX
Corps earthworks and had opened fire on the fleeing army.
"Almost every shell exploded in the midst of the crowded
masses before us," he wrote later. "Field pieces and caissons,
wagons and ambulances, were abandoned by their drivers and
dashed along the road in wild confusion, damaging or destroying each other by collisions, while swarms of the retreating
enemy left the road and scattered through the fields."[61]

DuPont's sport had been short-lived. Not only did Custer's
men appear across the creek to the right, but Merritt's cavalry
now arrived at the Valley Pike bridge. Tom Devin was in the
lead with the 6th New York Cavalry, which charged two at a
time across the bridge—just as Bennett led the charge from the
far right. Both Devin and Bennett were unaware of the presence of the other, and thus were a little surprised by their success.[62]

There may have been another reason for it. Henry Kyd
Douglas was in that line, and wrote later that "General Pegram
came and, believing we would be overrun, unfortunately ordered the line to retire. As it proceeded to do so, the enemy
came at us with a rush. The few of us who remained could
make little resistance and were virtually run over."[63]

Now Devin turned off to the left of the pike to organize his
brigade and direct the arriving units forward, while Custer did
likewise not far away, on the pike about a mile toward Stras-

burg. It was there that Custer's men captured their first gun of
the day. The lack of contact between Merritt's and Custer's
cavalry at this point would cast a long shadow.[64]

But it did not delay the pursuit. Riding now along the pike,
Custer's two regiments, followed at a distance by Devin's one,
galloped into the gathering darkness. According to Stevens,
"the broad macadamized limestone highway, compacted like a
solid rock, resounded and re-echoed under the iron-shod hoofs
of the galloping squadrons in the ears of the beaten and flying
rebels as if ten thousand Yankee troopers, sword in hand, were
thundering down upon their defenseless heads. Dropping their
muskets by thousands, abandoning their guns and teams in the
road, the terrified fugitives scattered right and left, seeking ref-
uge in the fields and woods, as the charging column with ringing hoof beats and clashing scabbards and shout and cheer and
carbine shot went thundering past."[65]

The number of Confederate prisoners taken by the cavalry
probably exceeded the number in Early's army; a Lieutenant
Isaacs of the 2nd South Carolina remembered surrendering five
times. A group of fleeing soldiers would be taken prisoner by a
small cavalry detachment, Isaacs explained later: "The chief of
the troop would order, 'Now you stay there!' and spur off after
more prisoners. Then we officers would tell our men, 'Now
scatter, boys; take to the bushes and hollows; get back to Fisher's Hill.' Well, what with the nightfall and the rough country,
the biggest part of us sneaked out of our scrape."[66]

General Gordon tried to organize a stand somewhere on
Hupp's Hill, at a spot where the pike ran "immediately on the
edge of one of those abrupt and ragged limestone cliffs down
which it was supposed not even a rabbit could plunge without
breaking its neck." Union cavalrymen—probably Custer's—
whirled in from three directions at once, and Gordon yelled to
his men to save themselves if they could. Then, "wheeling my
horse to the dismal brink, I drove my spurs into his flank, and
he plunged downward and tumbled headlong in one direction,
sending me in another. How I reached the bottom of that abyss
I shall never know." Man and animal lay unconscious for a
while, then staggered to their feet and limped away to safety in
the darkness.[67]

Even at this, Jubal Early's Confederates had one more disaster yet to endure. As Hazard Stevens recounted it, "Half a mile beyond Strasburg the pike crosses a small creek by a wooden bridge only 30 feet long. The left-hand or lower side of this bridge was broken down, but over half of it remained intact and afforded ample and safe room for anything on wheels. Some frightened teamster in his haste had driven too close to the broken side of the bridge, running his wheels on that side off the sound part, and left the wagon half upset, hanging on the edge, the lower wheels dangling over the broken planks and the stream. A single sturdy shove would have thrown it over and cleared the way. But this trifling obstruction, which any man who kept his head could have cleared away in a few minutes, blocked the whole retreating column of guns and trains behind it, by which the road was jammed full for a long distance in an almost solid mass."[68]

Others remembered it differently. Colonel Moses Granger wrote later that "the report current that night and next morning in our army was that some of Custer's cavalry, riding up to the bridge, forced the driver of the wagon then passing to make a short turn, which overturned the wagon and blocked the road."[69]

However it happened, the effect of the bottleneck at the bridge was calamitous. The resulting traffic jam congealed a mile or more back through the town and up onto Hupp's Hill, trapping virtually everything Jubal Early had on wheels. "Whole batteries were found standing in the pike, the horses all harnessed and ready to move at the word, but the drivers and cannoneers had fled. Ambulances, filled with wounded, had become jammed and locked together, and were abandoned. Wagons were overturned in the gutters, scattering their contents in every direction. The men stumbled over great piles of debris, or walked around innumerable heaps of dead horses and men."[70]

The confusion and the darkness forced an end to the cavalry pursuit, and the Federals turned their attention to securing the captures. Back across Cedar Creek where the Union infantry was, the shooting and the dying had stopped with disorienting suddenness; as Captain DeForest put it, "like a dream from which one is suddenly awakened." One minute he had been wrestling his panicky horse through deadly cannon fire; "half an hour later, the field was deserted by the Rebels, and our infantrymen were dragging back to their camps in perfect peace."[71]

The exultation of victory obscured the nightmarish quality of the walk. "Dead and wounded men, dead and wounded steeds, dismounted guns, shattered caissons, broken muskets, and pools or spatters of blood," wrote DeForest, testified "that the dragon of war had lately passed that way. Of the wounded a few lay still and silent; here and there one uttered quavering cries expressive of intense agony; others groaned from time to time, gently and patiently." The men were outraged to see how many of their dead had been stripped by scavengers; one cavalry officer counted 63 naked corpses as he rode across one section of the field.[72]

Corporal Charles M. Burr of the VI Corps' 2nd Connecticut Heavy Artillery had been shot in the leg just as the First Division had started to fall back, and in the regimental history he later recorded how the battle looked to him as he lay on the field. First the attacking Confederates swept past him. Before long a Confederate officer stopped and helped put a tourniquet on the leg to slow the bleeding. "Next came the noble army of stragglers and bummers with the question, 'Hello, Yank, have you got any Yankee notions about you?' and at the same time thrusting their hands into every pocket." Soon a fleet of wagons appeared into which detachments were gathering dropped weapons and useful equipment, and ambulances—for the Confederate wounded only, Yankees were left where they lay. After a time a curious civilian strolled by, having a look, followed by three local boys who gave Corporal Burr a drink of water.[73]

Thus the day passed until mid-afternoon when, as Burr saw it, "the tide of travel began to turn. The noble army of stragglers and bummers led the advance—then the roar of battle grew nearer and louder and more general, then came galloping officers and all kinds of wagons, then the routed infantry, artillery and cavalry, all mixed together, all on a full run, strewing the ground with muskets and equipments. Then came the shouting boys in blue and in a few minutes Pat Birmingham came up and said, 'Well, Charley, I'm glad to find you alive. I didn't expect it. We're back again in the old camp, and the Johnnies are whipped all to pieces.'"[74]

As Colonel William Emerson of VI Corps remembered with satisfaction, "The brigade went to its position of the morning, got its breakfast, and encamped, satisfied that it had done a good day's work before breakfast." The camps had been thoroughly picked over. "The ground was littered with ragged, lousy tatters of gray Rebel blouses and breeches," recalled the cannoneer Augustus Buell, "where they had just peeled themselves of their old duds to put on our spick-span artillery dress uniforms that we had left in our valises. Such of our stuff as they could not carry away they had thrown upon our smoldering campfires to be consumed; but in the evening of Cedar Creek we all surveyed this wreck with great complacency, reflecting, as we heard the incessant crash of the cavalry carbines in pursuit, that Johnny had paid pretty dear for his whistle!"[75]

At least Buell, and much of the infantry, still had a camp of some kind. Not so Crook's men. "What camping we did that night we did on the *sites* of our camps of the night before," wrote Colonel Wildes. "But our tents, blankets, rations, etc., were gone, the rebels having made clean work of our camps, and no rations came up to us until the next morning." Over to the right, XIX Corps had coffee, but not the time to enjoy it: "A halt of half an hour was made, for bringing in our wounded men, some of whom fell in the morning and had lain all day on the disputed field, and were shivering in the raw night air. Fire was built, and coffee prepared for the refreshment of the men after their long fast; but before it could be served, orders came to advance again, and, leaving the wounded to the surgeons, and the dead uncared for, on we went again, after the flying foe." They followed the cavalry to the other side of Strasburg, feeling their way into line in the dark below Fisher's Hill, to make sure there would be no Confederate counterattack in the morning.[76]

Cannoneer Buell showed a wounded Confederate prisoner how to manage a tourniquet on a wounded wrist, instructing him carefully how to relieve the pressure every so often. Buell reported with satisfaction that the bleeding soon stopped. "It was only in actual battle," he reflected, "that the veterans of the two armies were really enemies."[77]

"The hours flew on—8, 9, 10, 11 o'clock at night came, and still the fierce flashing of the cavalry carbines ever and anon lit up the dark fields and gloomy wood-edges away to our front and right. 'Will it ever end?' asked one of our men of another, as we stood by the roadside peering out into the gloom. 'Does the cavalry calculate to fight all night? There can't be much left of the Johnnies by this time!' And so on. But by midnight things quieted down. There is a limit to horseflesh if not human flesh, and so at last even Custer's troopers were silent."[78]

Belle Grove House was ablaze with light and awash in noise. Before the last Confederates were across Cedar Creek, the headquarters train rumbled back into the yard of the great house, and the clerks and orderlies commenced restoring order. With an enormous log fire painting the front of the house and its surroundings in lurid light, the men hauled the corpses and the litter out of the yard, erected the tents in crisp rows again, and soon had established as before the nerve center of the Army of the Shenandoah.

It would take a long time to do the sad bookkeeping required after a battle; to take the rolls, calculate the numbers absent, find the wounded, account for the dead. For the Union army—back in its old camp, in possession of its wounded and secure in its position—precision would be possible. It would eventually be determined that the Federal casualties that day totalled 5,764—569 men killed, 3,425 wounded, 1,770 missing.[79]

The Confederate toll could only be estimated. Bookkeepers are often asked to confirm that times are good, seldom to calculate the exact dimensions of loss; for some time, Confederate accounts had not been well kept. There is little doubt, however, that Early's casualties were both numerically fewer and proportionately less than Sheridan's. The Confederates lost roughly 1,860 men killed and wounded, 1,200 prisoners. The total of 3,100 represented a casualty rate of about 18 percent; the Federal casualty rate was 20 percent.[80]

Such grim details did not concern Sheridan as he came into his headquarters, sparking exultation, from Strasburg, where he had seen the final collapse of the enemy army. (To a prisoner being led past him, Sheridan had gloated, "What in the hell did you fellows run so for?" The sour reply: "We were flanked, and couldn't fly.") Captured guns and wagons began to roll up, the teamsters parking them in neat rows in front of the house for display. Before long the restlessly stalking Sheridan saw a familiar form appear out of the dark. "You have done it for me this time, Custer," he roared, and at the same time he strode over, reached up, and hauled Old Curly off his horse. Lieutenant T. W. White of the 10th Vermont happened to witness the meeting: "Custer seizing Sheridan around the waist lifted him high up and in wild glee danced and whirled him around and around, completely lost to military deportment in his intoxicating joy, exclaiming as their tears mingled, 'By God, Phil, we've cleaned them out of their guns and got ours back!' "[81]

Nearby, on the fields of dead and wounded, acres and acres of campfires winked up at the stars that were forming like crystals of frost on the black bowl of the clear October sky. Weary to the bone, 23,000 Federal soldiers held themselves awake for a few more delicious minutes of telling each other stories, savoring the scalding hot coffee, confirming that they were alive, and had won.

One of the wagons in the yard at Belle Grove was a Confederate ambulance that had been caught in the crush on the wrong side of the bridge below Strasburg. According to one story, it had been singled out for attention when its driver responded to Federal troopers demanding who was inside by saying, "The General says I must not tell." The passenger was Stephen Dodson Ramseur, his pallid face terribly aged by pain and weariness, his uniform jacket still displaying the wilted flower celebrating new life.

They carried him into a room in the mansion, where Sheridan's chief medical officer and a Confederate surgeon examined the young general and confirmed that the wound was mortal. They made him as comfortable as they could, and gave him as much laudanum as he could take.[82]

The word spread quickly. Ramseur's assistant adjutant general, Major R. R. Hutchinson, now also a prisoner, was given permission to join his former chief. Sheridan came in and awkwardly offered assistance. Then came a parade of old friends, once brother cadets and officers, now formal enemies, all deeply grieved. Henry DuPont came, and thoughtlessly sat on the bed. "DuPont," groaned Ramseur, "you don't know how I suffer." Captain George Sanford, who had not known Ramseur but was merely curious, looked in just as Custer strode in and "greeted Ramseur in his bluff, hearty manner, but he scarcely responded." After exuding chivalric sorrow for a time, Custer clanked away. Wesley Merritt came, and talked quietly for some time while Ramseur was conscious. They must have talked about Benny Havens's, and the party they had had there so long ago. They must have thought about the song: "They lie forgotten far away from Benny Havens, O."[83]

Then there was just Hutchinson, sitting stoically at the bedside as Ramseur drifted in and out of consciousness through the long hours of the night. Whenever he was awake Ramseur talked about Nellie and the baby, wished he could see them just once. But she would know, he murmured, that he had a firm hope in Christ and trusted that they would meet hereafter. Sometimes he mentioned friends; he wanted Hutchinson to tell one that he had died a Christian, and had done his duty; to tell Nellie he loved her; to send her a lock of his hair.

Gray light came in at the window as the morning came up cold and windy. At twenty-seven minutes past ten o'clock Hutchinson noted the time, picked up a pen, and addressed a letter to Ellen Ramseur: "I am writing at the side of him whose last thought was of you and his God, his country and his duty. The end was peaceful and quiet. He died as became a Confederate soldier and a firm believer."[84]

A little more than a mile away, Charles Russell Lowell lay in a modest house on the main street of Middletown. As soon as his cavalry had broken through to the town on the previous evening, men of the 2nd Massachusetts had carried their colonel forward, and he had seen the enemy break and run. Then they had taken him into the house, which had been turned into a makeshift hospital.

When the regimental surgeon got there he found Lowell stretched out on a table, paralyzed below the shoulders but conscious. There was nothing the surgeon could do, and Lowell knew it. "Four others were lying desperately wounded on the floor," recalled the surgeon. "One young officer was in great pain. Lowell spent much of his ebbing strength helping him through the straits of death. 'I have always been able to count on you, you were always brave. Now you must meet this as you have the other trials—be steady—I count on you.' "[85]

As for himself, Lowell had work to do before he died. He dictated some messages to friends; he gave detailed and explicit orders to complete his stewardship of the Reserve Brigade; with the help of the surgeon he scribbled a few words of farewell to Josephine. If he thought of, or mentioned, the child she was carrying, it was not recorded. Twice he sent the surgeons out to care for some wounded Confederates who had been laid in the yard.[86]

"As dawn approached," wrote a biographer who talked with the staff officers present, "he lay tranquil, his mind withdrawn, it seemed, into that chamber of still thought, known so imperfectly to the nearest of his friends, wherein was the seat of his deepest life. Even in his last hour he was fully conscious and seemed to retain his strength. But he spoke less and less often; and as the day rose into full morning he ceased to breathe the air of earth."[87]

Five miles or so to the southwest, along the dark ridges and cold hollows of Massanutten and Fisher's Hill, 14,000 beaten Confederates had been straggling through the woods, the strongest of them barely able to walk, the worst off hardly crawling. They were in squads, in pairs, and some of them were alone. They knew that Fisher's Hill, once their Gibraltar, would be no haven now, but that they must gather there before moving on.

By 3 A.M. they had tottered into ranks again and, astonishingly, began another forced march. Their objective now was New Market, thirty-five miles away. They had been marching or fighting almost continuously since midnight of the 18th, with little opportunity to rest and none to eat. "Up the valley this routed, disorganized rabble (it could not be called an army) marched," recalled Captain Dickert, "every man as he saw fit, here a General at the head of a few squads called regiments, or a Colonel or Captain with a few men at his heels, some with colors and some without; here a Colonel without a man, there a score or two of men without a commissioned officer."[88]

There were artillerymen with no guns, quartermasters without wagons. "Along the road loose horses roamed at will, while the sides of the pike were strewn with discarded blankets, tent flies, oil cloths and clothing, the men being forced to free themselves of all surplus encumbrances in order to keep up with the moving mass."[89]

"At one place we passed General Early, sitting on his horse by the roadside, viewing the motley crowd as it passed by. He looked sour and haggard. You could see by the expression of his face the great weight upon his mind, the deep disappointment, his unspoken disappointment."[90]

The brisk October winds swept across a bluff east of Richmond, a tent-clad rise overlooking the ruffled waters of the James and Appomattox rivers. Among the sprawling fields of tents below was an unending bustle of riverboats unloading at the wharves, of wagons loading and departing, of blueclad soldiers drilling, of staff officers and couriers coming and going. But the height of the bluff gave perspective and muted the noise. Inside his billowing headquarters tent, Lieutenant General Ulysses S. Grant was at work. Outside, an indolent little phalanx of staff officers sat and talked.

A telegraph operator bustled over with another telegram for the general in chief, and as usual simply took it into the tent himself. A few minutes passed, and then Grant emerged, looking grave. He had something to read to them, he told the staff. They braced themselves for bad news. The message, said Grant sadly, was from Phil Sheridan.[91]

"I have the honor to report," Grant read to his apprehensive officers, "that my army at Cedar Creek was attacked this morning before daylight, and my left was turned and driven in confusion; in fact, most of the line was driven in confusion, with the loss of 20 pieces of artillery. I hastened from Winchester, where I was on my return from Washington, and joined the army between Middletown and Newtown, having been driven back four miles."

Grant stopped, as if it were too hard to go on. He shook his head. "That's pretty bad, isn't it?" A deep breath, and then the rest: "I here took the affair in hand, and quickly united the corps, formed a compact line of battle, just in time to repulse an attack. . . . I attacked with great vigor, driving and routing the enemy . . . disaster has been converted into a splendid victory." The officers whooped and pounded one another, Grant grinned, and went back into the tent to continue working. A few hours later, no doubt recalling the difficulty he had had getting the administrative mess in the Valley straightened out and Sheridan appointed, Grant sent a crisp wire to Secretary Stanton: "I had a salute of 100 guns from each of the armies here fired in honor of Sheridan's last victory. Turning what bid fair to be a disaster into glorious victory stamps Sheridan what I have always thought him, one of the ablest of generals."[92]

No reply from Stanton is recorded, but President Lincoln was perfectly willing, even glad, to admit that he had been wrong to doubt Sheridan. He had always thought a cavalryman should be six feet four, mused the president, but now "five feet four seems about right." But there was no joking when, on October 22, the president penned a note to the plucky little general. "With great pleasure I tender to you and your brave army, the thanks of the nation, and my own personal admiration and gratitude, for the month's operations in the Shenandoah Valley; and especially for the splendid work of October 19, 1864."[93]

Nor was any humor intended when a delegation from Washington arrived at Belle Grove near midnight on October 23. Told that the commanding general was asleep, the civilian in charge of the group demanded that he be awakened. In a moment Sheridan, half dressed and more than half asleep, stumbled out of his tent near the mansion's front porch to find himself confronting the assistant secretary of war, Charles A. Dana. Flanked by officers, Dana whipped out and ceremoniously read a commission promoting Sheridan to the rank of major general in the regular army. It had been just thirty-three days since the president had appointed Sheridan to the regular rank of brigadier general after Third Winchester. Dana concluded with a bit of congratulatory rhetoric while the general stood squinty-eyed in the flickering torchlight. "Sheridan did not say much in reply to my little speech," Dana recalled ruefully. The commanding general simply pivoted on his heel and went back to bed.[94]

There was ample reason for Lincoln's gratitude. Sheridan's prior victories at Winchester and Fisher's Hill had begun to lift the pall of gloom from the president's reelection campaign, and now the sun of Middletown burned away the last of that fog. National enthusiasm for Sheridan and his miraculous victory was easily transmuted into renewed enthusiasm for the war, and for the president whose policies were at long last beginning to pay dividends. A minor poet named T. Buchanan Read penned a fanciful ode to "Sheridan's Ride" that immediately became the gospel of the Lincoln campaign; it was read to every gathering that would listen to it before the November election returned Lincoln to power with unequivocal authority to finish the business. ("The thing they seem to like best about it," said Sheridan about the ubiquitous poem, "is the horse.")

Of course General Early's report of the battle, and its reception, were quite different. When he reached New Market on the 20th, Early sent a preliminary wire to Lee in Richmond. It was a message that delayed as long as possible getting to the point. "The Sixth and Nineteenth Corps have not left the Valley," it began obliquely, "I fought them both yesterday. I attacked Sheridan's camp on Cedar Creek before day yesterday morning, and surprised and routed the Eighth and Nineteenth Corps, and then drove the Sixth Corps beyond Middletown, capturing 18 pieces of artillery and 1,300 prisoners." Only after having thus extracted every possible measure of good news from the day did Early turn, with a breathless rush of a sentence, to the rest of the story; "but the enemy subsequently made a stand on the pike, and, in turn, attacked my line, and my left gave way, and the rest of the troops took a panic and could not be rallied, retreating in confusion." And then, immediately, the blame: "But for *their* bad conduct *I* should have defeated Sheridan's whole force" (emphasis added).[95]

The next day Early wrote Lee "a fuller account of the matter." This detailed narrative was clear and complete in relating what had happened—up to the time when Early had taken over the attack from Gordon, at which point the report descended into confusion. Early thought he had been fighting the entire VI Corps at the cemetery west of Middletown, when only Getty's division was holding on; he believed Gordon and Kershaw had been incapable of advancing ("their ranks were so depleted by the number of men who had stopped in the camps to plunder") when in fact it was their advance that flanked Getty out of his position; and he thought his left had given way in the final attack "not because there was any pressure on them, but from an insane idea of being flanked."[96]

"We had within our grasp a glorious victory," Early wrote, "and lost it by the uncontrollable propensity of our men for plunder, in the first place, and the subsequent panic among those who had kept their places, which was without sufficient cause, for I believe the enemy had only made the movement against us as a demonstration, hoping to protect his stores, etc., at Winchester, and that the rout of our troops was a surprise to him."[97]

As he pored over his explanations, self-justifications and accusations, Early must have heard echoes of the account he had sent to Richmond just twelve days earlier. In it he had said of Winchester, "I have already defeated the enemy's infantry, and could have continued to do so, but the enemy's very great superiority in cavalry and the comparative inefficiency of ours turned the scale against us." And of Fisher's Hill; "the infantry got into a panic and gave way in confusion."[98]

Then Old Jube, reflecting on all the disappointments and failures, confronted his despair and saw, all of a sudden, that he could not blame anyone else. In a moment of stunning self-examination, he penned a passage that gives a glimpse of the mighty spirit lurking within that stooped and sour, prematurely old man: "It is mortifying to me, general, to have to make these explanations of my reverses. They are due to no want of effort on my part, though it may be that I have not the capacity or judgment to prevent them. I have labored faithfully to gain success, and I have not failed to expose my person and to set an example to my men. I know that I shall have to endure censure from those who do not understand my position and difficulties, but I am still willing to make renewed efforts. If you think, however, that the interests of the service would be prompted by a change of commanders, I beg you will have no hesitation in making the change."[99]

Had he been able to stop there, to put away his pen and meet his fate, even then Old Jube would have made people remember him differently. But he could not do it. He went on, the maddening note of self-justification creeping back in. The affair had been disastrous, yes, but was "not entirely without compensating benefits." Sheridan's army "is now so shattered that he will not be able to send Grant any efficient aid for some time." The enemy's loss "was very heavy"; Confederate losses, he thought, were "not more than 700 or 800" killed or wounded, and "very few prisoners were lost." In fact, he added, feeling better by the minute, "Except for the loss of my artillery the enemy has far the worst of it. The enemy is not pursuing, and I will remain here and organize my troops."[100]

By the time he dispatched the letter to Richmond with Jed Hotchkiss, Early had put out of his mind the momentary, jarring vision of total responsibility. Hotchkiss recalled that Early urged him "not to tell General Lee that we ought to have advanced in the morning at Middletown, for, said he, we ought to have done so."[101]

But there was nothing now that Early could say, or not say, to change the cast of the die. The main chance, for him as for the Southern cause, had slipped past. It is by no means certain that anyone else could have done better with Old Jube's famished little army and limited possibilities. He had, after all, cleared one Federal army out of the Valley, defeated another in Maryland, rattled the gates of Washington, plunged the Union into a frenzy of fear and dissension, drawn away from Lee's front five Federal divisions of infantry and two of cavalry, marched 1,670 miles by Jed Hotchkiss's reckoning, fought 75 battles and skirmishes and inflicted on his enemies 14,500 casualties—or more men than his army usually contained during the period.[102]

It was not enough. His cavalry had been routed at Toms Brook, his army at Third Winchester, again at Fisher's Hill, and now instead of getting it all back, instead of wrecking Lincoln's reelection and bringing on a collapse of Northern will, he had been routed again at Cedar Creek. Jubal Early's name was linked forevermore with failure. "The fact was generally conceded among the troops," one Cedar Creek veteran wrote later, "that the unfortunate result of the engagement was due to two mistakes; one was that General Sheridan was not at his headquarters with his army and [the other was] that General Early was present with his."[103]

As for the Cause, "one thing is certain," said Henry Kyd Douglas: Cedar Creek "was to us an irreparable disaster, the beginning of the end." With another starving winter coming on, the breadbasket of the Confederacy was a scorched and empty ruin. The last Southern army capable of inflicting harm on the North, the last distraction to Grant's Army of the Potomac, was gone. Lee, whose mobility had ever been his salvation, was pinned to Richmond and Petersburg.[104]

Lee was as kind as he could be under the circumstances. The Richmond public, with Extra Billy Smith in the lead, clamored for Early's head, but Lee would not give it to them. Neither did he dare bring Old Jube back to Richmond at the head of the Second Corps. So instead of removing Early from command, he gradually removed the command from Early. On November 15 Kershaw's division made the familiar march back to Richmond and went into the trenches north of the city under its old corps commander, James Longstreet, who had returned to the army on the day of the fighting along Cedar Creek (oblivious of the fact that he had been a ghostly presence throughout that battle, lurking over the shoulder of Phil Sheridan).

Three weeks later, more orders reached Early's army at New Market. John Gordon was to take his own and Pegram's divisions to Waynesboro and board trains for Petersburg. Bryan Grimes, now commanding Ramseur's division, was to follow later. Then the Second Corps would be in Petersburg, but the lieutenant general commanding would still be in the Valley.[105]

And so Jubal Early was required to watch, on a bitter cold December day, as the army he had led into the Shenandoah marched away up the Valley Pike. It trudged to Staunton, then turned eastward and climbed the Blue Ridge toward Waynesboro, retracing its steps of two months before; the Army of the Valley of Humiliation, bound for Petersburg and Appomattox.

Epilogue: Mustering Out

The guns of Cedar Creek reverberated through the lives of all the surviving combatants, and through the affairs of their sorely wounded country, for decades to come, and their echoes can still be heard. Disagreement about the outcome divided not only winners from losers, but to a remarkable degree embittered friends and colleagues against one another. To the last years of their lives Jubal Early and John Gordon trembled with rage when they thought of the other's actions during and after the battle, as did George Crook when he remembered how Phil Sheridan treated him. George Custer and Wesley Merritt were forever alienated by the apportionment of credit for the victory. On the other hand, one friendship unaffected by the battle was that of Tom Rosser and George Custer.

OLD JUBE

The unquiet winter passed, with Sheridan and Early stuck at their respective ends of the Valley with their truncated commands, Sheridan being prodded continually by Grant to do something about the Virginia Central Railroad, Early being ignored. Early stayed at New Market until the Second Corps left in December, then moved to Waynesboro with his command of fewer than 3,000 men—Wharton's brigade-sized division, along with some cavalry and artillery. There were a few excursions and alarms in the Valley, but on the whole Early's winter exile was a quiet one. In January he went to Richmond to complain to Lee about "the difficulties of my position," but accepted Lee's inventive mollification: "He told me he had left me there with the small command which still remained, in order to produce the impression that the force was much larger than it really was, and he instructed me to do the best I could."[1]

Early bore his disgrace with his own particular brand of dignity, still making contributions to the lore of the army with his mordant wit. Henry Kyd Douglas went to church with him in Waynesboro to hear a minister make an impassioned oration on the subject of the raising of the dead on judgment day. What would you do, the cleric thundered to his congregation, if the dead were to come marching forth today in their thousands and tens of thousands? The idea appealed to Old Jube, and he said so, hardly bothering to lower his voice: "I'd conscript every damned one of them."[2]

March came, its promise of spring and renewal mocking the desperate prospects of the Confederacy. Sherman was driving north through the Carolinas, Grant was snugging his iron noose around the Army of North Virginia, and now Sheridan moved. He came south with his entire cavalry corps, 6,000 strong, turned eastward at Staunton and approached Waynesboro on March 2. There Jubal Early awaited him. "I did not intend making my final stand on this ground," Early reported later, "yet I was satisfied that if my men would fight, which I had no reason to doubt, I could hold the enemy in check until night, and then cross the river and take position in Rockfish Gap; for I had done more difficult things than that during the war."[3]

This time all it took was Custer's division. He mounted what had become his standard charge on infantry, a couple of regiments circling out on the flank, and in a few stunning minutes it was all over. "I went to the top of a hill to reconnoitre," wrote Early, "and had the mortification of seeing the greater part of my command being carried off as prisoners." He escaped with an escort of perhaps 20 men, spent two weeks eluding the patrols of the triumphant Federal cavalry, and on March 16 arrived virtually alone at Lee's Petersburg headquarters.[4]

There was by now no hope of his resuming command of the Second Corps; Gordon was too well known and liked, Early's name had become anathema to the public, the politicians and much of the army. Lee, and only Lee, understood the burden Old Jube had carried and refused to revile a man whose best had proved to be not quite good enough. He dreamed up a new assignment—Early could go to southwestern Virginia, his native region, collect stragglers and deserters, put a force together, perhaps return to the Valley, now that Sheridan had moved on. Early left immediately to set about the task, but the crowd would not have it. In the newspapers, in the corridors of the capital and the streets of Richmond the chant for Early's head grew louder and more insistent.

Finally, on the 30th of March, it was done as gently as Lee could do it. Go home, he told his bad old man, go home and I will write you there. Early obeyed, but on the way was stricken with a cold that soon turned to something worse. Somewhere in Smyth County, far from his command and far from home, he lay incapacitated, coughing blood. After several days he had himself loaded on an ambulance and continued his journey, but before it was over a rider came along the road and paused to convey the awful news from Appomattox. Old Jube swore, turned on his side and groaned, "Blow your horn, Gabriel!"[5]

Then he went home to read the letter explaining why he had been deemed unworthy, by the man he had loved and served beyond all others, of participating in the final agony of the Army of Northern Virginia. As always, even in despair and anger, Lee had been considerate while being honest: "Your reverses in the Valley, of which the public and the army judge chiefly by the results, have, I fear, impaired your influence, both with the people and the soldiers, and would add greatly to the difficulties which will, under any circumstances, attend our military operations in Southwestern Virginia. While my own confidence in your ability, zeal, and devotion to the cause is unimpaired, I have nevertheless felt that I could not oppose what seems to be the current of opinion without injustice to your reputation and injury to the service."[6]

Old Jube began to wander the earth, a hunched and haggard exile feeding on dreams of hope. His dreams were tortured, his hope was for more war. He struggled west, planning to join the army of General Edmund Kirby Smith. Long before he got there he learned of its surrender, and fled east to Cuba. When he heard rumors of a possible war between the United States and Mexico he went immediately south, to fight with Mexico. "My hatred of the infernal Yankees is increasing daily," he wrote to Tom Rosser. "My motto is still, 'War to the death,' and I yet hope to have another chance at them." But the chance did not come in Mexico, and Early wandered on, back to Cuba and eventually to Ontario, in Canada.[7]

If he could not kill Yankees, he would maim their reputations, and few pens have dripped such venom as did Jubal Early's thereafter. In 1866 he published his memoir of the last year of the war, in which he placed the puny achievements of such upstarts as Phil Sheridan in their proper perspective. But even in this he was to see victory snatched from him; his spiteful account of agonizing defeat was largely ignored, while the reading public eagerly bought out the first history of Stonewall Jackson's already legendary exploits. It was First Bull Run all over again, with Early doing the work and Jackson getting the fame.

Doggedly, Early kept writing and launching across the border his vituperative missiles: the murdered Lincoln's estate of $100,000, said Early, proved that the president had been guilty of malfeasance in office; his successor, Andrew Johnson, was a "miserable, cowardly renegade"; Ulysses S. Grant was "a man of too little sense and too little character to be anything else than a mere tool in the hands of others." And the hatred burned undiminished. "There is scarce a night of my life," he wrote from Canada, "that I do not dream of being engaged in battle with the Yankees. I wish it was not all a dream."[8]

Early scorned applying for a pardon from the conquerors, and when amnesty was given anyway on Christmas Day of 1868 he accepted with typical ingratitude; he took it, he said, "not as a pardon for any offense committed," but rather "as a final acknowledgement by the government of its inability to hold us responsible for our resistance to its usurpations and encroachments." He went home to Rocky Mount, then moved to Lynchburg in search of better prospects for eking out a living by practicing law. But his financial situation remained precarious until 1877, when he was named a commissioner of the Louisiana lottery.

For lending his name and respectability to this unsavory enterprise, and for showing up to supervise the drawings, Early was eventually paid the handsome sum of $10,000 a year plus $150 per month in expenses. Various law enforcement and regulatory agencies eventually drove the lottery out of the country, but it took them sixteen years to do it, and by the time the embattled principals fled to the Honduras in 1893, Early was financially independent. He lived on, skewering Yankees and correcting history at every opportunity, contributing lavishly to fellow Confederates in need and to any Southern cause.

But it had to be purely Southern. He supported, for example, the commissioning of a statue to memorialize the beloved Lee. But on being shown a model of the monument, Old Jube went into a rage: "It is an abomination. The idea of representing General Lee on a bob tail horse, looking like an English jockey, is revolting, and if such a monument should ever be erected in my life time, I should feel like collecting the survivors of the Second Corps and going to Richmond to blow the thing up . . ."[9]

Several years later he was prepared to contribute to a Lee monument—presumably a more acceptable likeness—until he learned it was proposed to hew it out of granite from Maine. Henceforth he would have nothing to do with the project. As Fitz Lee observed with grudging admiration, for Old Jube the War Between the States had not ended: "When Early drew his sword in that conflict he threw the scabbard away and was never afterward able to find it."[10]

On February 16, 1894, while leaving the Lynchburg Post Office, Early slipped and fell on the stone steps. He got up immediately, made little of the fall, but that evening went into shock. There were no broken bones, not even an apparent bruise, but his condition deteriorated. Old Jube, now seventy-seven, did his best to declare a victory, but on March 2 the Grim Reaper turned Early's flank, the mischief could not be repaired, and he was required to quit the field. As he once said of the Army of Northern Virginia, he never was defeated; he simply wore himself out whipping the enemy.[11]

It doubtless would have embarrassed him, yet it might have done his soul good, to see a grizzled old veteran of the Second Corps, after all the deaths and defeats and recriminations and breaches of faith, step forward at the funeral and plant a tearful kiss on Old Jube's waxen brow.

LITTLE PHIL

In the spring of 1865, while Early had been lying ill and forgotten somewhere in southwestern Virginia, Phil Sheridan had been thundering across the blasted landscape of Virginia and onto ever more pages of history. East from Waynesboro he had led his eager cavalry, ignoring Grant's instructions to turn south and join Sherman, heading east instead, to Grant's side. Later, Sheridan was straightforward about his motives: "I wanted my cavalry to be in at the death." Grant was so glad to have a fighter with him for the final push into the formidable trenches at Petersburg that he overlooked the disobedience.

On March 29, while the Federal infantry began slogging through the spring mud toward Lee's last railroad connections to the south and west, Sheridan rode wide to the west, and on April 1 destroyed a desperate blocking force under George Pickett at a crossroads called Five Forks. The next dawn Grant unleashed his infantry against the Petersburg lines. It was VI Corps, with Getty's Second Division in the forefront, that smashed through the entrenchments first and saw their disheartened enemy, in the words of Hazard Stevens, "swept away and scattered like chaff before a tornado." But the Confederates held on until Lee could get most of his army away on a desperate run to the west in search of room to turn southward toward Johnston's army in North Carolina.

But Sheridan ran faster. He was there when Lee tried to turn south, and at Sayler's Creek on April 6 caught Anderson's Third Corps and Ewell's Richmond garrison between his cavalry and Horatio Wright's VI Corps. Together they enveloped the Confederate force, taking the surrender of 6,000 men and five generals—Ewell, Anderson, and Kershaw included. Meanwhile, the Federal infantry mauled Gordon's Second Corps and chased it across the Appomattox River at High Bridge, near Farmville.

Lee's army was desperate for food, and Sheridan found out where its cache was located; at a village called Appomattox, twenty-six miles to the west. He got there before Lee did. On the morning of April 8, John Gordon's Second Corps, supported by Fitz Lee's cavalry, advanced in a desperate breakthrough attempt, but Sheridan had held them long enough; the Federal Army of the James had got in front of the Confederates, while VI and II Corps were bearing down from behind. As one Federal soldier put it, Lee "couldn't go back, he couldn't go forward, and he couldn't go sideways."[12]

The white flag went up, and Lee began final negotiations with Grant toward the surrender of the Army of Northern Virginia. This enraged Sheridan, who had risked a great deal to be "in at the death," and now wanted to see death. A Federal staff officer bearing a letter from Grant to Lee heard Sheridan raging, "Damn them, I wish they had held out for an hour longer and I would have whipped hell out of them." To another officer he yelled, raising a clenched fist in protest of the pause for negotiations, "I've got 'em—got 'em like that!" Grant recalled that Sheridan "wanted to end the business by going in and forcing an absolute surrender by capture."[13]

But Grant leashed Sheridan firmly and arranged a surrender that had mercy in it, and dignity for the defeated; one that contributed to a faster, less bitter and far less deadly collapse of the doomed Confederacy than might otherwise have been the case. Sheridan stood fuming with disappointment in the parlor of the McLean House while men of larger spirit ended the war that had made him famous.

While others went home to savor the peace and enjoy their reputations as veterans, Sheridan the regular had hardly reached Washington City when he received new orders. There was still a Confederate army in the field out west, under Kirby Smith, and more ominously there was a French army in Mexico. Sheridan was needed out there, and there would not even be time for him to lead the cavalry corps in the May 23 Grand

Review of the victorious Army of the Potomac; Sheridan was to depart on May 22, with no delay permitted. Ever the dutiful regular, whether assigned to bookkeeping duty when there was a war on or to war duty when there was a parade on, Sheridan made his preparations. On the rainy Sunday afternoon of May 21 he was finishing his business when, from his room at the Willard Hotel, he heard the thrumming of horses' hooves. Thousands of them. And the blaring of bands.

He stepped onto a balcony to see his cavalry corps passing in impromptu review. They had been ordered to move their camps, so as to be closer to their jumpoff position for the review, and had decided to take a long detour to honor their chief. And so with their hats dripping and their guidons hanging limply in the rain, Merritt and Custer and Devin and Crook led their veterans past the man who had led them to victory and glory. It was the last time they would see each other, they all thought, and many a warrior was grateful to the rain that day for hiding unmanly tears.[14]

Sheridan went south to New Orleans, where his mere presence encouraged the surrender of Kirby Smith, then west to Texas to bluff the French out of Mexico. Sheridan would clearly have preferred blasting them out, but to his intense irritation he was kept under tight rein. Merritt and Custer and Crook and Wright soon joined him there, and although it took two years of maneuver and threat, they did the job.

Sheridan's next assignment was to take over as military governor of Louisiana and Texas. Seldom has there been a more spectacular mismatch of abilities to requirements. In the turbulent agony of reconstruction there was a desperate need for forgiveness, soft talk and delicacy of feeling; Sheridan came on the scene stamping, snarling and clanging his sword. His troops imposed his will at gunpoint, and when someone got in his way he had them removed—this included the elected governors of both states. When the president of the United States tried to restrain him, Sheridan ignored him. This was remarkable for a man who always spelled government with a capital *G*, but somehow Sheridan had decided that the demands of the radical Congress and the temporizing of his immediate commander,

Grant, were more important than the wishes of his president. After three months of this, Sheridan was removed from office.

In September of 1867 he was given a job to which he was much better suited by experience and temperament—the civilization of the western Indians. As commander of the Department of the Missouri he watched, unmoved, while the postwar, westward migration of whites pressed in on the Plains Indians with intolerable weight. When the Indians fought back with a summer of terror, Sheridan disdained to chase their ragged bands through their own territory. Instead, he waited until winter pinned the Indians to their villages, somewhat as Lee had been held at Petersburg. On November 27, 1868, he sent George Custer to attack a Cheyenne village on the Washita River. There Custer surprised and killed 103 warriors and an uncounted number of women and children.[15]

There were protests back east about the purported massacre, but U. S. Grant was elected president that month, and Grant liked firmness in military affairs. Sherman became general in chief of the army, and Sheridan took charge of the frontier. It was a desk job. The hero of Cedar Creek would never take the field again.

The hard pleasures of leading a campaign—the unquestioned authority over thousands of people, even in matters of life and death, the fawning attention of hundreds of men whose sole mission is seeing to one's personal comfort and safety, the admiration and recognition from all sides, the clarity of the problems, the finality of the solutions—were difficult to replicate in peacetime. After the wild, symphonic percussion of combat, the blood simply could not be made to race by a string quartet.

At his comfortable Chicago headquarters, Sheridan exercised his shrewd judgment but nothing else. There and on frequent trips east, he began to eat and drink and dance and keep company with the ladies to the extent that his face became even more florid and his little body began to swell. He took a liking to opulent hunting trips in his western territories, on one occasion with some visiting European royalty, on another with a scion of New York society. Sheridan smiled his approval on the mass butchery of the bison then being effected by unrestrained market hunting. It was not that he had anything against the

buffalo, but he saw their extermination as a solution to the
Indian problem. Every buffalo hunter should be given a medal,
Sheridan told the Texas legislature in 1875, engraved on one
side with a dead buffalo, on the other with a "discouraged-
looking Indian."[16] It was at about this time that Sheridan, on
being told by the Comanche chief Toch-a-way, "Me good Indian," shot back: "The only good Indians I ever saw were
dead." And gave birth to another frontier proverb.

In another misapplication of his shotgun diplomacy, he was
sent back to Louisiana to deal with unrest there. After suggesting to one congressman that "what you want to do is sus-
pend the what-do-you-call-it," by which he meant the writ of
habeas corpus, Sheridan sent troops with fixed bayonets into
two state legislative chambers. In fact, he was imposing the will
of the electorate, not his own, on an entrenched and intransi-
gent oligarchy, but he managed to do it in a way that offended
the North as well as the South. He was soon sent back to
Chicago to deal with Indians, who had no constituency.

In the spring of 1875 a Chicago newspaper ran the headline:
"Great Cavalry Leader Vanquished by a Blonde." The previous
spring, Sheridan had been smitten by an animated blond brides-
maid—Irene Rucker, his quartermaster's daughter. In June of
1875 they married, and the newspaper was right; Sheridan was
overcome. He lowered his voice, cleaned up his language and
modified his habits. At twenty-two she was exactly half his age
when they married, but his adoration and respect for her were
complete. Their marriage was close, stable and richly blessed—
by a daughter, then twin girls, and finally a son.[17]

For eight years he presided over the wearing down of the
Plains Indians and the relentless spread of civilization into the
West. Then, when Sherman retired in 1883, he became, inevita-
bly, general in chief of the United States Army. It was an army
with virtually nothing to do. Sheridan seemed to take deep
enjoyment from his family, but otherwise he was bored. For
years.

A newspaper reporter described the general as seen on the
streets of Washington in the 1880s: "He wore upon the back of
his round, bullet head a very slim, high, old-fashioned silk hat
of a style that was popular at the close of the Civil War. It was

about two sizes too small. His short, iron gray hair stood out from under the rim of his hat at nearly right angles with it. His red, weather-beaten face did not show any new lines of advancing age, but his grizzly, iron-gray mustache and imperial were whitening very fast. He wore a short, light, yellow-gray overcoat which had only two buttons on it, and they were nearly ready to fly off from the undue strain of Sheridan's round figure. The coat, like the hat, appeared to have been outgrown. The trousers were a gray plaid and fitted very snugly to the general's fat legs. His boots were thick soled and unblacked. He wore no gloves. The side and rear views of the general suggested a low comedy man who had walked off the stage all made up for a funny part; but when you came to look at the general square in the face, its stern, solemn, composed lines were enough to make one forget his grotesque figure and careless dress."[18]

In the spring of 1888 Sheridan was ravaged by a series of heart attacks. He was only fifty-seven, but his luck had run out; he knew the wound was mortal. He had himself set out on the porch of his just-built summer cottage at Nonquit, Massachusetts, and there he faced death with the cool aplomb of a seasoned combat veteran. On a Sunday afternoon, August 5, while he watched the waves roll in, it came to get him.

There were the obligatory eulogies. "He was a great soldier and a noble man," said Sherman, "and deserved all of the honors bestowed on him." Grant, who had died a poor and discredited man in 1885, had pronounced Sheridan "the embodiment of heroism, dash and impulse." Sheridan himself had devised a simpler and more accurate epitaph when he told a West Point class, "Whatever I took up, even if it were the simplest of duties, I tried to do it better than it had ever been done before. In the second place I always looked out for the common soldier. Trust your reputation to the private and he will never let your military fame suffer."[19]

But the most memorable tributes, perhaps because they unexpectedly belied the carapace of military hardness that had characterized his life, were those uttered indirectly and artlessly by his family. Asked by a friend why she did not remarry, Irene Sheridan snapped, "I would rather be the widow of Phil

Sheridan than the wife of any man alive." And after a statue of their husband and father—mounted on Rienzi, galloping toward the guns of Cedar Creek—was erected in Washington City, the Sheridans moved to a Massachusetts Avenue house in order to be near it. For years thereafter, apparently, the morning ritual of the Sheridan girls included stepping to the window and calling to the grim and motionless image of Phil Sheridan, "Good morning, Papa!"[20]

FANNY AND TEX

In his official report of the battle of Cedar Creek, George Custer boasted that his men had taken "colors, guns, caissons, wagons, ambulances, and immense numbers of prisoners." In fact, he claimed credit, on behalf of the 1st Vermont and 5th New York Cavalry regiments, for the capture of 45 guns—all 18 of the Union guns that had been lost early in the day, and all but three of the Confederate cannons taken in the evening. That claim did not square with the fact that on the night of the battle, Wesley Merritt had been given a receipt by the provost marshal for 22 guns taken by Devin (along with 3 battle flags, 8 caissons, 37 ambulances, 29 wagons, 95 horses and harness, 141 mules and harness and 389 prisoners of war). For a time, the discrepancy in the accounting for the guns went unnoticed.[21]

The taking of a gun in a stand-up fight was a matter of extreme pride to the individual or unit that accomplished it, signifying as it did the ultimate in courage and ability on the battlefield. But these guns had been rolled up in a rout, a confused stampede in the dark, during which the spoils went not to the bravest or the best but to whoever happened to be there to go through the technicalities of claiming the prize. Custer, however, knew and loved the effect of such numbers on newspaper readers and report collaters; it mattered to him, for example, that he had taken one more gun than Merritt had in the cavalry battle at Toms Brook.[22]

Merritt paid little attention to the arithmetic of the guns; for a time he was unaware of the conflicting reports, and did not know of Custer's congratulatory order to his troops, in which he spoke Napoleon-like of the "brilliant and glorious achievements" of his men. Among other things, Custer congratulated them for capturing "45 of the 48 pieces of artillery taken from the enemy on that day." This order, of course, was published in a New York newspaper, and when Merritt consequently found out about it, he blew up.[23]

By then he had heard rumors of the claim, he wrote, but here was "official recognition of over-weening greed of some of the Third Division for the rightful captures of my command." Custer's claim was "without foundation in truth," he wrote, it was "wholesale robbery." This correspondence also found its way to the New York press, hence to Custer, who in high dudgeon demanded either Torbert's official decision on the matter or a board of inquiry.[24]

Whatever the particulars had been of who put his hands on the guns, who posted guards over them and who escorted them to the rear—and Custer made a loud and laborious case of such stuff—Merritt had a far more serious claim to due credit for the outcome of Cedar Creek. While Custer had been waiting for orders on the right that morning, Devin of Merritt's division had been laboring to stop stragglers, then had been engaged on the left of the second position of VI Corps; after Custer had been moved to the left he had been held there in reserve, while Merritt's brigades had fought the enemy to a standstill west of Middletown; at the end, Merritt's advance had been bitterly contested by desperate men from good cover, while the lines in front of Custer had broken at his appearance. Custer deserved great credit for the initiative he took in getting across the creek and behind the retreating enemy, but in that entire day's battle his division had suffered two men killed and 24 wounded; Merritt had lost 22 dead, 86 wounded. "This division lost as many in killed and wounded on the south side of Cedar Creek"— where all the captures were made—"as the Third Division lost during the entire day," fumed Merritt. If Custer's claim were true, 45 of the 48 guns had been taken virtually without casualties, while the remaining three had cost "more bloodshed than that experienced by an entire division of cavalry in a pitch-battle."[25]

The issue was neither resolved nor contested further. Perhaps no one could be found who would take it seriously; more likely, Custer was mollified by the knightly duty to which Sheridan immediately assigned him, one that conveyed even more glory than the capture of 45 guns. On October 20 Sheridan sent Custer to Washington with the men who had captured all thirteen Confederate battle flags taken at Cedar Creek to present them to the secretary of war. Custer knew how to wring the most from such an assignment. He draped ten of the flags on the locomotive that pulled his train into the city. He marched his detail through the streets to the War Department while he dashed off to get his wife; this was too good for her to miss. But Libby had heard of his arrival and his mission, and knowing it was too good to miss had gone to the War Department. She attended the ceremony, but he missed it. She ended up standing in for him and making an impromptu speech. The press loved it all. The Custer legend grew.[26]

It is tempting to think that Wesley Merritt should have hugged his commanding general now and again, or somehow called attention to what he was doing. It was not necessary. Sheridan knew what was going on. He wired Grant on October 21 that the three people he wanted promoted for their role at Cedar Creek were "Getty, of the Sixth Corps, and the brave boys, Merritt and Custer." And while he gave command of the honor detail to Custer, when in the following spring he finally got rid of Torbert, it was Merritt to whom he gave command of all his cavalry.[27]

That winter, Libby joined her husband in Winchester, as did Tom Custer, assigned to his older brother as an aide. The three of them spent the idle months playing boisterous games of tag in the house they shared, or riding splendidly about the town, glowing self-consciously with animal vitality and studied handsomeness. Sheridan marveled at them. Custer was the only man in his experience who had not been ruined by marriage. (Perhaps he emulated them; there were strong rumors that winter that Little Phil had gone and got engaged, but nothing came of it.)

There was very little fighting in the Valley that winter, but Fanny and Tex did manage to get in one more round—with surprising results. On December 19 Sheridan responded to

Grant's continued nagging about the Confederate railroads by sending Torbert with two divisions of cavalry on a raid eastward toward the Virginia Central Railroad. Meanwhile, Custer's division rode south from Winchester, along the Valley Pike toward Staunton, whence he would strike for Lynchburg. Jubal Early was in Staunton when he received word of Custer's movement, from the signal station on Shenandoah Peak. Old Jube sighed, collected all the men of Wharton's division who could still walk and had Rosser gather those troopers who could still ride, and through bitter cold and alternating rain and hail they headed north.[28]

Rosser had somehow recovered the aggressiveness and dash that had been so conspicuously missing at Cedar Creek in October. This may have been related to the fact that his commission as a major general had been approved on November 4. On the night of December 20, while Wharton's men struggled toward Harrisonburg, Rosser found Custer camped at Lacey Spring, nine miles to the north. Rosser had perhaps 600 men with him, and even with Wharton present would still be outnumbered two to one; he decided that the only hope for stopping Custer would be a night attack. And Rosser, as Captain McDonald of the Laurel Brigade stressed in his recollection of that night, was "ever anxious to meet Custer."[29]

Whatever its source—military imperative or schoolboy competitiveness—a steelier brand of two-o'clock-in-the-morning courage than Rosser now displayed could not be imagined. Conditions were awful. "A cold wind blew and the rain froze as it fell," Captain McDonald wrote. "The hats and the clothes of the troopers soon became stiff with ice; while the horses were enveloped in frosty garments, the small icicles hanging from their bodies rattling as they staggered along. The road soon became icy smooth, and the horses not being rough shod traveled with much difficulty."[30]

By the time Rosser's men got in position, the Federals, who had slept on the wet ground, with saddles for pillows and rubber blankets their only cover, were struggling out from under six inches of new snow and trying to get a warm breakfast. The campfires extended over such a wide area that Rosser saw he could never surprise all of the camp, but he gathered his shivering men and, as he put it later, "without a yell or the sound of a bugle we swept down upon the half-sleeping foe like an avalanche."[31]

Private William Smith of the Federal Second Ohio Cavalry remembered how his colonel reacted to the sound of firing in the camp: "Instead of trying to form the regiment regular style," wrote Smith, the colonel bellowed "SECOND OHIO, MOUNT! FOURS RIGHT, MARCH! ON LEFT FRONT INTO LINE, GALLOP, MARCH!" In a few breathtaking minutes the half-frozen men were hacking at one another with sabers. "Business was lively for a short time," said Smith, "but we soon got them turned and started back down the hill." The Confederates killed or wounded 22 Federals and took 47 prisoners, and left 50 casualties behind. For once, Custer seemed to be completely unnerved. He abandoned his mission and retreated to Winchester. He was not afraid of Rosser, he explained lamely in his report, but "if it was decided to return, the sooner my return was accomplished the better it would be for my command." Among his casualties he reported 230 men frostbitten.[32]

Torbert, meanwhile, had found in Gordonsville more opposition than he cared to deal with, and withdrew without harming the railroad there. Sheridan placed another mark beside Torbert's name and laid his plans for replacing him, but somehow was not concerned about Custer's reverse. When the winter respite was over and the cavalry dashed off after Early's army at Waynesboro, Custer was in the van as usual.

Rosser had made some daring and successful raids into West Virginia that winter, but despite them General Early had found it impossible to feed his remaining men and horses. The Laurel Brigade had been disbanded temporarily, its men told to go home, take care of themselves and their families, and wait for a call to reassemble. That call came in haste on February 27, but Rosser had time to muster only a few hundred, with which he was able to make only a brief and feeble demonstration at Mount Crawford against Sheridan's hosts, on their way to finish the Army of the Valley.[33]

In March Rosser took his scanty division, now only about 1,200 men, to Petersburg, arriving just in time to take a somewhat unfortunate part in the decisive battle at Five Forks. On that April 1, Rosser had paused to scoop up some succulent shad from the Nottoway River. He invited George Pickett and Fitz Lee to join him for lunch. The generals were as hungry as anyone else in that gaunt army, and it may be that the prospect of a feast unbalanced all three of them; when Sheridan smashed into the Confederate line at Five Forks, the entire Confederate high command was secretly at lunch, unavailable to their subordinates, out of touch with the front until it was too late to do anything but retreat.

On April 6, during the desperate race away from Richmond, a force of 900 Federals got ahead of the fleeing Confederates and threatened to destroy two bridges at Farmville, thus severing one of the few lines of retreat and supply still open to Lee's army. Longstreet told Rosser to get to those bridges, save them, and hold them, if it cost every man in his command. With Munford's division as well as his own, Rosser raced to Farmville, arriving just as the Federal cavalry was about to destroy the High Bridge. Improvising his plans as he rode, Rosser launched a desperate attack. When it was over the Confederates held the bridge and 800 prisoners. They had won a few hours' more life for the Confederacy.

Rosser rode away from Appomattox to evade the surrender, disbanded his men until he could find a mission for them, and found what remained of the Confederate government at Lynchburg. By April 12 he was back in the Valley, at Staunton, where he issued a frenzied proclamation in which he urged the "veterans of the Old Dominion" to "shoulder your muskets and return to the field to meet the arrogant invader who has insulted you, robbed you, murdered your dearest friends and relatives, outraged your fair women, despoiled your homes and dishonored all that is most dear and sacred. I will lead you against them, and will never abandon or surrender you until the purple current ceases to flow from my heart, or until you are a free, independent and happy people!" Nothing came of these florid ravings, and Rosser decided to head west to join Kirby Smith. But first he visited his wife and daughter at their Hanover County home and there, on May 2, he was discovered and taken prisoner by a Federal cavalry detachment. His war was over.[34]

Custer's war, of course, ended with ruffles and flourishes. If Sheridan was overeager at Appomattox, Custer was positively manic on his behalf, at one point dashing into the Confederate lines demanding John Gordon's "immediate and unconditional surrender." Although Sheridan and Custer did not know it at the time, the generals in chief had already begun surrender negotiations, thus making any subordinate demands improper. Curtly informed of this by Gordon, Custer nevertheless pressed on to see Longstreet and repeat his demand. A Confederate onlooker recalled with disdain that Custer was wearing "the largest shoulder straps of a major general I ever saw," with his name and rank emblazoned on "a gold pin near two inches in length and breadth." But Old Curly was posturing in front of the wrong man. Longstreet dressed him down as if he were a cadet, and sent him back to his own lines.[35]

Several of the artists who later imagined the scene of Lee's surrender in the McLean House painted Custer into it; they could not imagine his not being there, but for once he did not manage to bull his way to the center of attention. Sheridan was there, though, apparently still thinking about Libby Custer. As soon as the formalities were over, he did a peculiar thing; with a gold coin he always carried in case he was captured, he bought one of Wilmer McLean's parlor tables and sent it to Libby, with an awkward, "my-dear-madam" note of admiration.[36]

The war was over, but Custer's lust for attention did not abate. On May 23, as the Army of the Potomac marched in triumphant (but individually anonymous) review down Pennsylvania Avenue, Custer's horse ran away with him. It is the only time on record that Custer ever lost control of a horse, and it happened just as the cavalry corps approached the reviewing stand. After the horse had plunged through Merritt's staff, had galloped in spectacular abandon past the reviewing stand whereon stood the president of the United States, Custer immediately regained control of his mount; rode back past the reviewing stand to his proper place in line; then rode a third time past the reviewing stand, this time with his men.[37]

Custer's gaudy courage and crafty success in battle had made his men love him, his peers endure him and his superiors advance him. But when there were no more battles to fight, no more charges to lead or bullets to face, Custer did not know what to do. In Texas, while Sheridan was daring the French to start another war, Custer tried frantically to hold on to the respect of volunteer soldiers who only wanted to go home. He played the martinet, insisting on a level of spit and polish that he had never attained himself. Within weeks all the glory was gone, and he was a hated man.

He had men whipped, shaved their heads, drummed them out of the service, but he could not make them respect him. With no one to kill and no death to defy, Custer's skills were irrelevant and his shortcomings as an officer and a man were obvious. Then he changed the situation into one he could deal with, by reintroducing death.

As a practical joke, some of his men showed up for parade one day with all their gear on backward, or inside out, or upside down. They deserved a dressing-down, but Custer had them arrested and ordered a sergeant he suspected of being their ringleader to face a firing squad. The response from the men was loud and clear; if the sergeant were shot, Custer would die on the same field. Now here was something Custer knew how to handle. He formed the men, had the sergeant and a deserter, also sentenced to death, brought out on their coffins and stood before their graves; had them blindfolded and ordered the firing squad's weapons loaded. Then Custer rode slowly up and down his lines, meeting the sullen stares of his men with his ice-blue eyes. At the last possible minute he had the sergeant led aside while the deserter was shot (but he failed to unbind the poor sergeant's eyes; when the rifles rang out, both condemned men fell to the ground, one dead, one in shock). Yet again, Custer's contempt for death had worked—he had little more trouble with those men."[38]

And so he rode on into a frenzied history, shooting deer and buffalo, Indian women and children and every once in a while his own men, killing as thoughtlessly and as happily as he had shot that first Confederate officer in 1861. Libby continued to love and follow him, with the breathless, palpitating adoration of the forever young, and it was still a perfect match; they both found him endlessly fascinating. Tom stayed with him, as unquestioning as a family dog, and the reporters still found him to be attentive company and good copy.

But Custer was cut off from the wellsprings of war, and found to his confusion that what people had celebrated then disgusted them now. Where there had been rapid promotions there were now courts-martial; where men had worn red ties to signify their fealty to him, they now reviled him, deserted his commands in droves. However, just as Grant remembered and protected the little man who had led his horsemen to red victory in the Valley and at Appomattox, so Sheridan remembered and sheltered the man who had embarrassed him with impetuous embraces, then galloped to irrepressible victory. And so the fiery partnership struck in the summer of 1864, confirmed by the guns of the Shenandoah, and culminated by the silence at Appomattox continued long past its obsolescence, with Grant the warrior king sheltering Sheridan the warrior administrator who protected Custer the warrior-turned-policeman. None of them was ever happy again, or forgot when they had all been at their best.

Like most Southern officers, Rosser had a great deal of trouble making a living after the war. He took a stab at studying the law, but quit; joined the National Express Company, which promptly failed; tried his hand as a salesman, but soon quit that; and was denied at least one decent job because he had been too prominent a Rebel. After three years of struggle he headed west, and took a job as an axman for the Lake Superior and Mississippi Railroad. But he had West Point education in engineering, and before long was an assistant construction engineer with the Northern Pacific.[39]

In 1871 Rosser was put in charge of a surveying party siting the Northern Pacific road westward from the Mississippi River across North Dakota and into Montana's Yellowstone country. This was disputed Indian territory, and a heavy military escort was required to protect the railroad workers. In the course of this years-long work, Rosser laid out the camp that would become Fargo, North Dakota. There in the fall of 1872 his infant son, named John Pelham Rosser in memory of the gallant Pelham of West Point days, died of cholera.

The survey continued westward, and when in June of 1873 the military escort joined the surveyors for an expedition to the Yellowstone, Rosser went to inquire about a lieutenant colonel of one of the regiments. From a nearby tent came a shout: "Haloo, old fellow! I haven't heard that voice in 13 years, but I know it!" And there, his dark brown velveteen replaced by equally extravagant buckskins, was George Custer. "Come in and welcome!"[40]

As the two men had laughed and tussled their way toward war thirteen years earlier, so they now enjoyed themselves while bringing on another war; they were on Sioux land, Indian ground forever by formal treaty, and the Sioux had denied permission for a railroad to be built across it. They were surveying the railroad anyway, and when that summer Rosser or Custer ran into hostile Indians there were brief combats. Rosser found himself and a small party of workmen surrounded once, but fought his way out, and Custer got in several similar scrapes. They lost a few of their men, but the Indians got the worst of it, and Custer became contemptuous of them. Because they would not stand up to his charges, refused to settle down and fight him when he was ready, he convinced himself that the Sioux were poor fighters. The conviction very probably killed him.

Meanwhile, the evenings were delightful that summer, with Custer and Rosser often stretched out on a buffalo hide in front of a tent reminiscing about who beat whom when during the war. Custer was the same callow glory-hound he had been at West Point, apparently little changed by all he had been through. A newspaper reporter who saw them together that summer thought Custer's manner "quick and nervous and somewhat eccentric." Custer leaned forward when he walked, the reporter wrote, was "intensely earnest and lively" in conversation, and was incapable of doing "anything by halves. He is a good soldier, but has the reputation of being rather reckless in his style of life." Rosser, on the other hand, no longer found life to be a coltish adventure. "He impresses you in his physical

presence as a man of great strength and endurance," the reporter wrote of the six-foot-two, 220-pound Rosser. "In conversation his voice is never pitched on a high key, but is deliberate
without being slow, energetic without being demonstrative. He
is one who is eminently fitted to exert great influence over
men."[41]

Perhaps so; but he never would again. As soon as he had
made his stake in the West he bought an estate near Charlottesville and left the harsh plains (leaving behind as markers the
grave of his son and a town called Rosser on the Canadian
Pacific line west of Winnipeg, Manitoba) to spend the rest of
his days among the gentle, tree-clad folds of the Virginia Piedmont.

There was, however, nothing particularly gentle about Rosser's later life. He lost another child to illness; tried politics as a
Democrat and failed; tried again as a Republican and achieved
only a postmaster's appointment; tried not to drink so much
and often failed at that. And above all he fought lost battles,
over and over again, nastily and publicly chastising those who,
in his view, had failed.

He was frequently as vitriolic as Jubal Early, but without the
latter's sweeping, Jovian rage against all things Northern.
Rosser paid public tribute to Ulysses Grant, and publicly vilified his old rival Tom Munford (who had been kept waiting for
his general officer's wreath until November of 1864). Rosser
waded into the public controversy that followed Custer's spectacular end at the Little Bighorn, savaging Marcus Reno for
deserting his commander, defending Custer against all comers:
"As a soldier I would sooner today lie in the grave of General
Custer and his gallant comrades alone in that distant wilderness," he wrote, "than to live in the place of the survivors of the
siege on the hills."[42]

But Rosser reserved his harshest language for the two princi-
pal actors on the stage of Cedar Creek. Not surprisingly,
Rosser never had much to say about Cedar Creek itself, but he
had plenty to say about Old Jube and Little Phil. On hearing a
mistaken report that Sheridan planned to visit the Shenandoah
in 1887, Rosser published a response: "I had hoped that our

beautiful valley would never again be desecrated by his foot-prints. Cold, cruel and brutal must be the character of this soldier who fondly cherishes memories of the wild wanton waste and desolation which his barbarous torch spread through the valley."[43]

Rosser blamed Early for posting the cavalry too far away from infantry support at Toms Brook; for general misuse of the cavalry during the 1864 Valley Campaign; and—expressly and oddly—for not putting all his cavalry at that time under the command of the ranking cavalry officer, Lunsford Lomax. In an 1884 letter to Early, Rosser summed up his case against his former commander with appalling lack of grace: "Incompentency is not a crime, and that you failed in the Valley is not due to your neglect or carelessness, for I know you were assiduous, but God did not make you a general, and it was Gen. R. E. Lee's mistake in trusting so important a command as that you had to you before you had been more fully tried."[44]

In 1898 the United States stepped onto the stage of world politics with a brief war with Spain over Cuba. Rosser heard the trumpets, and although his health and age would not permit active service, he donned a uniform again—a blue Federal coat this time, bearing the stars of a brigadier general of volunteers. Three other former Confederate generals did similar service in the Spanish-American War, including "Fightin' Joe" Wheeler and Fitz Lee. An unreconstructed Rebel from Alabama wrote that he heard a former comrade declare, "I'm a Confederate and a Christian, and I always aimed to live right so's I'd go to Heaven, but if them newspapers ain't lyin', and this here is true, I ain't so sure. Now, I reckon I'd ruther go to Hell and see the Devil rip them blue coats off Tom Rosser and Fitz Lee!"[45]

There was even worse to come. On returning to his Charlottesville home, Rosser forsook the Democratic Party and became a Republican. He ran for governor of Virginia in 1901, but was soundly defeated. In 1905 he was appointed postmaster at Charlottesville by President Theodore Roosevelt. Five years later he died quietly in bed.

THE *CHEVALIER* AND UNCLE GEORGE

Jed Hotchkiss recorded in his diary that on Saturday, October 29, 1864, a "fine October day" in New Market, there was "a contention between Generals Gordon and Early about the battle of Cedar Creek, etc." The immediate cause of the dispute was the savage treatment Early was getting in the Southern press— "papers abusing General Early roundly," Hotchkiss had noted the previous day. The abuse directed at Early stood in marked contrast to the kind treatment Gordon was receiving, and Early muttered something about Gordon being responsible for the articles. This at last was something over which Gordon could take umbrage—one could not, after all, go around accusing one's commanding officer of incompetence— and he took the opportunity to flare up. It was a small spark, but it fell on dry tinder, and the fires of dissension between them would never go out.[46]

John Gordon was spared the final humiliation of the Army of the Valley, having been called east with the Second Corps to stand with Longstreet and A. P. Hill at the side of Lee. During the last anguished days of the Army of Northern Virginia, Gordon fought as well as anyone did or could have done. In the spring of 1865 he masterminded a breakout attempt that failed but was foredoomed, and when the last, overwhelming Union assault overbore the trenches, his line held longer than anyone's. He commanded the last advance at Appomattox. And he was given the somewhat dubious honor of leading the Army of Northern Virginia to its surrender; Hill was dead, and neither Lee nor Longstreet was anywhere to be seen on that day.

And with that there were no more drums or bugles. Suddenly bereft of power, virtually penniless, private citizen John Gordon joined the masses stumbling away into the ravaged Southland. He found his wife and his infant daughter, born in the fires of Richmond's falling, and took them back to Georgia —a long and difficult journey on the remnants of the blasted Southern railroads.

He returned home a hero, idolized by his state as its foremost soldier in the war for independence. When he turned his attention to making a living, he found ample financial support and soon built two sawmills and bought a rice plantation at Bruns-, wick, on the Georgia coast. But he who had been an indifferent lawyer before the war turned out to be an indifferent business-man afterward, and the enterprises failed. In 1867 he returned to Atlanta to become president of the Southern Life Insurance Company, which was to do well for a time but would declare bankruptcy within ten years.

He was much more successful, and even more avidly sup-ported, in the application of his newly discovered aptitude for politics. Apparently this set of skills was at first nurtured clandestinely, and succeeded in raising him to the exalted posi-tion of Grand Dragon of the Realm of Georgia in that new, private gentleman's club known as the Ku Klux Klan. From that odious base—one whose existence he blandly denied in the North but benefited from in the South—he aspired to a more exclusive gentleman's club—the United States Senate.

This membership was conferred on him in 1873 by his peers in the Georgia General Assembly, and Gordon soon became a powerful voice for Southern rights in a Congress still bent on a vengeful reconstruction. His eloquence and his large view of history set him apart from other, more mean-minded represen-tatives of the Southern oligarchy. Although he became a leader of the Southern Democrats who strove with remarkable success to restore white rule and de facto slavery to the South, his voice was ever raised for justice and union, not for repression and retribution. He addressed every audience, North and South, as "my countrymen," he never recalled the war without stressing the bravery and gallantry of the men on both sides. He stated his postwar creed in a speech in Boston in 1878: "The causes that divided us are gone, and gone forever. The interests which now unite us will unite us forever."[47]

Senator Gordon soon became a leading spokesman for the South in the Congress, and it was in that role that he took the lead in trying to prevent the election to the presidency in 1877 of the man whose division had been the first overrun by Gor-don's forces at Cedar Creek—Rutherford B. Hayes. This time it was Hayes who prevailed, winning a chaotic, long-delayed and probably fraudulent election that had to be decided finally by a special congressional commission. It was a bad beginning to a respectable administration, in which Hayes withdrew Federal troops from the South, ended Reconstruction, admitted the former Confederate states to full partnership in the Union, and won the admiration and support of the general whose men had rolled over his lines on that long-ago October morning.

Meanwhile, the officer to whom Hayes had given his unstinting devotion and admiration during the war—George Crook—was leading a star-crossed life. And the stars that shone balefully on his career glittered from the shoulder straps of his old friend Phil Sheridan.

The two had been close friends still when, according to long custom, they had hashed over the events of the battle around a campfire in front of Belle Grove, late on the night of October 19, 1864. "Crook, I am going to get much more credit for this than I deserve," Sheridan said, "for had I been here in the morning the same thing would have taken place." Whether Sheridan really felt that way—and he made no public or official statement that would indicate he did—or was simply trying to comfort a comrade who had had a bad day, cannot be known. "The saying was full of meat," Crook wrote years later, "but it made little impression on me at the time."[48]

At the time, Crook still thought his commanding officer was a friend who understood and valued Crook's contributions to the victories at Winchester and Fisher's Hill and understood the reverses at Kernstown and Cedar Creek. As they reflected in the glow of their fire that night, Crook probably explained his rout to Sheridan in something like the heated outburst with which he wrote about it long afterward: "We were assigned to duties that required a corps to perform, and then were not properly supported, and have been held responsible for the surprise that does not belong to us, for had the cavalry pickets been where we had every reason to expect them, the surprise never could have happened, and without the surprise the enemy would never have dared to have gotten so near to us with their small force."[49]

The sting of Crook's defeats was soothed somewhat by his promotion on October 21 to major general. No doubt the extra star helped him dwell, Jubal-like, on his substantial triumphs at Third Winchester and Fisher's Hill, while ascribing to others his failures at Kernstown and Cedar Creek. But George Crook's successes had many fathers; his failures were orphans with a knack for garnering publicity.

Crook returned to command of the department of West Virginia, where before Sheridan's advent he had done so well leading small units in pursuit of bushwhackers. He was probably relieved to be back on his own, in familiar territory, and he may have had another reason to relish his return to his old headquarters at Cumberland, Maryland: it was the residence of one Mary Dailey, whom he would marry the next year, and who may already have caught the general's eye. But Crook's stay this time was to be involuntarily brief; a party of guerrillas snatched him from his hotel room and deposited him in Richmond's infamous Libby Prison. A few days later he was exchanged and back in his own lines a few miles away.[50]

On his return, Crook was given command of the Second Division of the Cavalry Corps, Army of the Potomac. ("General Grant intended giving me command of all the cavalry of the Potomac at the final struggle," Crook wrote, without a shred of substantiating evidence.) Once again, instead of being out where he could succeed or fail in solitary splendor, he was surrounded by flashy superiors and peers: Sheridan, Custer, Devin and the quieter but supremely competent Merritt.[51]

During the Appomattox Campaign, Crook fought well and made a significant contribution to the ending of the war. But with Sheridan blazing up and down the lines and Custer striking up his bands and galloping about, the dour Crook had no chance for public recognition. At Sayler's Creek after a hard fight Crook noted in mortal disgust that "as soon as the enemy hoisted the white flag, General Custer's division rushed up the hill and turned in more prisoners and battle flags than any of the cavalry, and probably had less to do with their surrender than any of the rest of us."[52]

After the war, still only a captain in the regular army, Crook was promoted to lieutenant colonel. It was a hard fall from corps commander and major general of volunteers, especially when two men who had commanded brigades under him, as he noted sourly, were made full colonels: "I learned too late that it was not what a person did, but what he got the credit of doing that gave him a reputation and at the close of the war gave him position."[53]

With that, however, Crook returned to doing what he did best: leading small groups of men through difficult terrain and harsh weather with the object of killing other small groups of men. He became, and was acknowledged by President Grant to be, "the best, wiliest Indian fighter in this country." He contributed mightily to the subduing of the Paiute and Snake Indians in the Northwest, and then operated with singular success against the Apaches in Arizona. In 1873 George Crook was once again a general, this time in the regular army.[54]

He was not very regular, however. He affected a splendidly sloppy style of dress, trained his beard into a strange, forked shape and treated the Indians with honesty and a measure of respect. None of these eccentricities helped his career, and his reasonableness toward Indians especially vexed his old friend Phil Sheridan. But Sheridan liked success more than he disliked sentimentality, and Crook was a successful Indian fighter; when war with the undefeated Sioux nation loomed in 1875, Sheridan made Crook a department commander in his Division of the Missouri. Soon afterward, Crook attended Sheridan's wedding. Times had changed; the reception for the formerly hard-drinking, cigar-smoking, blaspheming bridegroom featured ice cream and cookies and was, Crook said with obvious surprise, "rather a quiet affair."[55]

Return to Sheridan's command meant a return to the complicated teamwork and large-scale movements that had been Crook's downfall before—and were again. In fact, the summer of 1876 found Crook embroiled to his disadvantage in a campaign against the Indians that had a great deal in common with the battle of Cedar Creek—especially in its cast of characters. Sheridan had overall command and responsibility but was not present. Crook's command was the first to meet the enemy. Wesley Merritt and George Custer had equivalent cavalry commands (Merritt having replaced William Emory, the former XIX Corps commander, who was in the process of retiring from the army), but Custer captured the greater part of the fame with a showy, final charge against the enemy.

Crook's lumbering column of more than a thousand men,

one of three ordered in from different directions to converge on the rebellious Sioux, was fought to a standstill by Crazy Horse at the battle of the Rosebud River in June of 1876. General in Chief Sherman was among those who believed Crook was partly responsible for the disaster that befell Custer's regiment a week and a day later at the Little Bighorn (a disaster survived by the command of one Marcus Reno—who had been on Trobert's staff at Cedar Creek). Division commander Sheridan was among those who thought that Crook's subsequent pursuit of the Indians was clumsy and ineffective. And Sheridan was enraged when, instead of exterminating the Indians who remained off the reservation after the massacre, Crook recruited some of them to help him negotiate with the others. When, after a long, blundering campaign the Great Sioux War was finally brought to a sad end, neither Crook nor anyone else in the army was covered with glory.[56]

Years later, Crook was sent back to Arizona, where government mistreatment had led to a new Apache uprising. In 1882 he chased the insurgents down and returned them to the reservation. But in 1885, spurred by government mismanagement and duplicity, the legendary Geronimo took his band back out into the mountains of Mexico. Crook ran him down again and persuaded him to surrender. Sheridan repudiated the terms, Geronimo escaped, and at that the increasingly strained friendship of Crook and Sheridan came to a bitter end. Crook resigned from his command and returned to Nebraska.

On December 26, 1889, in the year after Sheridan's death and the year before his own, George Crook returned to Middletown and walked the quiet fields near Belle Grove, seeing the fog and smoke again, hearing the guns of Cedar Creek and thinking about what, in the end, they signified. His conclusion, inscribed in gall that night in his diary, was not a pleasant one: "After examining the grounds and the position of the troops after 25 years which have elapsed and in the light of subsequent events, it renders General Sheridan's claims and his subsequent actions in allowing the general public to remain under the impressions regarding his part in these battles, when he knew they were fiction, all the more contemptible. The adulations heaped on him by a grateful nation for his supposed genius turned his

head, which, added to his natural disposition, caused him to
bloat his little carcass with debauchery and dissipation, which
carried him off prematurely."[57]

A month later, on a train journey to Washington from Florida, Crook was delayed in Lynchburg, and to fill the time went
to visit Jubal Early. Crook saw nothing familiar in Early's biliousness. "He is much stooped and enfeebled," Crook wrote
without compassion, "but as bitter and virulent as an adder. He
has survived his usefulness, and is living entirely in the past. He
has fought his battles over so many times that he has worked
himself into the belief that many of the exaggerated, and some
ridiculous stories he tells are true." Still, the conversation could
not have been all that distasteful to Crook: "We sat up with him
until long after 12 M., taking a hot scotch with him the last
thing." Ten weeks later Crook dropped dead of a heart attack.[58]

THE FIREBRAND AND
THE FUTURE KING

In the march to their widely separated graves, the men of
Cedar Creek were led, as they had been led so often in the past,
by Dodson Ramseur and Charles Russell Lowell. Ramseur's
body was embalmed and taken to the lines outside Richmond
by the Federals, and there passed through to Ramseur's friend
and fellow North Carolinian Major General Robert F. Hoke.
The remains were laid in state in the capitol at Richmond,
mourned by the entire South. Dodson Ramseur had represented the future, and he was dead.

A train took the casket home to Lincolnton for a funeral that
Ellen and her daughter—Mary Dodson Ramseur, by then three
weeks old—could not attend. Ramseur's sister Luly wrote to
Ellen in sorrow and in pride to wish that Nellie could have had
the "sad, sweet privilege of kissing his dear face once more,"
and to remind her that "the whole country mourns his death,
and every earthly honor is paid to him."[59]

Similarly, in Massachusetts, they said farewell to the promise
that had been Charles Russell Lowell. Edward Emerson attended the ceremonies at Harvard: "I remember, one rainy day

when the sudden gusts blew the yellow leaves in showers from the College elms, hearing the beautiful notes of Pleyel's Hymn, which was the tune to which soldiers were borne to burial, played by the band as the procession came, bearing Charles Lowell's body from his mother's house to the College Chapel; and seeing his coffin, wrapped in the flag, carried to the altar by soldiers; and how strangely in contrast with the new blue overcoats and fresh red and white bunting were the campaign-soiled cap and gauntlets, the worn hilt and battered scabbard of the sword that lay on the coffin."[60]

He was buried a general, a title he never carried in life. The commission had come through a few days after Cedar Creek, in the same mail that had brought Wesley Merritt promotion to major general. Merritt had accepted his commission, listened to the congratulations, then gestured to the other paper lying there unclaimed. "I would gladly give up *this,*" he said with feeling, "if he could only take *that.*"[61]

"He led a crowded life," wrote Edward Emerson, "never drowned by his work—and found all in the day's work *good:* filed iron or kept his ledger, rode in the rain or kept his men quiet under fire, or fought hand to hand with sabre among, or before them." He was sorely missed, not only by his family and his comrades, but by people in high places who had seen, as John Murray Forbes had seen, that nothing was "too good or too high for him." Sheridan said that Lowell, "would have commanded all my cavalry" had he lived. Others talked about the presidency.

Twenty-five years later, Henry Lee Higginson (he whose face bore the mark of Tom Rosser's saber) still missed his friend. Incalculably rich by then, he made a present to his alma mater of Soldiers Field, in memory of Lowell and five others who did not come back. They were, said Higginson, "dear friends, who gave freely and eagerly all that they had or hoped for."[62]

Sheridan's Ride
October 19, 1864

Up from the South at break of day,
Bringing to Winchester fresh dismay,
The affrighted air with a shudder bore,
Like a herald in haste, to the chieftain's door,
The terrible grumble and rumble and roar,
Telling the battle was on once more,
And Sheridan twenty miles away.

And wider still those billows of war
Thundered along the horizon's bar;
And louder yet into Winchester rolled
The roar of that red sea uncontrolled,
Making the blood of the listener cold
As he thought of the stake in that fiery fray,
With Sheridan twenty miles away.

But there is a road from Winchester town,
A good, broad highway, leading down;
And there, through the flash of the morning light,
A steed as black as the steeds of night
Was seen to pass as with eagle flight.
As if he knew the terrible need,
He stretched away with the utmost speed;
Hills rose and fell,—but his heart was gay,
With Sheridan fifteen miles away.

Still sprung from those swift hoofs, thundering South,
The dust, like smoke from the cannon's mouth;
Or the trail of a comet, sweeping faster and faster,
Foreboding to traitors the doom of disaster.
The heart of the steed and the heart of the master
Were beating, like prisoners assaulting their walls,
Impatient to be where the battle-field calls;
Every nerve of the charger was strained to full play,
With Sheridan only ten miles away.

Under his spurning feet, the road
Like an arrowy Alpine river flowed,
And the landscape sped away behind,
Like an ocean flying before the wind;
And the steed, like a bark fed with furnace ire,
Swept on, with his wild eyes full of fire;
But, lo! he is nearing his heart's desire,
He is snuffing the smoke of the roaring fray,
With Sheridan only five miles away.

The first that the General saw were the groups
Of stragglers, and then the retreating troops;
What was done,—what to do,—a glance told him both,
And, striking his spurs with a terrible oath,
He dashed down the line mid a storm of huzzas,
And the wave of retreat checked its course there, because
The sight of the master compelled it to pause.
With foam and with dust the black charger was gray;
By the flash of his eye, and his nostril's play,
He seemed to the whole great army to say,
"I have brought you Sheridan all the way
From Winchester town, to save the day!"

Hurrah, hurrah for Sheridan!
Hurrah, hurrah, for horse and man!
And when their statues are placed on high,
Under the dome of the Union sky,—
The American soldier's Temple of Fame,—
There with the glorious General's name

Be it said in letters both bold and bright:
"Here is the steed that saved the day
By carrying Sheridan into the fight,
From Winchester,—twenty miles away!"

—THOMAS BUCHANAN READ

Appendix: Forces Engaged Battle of Cedar Creek, Va.: October 19, 1864

Union Forces: Army of the Shenandoah

Maj. Gen. Philip H. Sheridan

Maj. Gen. HORATIO G. WRIGHT*

Escort

17th Pennsylvania Cavalry (detachment), Maj. Weidner H. Spera
6th U.S. Cavalry, Capt. Ira W. Claflin

SIXTH ARMY CORPS

Brig. Gen. JAMES B. RICKETTS
Brig. Gen. GEORGE W. GETTY
Maj. Gen. HORATIO G. WRIGHT

Escort

1st Michigan Cavalry, Company G, Lieut. William H. Wheeler

* Commanded during General Sheridan's temporary absence in the early part of the battle.

First Division

Brig. Gen. FRANK WHEATON

First Brigade

Col. WILLIAM H. PENROSE
Lieut. Col. EDWARD L. CAMPBELL
Capt. BALDWIN HUFTY

4th	New Jersey, Capt. Baldwin Hufty
10th	New Jersey:
	Maj. Lambert Boeman
	Capt. Charles D. Claypool
15th	New Jersey:
	Lieut. Col. Edward L. Campbell
	Capt. James W. Penrose

Second Brigade

Col. JOSEPH E. HAMBLIN
Col. RANALD S. MACKENZIE
Lieut. Col. EGBERT OLCOTT

2d	Connecticut Heavy Artillery:
	Col. Ranald S. Mackenzie
	Maj. Edward W. Jones
65th	New York:
	Lieut. Col. Thomas H. Higinbotham
	Capt. Henry C. Fisk
121st	New York:
	Lieut. Col. Egbert Olcott
	Capt. Daniel D. Jackson
95th	Pennsylvania ⎫
96th	Pennsylvania ⎬ Capt. John Harper

Third Brigade*

Col. OLIVER EDWARDS

37th Massachusetts, Lieut. Col. George L. Montague
49th Pennsylvania, Lieut. Col. Baynton J. Hickman
82d Pennsylvania, Col. Isaac C. Bassett
119th Pennsylvania, Lieut. Col. Gideon Clark
2d Rhode Island (battalion), Capt. Elisha H. Rhodes
5th Wisconsin (battalion), Maj. Charles W. Kempf
17th Pennsylvania Cavalry, Maj. Coe Durland

Second Division

Brig. Gen. GEORGE W. GETTY
Brig. Gen. LEWIS A. GRANT

First Brigade

Col. JAMES M. WARNER

62d	New York, Lieut. Col. Theodore B. Hamilton
93d	Pennsylvania, Capt. David C. Keller
98th	Pennsylvania:
	Lieut. Col. John B. Kohler
	Capt. Gottfried Bauer
102d	Pennsylvania:
	Maj. James H. Coleman
	Capt. James Patchell
139th	Pennsylvania, Lieut. Col. John G. Parr

Second Brigade

Brig. Gen. LEWIS A. GRANT
Lieut. Col. AMASA S. TRACY

2d   Vermont:

* At Winchester, Va., and not engaged in the battle.

Lieut. Col. Amasa S. Tracy
Capt. Elijah Wales

3d   Vermont (battalion), Maj. Horace W. Floyd
4th   Vermont:

Maj. Horace W. Floyd
Col. George P. Foster*

5th   Vermont, Maj. Enoch E. Johnson
6th   Vermont (battalion):

Capt. Edwin R. Kinney
Capt. William J. Sperry

11th   Vermont (1st Heavy Artillery), Lieut. Col. Charles
Hunsdon

Third Brigade

Brig. Gen. DANIEL D. BIDWELL
Lieut. Col. WINSOR B. FRENCH

1st   Maine (Veteran), Maj. Stephen C. Fletcher
43d   New York (battalion), Maj. Charles A. Milliken
49th   New York (battalion), Lieut. Col. Erastus D. Holt
77th   New York, Lieut. Col. Winsor B. French
122d   New York:

Lieut. Col. Augustus W. Dwight
Maj. Jabez M. Brower

61st   Pennsylvania (battalion), Capt. David J. Taylor

* Corps officer of the day at the beginning of the battle; later rejoined brigade and commanded the left of its line.

Third Division

Col. J. WARREN KEIFER

First Brigade

Col. WILLIAM EMERSON

14th	New Jersey, Capt. Jacob J. Janeway
106th	New York:
	Capt. Alvah W. Briggs
	Capt. Peter Robertson
151st	New York:
	Capt. Browning N. Wiles
	Capt. Hiram A. Kimball
184th	New York (battalion), Maj. William D. Ferguson
87th	Pennsylvania (battalion):
	Capt. Edgar M. Ruhl
	Capt. John A. Salsbury
10th	Vermont:
	Col. William W. Henry
	Capt. Henry H. Dewey

Second Brigade

Col. WILLIAM H. BALL

6th	Maryland, Maj. Joseph C. Hill
9th	New York Heavy Artillery,
	Maj. James W. Snyder
110th	Ohio, Lieut. Col. Otho H. Binkley
122d	Ohio, Lieut. Col. Moses M. Granger
126th	Ohio:
	Maj. George W. Voorhes
	Capt. George W. Hoge
67th	Pennsylvania, Lieut. John F. Young
138th	Pennsylvania, Maj. Lewis A. May

Artillery Brigade

Col. CHARLES H. TOMPKINS

Maine Light, 5th Battery (E), Capt. Greenleaf T. Stevens
New York Light, 1st Battery, Lieut. Orsamus R. Van Etten
1st Rhode Island Light, Battery C, Lieut. Jacob H. Lamb
1st Rhode Island Light, Battery G, Capt. George W. Adams
5th United States, Battery M, Capt. James McKnight

NINETEENTH ARMY CORPS

Bvt. Maj. Gen. WILLIAM H. EMORY

First Division

Brig. Gen. JAMES W. MCMILLAN
Brig. Gen. WILLIAM DWIGHT

First Brigade

Col. EDWIN P. DAVIS

29th	Maine	{ Maj. George H. Nye { Capt. Alfred L. Turner
30th	Massachusetts, Capt. Samuel D. Shipley	
90th	New York	{ Lieut. Col. Nelson Shaurman { Capt. Honore De La Paturelle
114th	New York, Lieut. Col. Henry B. Morse	
116th	New York, Col. George M. Love	
153d	New York	{ Lieut. Col. Alexander Strain { Capt. George H. McLaughlin

Second Brigade

Col. STEPHEN THOMAS
Brig. Gen. JAMES W. MCMILLAN

12th	Connecticut, Lieut. Col. George N. Lewis

| 160th | New York, Capt. Henry P. Underhill |
| 47th | Pennsylvania, Maj. J. P. Shindel Gobin |

8th Vermont { Maj. John B. Mead
                Capt. Moses McFarland
                Col. Stephen Thomas

*Third Brigade**

Col. LEONARD D. H. CURRIE

30th	Maine, Col. Thomas H. Hubbard
133d	New York, Maj. Anthony J. Allaire
162d	New York, Col. Justus W. Blanchard
165th	New York (six companies), Lieut. Col. Gouverneur Carr
173d	New York, Maj. George W. Rogers

Artillery

New York Light, 5th Battery, Capt. Elijah D. Taft

Second Division

Brig. Gen. CUVIER GROVER
Brig. Gen. HENRY W. BIRGE

First Brigade

Brig. Gen. HENRY W. BIRGE
Col. THOMAS W. PORTER

9th	Connecticut (battalion), Capt. John G. Healy
12th	Maine, Lieut. Col. Edwin Ilsley
14th	Maine:

Col. Thomas W. Porter
Capt. John K. Laing

* Guarding wagon trains, and not engaged in the battle.

| 26th | Massachusetts (battalion), Lieut. John S. Cooke |
| 14th | New Hampshire: |

> Capt. Theodore A. Ripley
> Capt. Oliver H. Marston

| 75th | New York, Maj. Benjamin F. Thurber |

Second Brigade

Col. EDWARD L. MOLINEUX

13th	Connecticut, Col. Charles D. Blinn
11th	Indiana, Lieut. Col. William W. Darnall
22d	Iowa, Col. Harvey Graham
3d	Massachusetts Cavalry (dismounted), Col. Lorenzo D. Sargent
131st	New York, Col. Nicholas W. Day
159th	New York, Lieut. Col. William Waltermire

Third Brigade

Col. DANIEL MACAULEY
Lieut. Col. ALFRED NEAFIE

38th	Massachusetts, Maj. Charles F. Allen
128th	New York, Capt. Charles R. Anderson
156th	New York:

> Lieut. Col. Alfred Neafie
> Capt. Alfred Cooley

| 175th | New York (battalion), Capt. Charles McCarthey |
| 176th | New York, Maj. Charles Lewis |

Fourth Brigade

Col. DAVID SHUNK

| 8th | Indiana: |

> Lieut. Col. Alexander J. Kenny
> Maj. John R. Polk

18th   Indiana, Lieut. Col. William S. Charles
24th   Iowa:
           Lieut. Col. John Q. Wilds
           Capt. Leander Clark
           Maj. Edward Wright
28th   Iowa:
           Lieut. Col. Bartholomew W. Wilson
           Maj. John Meyer

Artillery

Maine Light, 1st Battery (A):
Lieut. Eben D. Haley
Lieut. John S. Snow

Reserve Artillery

Maj. ALBERT W. BRADBURY

Indiana Light, 17th Battery, Lieut. Hezekiah Hinkson
1st Rhode Island Light, Battery D, Lieut. Frederick Chase

ARMY OF WEST VIRGINIA

Bvt. Maj. Gen. GEORGE CROOK

First Division
Col. JOSEPH THOBURN
Col. THOMAS M. HARRIS

First Brigade

Lieut. Col. THOMAS F. WILDES

34th   Massachusetts, Capt. Andrew Potter
5th   New York Heavy Artillery,
           2d Battalion,
           Capt. Frederick C. Wilkie

116th   Ohio:
        Capt. Wilbert B. Teters
        Capt. John Hull
123d   Ohio, Maj. Horace Kellogg

Second Brigade*

Col. WILLIAM B. CURTIS

1st   West Virginia, Lieut. Col. Jacob Weddle
4th   West Virginia, Capt. Benjamin D. Boswell
12th West Virginia, Lieut. Col. Robert S. Northcott

Third Brigade

Col. THOMAS M. HARRIS
Col. MILTON WELLS

23d   Illinois (battalion),* Capt. Samuel A. Simison
54th Pennsylvania, Capt. John Suter
10th West Virginia:
        Lieut. Col. Moses S. Hall
        Maj. Henry H. Withers
11th West Virginia, Lieut. Col. Van H. Bukey
15th West Virginia:
        Col. Milton Wells
        Maj. John W. Holliday

Second Division

Col. RUTHERFORD B. HAYES

First Brigade

Col. HIRAM F. DEVOL

* At Winchester, Va., and not engaged in the battle.

23d Ohio, Lieut. Col. James M. Comly
36th Ohio, Lieut. Col. William H. G. Adney
5th West Virginia (battalion), Lieut. Col. William H.
        Enochs
13th West Virginia { Col. William R. Brown*
                      { Lieut. Col. James R. Hall

Second Brigade

Lieut. Col. BENJAMIN F. COATES

34th Ohio (battalion), Lieut. Col. Luther Furney
91st Ohio, Maj. Lemuel Z. Cadot
9th West Virginia, Capt. John S. P. Carroll
14th West Virginia, Maj. Shriver Moore

Artillery Brigade

Capt. HENRY A. DuPONT

1st Ohio Light, Battery L, Capt. Frank C. Gibbs
1st Pennsylvania Light, Battery D, Lieut. William Munk
5th United States, Battery B:
        Lieut. Henry F. Brewerton
        Lieut. Charles Holman

Provisional Division†

Col. J. HOWARD KITCHING

CAVALRY

Bvt. Maj. Gen. ALFORD T. A. TORBERT

* Corps officer of the day.
† Only a small detachment from the First Brigade, and the 6th New York Heavy Artillery, from the Second Brigade, engaged in the battle.

Escort

1st Rhode Island, Maj. William Turner, Jr.

First Division

Brig. Gen. WESLEY MERRITT

First Brigade

Col. JAMES H. KIDD

1st	Michigan, Capt. Andrew W. Duggan
5th	Michigan, Maj. Smith H. Hastings
6th	Michigan, Maj. Charles W. Deane
7th	Michigan, Maj. Daniel H. Darling
	New York Light Artillery, 6th Battery, Capt. Joseph W. Martin

Second Brigade

Bvt. Brig. Gen. THOMAS C. DEVIN

4th	New York,* Maj. Edward Schwartz
6th	New York, Capt. George E. Farmer
9th	New York, Col. George S. Nichols
19th	New York (1st Dragoons), Col. Alfred Gibbs
1st	U.S. Artillery, Batteries K and L, Lieut. Franck E. Taylor

Reserve Brigade

Col. CHARLES R. LOWELL, Jr.
Lieut. Col. CASPER CROWNINSHIELD

* Detailed for duty at General Sheridan's headquarters.

2d   Massachusetts:
       Lieut. Col. Casper Crowninshield
       Capt. Archibald McKendry
1st   United States, Capt. Eugene M. Baker
2d   United States, Capt. Robert S. Smith
5th   United States, Lieut. Gustavus Urban

Second Division†

Col. WILLIAM H. POWELL

First Brigade

Col. ALPHEUS S. MOORE

8th   Ohio (detachment)
14th   Pennsylvania, Maj. Thomas Gibson
22d   Pennsylvania, Lieut. Col.
       Andrew J. Greenfield

Second Brigade

Col. HENRY CAPEHART

1st   New York, Maj. Timothy Quinn
1st   West Virginia, Maj. Harvey Farabee
2d   West Virginia, Lieut. Col. John J. Hoffman
3d   West Virginia, Lieut. Col. John L. McGee

Artillery
5th United States, Battery L, Lieut. Giulian V. Weir

Third Division

Brig. Gen. GEORGE A. CUSTER

† From Department of West Virginia.

First Brigade

Col. ALEXANDER C. M. PENNINGTON

1st	Connecticut, Capt. Edwin W. French
3d	New Jersey, Lieut. Col. Charles C. Suydam
2d	New York, Capt. Andrew S. Glover
5th	New York, Maj. Theodore A. Boice
2d	Ohio, Lieut. Col. George A. Purington
18th	Pennsylvania, Maj. John W. Phillips

Second Brigade

Col. WILLIAM WELLS

3d	Indiana (two companies), Lieut. Benjamin F. Gilbert
1st	New Hampshire (battalion), Col. John L. Thompson
8th	New York, Lieut. Col. William H. Benjamin
22d	New York, Maj. Charles C. Brown
1st	Vermont, Lieut. Col. John W. Bennett

Horse Artillery

2d United States, Batteries B and L, Capt. Charles H. Pierce
3d United States, Batteries C, F, and K, Capt. Dunbar R. Ransom

CONFEDERATE FORCES: ARMY OF THE VALLEY

Lieut. Gen. Jubal A. Early

Ramseur's Division

Maj. Gen. S. D. RAMSEUR

Battle's Brigade

Brig. Gen. C. A. BATTLE
Lieut. Col. E. L. HOBSON

3d Alabama:
      Brig. Gen. C. A. Battle
      Lieut. Col. E. L. Hobson
5th Alabama, Lieut. Col. E. L. Hobson
6th Alabama, Capt. J. Green
12th Alabama, Capt. P. D. Rose
61st Alabama, Maj. W. E. Pinckard

Grimes Brigade

Brig. Gen. BRYAN GRIMES

32d, 53d, and 2d N.C. Battalions: Col. D. G. Cowand
43d and 45th N.C., Col. John R. Winston

Cook's Brigade

Brig. Gen. PHILIP COOK

4th Georgia, Lieut. Col. W. H. Willis
12th Georgia, Capt. James Everett
21st Georgia, Capt. H. T. Battle
44th Georgia, Lieut. Col. J. W. Beck

Cox's Brigade

Brig. Gen. WILLIAM R. COX

1st N.C., Capt. W. H. Thomson
2d N.C., Capt. T. B. Beall
3d and 4th N.C., Capt. W. H. Thomson
14th N.C., Capt. Joseph Jones
30th N.C., Capt. J. C. McMillan

Pegram's (Early's) Division

Brig. Gen. JOHN PEGRAM

Godwin's Brigade

6th, 21st, 54th, and 57th N.C.

Johnston's Brigade

Brig. Gen. ROBERT D. JOHNSTON

5th	and 12th N.C., Brig. Gen. Robert D. Johnston
20th	and 23d N.C., Col. T. F. Toon
1st	N.C. Battalion Sharpshooters, Capt. R. E. Wilson

Pegram's Brigade

Col. JOHN S. HOFFMAN

13th	Va., Capt. Felix Heiskell
31st	Va., Lieut. Col. J. S. K. McCutchen
49th	Va., Capt. John G. Lobban
52d	Va., Capt. J. M. Humphreys
58th	Va., Capt. L. C. James

Gordon's Division

Maj. Gen. JOHN B. GORDON

Evans's Brigade

Brig. Gen. C. A. EVANS

Hays's Brigade

5th, 6th, 7th, 8th, and 9th La.

13th, 26th, 31st, 38th, 60th, and
61st Ga. and 12th Ga. Battalion.

Terry's Brigade

Brig. Gen. WILLIAM TERRY

(Composed of the fragmentary remains of fourteen regiments of Edward Johnson's division, most of which was captured by the enemy, May 12th, 1864.)

Stonewall Brigade

Col. J. H. S. FUNK

2d, 4th, 5th, 27th, and 33d Va.

J. M. Jones's Brigade

Col. R. H. DUNGAN
21st, 25th, 42d, 44th, 48th, and 50th Va.

Stewart's Brigade

Lieut. Col. S. H. SAUNDERS

10th, 23d, and 37th Va.

Stafford's Brigade

1st, 2d, 10th, 14th, and 15th La.

Kershaw's Division
Maj. Gen. J. B. KERSHAW

Conner's Brigade

Brig. Gen. JAMES CONNER
Maj. JAMES M. GOGGIN

2d   S.C., Maj. B. R. Clyburn

3d, 　　7th, 8th, and 15th S.C., Maj. R. T. Todd
20th　　S.C. and 3d S.C. Battalion, Col. S. M. Boykin

Humphreys's Brigade

Brig. Gen. BENJAMIN G. HUMPHREYS

13th, 17th, 18th, and 21st Miss.

Wharton's Brigade

45th, 　50th, and 51st Va., and 30th Va. Battalion Sharp-
　　　　Shooters

Wofford's Brigade

16th, 　18th, and 24th Ga.; 3d Ga. Battalion; Cobb's Ga.
　　　　Legion and Phillips's Ga. Legion

Bryan's Brigade

Col. JAMES P. SIMMS

10th　　Ga., Col. W. C. Holt
50th　　Ga., Col. P. McGlashan
51st　　and 53d Ga., Col. E. Ball

Echols's Brigade

22d Va., and 23d and 26th Va. Battalions

Smith's Brigade

Col. THOMAS SMITH

36th and 60th Va., Capt. A. G. P. George
45th Va. Battalion, Capt. W. B. Hensley
Thomas Legion, Lieut. Col. James R. Lowe

CAVALRY

Lomax's Division

Maj. Gen. LUNSFORD L. LOMAX

Imboden's Brigade

18th, 23d, and 62d Va.

B. T. Johnson's Brigade

8th,   21st, and 22d Va., and 34th and 35th Va. Battalions

McCausland's Brigade

Brig. Gen. JOHN McCAUSLAND
14th,   16th, 17th, and 25th Va., and 37th Va. Battalion

Jackson's Brigade

Brig. Gen. H. B. DAVIDSON

1st   Md. 19th and 20th Va., and 46th and 47th Va.
Battalions

Rosser's (Fitz Lee's) Division

Maj. Gen. THOMAS L. ROSSER

Wickham's Brigade

1st, 2d, 3d, and 4th Va.

Rosser's Brigade

7th,   11th, and 12th Va., and 35th Va. Battalion

Payne's Brigade

Col. WILLIAM H. PAYNE

5th, 6th, and 15th Va.

ARTILLERY

Col. T. H. CARTER

Braxton's Battalion

Carpenter's, Cooper's, and Hardwicke's Va. Batteries

Cutshaw's Battalion

Carington's, Garber's and Tanner's Va. Batteries

Carter's Battalion

Reese's Ala. Battery, and W. P. Carter's, Fry's, and Pendleton's Va. Batteries

Nelson's Battalion

Lieut. Col. WILLIAM NELSON

Milledge's Ga. Battery, and Kirkpatrick's and Massie's Va. Batteries

King's Battalion

Lieut. Col. J. FLOYD KING

Bryan's, Chapman's, and Lowry's Va. Batteries

Horse Artillery

Griffin's Md. Battery, and Jackson's, Johnston's, Lurty's, McClanahan's, Shoemaker's, and Thomson's Va. Batteries

Notes

References in the Notes are by short title; the complete citation can be found in the Bibliography.

Chapter One

1. Coulter, E. Merton, *The Confederate States of America,* quoted in Bushong, *Old Jube,* p. 247.
2. *Confederate Veteran,* vol. 10, no. 4, p. 165.
3. Wise, *End of an Era,* p. 226.
4. *Confederate Veteran,* vol. 31, no. 3, p. 881.
5. Bushong, *Old Jube,* p. 104.
6. Douglas, *I Rode with Stonewall,* p. 33.
7. Wise, *End of an Era,* p. 226.
8. Douglas, *I Rode with Stonewall,* p. 33.
9. Early, *Narrative,* p. xi; Bushong, *Old Jube,* pp. 12–14.
10. The story is related in Bushong, *Old Jube,* pp. 18–19.
11. Wise, *End of an Era,* p. 227.
12. Bushong, *Old Jube,* p. 30; Stiles, *Marse Robert,* p. 50.
13. Bushong, *Old Jube,* p. 32.
14. Stiles, *Marse Robert,* p. 50.
15. *Southern Historical Society Papers,* vol. 20, p. 287.
16. Bushong, *Old Jube,* p. 69.
17. *Southern Historical Society Papers,* vol. 22, p. 288.

18. Stiles, *Marse Robert,* p. 190.
19. *Battles and Leaders,* vol. 3, p. 140; *Southern Historical Society Papers,* vol. 22, p. 288.
20. Bushong, *Old Jube,* p. 115.
21. *Southern Historical Society Papers,* vol. 22, p. 289.
22. Goolrick, *Rebels Resurgent,* p. 14.
23. Ibid., p. 24.
24. Ibid., pp. 116–18; Bushong, *Old Jube,* p. 150; *Southern Historical Society Papers,* vol. 22, p. 289.
25. Freeman, *Lee's Lieutenants,* vol. 3, p. 264.
26. Boatner, *Civil War Dictionary,* p. 680; Freeman, *Lee's Lieutenants,* vol. 3, p. 267; *Battles and Leaders,* vol. 4, p. 87.
27. Early, *Narrative,* p. 316; Freeman, *Lee's Lieutenants,* vol. 3, p. 268; *Official Records,* vol. 29, pp. 623–26.
28. Freeman, *Lee's Lieutenants,* vol. 3, p. 326; *Official Records,* vol. 33, pp. 1167–68; Early, *Narrative,* pp. 326–42.
29. Freeman, *Lee's Lieutenants,* vol. 3, p. 328.
30. Ibid., p. 333; Bushong, *Old Jube,* p. 170.
31. The numbers cited approximate the conditions of 1864; actual sizes of units varied widely from one year to the next, one theater to the next, and so forth. See Boatner, *Civil War Dictionary,* p. 611.
32. *Battles and Leaders,* vol. 4, p. 524; Stackpole, *Sheridan in the Shenandoah,* p. 239; Pond, *Shenandoah Valley,* p. 184.
33. *Confederate Veteran,* vol. 10, no. 4, p. 165.
34. Freeman, *Lee's Lieutenants,* vol. 3, p. 585; *Official Records,* vol. 43, part 2, p. 880.
35. The story, from Stiles, *Marse Robert,* is recounted in Clark, *Gettysburg,* p. 30.
36. The exchange of letters is reproduced in *Official Records,* vol. 43, part 2, pp. 894–98.
37. Ibid., p. 892.

Chapter Two

1. *Official Records,* vol. 43, part 2, p. 249.

2. Taylor, "With Sheridan," p. 37; Hutton, *Sheridan's Army,* p. 2.

3. Taylor, "With Sheridan," p. 37; Newhall, *With General Sheridan,* pp. 13, 27.

4. Newhall, *With General Sheridan,* p. 17.

5. Ibid., p. 18.

6. Burr, *Life of Sheridan,* p. 18.

7. Newhall, *With General Sheridan,* p. 14.

8. Stackpole, *Sheridan in the Shenandoah,* pp. 123–24.

9. Kidd, *Recollections,* p. 299.

10. Sheridan, *Memoirs,* vol. 1, p. 94.

11. Ibid., p. 1; Hutton, *Sheridan's Army,* p. 2.

12. Burr, *Life of Sheridan,* p. 24.

13. Hutton, *Sheridan's Army,* p. 3; Sheridan, *Memoirs,* vol. 1, p. 7; O'Connor, *Sheridan,* p. 23.

14. O'Connor, *Sheridan,* p. 29.

15. Sheridan, *Memoirs,* vol. 1, p. 7.

16. Ibid., p. 10.

17. Hutton, *Sheridan's Army,* p. 6.

18. Sheridan, *Memoirs,* vol. 1, pp. 44–46.

19. Ibid., pp. 105–20; Hutton, *Sheridan's Army,* p. 10.

20. Sheridan, *Memoirs,* vol. 1, p. 123.

21. Ibid., pp. 122–23; Hutton, *Sheridan's Army,* p. 11.

22. Sheridan, *Memoirs,* vol. 1, pp. 125–27; Boatner, *Civil War Dictionary,* p. 215.

23. O'Connor, *Sheridan,* p. 60.

24. Sheridan, *Memoirs,* vol. 1, p. 135.

25. Ibid., pp. 140–43, 150.

26. Ibid., pp. 153–54.

27. Ibid., pp. 166.

28. Ibid., pp. 175–77.

29. Ibid., pp. 181–82.

30. Street, *Struggle for Tennessee,* p. 54.

31. Sheridan, *Memoirs,* vol. 1, p. 195.

32. Ibid., pp. 12–13; Street, *Struggle for Tennessee,* p. 58; Boatner, *Civil War Dictionary,* p. 830.

33. Sheridan, *Memoirs*, vol. 1, pp. 199–200; Street, *Struggle for Tennessee*, p. 62–67.

34. Street, *Struggle for Tennessee*, pp. 80–81; Sheridan, *Memoirs*, vol. 1, pp. 211–12.

35. Street, *Struggle for Tennessee*, p. 124.

36. Sheridan, *Memoirs*, vol. 1, pp. 241–42.

37. Ibid., pp. 154, 236.

38. Korn, *Chattanooga*, p. 49.

39. Sheridan, *Memoirs*, vol. 1, p. 286.

40. Ibid., pp. 297, 311; O'Connor, *Sheridan*, p. 136.

41. Sheridan, *Memoirs*, vol. 1, p. 339.

42. Ibid., pp. 339, 342.

43. Ibid., p. 346; Porter, *With Grant*, p. 24.

44. Sheridan, *Memoirs*, vol. 1, p. 347; Hutton, *Sheridan's Army*, p. 2; Porter, *With Grant*, p. 24.

45. Starr, *Union Cavalry*, vol. 2, pp. 75, 78–79; Davies, *General Sheridan*, pp. 93–95.

46. *Battles and Leaders*, p. 188.

47. Ibid.

48. Sheridan, *Memoirs*, vol. 1, p. 354.

49. *Battles and Leaders*, p. 189.

50. Kidd, *Recollections*, p. 286; Porter, *With Grant*, p. 84.

51. Porter, *With Grant*, p. 84.

52. *Battles and Leaders*, p. 189; Kidd, *Recollections*, p. 287.

53. Kidd, *Recollections*, p. 291; Starr, *Union Cavalry*, vol. 2, p. 99.

54. Sheridan, *Memoirs*, vol. 1, pp. 390–93; Freeman, *Lee's Lieutenants*, vol. 3, p. 419; Starr, *Union Cavalry*, vol. 2, pp. 102–3.

55. Sheridan, *Memoirs*, vol. 1, pp. 384–85.

56. Beecher, *Record of the 114th New York*, p. 396; Walker, *The Vermont Brigade*, pp. 54, 60, 72.

57. *Battles and Leaders*, p. 522.

58. Catton, *Grant Takes Command*, pp. 362–63; Pond, *Shenandoah Valley*, p. 151.

59. O'Connor, *Sheridan*, p. 206; Burr, *Life of Sheridan*, p. 203.

60. Catton, *Grant Takes Command*, p. 171; Freeman, *Lee's Lieutenants*, vol. 3, p. 477.
61. *Official Records*, vol. 43, part 2, p. 177.
62. Ibid., p. 170.
63. Sheridan, *Memoirs*, vol. 2, p. 54.
64. Ibid., p. 55.
65. Ibid.
66. *Official Records*, vol. 43, part 2, p. 366.
67. Ibid., pp. 37, 2, 301; Pond, *Shenandoah Valley*, pp. 192–93.
68. DuPont, *Campaign of 1864*, pp. 37–40; Taylor, "With Sheridan," p. 34; Williams, *Hayes of the Twenty-third*, p. 192.

Chapter Three

1. Newhall, *With General Sheridan*, p. 22.
2. *Official Records*, vol. 43, part 1, p. 30.
3. Douglas, *I Rode with Stonewall*, pp. 315–16; *Official Records*, vol. 43, part 1, p. 302.
4. McDonald, *The Laurel Brigade*, p. 300; *Battles and Leaders*, p. 525; Pond, *Shenandoah Valley*, p. 201; Myers, *The Commanches*, p. 335.
5. Evans, *Confederate Military History*, vol. 3, pp. 628, 686.
6. Clark, *Histories of Regiments from North Carolina*, vol. 2, p. 258.
7. Myers, *The Commanches*, p. 335.
8. McDonald, *The Laurel Brigade*, p. 300.
9. Ibid.
10. Myers, *The Commanches*, p. 335; Bushong, *Fightin' Tom Rosser*, p. 68.
11. *Official Records*, vol. 43, part 1, pp. 56–57; ibid., part 2, pp. 158, 177, 218.
12. Sanford, *Rebels and Redskins*, p. 302.
13. Ibid., p. 303; *Battles and Leaders*, p. 525; *Confederate Veteran*, vol. 22, no. 3, p. 128.
14. *Official Records*, vol. 43, part 1, pp. 30, 99.
15. Kersheval, *Valley of Virginia*, p. 60; Taylor, "With Sheridan," p. 411.

16. Mosby, *Memoirs*, pp. 300–313; Charles Brewster, "Captured by Mosby's Guerrillas," *National Tribune*, Thursday, September 26, 1901.

17. Van de Water, *Glory Hunter*, p. 43.

18. Sanford, *Rebels and Redskins*, pp. 225–26.

19. Van de Water, *Glory Hunter*, p. 30; Urwin, *Custer Victorious*, p. 44.

20. Connell, *Morning Star*, p. 108.

21. Van de Water, *Glory Hunter*, pp. 20–22; Sanford, *Rebels and Redskins*, p. 302.

22. Sergent, *They Lie Forgotten*, p. 168.

23. Bushong, *Fightin' Tom Rosser*, p. 15.

24. Urwin, *Custer Victorious*, p. 46.

25. Ibid.; Van de Water, *Glory Hunter*, p. 39.

26. Connell, *Morning Star*, p. 109; *Civil War Times Illustrated*, December 1967, p. 25.

27. Urwin, *Custer Victorious*, p. 47.

28. Freeman, *Lee's Lieutenants*, vol. 3, p. 212; Bushong, *Fightin' Tom Rosser*, p. 36.

29. Thomas, *Bold Dragoon*, p. 206; Goolrick, *Rebels Resurgent*, p. 109.

30. Thomas, *Bold Dragoon*, pp. 206–7; Goolrick, *Rebels Resurgent*, p. 111.

31. Bushong, *Fightin' Tom Rosser*, p. 42.

32. Ibid., pp. 43, 47.

33. Urwin, *Custer Victorious*, p. 53.

34. Thomas, *Bold Dragoon*, p. 228.

35. Van de Water, *Glory Hunter*, pp. 50–51.

36. Ibid., p. 50; Thomas, *Bold Dragoon*, p. 234.

37. Van de Water, *Glory Hunter*, p. 50.

38. Clark, *Gettysburg*, pp. 27–29.

39. Urwin, *Custer Victorious*, p. 43.

40. Ibid., p. 65.

41. Ibid., p. 68; Kidd, *Recollections*, pp. 126, 133.

42. Urwin, *Custer Victorious*, pp. 71–75.

43. Kidd, *Recollections*, pp. 137, 145–48.

44. Ibid., p. 153.

45. Clark, *Gettysburg,* p. 132.
46. Urwin, *Custer Victorious,* p. 81.
47. Ibid.
48. Urwin, *Custer Victorious,* p. 95.
49. Bushong, *Fightin' Tom Rosser,* pp. 55–56.
50. Freeman, *Lee's Lieutenants,* vol. 3, pp. 212–13; Bushong, *Fightin' Tom Rosser,* pp. 58–60; Thomas, *Bold Dragoon,* pp. 260–61.
51. *Official Records,* vol. 29, part 2, p. 779; Freeman, *Lee's Lieutenants,* vol. 3, p. 249; Bushong, *Fightin' Tom Rosser,* p. 59.
52. Freeman, *Lee's Lieutenants,* vol. 3, p. 260.
53. Kidd, *Recollections,* p. 216.
54. Van de Water, *Glory Hunter,* p. 61; Thomas, *Bold Dragoon,* p. 269.
55. Bushong, *Fightin' Tom Rosser,* pp. 74–75.
56. *Official Records,* vol. 33, part 1, pp. 43–46.
57. Van de Water, *Glory Hunter,* p. 60.
58. Urwin, *Custer Victorious,* p. 116.
59. Catton, *Grant Takes Command,* pp. 21–23; Connell, *Morning Star,* p. 115.
60. McDonald, *The Laurel Brigade,* p. 225.
61. Van de Water, *Glory Hunter,* p. 66; Thomas, *Bold Dragoon,* p. 287.
62. Urwin, *Custer Victorious,* pp. 140–41.
63. Sheridan, *Memoirs,* vol. 1, p. 378; Urwin, *Custer Victorious,* pp. 142–45; Freeman, *Lee's Lieutenants,* vol. 3, p. 413.
64. Starr, *Union Cavalry,* vol. 2, pp. 109–10.
65. Thomas, *Bold Dragoon,* pp. 270–72.
66. *Official Records,* vol. 36, part 1, p. 823.
67. Knapp, *Confederate Horsemen,* pp. 48–49.
68. *Official Records,* vol. 36, part 1, p. 1095.
69. Urwin, *Custer Victorious,* pp. 159–60.
70. *Official Records,* vol. 26, part 1, p. 832; Knapp, *Confederate Horsemen,* p. 49.
71. Starr, *Union Cavalry,* vol. 2, p. 141.
72. Bushong, *Fightin' Tom Rosser,* pp. 102–3.
73. Ibid., pp. 103, 188.

74. Ibid., p. 103.
75. *Official Records,* vol. 43, part 1, p. 1029; McDonald, *The Laurel Brigade,* p. 301.
76. McDonald, *The Laurel Brigade,* p. 301; Urwin, *Custer Victorious,* p. 195.
77. McDonald, *The Laurel Brigade,* p. 302.
78. Ibid., pp. 302–3.
79. Ibid., p. 303.
80. Ibid., pp. 304–5.
81. *Official Records,* vol. 43, part 1, pp. 430–31.
82. Urwin, *Custer Victorious,* pp. 196–97; Sanford, *Rebels and Redskins,* pp. 282–83.
83. Urwin, *Custer Victorious,* p. 198; *Official Records,* vol. 43, part 1, p. 520.
84. *Official Records,* vol. 43, part 1, p. 567; McDonald, *The Laurel Brigade,* p. 306.
85. Starr, *Union Cavalry,* vol. 2, p. 194.
86. Urwin, *Custer Victorious,* p. 199.
87. Taylor, "With Sheridan," p. 429.
88. Urwin, *Custer Victorious,* p. 200.
89. Starr, *Union Cavalry,* vol. 2, p. 298.
90. Urwin, *Custer Victorious,* p. 200.
91. Taylor, "With Sheridan," p. 429; Urwin, *Custer Victorious,* p. 200.
92. Sanford, *Rebels and Redskins,* p. 284.
93. *Official Records,* vol. 43, part 1, p. 521.
94. *Southern Historical Society Papers,* vol. 13, p. 135.
95. Urwin, *Custer Victorious,* p. 201.
96. Bushong, *Fightin' Tom Rosser,* pp. 142–43.
97. Urwin, *Custer Victorious,* p. 202.

Chapter Four

1. Tankersley, *Gordon,* p. vii.
2. Ibid., pp. 13–15.
3. Schmitt, *General George Crook,* pp. vii–viii.
4. Gordon, *Reminiscences,* p. 333.

5. Stevens, "Cedar Creek," p. 89; Sheridan, *Memoirs,* vol. 1, p. 472.

6. *Official Military Atlas,* plate 72, no. 9 (made by Jed Hotchkiss to accompany Early's report of the battle of Cedar Creek), and plate 99 (a reconstruction made nine years after the battle by Federal engineers). The Hotchkiss map is of course more reliable on the Confederate positions and movements, while the Federal map offers more detail on the terrain and the Federal units.

7. Lincoln, *Life with the 34th Massachusetts,* p. 371; Taylor, "With Sheridan," p. 437.

8. Lincoln, *Life with the 34th Massachusetts,* p. 372; Taylor, "With Sheridan," p. 437.

9. Early, *Memoir,* pp. 99–100.

10. Lincoln, *Life with the 34th Massachusetts,* p. 372; Williams, *Hayes of the Twenty-third,* pp. 33–37; *Official Records,* vol. 43, part 1, pp. 128, 11.

11. Gordon, *Reminiscences,* p. 331; *Official Records,* vol. 43, part 1, p. 579.

12. Dickert, *Kershaw's Brigade,* p. 438; *Official Records,* vol. 43, part 1, p. 579; *Official Military Atlas,* plate 85, nos. 36 and 37.

13. Dickert, *Kershaw's Brigade,* p. 438.

14. Lincoln, *Life with the 34th Massachusetts,* p. 373.

15. *Official Records,* vol. 43, part 1, p. 371.

16. Taylor, "With Sheridan," p. 437.

17. Lincoln, *Life with the 34th Massachusetts,* p. 373, 375.

18. Ibid.

19. *Official Records,* vol. 43, part 1, p. 372.

20. Tankersley, *Gordon,* p. 5.

21. Stiles, *Marse Robert,* pp. 211–12.

22. See Worthington, *Fighting for Time.*

23. Gordon, *Reminiscences,* p. 151.

24. Ibid., pp. 153–54.

25. Ibid., p. 243.

26. Ibid., p. 258.

27. Ibid., pp. 249–51.

28. Tankersley, *Gordon*, pp. 64–65, 82; Gordon, *Reminiscences*, pp. 4–9.
29. Tankersley, *Gordon*, pp. 64–67.
30. Ibid., p. 75.
31. Ibid., pp. 1–2.
32. Gordon, *Reminiscences*, p. 319.
33. Ibid.
34. Ibid.
35. Early, *Narrative*, p. 438.
36. Gordon, *Reminiscences*, pp. 301, 333; *Official Records*, vol. 43, part 1, p. 580.
37. Gordon, *Reminiscences*, p. 334.
38. Ibid., pp. 334–35.
39. Ibid.
40. Taylor, "With Sheridan," p. 462.
41. Stevens, "Cedar Creek," p. 98.
42. Schmitt, *General George Crook*, p. xiv.
43. Williams, *Hayes of the Twenty-third*, p. 167.
44. Ibid., pp. 176–77.
45. Schmitt, *General George Crook*, p. xvi.
46. Sheridan, *Memoirs*, vol. 1, p. 70.
47. Schmitt, *General George Crook*, p. 16.
48. Ibid., pp. 40–42.
49. Ibid., pp. 40, 37; Newhall, *With General Sheridan*, pp. 16–17.
50. Schmitt, *General George Crook*, p. 126.
51. Ibid., p. 127.
52. Ibid., p. 10.
53. Ibid., p. 98.
54. Ibid., p. 107.
55. Ibid., p. 111 and 111n.
56. Williams, *Hayes of the Twenty-third*, pp. 170–71; Pond, *Shenandoah Valley*, pp. 9–10; Schmitt, *General George Crook*, p. 114.
57. Williams, *Hayes of the Twenty-third*, pp. 174–82; Schmitt, *General George Crook*, pp. 115–18.
58. Lewis, *Shenandoah in Flames*, p. 89.

59. Williams, *Hayes of the Twenty-third*, pp. 211–13; Schmitt, *General George Crook*, p. 122.

60. Williams, *Hayes of the Twenty-third*, pp. 217–23; Schmitt, *General George Crook*, p. 123.

61. DuPont, *Campaign of 1864*, p. 135.

62. Schmitt, *General George Crook*, pp. 128–29.

63. *Official Records*, vol. 43, part 1, p. 314; Carpenter, *History of the Eighth Vermont*, p. 181; Schmitt, *General George Crook*, p. 128n.

64. *Official Records*, vol. 43, part 1, pp. 295–307.

65. Ibid., p. 47; Schmitt, *General George Crook*, p. 127.

66. Schmitt, *General George Crook*, p. 130.

67. Sergent, *They Lie Forgotten*, p. 129.

68. Schmitt, *General George Crook*, p. 132.

69. Catton, *Grant Takes Command*, p. 378.

70. *Official Records*, vol. 43, part 2, p. 339.

71. Catton, *Grant Takes Command*, p. 362.

72. Stevens, "Cedar Creek," pp. 91–92.

73. *Official Records*, vol. 43, part 2, p. 345; Forsyth, *Thrilling Days*, p. 128; Stevens, "Cedar Creek," p. 93.

74. Forsyth, *Thrilling Days*, p. 128; *Official Records*, vol. 43, part 2, pp. 339, 355, 363.

75. *Official Records*, vol. 43, part 2, p. 355.

76. Ibid., p. 389.

77. Sheridan, *Memoirs*, vol. 2, pp. 63–64; Forsyth, *Thrilling Days*, p. 132; *Official Records*, vol. 43, part 2, p. 390.

78. Stevens, "Cedar Creek," pp. 95–96.

79. Sheridan, *Memoirs*, vol. 1, p. 484; Pond, *Shenandoah Valley*, p. 128.

80. Sheridan, *Memoirs*, vol. 1, p. 472.

81. *Dictionary of American Biography*.

82. DuPont, *Campaign of 1864*, pp. 143–45.

83. Stevens, "Cedar Creek," pp. 96–97.

84. Carpenter, *History of the Eighth Vermont*, p. 207.

85. Ibid., p. 208.

86. DuPont, *Campaign of 1864*, p. 152.

87. Putnam, *Memories*, pp. 365–66.

88. Carpenter, *History of the Eighth Vermont,* p. 208.
89. Schmitt, *General George Crook,* p. 133.

Chapter Five

1. Nettleton, "How the Day Was Saved," p. 265.
2. Ibid.
3. Gallagher, *Ramseur,* p. 119.
4. *Official Records,* vol. 43, part 1, pp. 580, 598.
5. Ibid., pp. 365, 403.
6. Gordon, *Reminiscences,* p. 336; Stevens, "Cedar Creek," p. 98.
7. *Southern Historical Society Papers,* vol. 30, p. 105; *Official Records,* vol. 43, part 1, p. 606.
8. *Confederate Veteran,* vol. 27, no. 10, p. 390; vol. 2, no. 3, p. 75.
9. Gallagher, *Ramseur,* pp. 10, 20.
10. Cox, "Ramseur," p. 226.
11. Gallagher, *Ramseur,* p. 15.
12. Ibid., pp. 17–18.
13. Ibid., p. 22.
14. Sergent, *They Lie Forgotten,* p. 1; Gallagher, *Ramseur,* pp. 26–27.
15. Cox, "Ramseur," p. 226; Gallagher, *Ramseur,* pp. 30–31.
16. Cox, "Ramseur," pp. 227–28; Gallagher, *Ramseur,* pp. 31–36.
17. Gallagher, *Ramseur,* pp. 42–44.
18. Cox, "Ramseur," p. 231; Gallagher, *Ramseur,* p. 55.
19. Goolrick, *Rebels Resurgent,* p. 147.
20. Gallagher, *Ramseur,* p. 64.
21. Cox, "Ramseur," p. 237.
22. Gallagher, *Ramseur,* p. 66.
23. Ibid., p. 73n.
24. Ibid., p. 76.
25. Ibid., p. 84.
26. Ibid.
27. Ibid., p. 95.

28. Ibid., pp. 95–96.
29. Freeman, *Lee's Lieutenants,* vol. 3, p. 394; Boatner, *Dictionary,* pp. 784–86; Gallagher, *Ramseur,* p. 105.
30. Freeman, *Lee's Lieutenants,* vol. 3, p. 406; *Southern Historical Society Papers,* vol. 18, p. 242.
31. Gallagher, *Ramseur,* p. 108.
32. Freeman, *Lee's Lieutenants,* vol. 3, pp. 406–7.
33. Ibid., p. 440.
34. Catton, *Grant Takes Command,* p. 257; Early, *Narrative,* p. 362; *Southern Historical Society Papers,* vol. 33, p. 59; Gallagher, *Ramseur,* p. 116.
35. Gallagher, *Ramseur,* p. 130.
36. Ibid., p. 133.
37. Ibid.; Freeman, *Lee's Lieutenants,* vol. 3, p. 570; Douglas, *I Rode with Stonewall,* p. 288.
38. Gallagher, *Ramseur,* p. 135.
39. Ibid., pp. 139–40.
40. Ibid., p. 155; Freeman, *Lee's Lieutenants,* vol. 3, p. 599.
41. Gordon, *Reminiscences,* p. 337.
42. Ibid., p. 336.
43. Ibid., pp. 64, 338.
44. Ibid., p. 337.
45. Humphreys, *Field, Camp, Hospital and Prison,* p. 169.
46. Kidd, *Recollections,* pp. 409–10.
47. Emerson, *Lowell,* p. 482.
48. Ibid., pp. 40–41; Higginson, "Lowell," p. 318.
49. Ibid., pp. 41, 45.
50. Ibid., pp. 40, 51.
51. Ibid., pp. 53, 42.
52. Ibid., pp. 49–50.
53. Ibid., pp. 46–47.
54. Higginson, "Lowell," p. 297.
55. Emerson, *Lowell,* p. 371.
56. Greenslet, *The Lowells,* pp. 274–75.
57. Emerson, *Lowell,* p. 387.
58. Ibid., pp. 398–99.
59. Greenslet, *The Lowells,* p. 276.

60. Emerson, *Lowell*, p. 19; Greenslet, *The Lowells*, p. 276.
61. Greenslet, *The Lowells*, p. 277.
62. Emerson, *Lowell*, pp. 183–85.
63. Greenslet, *The Lowells*, p. 267; Whitman, *Leaves of Grass*, pp. 404, 1348.
64. Emerson, *Lowell*, p. 196.
65. Ibid., p. 210.
66. Ibid., pp. 23–24.
67. Ibid., p. 373.
68. Ibid., pp. 26–27, 407; Greenslet, *The Lowells*, p. 283.
69. Emerson, *Lowell*, pp. 221–22.
70. Ibid., pp. 29, 225, 411.
71. Ibid., p. 30.
72. Ibid., p. 375.
73. Greenslet, *The Lowells*, p. 289.
74. Emerson, *Lowell*, pp. 234–35.
75. Ibid., p. 241.
76. Ibid., pp. 241–42.
77. Ibid., p. 35.
78. Ibid., p. 421.
79. Ibid., pp. 244, 254, 419.
80. Ibid., p. 246.
81. Ibid., p. 36–37, 430–33.
82. Ibid., pp. 284–85, 433.
83. Ibid., pp. 37–39.
84. Sanford, *Rebels and Redskins*, p. 266; Emerson, *Lowell*, pp. 54, 338.
85. Starr, *Union Cavalry*, vol. 2, p. 272.
86. Emerson, *Lowell*, pp. 56–57.
87. Ibid., p. 61.
88. Ibid., pp. 339, 359.
89. Alberts, *Brandy Station*, p. 131; Emerson, *Lowell*, pp. 363–64.
90. Emerson, *Lowell*, p. 364.
91. Ibid., pp. 354–55.
92. Ibid., pp. 357–58.

Chapter Six

1. Stevens, "Cedar Creek," pp. 89–90. No one will ever know exactly how many men were engaged at Cedar Creek. I have accepted the Federal numbers worked out by Hazard Stevens, who was assistant adjutant general and acting assistant inspector general of the Second Division, VI Corps; and the Confederate tally of J. S. McNeily, an officer in the Twenty-first Mississippi of Kershaw's division, who made a later study of the battle.

2. McDonald, *The Laurel Brigade*, p. 310; *Official Records*, vol. 43, part 1, p. 449; *Southern Historical Society Papers*, vol. 32, pp. 225–26; *Official Military Atlas*, plate 99.

3. Bushong, *Fightin' Tom Rosser*, p. 131.

4. Starr, *Union Cavalry*, vol. 2, p. 306; *Official Records*, vol. 43, part 1, p. 432.

5. Dickert, *Kershaw's Brigade*, p. 446.

6. Stevens, "Cedar Creek," p. 99; *Battles and Leaders*, p. 526.

7. Wise, *Long Arm of Lee*, pp. 881–82.

8. *Battles and Leaders*, p. 526.

9. Ibid.

10. Carpenter, *History of the Eighth Vermont*, p. 208.

11. Grant, "Sixth Corps at Cedar Creek," p. 13; *Official Records*, vol. 43, part 1, p. 449; Dickert, *Kershaw's Brigade*, p. 447; McDonald, *The Laurel Brigade*, p. 310.

12. Kidd, *Recollections*, p. 410.

13. Ibid., pp. 410–11; *Official Records*, vol. 43, part 1, pp. 522, 449.

14. Kidd, *Recollections*, p. 411; *Official Records*, vol. 43, part 1, pp. 449, 130.

15. *Confederate Veteran*, vol. 20, p. 315; vol. 14, p. 501.

16. Gordon, *Reminiscences*, pp. 338–39; DuPont, *Campaign of 1864*, p. 145.

17. Dickert, *Kershaw's Brigade*, p. 447.

18. Ibid.; Stevens, "Cedar Creek," p. 101; Wildes, *Record of the 116th Ohio*, p. 203.

19. DuPont, *Campaign of 1864*, p. 153.

20. Ibid., p. 154.
21. Wildes, *Record of the 116th Ohio,* p. 203; *National Tribune,* October 14, 1909.
22. Dickert, *Kershaw's Brigade,* p. 447.
23. *National Tribune,* August 29, 1901.
24. Dickert, *Kershaw's Brigade,* p. 448; Williams, *Hayes of the Twenty-third,* p. 299.
25. Wildes, *Record of the 116th Ohio,* pp. 203–4.
26. DuPont, *Campaign of 1864,* p. 156; Dickert, *Kershaw's Brigade,* p. 448.
27. DuPont, *Campaign of 1864,* pp. 157–59.
28. Ibid., p. 160.
29. Dickert, *Kershaw's Brigade,* p. 448.
30. Ibid.; Wildes, *Record of the 116th Ohio,* p. 204.
31. Dickert, *Kershaw's Brigade,* p. 449; *Confederate Veteran,* vol. 27, p. 390.
32. Early, *Memoir,* p. 105.
33. DuPont, *Campaign of 1864,* p. 161.
34. Ibid., pp. 158–59.
35. Ibid., p. 163.
36. Howard, "The Morning Surprise," p. 417.
37. DeForest, *Volunteer's Adventures,* p. 208.
38. Ibid., pp. 208–9; Crowninshield, *Cedar Creek,* p. 15.
39. *Official Records,* vol. 43, part 1, p. 403.
40. Ibid.; DuPont, *Campaign of 1864,* p. 163.
41. *Official Records,* vol. 43, part 1, pp. 158, 333.
42. Stevens, "Cedar Creek," p. 106.
43. Hayes, "Incidents at Cedar Creek," p. 238.
44. DeForest, *Volunteer's Adventures,* p. 210.
45. *Official Records,* vol. 43, part 1, p. 403; Gordon, *Reminiscences,* p. 339; Stackpole, *Sheridan in the Shenandoah,* p. 301.
46. *Confederate Veteran,* vol. 27, p. 411.
47. Wildes, *Record of the 116th Ohio,* p. 205.
48. Ibid.
49. Ibid., pp. 205–6.
50. Stevens, "Cedar Creek," p. 103.

51. DuPont, *Campaign of 1864,* p. 163.

52. Hayes, "Incidents at Cedar Creek," p. 239.

53. Williams, *Hayes of the Twenty-third,* pp. 302–3.

54. Howard, "The Morning Surprise," pp. 417–18.

55. DeForest, *Volunteer's Adventures,* p. 220.

56. Pollard, "Recollections of Cedar Creek," p. 280.

57. DeForest, *Volunteer's Adventures,* p. 211; Wildes, *Record of the 116th Ohio,* p. 206.

58. Pellett, *History of the 114th New York,* p. 268.

59. *Battles and Leaders,* p. 531; Carpenter, *History of the Eighth Vermont,* p. 215; Howard, "The Morning Surprise," p. 418.

60. DeForest, *Volunteer's Adventures,* p. 214; Carpenter, *History of the Eighth Vermont,* p. 210.

61. Carpenter, *History of the Eighth Vermont,* pp. 212, 215.

62. Ibid., pp. 215–16.

63. Ibid., p. 218; Stevens, "Cedar Creek," p. 104.

64. Howard, "The Morning Surprise," p. 420.

65. DeForest, *Volunteer's Adventures,* p. 212.

66. *Official Records,* vol. 43, part 1, pp. 284, 342.

67. DeForest, *Volunteer's Adventures,* p. 211.

68. Putnam, *Memories,* p. 371.

69. *Official Records,* vol. 43, part 1, p. 342.

70. DeForest, *Volunteer's Adventures,* p. 213.

71. Ibid.

72. *Official Records,* vol. 43, part 1, pp. 284–85.

73. Wildes, *Record of the 116th Ohio,* p. 206.

74. Sanford, *Rebels and Redskins,* pp. 287–88.

75. Wildes, *Record of the 116th Ohio,* p. 206; Taylor, "With Sheridan," pp. 13, 466.

76. DeForest, *Volunteer's Adventures,* p. 217.

77. Sanford, *Rebels and Redskins,* p. 288; Alberts, *Brandy Station,* p. 128.

78. Nettleton, "How the Day Was Saved," pp. 266–67.

79. *Official Records,* vol. 43, part 1, p. 449; Pond, *Shenandoah Valley,* p. 231; Stevens, "Cedar Creek," p. 112.

80. Dickert, *Kershaw's Brigade,* pp. 449–50.

81. DeForest, *Volunteer's Adventures,* p. 215.
82. Ibid., p. 217.

Chapter Seven

1.   Granger, "Cedar Creek," p. 116.
2.   Walker, *The Vermont Brigade,* p. 138.
3.   Granger, "Cedar Creek," p. 116.
4.   Ibid., p. 117.
5.   Ibid.; Stevens, "Cedar Creek," p. 107.
6.   Stevens, "Cedar Creek," p. 107.
7.   Ibid., p. 108.
8.   Granger, "Cedar Creek," p. 118.
9.   Ibid., p. 119.
10. *Official Military Atlas;* Best, *History of the 121st New York,* pp. 193–94; Vaill, *History of the 2nd Connecticut Heavy Artillery,* p. 121.
11. Best, *History of the 121st New York,* p. 194.
12. *Official Records,* vol. 43, part 1, p. 720; Crowninshield, *Cedar Creek,* p. 22.
13. Walker, *The Vermont Brigade,* pp. 139–40.
14. Stevens, "Cedar Creek," pp. 114–15; Walker, *The Vermont Brigade,* pp. 140–41.
15. Vaill, *History of the 2nd Connecticut Heavy Artillery,* pp. 121–22.
16. Gordon, *Reminiscences,* p. 340.
17. *Confederate Veteran,* vol. 31, p. 169; Gordon, *Reminiscences,* p. 341.
18. Stevens, "Cedar Creek," p. 109.
19. Best, *History of the 121st New York,* p. 195.
20. *Official Records,* vol. 43, part 1, p. 233.
21. Buell, *The Cannoneer,* p. 286; *Official Records,* vol. 43, part 1, p. 233.
22. Walker, *The Vermont Brigade,* p. 141.
23. Gallagher, *Ramseur,* p. 158; Douglas, *I Rode with Stonewall,* p. 303.
24. Stevens, "Cedar Creek," p. 115.

25. Ibid., pp. 108–9.
26. Vaill, *History of the Second Connecticut Heavy Artillery,* pp. 122–23.
27. Buell, *The Cannoneer,* pp. 286–87.
28. *National Tribune,* September 23, 1897.
29. Stevens, "Cedar Creek," p. 110.
30. Walker, *The Vermont Brigade,* p. 141; Buell, *The Cannoneer,* p. 287.
31. Buell, *The Cannoneer,* p. 287.
32. Gordon, *Reminiscences,* p. 359.
33. The entire exchange is from Gordon, *Reminiscences,* p. 341.
34. Early, *Memoir,* p. 106.
35. Stevens, "Cedar Creek," p. 117; *Official Records,* vol. 43, part 1, p. 201.
36. Stevens, "Cedar Creek," p. 117; Walker, *The Vermont Brigade,* p. 142; Buell, *The Cannoneer,* p. 287.
37. Buell, *The Cannoneer,* pp. 288, 295; *Official Records,* vol. 43, part 1, p. 599.
38. Buell, *The Cannoneer,* p. 296.
39. Ibid., pp. 288, 295.
40. Ibid., p. 290.
41. Walker, *The Vermont Brigade,* p. 143.
42. Brewer, *History, 61st Pennsylvania,* p. 128.
43. Walker, *The Vermont Brigade,* p. 143; Stevens, "Cedar Creek," p. 117.
44. Early, *Memoir,* p. 106.
45. Ibid.
46. *Official Records,* vol. 43, part 1, p. 194; Buell, *The Cannoneer,* p. 292.
47. Buell, *The Cannoneer,* pp. 290–91, 299.
48. *Official Records,* vol. 43, part 1, p. 210.
49. Stevens, "Cedar Creek," p. 118; *Official Records,* vol. 43, part 1, pp. 209–10, 599.
50. Early, *Memoir,* p. 107.
51. *Official Records,* vol. 43, part 1, p. 478.
52. Crowninshield, *Cedar Creek,* p. 23.
53. *Official Records,* vol. 43, part 1, p. 433.

54. Kidd, *Recollections*, p. 412.
55. Ibid.
56. Ibid., p. 414.
57. Emerson, *Lowell*, p. 63.
58. Kidd, *Recollections*, p. 416; *Official Records*, vol. 43, part 1, p. 449.
59. Early, *Memoir*, p. 107.
60. Ibid., p. 108.
61. Ibid.
62. *Official Records*, vol. 43, part 1, p. 509.
63. Early, *Memoir*, p. 107.
64. Ibid., p. 108.
65. Stevens, "Cedar Creek," p. 121.
66. Walker, *The Vermont Brigade*, p. 142; *Official Records*, vol. 43, part 1, p. 194.
67. Stevens, "Cedar Creek," p. 120.
68. Walker, *The Vermont Brigade*, p. 144.
69. Stevens, "Cedar Creek," p. 120.
70. Crowninshield, *Cedar Creek*, p. 24; Stevens, "Cedar Creek," p. 121.
71. Stevens, "Cedar Creek," p. 122; Kidd, *Recollections*, p. 416.
72. Early, *Memoir*, pp. 107–8.
73. Stevens, "Cedar Creek," p. 122.
74. Ibid., pp. 123–24; Crowninshield, *Cedar Creek*, p. 24.
75. Granger, "Cedar Creek," pp. 123–24.
76. Nettleton, "How the Day Was Saved," p. 269.
77. *Official Records*, vol. 43, part 1, p. 449; Early, *Memoir*, p. 108.
78. *Official Records*, vol. 43, part 1, p. 449; Humphreys, *Field, Camp, Hospital and Prison*, p. 170.
79. *Official Records*, vol. 43, part 1, p. 449.
80. Ibid., p. 450; Stevens, "Cedar Creek," p. 122.
81. Kidd, *Recollections*, p. 418.
82. Wildes, *Record of the 116th Ohio*, p. 208.
83. Nettleton, "How the Day Was Saved," p. 269.
84. *Official Records*, vol. 43, part 1, p. 562.
85. Wildes, *Record of the 116th Ohio*, p. 209.

86. Gordon, *Reminiscences,* p. 344.
87. Ibid.
88. Douglas, *I Rode with Stonewall,* p. 305.

Chapter Eight

1. Sheridan, *Memoirs,* vol. 2, p. 65.
2. *Official Records,* vol. 43, part 1, p. 386; Sheridan, *Memoirs,* vol. 2, p. 65.
3. Sheridan, *Memoirs,* vol. 2, p. 66.
4. *Official Records,* vol. 43, part 1, p. 393.
5. Forsyth, *Thrilling Days,* p. 134.
6. Ibid., p. 135.
7. Taylor, "With Sheridan," p. 475.
8. Sheridan, *Memoirs,* vol. 2, pp. 68–69.
9. Ibid., pp. 69–71.
10. Forsyth, *Thrilling Days,* p. 136; Sheridan, *Memoirs,* vol. 2, pp. 74–75; Taylor, "With Sheridan," p. 475.
11. Forsyth, *Thrilling Days,* p. 136.
12. Sheridan, *Memoirs,* vol. 2, p. 78.
13. Ibid., p. 79.
14. Forsyth, *Thrilling Days,* pp. 137–38.
15. Ibid.
16. Ibid., pp. 138–39.
17. Ibid., p. 142.
18. Ibid., p. 140.
19. Ibid., pp. 139–40.
20. Ibid., p. 141.
21. Sheridan, *Memoirs,* vol. 2, p. 80.
22. Forsyth, *Thrilling Days,* p. 143.
23. Sheridan, *Memoirs,* vol. 2, p. 81.
24. Stackpole, *Sheridan in the Shenandoah,* p. 325; Hayes, "Incidents at Cedar Creek," p. 238.
25. Forsyth, *Thrilling Days,* pp. 144–45; Howard, "The Morning Surprise," p. 424.
26. Forsyth, *Thrilling Days,* p. 145.
27. Walker, *The Vermont Brigade,* pp. 146–47.

28. Taylor, "With Sheridan," p. 442.
29. Ibid., p. 474.
30. Ibid., p. 476.
31. Stevens, "Cedar Creek," p. 125.
32. Ibid.
33. Sheridan, *Memoirs,* vol. 2, p. 83; Walker, *The Vermont Brigade,* p. 148.
34. Taylor, "With Sheridan," p. 478.
35. Sheridan, *Memoirs,* vol. 2, p. 83; Hayes, "Incidents at Cedar Creek," p. 235.
36. Taylor, "With Sheridan," pp. 482–83.
37. Sanford, *Rebels and Redskins,* p. 291.
38. Sheridan, *Memoirs,* vol. 2, p. 84.
39. Forsyth, *Thrilling Days,* p. 147.
40. Ibid., p. 148.
41. Ibid., p. 149; *Official Records,* vol. 43, part 1, p. 53.
42. Stevens, "Cedar Creek," p. 128; *Official Records,* vol. 43, part 1, p. 53.
43. Emerson, *Lowell,* p. 376.
44. Ibid., p. 64.
45. *Official Records,* vol. 43, part 1, p. 523.
46. McDonald, *The Laurel Brigade,* p. 311.
47. Ibid., p. 312.
48. Ibid.
49. *Official Records,* vol. 43, part 1, p. 523.
50. Forsyth, *Thrilling Days,* p. 151.
51. Beecher, *Record of the 114th New York,* p. 449; Walker, *The Vermont Brigade,* p. 148.
52. Forsyth, *Thrilling Days,* p. 152.
53. *National Tribune,* August 29, 1901.
54. Gordon, *Reminiscences,* p. 359.
55. Ibid., p. 361.
56. *Official Records,* vol. 43, part 1, p. 562.
57. Ibid.; Early, *Memoir,* pp. 108–9.
58. Gordon, *Reminiscences,* p. 363.
59. Ibid., pp. 365–66.
60. Ibid.

61. Ibid., p. 368.
62. Ibid., p. 365.
63. Early, *Memoir,* p. 109.
64. *Official Records,* vol. 43, part 1, p. 562; Early, *Memoir,* p. 109.
65. Early, *Memoir,* p. 109.
66. Ibid.
67. Stevens, "Cedar Creek," p. 130.
68. Forsyth, *Thrilling Days,* p. 152.
69. DeForest, *Volunteer's Adventures,* p. 222.
70. Ibid., pp. 222–23.
71. Forsyth, *Thrilling Days,* p. 154.
72. Ibid.
73. Ibid., pp. 155–56.
74. Ibid., pp. 157–58.
75. Sheridan, *Memoirs,* vol. 2, pp. 87–88.
76. Forsyth, *Thrilling Days,* p. 158; Stevens, "Cedar Creek," p. 132.
77. Stevens, "Cedar Creek," p. 132.
78. Forsyth, *Thrilling Days,* p. 160.
79. Ibid., p. 161.
80. Beecher, *Record of the 114th New York,* p. 450.
81. DeForest, *Volunteer's Adventures,* p. 223.

Chapter Nine

1. Stevens, "Cedar Creek," p. 133; Granger, "Cedar Creek," p. 132.
2. Kidd, *Recollections,* p. 422.
3. Walker, *The Vermont Brigade,* p. 151.
4. *Official Records,* vol. 43, part 1, p. 599.
5. Kidd, *Recollections,* p. 423.
6. Emerson, *Lowell,* pp. 65–66.
7. Kidd, *Recollections,* p. 423.
8. Stevens, "Cedar Creek," p. 133; Sheridan, *Memoirs,* vol. 2, p. 90.

9. Stevens, "Cedar Creek," p. 133; *Official Records,* vol. 43, part 1, p. 599; Walker, *The Vermont Brigade,* p. 150.

10. Walker, *The Vermont Brigade,* p. 150; Stevens, "Cedar Creek," p. 133.

11. Stevens, "Cedar Creek," p. 134.

12. Kidd, *Recollections,* p. 423.

13. Ibid.

14. Walker, *The Vermont Brigade,* pp. 151–52.

15. *Official Records,* vol. 43, part 1, p. 599.

16. Walker, *The Vermont Brigade,* pp. 151–52.

17. *Official Records,* vol. 43, part 1, pp. 523–24.

18. Ibid., p. 524.

19. Ibid.

20. Gordon, *Reminiscences,* p. 347.

21. McNeily in *Southern Historical Society Papers,* vol. 32, p. 232.

22. Forsyth, *Thrilling Days,* p. 161.

23. Ibid., p. 162.

24. Beecher, *Record of the 114th New York,* p. 451.

25. Forsyth, *Thrilling Days,* p. 162.

26. Carpenter, *History of the Eighth Vermont,* p. 221.

27. Beecher, *Record of the 114th New York,* pp. 451–52.

28. Ibid., p. 452; Carpenter, *History of the Eighth Vermont,* p. 221.

29. Carpenter, *History of the Eighth Vermont,* pp. 221–22.

30. Forsyth, *Thrilling Days,* p. 163.

31. Carpenter, *History of the Eighth Vermont,* p. 222.

32. Forsyth, *Thrilling Days,* p. 163.

33. Ibid.

34. Carpenter, *History of the Eighth Vermont,* p. 223; *Official Records,* vol. 43, part 1, p. 310.

35. Sheridan, *Memoirs,* vol. 2, p. 89.

36. Beecher, *Record of the 114th New York,* p. 452; Forsyth, *Thrilling Days,* p. 165.

37. *Official Records,* vol. 43, part 1, p. 524.

38. Ibid.

39. Carpenter, *History of the Eighth Vermont,* p. 224.

40. Ibid.
41. *Official Records,* vol. 43, part 1, p. 524.
42. Carpenter, *History of the Eighth Vermont,* p. 224; Forsyth, *Thrilling Days,* p. 165.
43. Stevens, "Cedar Creek," p. 134.
44. Dickert, *Kershaw's Brigade,* p. 451.
45. Stevens, "Cedar Creek," p. 137; Gallagher, *Ramseur,* p. 161.
46. Stevens in *Confederate Veteran,* vol. 27, no. 10, p. 390.
47. Clark, *Histories of Regiments from North Carolina,* vol. 2, p. 143; Gallagher, *Ramseur,* p. 162.
48. Carpenter, *History of the Eighth Vermont,* p. 225.
49. Forsyth, *Thrilling Days,* p. 166.
50. Carpenter, *History of the Eighth Vermont,* p. 225.
51. Ibid., pp. 225–26.
52. Stevens, "Cedar Creek," p. 136; Early, *Memoir,* p. 110; Crowninshield, *Cedar Creek,* p. 28.
53. Benson in *Confederate Veteran,* vol. 27, no. 10, p. 390.
54. Gordon, *Reminiscences,* p. 348.
55. Pollard, *Recollections,* p. 284; Beecher, *Record of the 114th New York,* pp. 452–53.
56. *Official Records,* vol. 43, part 1, p. 525; Hamlin, "Who Recaptured the Guns?" p. 201.
57. Vaill, *History of the Second Connecticut Heavy Artillery,* p. 127.
58. Hamlin, "Who Recaptured the Guns?" p. 201.
59. Ibid.
60. Ibid., p. 202.
61. DuPont, *Campaign of 1864,* p. 172.
62. *Official Records,* vol. 43, part 1, pp. 479, 525.
63. Douglas, *I Rode with Stonewall,* p. 304.
64. *Official Records,* vol. 43, part 1, pp. 479, 525.
65. Stevens, "Cedar Creek," p. 139.
66. DeForest, *Volunteer's Adventures,* p. 229.
67. Gordon, *Reminiscences,* p. 350.
68. Stevens, "Cedar Creek," p. 140.
69. Granger, "Cedar Creek," p. 135.
70. Beecher, *Record of the 114th New York,* p. 455.

71. DeForest, *Volunteer's Adventures*, p. 228.

72. Ibid.; Nettleton, "How the Day Was Saved," p. 275.

73. Vaill, *History of the Second Connecticut Heavy Artillery*, pp. 129–30.

74. Ibid.

75. *Official Records*, vol. 43, part 1, p. 234; Buell, *The Cannoneer*, p. 304.

76. Wildes, *Record of the 116th Ohio*, p. 212; Carpenter, *History of the Eighth Vermont*, p. 226.

77. Buell, *The Cannoneer*, p. 305.

78. Ibid., p. 306.

79. Pond, *Shenandoah Valley*, p. 240.

80. Ibid., p. 239.

81. *Confederate Veteran*, vol. 14, p. 502; Taylor, "With Sheridan," p. 496.

82. DuPont, *Campaign of 1864*, p. 175.

83. Sanford, *Rebels and Redskins*, p. 296.

84. Gallagher, *Ramseur*, p. 165; Cox, "Ramseur," pp. 257–58.

85. Emerson, *Lowell*, p. 66.

86. Ibid., p. 67.

87. Higginson, "Lowell," p. 326.

88. Dickert, *Kershaw's Brigade*, p. 468.

89. Ibid., p. 469.

90. Ibid.

91. Porter, *Campaigning with Grant*, pp. 306–8.

92. *Official Records*, vol. 43, part 2, pp. 410, 423.

93. *Official Records*, vol. 43, part 1, p. 62.

94. O'Connor, *Sheridan*, p. 233.

95. *Official Records*, vol. 43, part 1, p. 560.

96. Ibid., p. 562.

97. Ibid., p. 563.

98. Ibid., pp. 555–56.

99. Ibid., p. 563.

100. Ibid.

101. Ibid., p. 582.

102. Freeman, *Lee's Lieutenants*, vol. 3, p. 628.

103. *Confederate Veteran*, vol. 31, p. 169.

104.   Douglas, *I Rode with Stonewall,* p. 305.
105.   *Official Records,* vol. 43, part 1, pp. 584, 586.

Epilogue

1.   Early, *Memoir,* p. 121.
2.   Douglas, *I Rode with Stonewall,* p. 310.
3.   Early, *Narrative,* p. 462.
4.   Ibid., p. 463; Freeman, *Lee's Lieutenants,* vol. 3, p. 635.
5.   Bushong, *Old Jube,* p. 280; Freeman, *R. E. Lee,* vol. 4, pp. 507–9.
6.   Bushong, *Old Jube,* p. 281.
7.   Ibid., p. 290.
8.   Ibid., pp. 289, 293.
9.   Ibid., p. 296.
10.   Ibid., pp. 288, 296.
11.   Ibid., pp. 297, 304.
12.   Korn, *Pursuit to Appomattox,* p. 140.
13.   Catton, *Grant Takes Command,* p. 462.
14.   O'Connor, *Sheridan,* p. 279.
15.   Ibid., p. 303.
16.   Ibid., p. 325.
17.   Ibid., pp. 333–34.
18.   Ibid., p. 349.
19.   Ibid., pp. 355–56.
20.   Ibid., p. 357.
21.   *Official Records,* vol. 43, part 1, pp. 526, 451.
22.   Alberts, *Brandy Station,* p. 132.
23.   *Official Records,* vol. 43, part 1, pp. 527–28.
24.   Ibid., pp. 453, 528–29.
25.   Kidd, *Recollections,* p. 432; *Official Records,* vol. 43, part 1, p. 453.
26.   Urwin, *Custer Victorious,* p. 217; Leech, *Reveille,* p. 350; Taylor, "With Sheridan," p. 512.
27.   *Official Records,* vol. 43, part 1, p. 33.
28.   Hale, *Four Valiant Years,* p. 480.
29.   McDonald, *The Laurel Brigade,* p. 332.

30. Ibid., pp. 332–33.
31. Urwin, *Custer Victorious,* p. 221; McDonald, *The Laurel Brigade,* pp. 480–81.
32. Pond, *Shenandoah Valley,* p. 250; McDonald, *The Laurel Brigade,* pp. 480–81; Urwin, *Custer Victorious,* p. 222.
33. Pond, *Shenandoah Valley,* p. 252.
34. Bushong, *Fightin' Tom Rosser,* p. 183.
35. Gordon, *Reminiscences,* p. 439; Korn, *Pursuit to Appomattox,* p. 144.
36. Van de Water, *Glory Hunter,* p. 115.
37. Ibid., p. 126; O'Connor, *Sheridan,* p. 279.
38. Van de Water, *Glory Hunter,* pp. 130–33.
39. Bushong, *Fightin' Tom Rosser,* p. 186.
40. Ibid., p. 189.
41. Ibid., p. 190.
42. Ibid., p. 192.
43. Ibid., p. 199.
44. Ibid., p. 198.
45. Ibid., p. 202.
46. *Official Records,* vol. 43, part 1, p. 583.
47. Tankersley, *Gordon,* p. 360.
48. Schmitt, *General George Crook,* p. 134.
49. Ibid.
50. Ibid., p. 303; Starr, *Union Cavalry,* vol. 2, p. 364.
51. Schmitt, *General George Crook,* p. 136.
52. Ibid., p. 139.
53. Ibid., p. 141.
54. Hutton, *Sheridan's Army,* p. 128.
55. Ibid., p. 129; Schmitt, *General George Crook,* p. 187.
56. Hutton, *Sheridan's Army,* pp. 313, 326.
57. Schmitt, *General George Crook,* p. 134.
58. Ibid., p. 294.
59. Gallagher, *Ramseur,* pp. 166–67; Cox, *Ramseur.*
60. Emerson, *Lowell,* p. 68.
61. Sanford, *Rebels and Redskins,* p. 298.
62. Adams, *Boston Money Tree,* p. 159.

Bibliography

Adams, Russell B., Jr. *The Boston Money Tree.* New York: Thomas Y. Crowell Company 1977.

Alberts, Don. E. *Brandy Station to Manila Bay: A Biography of General Wesley Merritt.* Austin, Texas: Presidial Press 1980.

Battles and Leaders of the Civil War. Vol. 4. New York: Castle Books 1956.

Beecher, Dr. Harris H. *Record of the 114th Regiment, N.Y.S.V.* Norwich, Vt.: J. F. Hubbard, Jr. 1866.

Best, Isaac O. *History of the 121st New York State Infantry.* Privately printed. Chicago 1921.

Boatner, Mark. *The Civil War Dictionary.* New York: David McKay Company 1959.

Brewer, Abraham T. *History, 61st Regiment Pennsylvania Volunteers, 1861–1865.* Pittsburgh: Art engrav. and print. co. 1911.

Brewster, Charles. "Captured by Mosby's Guerillas." *National Tribune,* Thursday, September 26, 1901, and Thursday, October 3, 1901.

Buell, Augustus. *The Cannoneer: Recollections of Service in the Army of the Potomac by a Detached Volunteer in the Regular Artillery.* Washington, D.C.: The National Tribune 1890.

Burr, Frank A., and Richard J. Hinton. *The Life of General Philip H. Sheridan: Its Romance and Reality.* Providence, R.I.: J. A. & R. A. Reid, Publishers 1888.

Bushong, Millard K. *Old Jube: A Biography of General Jubal A. Early.* Shippensburg, Pa.: Beidel Printing House 1955.

Bushong, Millard K. and Dean M. *Fightin' Tom Rosser, C.S.A.* Shippensburg, Pa.: Beidel Printing House 1983.

Carpenter, George N. *History of the Eighth Regiment, Vermont Volunteers.* Boston: Deland and Barta 1886.

Casler, John O. *Four Years in the Stonewall Brigade.* 1893. Reprint. Dayton, Ohio: Morningside Bookshop 1981.

Catton, Bruce. *Grant Takes Command.* Boston: Little, Brown & Company 1969.

Clark, Champ. *Gettysburg: The Confederate High Tide.* Alexandria, Va.: Time-Life Books 1985.

Clark, Walter, ed. *Histories of the Several Regiments and Battalions from North Carolina in the Great War 1861–65.* vols. I–V. Raleigh, N.C.: E. M. Uzzell, printer and binder 1901.

Connell, Evan S. *Son of the Morning Star.* New York: Harper & Row 1985.

Cox, William R. "Major General Stephen D. Ramseur: His Life and Character." Address before the Ladies' Memorial Association of Raleigh, N.C., May 10, 1891. In *Southern Historical Society Papers,* vol. 18, pp. 217–60.

Crook, George C. *General George Crook: His Autobiography.* Edited by Martin F. Schmitt. Norman, Okla.: University of Oklahoma Press 1946.

Crowninshield, Col. B. W. *The Battle of Cedar Creek, October 19, 1864.* Paper read before the Massachusetts Military Historical Society, December 8, 1879. Cambridge: Riverside Press 1879.

Davies, Henry E. *General Sheridan.* New York: D. Appleton & Company 1909.

Davis, James A. *51st Virginia Infantry.* Lynchburg: H. E. Howard, Inc. 1986.

Davis, William C. *Breckinridge: Statesman, Soldier, Symbol.* Baton Rouge: Louisiana State University Press 1974.

DeForest, John William. *A Volunteer's Adventures: A Union Captain's Record of the Civil War.* New Haven: Yale University Press 1946.

Delauter, Roger U., Jr. *18th Virginia Cavalry.* Lynchburg: H. E. Howard, Inc. 1985.

———. *McNeil's Rangers.* Lynchburg: H. E. Howard, Inc. 1986.

Dickert, D. Augustus. *History of Kershaw's Brigade.* 1899. Reprint. Dayton, Ohio: Morningside Bookshop 1976.

Dictionary of American Biography. 20 vols. New York: Charles Scribner's Sons 1928.

Douglas, Henry Kyd. *I Rode with Stonewall.* Chapel Hill: University of North Carolina Press 1980.

DuPont, H. A. *The Campaign of 1864 in the Valley of Virginia and the Expedition to Lynchburg.* New York: J. J. Little & Ives Company 1925.

Early, Jubal A. *Autobiographical Sketch and Narrative of the War Between the States.* Philadelphia: J. B. Lippincott Company 1912.

———. *A Memoir of the Last Year of the War for Independence in the Confederate States of America.* Lynchburg: Charles W. Button 1867.

Emerson, Edward W. *Life and Letters of Charles Russell Lowell.* Houghton, Mifflin & Company 1907.

Evans, Clement A., ed. *Confederate Military History.* vols. 1–12. Atlanta, Ga.: Confederate Publishing Company 1899.

Fisk, Wilbur. *Anti-Rebel: The Civil War Letters of Wilbur Fisk.* New York: Emil Rosenblatt 1983.

Forsyth, George A. *Thrilling Days in Army Life.* New York: Harper & Bros. 1900.

Freeman, Douglas Southall. *Lee's Lieutenants.* vols. 1–3. New York: Charles Scribner's Sons 1944.

———. *R. E. Lee: A Biography.* vols. 1–4. New York: Charles Scribner's Sons 1935.

Gallagher, Gary W. *Stephen Dodson Ramseur: Lee's Gallant General.* Chapel Hill: University of North Carolina Press 1985.

Gilham, William. *Manual of Instruction for the Volunteers and Militia of the Confederate States.* Richmond, Va.: West & Johnson 1861.

Goolrick, William K. *Rebels Resurgent: Fredericksburg to Chancellorsville.* Alexandria, Va.: Time-Life Books 1985.

Gordon, John B. *Reminiscences of the Civil War.* New York: Charles Scribner's Sons 1903.

Granger, Moses M. "The Battle of Cedar Creek." Item 18 in *Sketches of War History,* vol. 3. pp. 100–143. Military Order of the Loyal Legion of the United States, Ohio Commandery, Cincinnati: R. Clarke & Co. 1888.

Grant, General L. A. "The Second Division of the Sixth Corps at Cedar Creek." In *Glimpses of the Nation's Struggle,* 6th ser. Military Order of the Loyal Legion of the United States, Minnesota Commandery. Minneapolis: Aug. Davis 1909.

Greenslet, Ferris. *The Lowells and Their Seven Worlds.* Boston: Houghton Mifflin 1946.

Hale, Laura Virginia. *Four Valiant Years in the Lower Shenandoah Valley 1861–1865.* Front Royal, Va.: Hathaway Publishing 1986.

Hale, Laura Virginia, and Stanley S. Phillips. *History of the 49th Virginia Infantry C.S.A.* Lanham, Md.: S. S. Phillips 1981.

Hamlin, Augustus C. "Who Recaptured the Guns at Cedar Creek?" *Papers of the Military Historical Society of Massachusetts,* vol. 6, 1907.

Hayes, Rutherford B. "Incidents at the Battle of Cedar Creek." Item 19 in *Sketches of War History,* vol. 4. pp. 235–45. Military Order of the Loyal Legion of the United States, Ohio Commandery. Cincinnati: R. Clarke & Co. 1889.

Haynes, E. M. *A History of the 10th Regiment, Vermont Volunteers.* Rutland, Vt.: Tuttle Company 1894.

Higginson, Henry Lee. "Charles Russell Lowell." *Harvard Memorial Biographies.* Cambridge: Sever and Francis 1866.

Howard, Captain S. E. "The Morning Surprise at Cedar Creek." *Civil War Papers,* vol. 2 pp. 415–24. Military Order of the Loyal Legion of the United States, Massachusetts Commandery. Boston 1900.

Humphreys, Charles A. *Field, Camp, Hospital and Prison in the Civil War, 1863–1865.* Boston: Press of Geo. H. Ellis Co. 1918.

Hutton, Paul Andrew. *Phil Sheridan and His Army.* Lincoln, Neb.: University of Nebraska Press 1985.

Kellogg, Sanford C. *The Shenandoah Valley and Virginia 1861 to 1865: A War Study*. New York: The Neale Publishing Company 1903.

Kersheval, Samuel. *A History of the Valley of Virginia*. 1925. Reprint. Strasburg: Shenandoah Publishing House 1981.

Kidd, J. H. *Personal Recollections of a Cavalryman*. Grand Rapids, Mich.: Black Letter Press 1969.

Knapp, David Jr. *The Confederate Horsemen*. New York: Vantage Press 1966.

Korn, Jerry. *The Fight for Chattanooga: Chickamauga to Missionary Ridge*. Alexandria, Va.: Time-Life Books 1985.

———. *Pursuit to Appomattox*. Alexandria, Va.: Time-Life Books 1987.

Leech, Margaret. *Reveille in Washington 1860–65*. New York: Harper & Bros. 1941.

Lewis, Thomas A. *The Shenandoah in Flames: The Valley Campaign of 1864*. Alexandria, Va.: Time-Life Books 1987.

Lincoln, William S. *Life with the 34th Massachusetts Infantry in the War of the Rebellion*. Worcester: Press of Noyes, Snow & Company 1879.

Maine at Gettysburg: Report of Maine Commissioners. Boston 1898.

McDonald, Capt. William N. *A History of the Laurel Brigade*. Baltimore: Mrs. Kate S. McDonald 1907.

Military Analysis of the Civil War. Editors of Military Affairs. Millwood, N.Y.: KTO Press 1977.

Mosby, John S. *The Memoirs of Colonel John S. Mosby*. Bloomington: Indiana University Press 1959.

Myers, Frank M. *The Commanches: A History of White's Battalion, Virginia Cavalry*. Baltimore: Kelly, Piet & Company 1871.

Nettleton, A. Bayard. "How the Day Was Saved at the Battle of Cedar Creek." *Glimpses of the Nation's Struggle*. Military Order of the Loyal Legion of the United States, Minnesota Commandery. St. Paul, Minn.: St. Paul Book & Stationery Company 1887.

Newhall, F. C. *With General Sheridan in Lee's Last Campaign*. Philadelphia: J. B. Lippincott & Company 1866.

O'Connor, Richard. *Sheridan the Inevitable.* Indianapolis: Bobbs-Merrill Company 1953.

The Official Military Atlas of the Civil War. New York: Fairfax Press 1983.

Official Records: *The War of the Rebellion: A Compilation of the Official Records of the Union and Confederate Armies.* Series 1, 128 vols.

Olcott, Mark. *The Civil War Letters of Lewis Bissell: A Curriculum.* Washington, D.C.: Field School Educational Foundation Press 1981.

Pellett, Elias P. *History of the 114th Regiment, New York State Volunteers.* Norwich, N.Y.: Telegraph and Chronicle 1866.

Pollard, Maj. H. M. "Recollections of Cedar Creek." *War Papers and Personal Reminiscences.* Vol. 1. Military Order of the Loyal Legion of the United States, Missouri Commandery. St. Louis: Becktold & Company 1892.

Pond, George E. *The Shenandoah Valley in 1864.* New York: Charles Scribner's Sons 1901.

Porter, Gen. Horace. *Campaigning with Grant.* Bloomington: Indiana University Press 1961.

Putnam, George Haven. *Memories of My Youth, 1844–1865.* New York: G. P. Putnam's Sons 1914.

Sandburg, Carl. *Abraham Lincoln: The Prairie Years and the War Years.* New York: Harcourt, Brace & World 1954.

Sanford, George B. *Fighting Rebels and Redskins.* Norman, Okla.: University of Oklahoma Press 1969.

Schmitt, Martin F., ed. *General George Crook: His Autobiography.* Norman, Okla.: University of Oklahoma Press 1946.

Sergent, Mary Elizabeth. "Classmates Divided." *American Heritage,* February 1958.

———. *They Lie Forgotten.* Middletown, N.Y.: Prior King Press 1986.

Sheridan, Philip H. *Personal Memoirs.* vols. 1 and 2. New York: Charles L. Webster & Company 1888.

Southern Historical Society Papers. 47 vols. Richmond, Va.: 1876–1930.

Stackpole, Edward J. *Sheridan in the Shenandoah.* Harrisburg, Pa.: Stackpole Company 1961.

Starr, Stephen Z. *The Union Cavalry in the Civil War.* vols. 1 and 2. Baton Rouge: Louisiana State University Press 1981.

Starr, William C. "Cedar Creek." In *War Papers Read before the Indiana Commandery.* Military Order of the Loyal Legion of the United States. Indianapolis 1898.

Stevens, Hazard. "The Battle of Cedar Creek." *Papers of the Military Historical Society of Massachusetts,* vol. 6, 1907.

Stiles, Robert. *Four Years under Marse Robert.* New York and Washington: Neale Publishing Company 1903.

Street, James Jr. *The Struggle for Tennessee.* Alexandria, Va.: Time-Life Books 1985.

Strother, David Hunter. *A Virginia Yankee in the Civil War.* Chapel Hill: University of North Carolina Press 1961.

Tankersley, Allen P. *John B. Gordon: A Study in Gallantry.* Atlanta: Whitehall Press 1955.

Taylor, James. "With Sheridan up the Shenandoah Valley in 1864." Unpublished manuscript in the collection of the Western Reserve Historical Society, Cleveland, Ohio.

Thomas, Emory M. *Bold Dragoon: The Life of J.E.B. Stuart.* New York: Harper & Row 1986.

Urwin, Gregory J. W. *Custer Victorious: The Civil War Battles of George Armstrong Custer.* East Brunswick, N.J.: Associated University Presses 1983.

Vaill, Dudley Landon. *The County Regiment: A Sketch of the Second Regiment of Connecticut Volunteer Heavy Artillery,* etc. Winsted, Conn.: Litchfield County University Club 1908.

Vaill, Theodore F. *History of the Second Connecticut Volunteer Heavy Artillery,* etc. Winsted, Conn.: Winsted Printing Company 1868.

Van de Water, Frederic F. *Glory Hunter: A Life of General Custer.* New York: Argosy-Antiquarian Ltd. 1963.

Walker, Aldace F. *The Vermont Brigade in the Shenandoah Valley.* Burlington, Vt.: Free Press Association 1869.

Wert, Jeffry D. "Woodstock Races." *Civil War Times,* May 1980.

Whitman, Walt. *Leaves of Grass.* Garden City, N.Y.: Doubleday 1926.

Wildes, Thomas F. *Record of the 116th Regiment, Ohio Infantry Volunteers, in the War of the Rebellion.* Sandusky, Ohio: I. F. Mack & Bro. 1884.

Williams, T. Harry. *Hayes of the Twenty-third.* New York: Alfred A. Knopf 1965.

Wise, Jennings Cropper. *The Long Arm of Lee.* New York: Oxford University Press 1959.

Wise, John Sergeant. *The End of an Era.* New York: Thomas Yoseloff 1965.

Worthington, Glenn H. *Fighting for Time.* Shippensburg, Pa.: Beidel Printing House 1985.

Index